ACCA

Applied Skills

Taxation (TX – UK) FA 2020

Workbook

For exams in June 2021, September 2021, December 2021 and March 2022

WITHDRAWN

BPP
LEARNING
MEDIA

First edition 2020

ISBN 9781 5097 3442 9

ISBN (for internal use only): 9781 5097 3441 2

e-ISBN 9781 5097 3490 0

British Library Cataloguing-in-Publication Data

A catalogue record for this book is available from the British Library.

Published by

BPP Learning Media Ltd

BPP House, Aldine Place

142–144 Uxbridge Road

London W12 8AA

learningmedia.bpp.com

Printed in the United Kingdom

Your learning materials, published by BPP Learning Media Ltd, are printed on paper sourced from sustainable, managed forests.

We are grateful to the Association of Chartered Certified Accountants for permission to reproduce past examination questions and extracts from the syllabus. The suggested solutions in the practice answer bank have been prepared by BPP Learning Media Ltd, except where otherwise stated.

Contents

Helping you to pass

BPP Learning Media – ACCA Approved Content Provider

As an ACCA Approved Content Provider, BPP Learning Media gives you the opportunity to use study materials reviewed by the ACCA examining team. By incorporating the examining team's comments and suggestions regarding the depth and breadth of syllabus coverage, the BPP Learning Media Workbook provides excellent, ACCA-approved support for your studies.

These materials are reviewed by the ACCA examining team. The objective of the review is to ensure that the material properly covers the syllabus and study guide outcomes, used by the examining team in setting the exams, in the appropriate breadth and depth. The review does not ensure that every eventuality, combination or application of examinable topics is addressed by the ACCA Approved Content. Nor does the review comprise a detailed technical check of the content as the Approved Content Provider has its own quality assurance processes in place in this respect.

BPP Learning Media do everything possible to ensure the material is accurate and up to date when sending to print. In the event that any errors are found after the print date, they are uploaded to the following website: www.bpp.com/learningmedia/Errata.

The PER alert

Before you can qualify as an ACCA member, you not only have to pass all your exams but also fulfil a three-year practical experience requirement (PER). To help you to recognise areas of the syllabus that you might be able to apply in the workplace to achieve different performance objectives, we have introduced the 'PER alert' feature (see the next section). You will find this feature throughout the Workbook to remind you that what you are learning to pass your ACCA exams is equally useful to the fulfilment of the PER requirement. Your achievement of the PER should be recorded in your online My Experience record.

Chapter features

Studying can be a daunting prospect, particularly when you have lots of other commitments. This Workbook is full of useful features, explained in the key below, designed to help you get the most out of your studies and maximise your chances of exam success.

Key term

Central concepts are highlighted and clearly defined in the Key terms feature. Key terms are also listed in bold in the Index, for quick and easy reference.

Formula to learn

This boxed feature will highlight important formula which you need to learn for your exam.

PER alert

This feature identifies when something you are reading will also be useful for your PER requirement (see 'The PER alert' section above for more details).

Real world examples

These will give real examples to help demonstrate the concepts you are reading about.

Illustration

Illustrations walk through how to apply key knowledge and techniques step by step.

Activity

Activities give you essential practice of techniques covered in the chapter.

Essential reading

Links to the Essential reading are given throughout the chapter. The Essential reading is included in the free eBook, accessed via the Exam Success Site (see inside cover for details on how to access this).

At the end of each chapter you will find a Knowledge diagnostic, which is a summary of the main learning points from the chapter to allow you to check you have understood the key concepts. You will also find a Further study guidance which contains suggestions for ways in which you can continue your learning and enhance your understanding. This can include: recommendations for question practice from the Further question practice and solutions, to test your understanding of the topics in the Chapter; suggestions for further reading which can be done, such as technical articles; and ideas for your own research.

Introduction to the Essential reading

The electronic version of the Workbook contains additional content, selected to enhance your studies. Consisting of revision materials and further explanations of complex areas (including illustrations and activities), it is designed to aid your understanding of key topics which are covered in the main printed chapters of the Workbook.

A summary of the content of the Essential reading is given below.

Chapter		Summary of Essential reading content
1	Introduction to the UK tax system	• Function and purpose of tax • Economic factors ie to discourage/encourage certain types of activity • Social factors - different taxes, different effects • Environmental factors - eg climate change levy • Tax avoidance and tax evasion
2	Computing taxable income and the income tax liability	• Steps in computing the tax liability and tax payable • Working at the margin examples • Qualifying interest - loan purposes that qualify for relief • Examples of income tax planning for spouses/civil partners
3	Employment income	There is no essential reading for this chapter
4	Taxable and exempt benefits. The PAYE system	• Detailed example on car and fuel benefit • Further detail on beneficial loans • Further detail on expenses and exempt benefits
5	Pensions	• Contributions not attracting tax relief
6	Property income	There is no essential reading for this chapter
7	Computing trading income	• Further reading on the badges of trade • Case law information on the distinction between capital and revenue expenditure • The application of the 'wholly and exclusively' rule - the remoteness and duality tests • Table of sundry allowable and disallowable items • Detail of the operation of fixed rate expenses in the cash basis
8	Capital allowances	• Rule concerning date of expenditure for capital allowance purposes • Detailed definition of plant and machinery, buildings, and structures • Treatment of land and computer software • Relevant case law on function vs setting
9	Assessable trading income	• Basis period rules where cessation occurs in the first two years of trading • Illustration of basis periods over the life of a business • Detailed analysis of factor influencing choice of accounting date

Chapter		Summary of Essential reading content
10	Trading losses	• Loss relief against capital gains • Further example of basis period rules applicable to losses in early years of trading • Disclaiming capital allowances as a tax planning tool
11	Partnerships and limited liability partnerships	• Additional illustration of the use of losses in a partnership
12	National insurance contributions	• Detailed definition of 'earnings' for NIC • Operation of earnings periods for directors including an example comparing a director to an employee
13	Computing chargeable gains	• Further detail/example on computing a gain or loss
14	Chattels and private residence relief	• Business use of a residence
15	Business reliefs	• More detail on the business asset disposal relief lifetime limit • Rollover relief - non-business use
16	Shares and securities	There is no essential reading for this chapter
17	Self assessment and payment of tax by individuals	• Penalties for failure to notify chargeability • Penalties for late filing exceeding 12 months • Circumstances where payments on account are not required or may be reduced • HMRC powers - Determinations, discovery assessments and investigating dishonest conduct by tax agents • Detail regarding appeals and Tax Tribunal hearings
18	Inheritance tax: scope and transfers of value	• Deductibility of debts and funeral expenses
19	Computing taxable total profits and the corporation tax liability	• Loan relationships - accounting methods, tax treatment of incidental costs of loan finance, and capital costs • Illustration showing the calculation of property business profit for a company • Comprehensive illustration of the computation of TTP • Comparison of running a business as a sole trader vs a company
20	Chargeable gains for companies	• Detail, including an example, of the impact of bonus and rights issues on the FA 1985 share pool for a company • Treatment of reorganisations and takeovers for a corporate shareholder
21	Loss relief for single companies	There is no essential reading for this chapter
22	Groups	• The order of offset of losses for a claimant company • Illustration showing the different definitions of a group relief and chargeable gains group

Chapter		Summary of Essential reading content
23	Self assessment and payment of tax by companies	• Detail of iXBRL • Detail of how a company can make and amend claims
24	An introduction to VAT	• Example with standard and zero-rated and exempt supplies • Meaning of supplies of goods/services/taxable persons • Categorising a supply • Examples of zero-rated and exempt supplies
25	Further aspects of VAT	• VAT records

Introduction to Taxation (TX)

Overall aim of the syllabus

You are introduced to the rationale behind – and the functions of – **the tax system**. The syllabus then considers the **separate taxes** that an accountant would need to have a detailed knowledge of, such as **income tax from self-employment, employment and investments**, the **corporation tax** liability of individual companies and groups of companies, the **national insurance contribution** liabilities of both employed and self employed persons, the **value added tax** liability of businesses, the **chargeable gains** arising on disposals of investments by both individuals and companies, and the **inheritance tax** liabilities arising on chargeable lifetime transfers and on death.

You will be expected to have a **detailed knowledge** of these taxes, but **no previous knowledge is assumed**. You should **study the basics** carefully and **learn the pro forma computations**. It then becomes straightforward to complete these by slotting in figures from your detailed workings.

As well as being able to calculate tax liabilities, you may be required to **explain the basis of the calculations, apply tax planning techniques** for individuals and companies and **identify the compliance issues** for each major tax through a variety of business and personal scenarios and situations

Members of the Taxation (TX – UK) examining team have written several technical articles including two on Inheritance Tax, two on chargeable gains, one on groups, two on VAT, one on benefits, one on motor cars, one on adjustment of profit, one on higher skills and one on Finance Act 2020. All these articles are available on the ACCA website. Make sure you read them to gain further insight into what the Taxation (TX – UK) examining team is looking for.

The syllabus

The broad syllabus headings are:

A	The UK tax system and its administration
B	Income tax and NIC liabilities
C	Chargeable gains for individuals
D	Inheritance tax
E	Corporation tax liabilities
F	Value added tax (VAT)
G	Employability and technology skills

Main capabilities

On successful completion of this exam, you should be able to:

A	Integrate knowledge and understanding from across the syllabus to enable you to complete detailed computations of tax liabilities
B	Explain the underlying principles of taxation by providing a simple summary of the rules and how they apply to the particular situation
C	Apply tax planning techniques by identifying available options and testing them to see which has the greater effect on tax liabilities

Links with other exams

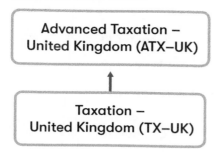

Advanced Taxation –
United Kingdom (ATX–UK)

↑

Taxation –
United Kingdom (TX–UK)

The diagram shows where direct (solid line arrows) and indirect (dashed line arrows) links exist between this exam and other exams preceding or following it.

TX-UK provides a **foundation for Advanced Taxation (ATX – UK)** which will be chosen by those who work in a tax environment.

Achieving ACCA's Study Guide Learning Outcomes

This BPP Workbook covers all the Taxation (TX) syllabus learning outcomes. The tables below show in which chapter(s) each area of the syllabus is covered.

A	The UK tax system and its administration	
A1	The overall function and purpose of taxation in a modern economy	Chapter 1
A2	Principal sources of revenue law and practice	Chapter 1
A3	The systems for self-assessment and the making of returns	Chapters 17, 23
A4	The time limits for the submission of information, claims and payment of tax, including payments on account	Chapters 17,23
A5	The procedures relating to compliance checks, appeals and disputes	Chapters 17,23
A6	Penalties for non-compliance	Chapters 17, 23

B	Income tax and NIC liabilities	
B1	The scope of income tax	Chapter 2
B2	Income from employment	Chapters 3, 4
B3	Income from self-employment	Chapters 7, 8, 9, 10, 11
B4	Property and investment income	Chapters 2, 6
B5	The comprehensive computation of taxable income and income tax liability	Chapters 2, 3
B6	National insurance contributions for employed and self-employed persons	Chapter 12
B7	The use of exemptions and reliefs in deferring and minimising income tax liabilities	Chapters 2, 5

C	Chargeable gains for individuals	
C1	The scope of the taxation of capital gains	Chapter 13
C2	The basic principles of computing gains and losses	Chapter 13
C3	Gains and losses on the disposal of movable and immovable property	Chapter 14
C4	Gains and losses on the disposal of shares and securities	Chapter 16
C5	The computation of capital gains tax	Chapters 13, 15
C6	The use of exemptions and reliefs in deferring and minimising tax liabilities arising on the disposal of capital assets	Chapters 13, 15

D	Inheritance tax	
D1	The basic principles of computing transfers of value	Chapter 18
D2	The liabilities arising on chargeable lifetime transfers and on the death of an individual	Chapter 18
D3	The use of exemptions in deferring and minimising inheritance tax liabilities	Chapter 18
D4	Payment of inheritance tax	Chapter 18

E	Corporation tax liabilities	
E1	The scope of corporation tax	Chapter 19
E2	Taxable total profits	Chapter 19, 21
E3	Chargeable gains for companies	Chapters 20, 21
E4	The comprehensive computation of corporation tax liability	Chapter 19
E5	The effect of a group corporate structure for corporation tax purposes	Chapter 22
E6	The use of exemptions and reliefs in deferring and minimising corporation tax liabilities	Chapters 19, 20, 21, 22

F	Value added tax (VAT)	
F1	The VAT registration requirements	Chapter 24
F2	The computation of VAT liabilities	Chapters 24, 25
F3	The effect of special schemes	Chapter 25

G	Employability and technology skills	
G1	Use computer technology to efficiently access and manipulate relevant information	Skills checkpoint 2 and 4

BPP LEARNING MEDIA

G2	Work on relevant response options, using available functions and technology, as would be required in the workplace.	Skills checkpoint 2 and 4
G3	Navigate windows and computer screens to create and amend responses to exam requirements, using the appropriate tools.	Skills checkpoint 2 and 4
G4	Present data and information effectively using the appropriate tools.	Skills checkpoint 2 and 4

The complete syllabus and study guide can be found by visiting the exam resource finder on the ACCA website: www.accaglobal.com/gb/en.html.

The exam

Computer-based exams

Applied Skills exams are all computer-based exams (CBE).

Approach to examining the syllabus

The Taxation (TX) syllabus is assessed by a 3 hour exam. The pass mark is **50%**. All questions in the exam are **compulsory**.

There is no choice in this exam, all questions have to be answered. You must therefore study the **entire syllabus**, there are no short-cuts.

The first section of the exam consists of 15 **objective test questions**, worth two marks each. These will inevitably cover a **wide range of the syllabus**.

The second section of the exam consists of three scenarios each being tested with five **objective test questions,** worth two marks each. You must make sure you **understand the scenario** before attempting the related questions.

The third section of the exam consists of three **constructed response questions**, one 10 mark question and two 15 mark questions.

Practising longer questions set in the third section of the exam under **timed conditions** is essential. BPP's **Practice & Revision Kit** contains 10 mark and 15 mark questions on all areas of the syllabus.

Answer all parts of the question. Even if you cannot do all of the calculation elements, you will still be able to gain marks in the discussion parts.

Answer selectively – the examining team will expect you to consider carefully what is relevant and significant enough to include in your answer. Don't include unnecessary information.

Keep an eye out for **articles** as the **examining team** will use **Student Accountant** to communicate with students.

Tax rates, allowances and information on certain reliefs will be given in the exam. You should familiarise yourself with the information provided so that you know how to find it quickly in the exam.

Format of the exam		Marks
Section A	Objective test (OT) 15 questions × 2 marks	30
Section B	Objective test (OT) case 3 questions × 10 marks Each question will contain 5 subparts each worth 2 marks	30

Format of the exam		Marks
Section C	Constructed response (long questions) 1 question × 10 marks 2 questions × 15 marks	40
		100

Section A and B questions will be selected from the entire syllabus. The responses to each question or subpart in the case of OT cases are marked automatically as either correct or incorrect by computer.

The 10 mark Section C questions can come from any part of the syllabus. The 15 mark Section C questions will mainly focus on the following syllabus areas but a minority of marks can be drawn from any other area of the syllabus:

• Income tax (syllabus area B)

• Corporation tax (syllabus area E)

The responses to these questions are human marked.

Essential skills areas to be successful in Taxation (TX – UK)

We think there are three areas you should develop in order to achieve exam success in TX:

(a) Knowledge application

(b) Specific Taxation skills

(c) Exam success skills

These are shown in the diagram below.

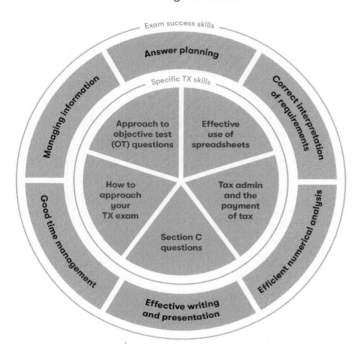

Specific TX skills

These are the skills specific to TX that we think you need to develop in order to pass the exam.

In this Workbook, there are five **Skills Checkpoints** which define each skill and show how it is applied in answering a question. A brief summary of each skill is given below.

Skill 1: Approach to objective test (OT) questions

Section A of the exam will include 15 OT questions worth two marks each. Section B of the exam will include three OT cases, worth 10 marks each. Each OT case contains a group of five OT questions based around a single scenario. 60% of your TX exam is therefore made up of OT questions. It is essential that you have a good approach to answering these questions. OT questions are auto-marked; your workings will therefore not be considered; you have to answer the whole question correctly to earn their two marks.

A step-by-step technique for tackling OT questions is outlined below:

General guidance for approaching OT questions

STEP 1: Answer the questions you know first.

If you're having difficulty answering a question, move on and come back to tackle it once you've answered all the questions you know.

It is often quicker to answer discursive style OT questions first, leaving more time for calculations.

General guidance for approaching OT questions

STEP 2: Answer all questions.

There is no penalty for an incorrect answer in ACCA exams; there is nothing to be gained by leaving an OT question unanswered. If you are stuck on a question, as a last resort, it is worth selecting the option you consider most likely to be correct and moving on. Make a note of the question, so if you have time after you have answered the rest of the questions, you can revisit it.

Guidance for answering specific OT questions

STEP 3: Read the requirement first!

The requirement will be stated in bold text in the exam. Identify what you are being asked to do, any technical knowledge required and **what type of OT question** you are dealing with. Look for key words in the requirement such as "which **TWO** of the following," "which of the following is **NOT**"

Guidance for answering specific OT questions

STEP 4: Apply your technical knowledge to the data presented in the question.

Take your time working through questions, and make sure to read through each answer option with care. OT questions are designed so that each answer option is plausible. Work through each response option and eliminate those you know are incorrect.

Skills Checkpoint 1 covers this technique in detail through application of an OT case question.

Skill 2: Effective use of spreadsheets

It is very likely that you will be required to use the spreadsheet response option in the constructed workspace for Section C questions. It is imperative that you know how to use the spreadsheet functions to prepare accurate and easy to follow calculations.

The key steps are outlined below.

Step 1	Start by setting up the spreadsheet.
Step 2	Ensure the numbers are in a separate cell from the label.
Step 3	Always use formulae to perform calculations.
Step 4	Make efficient use of the SUM function.
Step 5	Only use separate workings for longer calculations and cross reference any workings using '=' rather than re-typing the numbers.
Step 6	Does your answer look reasonable?

Skills Checkpoint 2 covers this technique in detail through application to a question.

Skill 3: The UK tax system and its administration

You must study the whole syllabus in order to pass the TX exam, but having the administration knowledge at your fingertips will give you extra time in the exam to answer the more difficult questions.

This skills checkpoint gives you a list of quick fire questions to help you learn the basic information.

Skill 4: Section C questions

Section C questions contain one 10-mark question and two 15-mark questions. One 15-mark question will focus on income tax and the other one will focus on corporation tax. This means that you know roughly what to expect and you can use proformas where relevant to help with the long calculations. Discursive elements will be relatively short. 10-mark questions often cover more than one tax and are designed to act as a bridge question between TX and the higher level exam, ATX.

A step-by-step technique for attempting these questions is outlined below.

Step 1	Read the requirements first and read them carefully.
Step 2	Learn and use the proformas where relevant.
Step 3	Input easy numbers from the question directly into your proforma.
Step 4	Always use formulae to perform basic calculations.
Step 5	Show longer workings separately.

Skills Checkpoint 4 covers this technique in detail through application to a question.

Skill 5: How to approach your TX exam

You can answer your TX exam in whatever order you prefer. It is important that you adopt a strategy that works best for you. We would suggest that you decide on your preferred approach and practise it by doing a timed mock exam before your real exam.

A suggested approach to tackling your TX exam is outlined below.

Complete Section A first - allocated time 54 minutes

Tackle any easier OT questions first. Often discursive style questions can be answered quickly, saving more time for calculations. Do not leave any questions unanswered. Even if you are unsure make a reasoned guess.

Complete Section B next - allocated time 54 minutes

You will have 18 mins of exam time to allocate to each of the three OT case questions in Section B. Use the same approach to OT questions as discussed for Section A.

There will normally be discursive and numerical questions within each case. Again, it is better to tackle the discursive type questions first and make a reasoned guess for any questions you are unsure on.

Finally, complete Section C - allocated time 72 minutes

Start with the question you feel most confident with.

Skills Checkpoint 5 covers this technique in more detail.

Exam success skills

Passing the TX exam requires more than applying syllabus knowledge and demonstrating the specific TX skills; it also requires the development of excellent exam technique through question practice.

We consider the following six skills to be vital for exam success. The Skills Checkpoints show how each of these skills can be applied in the exam.

1 Exam success skill 1

Managing information

Questions in the exam will present you with a lot of information. The skill is how you handle this information to make the best use of your time. The key is determining how you will approach the exam and then actively reading the questions.

Advice on developing Managing information

Approach

The exam is 3 hours long. There is no designated 'reading' time at the start of the exam, however, one approach that can work well is to start the exam by spending 10–15 minutes carefully reading through all of the questions to familiarise yourself with the exam.

Once you feel familiar with the exam, consider the order in which you will attempt the questions; always attempt them in your order of preference. For example, you may want to leave to last the question you consider to be the most difficult.

If you do take this approach, remember to adjust the time available for each question appropriately – see Exam success skill 6: Good time management.

If you find that this approach doesn't work for you, don't worry – you can develop your own technique.

Active reading

You must take an active approach to reading each question. Focus on the requirement first, underlining/ highlighting key verbs such as 'prepare', 'comment', 'explain', 'discuss', to ensure you answer the question properly. Then read the rest of the question, underlining/highlighting and annotating important and relevant information, and making notes of any relevant technical information you think you will need.

2 Exam success skill 2

Correct interpretation of the requirements

The active verb used often dictates the approach that written answers should take (eg 'explain', 'discuss', 'evaluate'). It is important you identify and use the verb to define your approach. The **correct interpretation of the requirements** skill means correctly producing only what is being asked for by a requirement. Anything not required will not earn marks.

Advice on developing correct interpretation of the requirements

This skill can be developed by analysing question requirements and applying this process:

Step 1	**Read the requirement** Firstly, read the requirement a couple of times slowly and carefully and highlight the active verbs. Use the active verbs to define what you plan to do. Make sure you identify any sub-requirements and any topics which you are specifically told you do not need to cover in your answer. Also note the number of marks available for each requirement or sub-requirement, as this will indicate the time available and hence the level of depth required in your answer.
Step 2	**Read the rest of the question** By reading the requirement first, you will have an idea of what you are looking out for as you read through the scenario. This is a great time saver and means you don't end up having to read the whole question in full twice. You should do this in an active way – see Exam success skill 1: Managing Information.
Step 3	**Read the requirement again** Read the requirement again to remind yourself of the exact wording before starting your answer. This will capture any misinterpretation of the requirements or any missed requirements entirely. This should become a

> habit in your approach and, with repeated practice, you will find the focus, relevance and depth of your answer plan will improve.

3 Exam success skill 3

Answer planning: Priorities, structure and logic

This skill requires the planning of the key aspects of an answer which accurately and completely responds to the requirement.

Advice on developing Answer planning: Priorities, structure and logic

Everyone will have a preferred style for an answer plan. For example, it may be a mind map, bullet-pointed lists or simply making some notes. Choose the approach that you feel most comfortable with, or, if you are not sure, try out different approaches for different questions until you have found your preferred style.

For 10 mark Section C questions, it can be useful to draw up a separate answer plan in the format of your choosing (eg a mind map or bullet-pointed lists). You will want to remind yourself of key facts from the scenario to avoid having to re-read the question – you should at the very least make a few notes including vital information such as the following key factors:

- Nature of the taxpayer: is it an individual or a company?
- For individuals: their age, any family relationships, their residence and domicile status, whether they're a basic, higher or additional rate taxpayer, and whether they've used their CGT annual exempt amount /IHT exemptions
- For companies: their ownership structure and group relationships
- Relevant dates: the year end(s) of businesses, dates of actual or proposed transactions, the date that a business started, dates of gifts (or death!) for IHT

4 Exam success skill 4

Efficient numerical analysis

This skill aims to maximise the marks awarded by making clear to the marker the process of arriving at your answer. This is achieved by laying out an answer such that, even if you make a few errors, you can still score subsequent marks for follow-on calculations. It is vital that you do not lose marks purely because the marker cannot follow what you have done.

Advice on developing Efficient numerical analysis

This skill can be developed by applying the following process:

Step 1	**Use a standard proforma working where relevant** If answers can be laid out in a standard proforma then always plan to do so. This will help the marker to understand your working and allocate the marks easily. It will also help you to work through the figures in a methodical and time-efficient way.
Step 2	**Show your workings** Keep your workings as clear and simple as possible and ensure they are cross-referenced to the main part of your answer.
Step 3	**Keep moving!** It is important to remember that, in an exam situation, it is difficult to get every number 100% correct. The key is therefore ensuring you do not spend too long on any single calculation. If you are struggling with a solution then make a sensible assumption, state it and move on.

5 Exam success skill 5

Effective writing and presentation

Written answers should be presented so that the marker can clearly see the points you are making, presented in the format specified in the question. The skill is to provide efficient written answers with sufficient breadth of points that answer the question, in the right depth, in the time available.

Advice on developing Effective writing and presentation

Step 1	**Use headings** Using the headings and sub-headings from your answer plan will give your answer structure, order and logic. This will ensure your answer links back to the requirement and is clearly signposted, making it easier for the marker to understand the different points you are making. Underlining your headings will also help the marker.
Step 2	**Write your answer in short, but full, sentences** Use short, punchy sentences with the aim that every sentence should say something different and generate marks. Write in full sentences, ensuring your style is professional.
Step 3	**Do your calculations first and explanation second** Questions sometimes ask for an explanation with supporting calculations. The best approach is to prepare the calculation first then add the explanation. Performing the calculation first should enable you to explain what you have done.

6 Exam success skill 6

Good time management

This skill means planning your time across all the requirements so that all tasks have been attempted at the end of the 3 hours available and actively checking on time during your exam. This is so that you can flex your approach and prioritise requirements which, in your judgement, will generate the maximum marks in the available time remaining.

Advice on developing Good time management

The exam is 3 hours long, which translates to 1.8 minutes per mark. At the beginning of a question, work out the amount of time you should be spending on each requirement If you take the approach of spending 10–15 minutes reading and planning at the start of the exam, adjust the time allocated to each question accordingly.

Keep an eye on the clock

Aim to attempt all requirements, but be ready to be ruthless and move on if your answer is not going as planned. The challenge for many is sticking to planned timings. Be aware this is difficult to achieve in the early stages of your studies and be ready to let this skill develop over time.

Question practice

Question practice is a core part of learning new topic areas. When you practise questions, you should focus on improving the Exam success skills – personal to your needs – by obtaining feedback or through a process of self-assessment.

Sitting this exam as a computer-based exam and practicing as many exam-style questions as possible in the ACCA CBE practice platform will be the key to passing this exam. You should attempt questions under timed conditions and ensure you produce full answers to the discussion parts as well as doing the calculations. Also ensure that you attempt all mock exams under exam conditions.

ACCA have launched a free on-demand resource designed to mirror the live exam experience helping you to become more familiar with the exam format. You can access the platform via the Study Support Resources section of the ACCA website navigating to the CBE question practice section and logging in with your myACCA credentials.

1

Introduction to the UK tax system

Learning objectives

On completion of this chapter, you should be able to:

	Syllabus reference no.
Describe the purpose (economic, social etc) of taxation in a modern economy.	A1(a)
Explain the difference between direct and indirect taxation.	A1(b)
Identify the different types of capital and revenue tax.	A1(c)
Describe the overall structure of the UK tax system.	A2(a)
State the different sources of revenue law.	A2(b)
Describe the organisation HM Revenue & Customs (HMRC) and its terms of reference.	A2(c)
Explain the difference between tax avoidance and tax evasion, and the purposes of the General Anti-Abuse Rule (GAAR).	A2(d)
Appreciate the interaction of the UK tax system with that of other tax jurisdictions.	A2(e)
Appreciate the need for double taxation agreements.	A2(f)
Explain the need for an ethical and professional approach.	A2(g)

Exam context

You may be asked a question on a specific topic in the UK tax system in either Section A or Section B. An example would be to identify sources of revenue law. You are unlikely to be asked a whole Section C question on this part of the syllabus. You may, however, be asked to comment on one aspect, such as the difference between tax avoidance and tax evasion or how to act if a client has failed to disclose information to the tax authorities, as part of a question.

Chapter overview

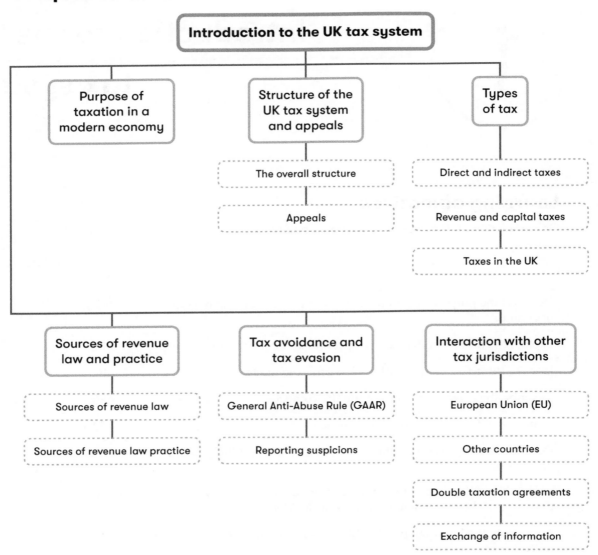

BPP
LEARNING
MEDIA

1 Purpose of taxation in a modern economy

There are many factors which will influence the government's tax policy:

(a) **Economic factors:** Tax can be used to encourage and discourage certain types of activity.

Encourages	Discourages
Saving (ISA/pension)	Smoking
Charitable donations	Alcohol
Entrepreneurs	Motoring
Investment in plant and machinery	

Tax also raises money for defence, law and order, overseas aid and government and parliamentary costs.

(b) **Social factors:** Tax can be used in the redistribution of income and wealth. Different taxes have different social effects:

Tax	Social effect
Direct taxes (based on income, gains and wealth)	Tax only those who have these resources
Indirect taxes (tax on consumption eg VAT on products/services purchases)	Discourage spending (VAT) and encourage saving. Lower or nil rates of tax can be levied on essentials like food.
Progressive taxes (ie where the proportion of income paid increases as income or gains rise)	Target those who can afford to pay.

(c) **Environmental factors:** Taxes may be levied for environmental reasons (for example, a climate change levy or landfill tax).

Essential reading

See Chapter 1 Section 1 of the Essential reading for more detail on the purpose of taxation.

The Essential reading is available as an Appendix of the digital edition of the Workbook.

2 Structure of the UK tax system and appeals

2.1 The overall structure

HM Treasury formally **imposes and collects** tax.

HM Revenue & Customs (HMRC) is a part of HM Treasury and has responsibility for the

administrative function for the collection of tax. HMRC staff are referred to in the tax legislation as **'Officers of Revenue and Customs'** and are responsible for supervising the self-assessment system and raising queries about tax liabilities.

The Crown Prosecution Service (CPS) provides legal advice and institutes and conducts criminal prosecutions in England and Wales where there has been an investigation by HMRC.

2.2 Appeals

A taxpayer can appeal against a decision of HMRC. Appeals relating to direct taxes (see next section) must first be made to HMRC. Appeals relating to indirect taxes must be made directly to the Tax Tribunal.

The Tribunal hears appeals and is in two tiers:

- First Tier Tribunal - deals with **most cases**
- Upper Tribunal - deals with **complex cases** (important issue of tax law or large financial sums) or appeals against decisions of the First Tier Tribunal

Before an appeal is heard by the Tax Tribunal, there is an option for the taxpayer to request an internal review of a decision by a HMRC review officer.

3 Types of taxes

3.1 Direct and indirect taxes

> **Direct tax:** Direct taxes are those charged on income, gains and wealth. Income tax, national insurance, corporation tax, capital gains tax and inheritance tax are direct taxes. Direct taxes are collected directly from the taxpayer.
>
> **Indirect tax:** Indirect taxes are those paid by the consumer to the supplier who then passes the tax to the HMRC. Value added tax is an indirect tax.

3.2 Revenue and capital taxes

> **Revenue tax:** Revenue taxes are those charged on income.
>
> **Capital tax:** Capital taxes are those charged on capital gains or on wealth.

Note that corporation tax is charged on both income and capital gains of UK companies.

3.3 Taxes in the UK

The main taxes in the UK are:

Tax	Direct or indirect	Capital or revenue	Suffered by
Income tax	Direct	Revenue	Individuals and partners
National insurance	Direct	Revenue	Employees, employers, self-employed
Corporation tax	Direct	Both	UK companies
Capital gains tax	Direct	Capital	Individuals and partners
Inheritance tax	Direct	Capital	Individuals
VAT	Indirect	Neither	Businesses

4 Sources of revenue law and practice

4.1 Sources of revenue law

There are three sources of revenue law:

(a) Primary legislation (Acts of Parliament) which sets out the basic principles

(b) Secondary legislation (Statutory Instruments) which gives the detail of how the law applies

(c) Case law, which is the interpretation of legislation by the courts

At least one Finance Act is passed by Parliament each year to update the various rules governing the calculation and collection of tax for the current tax year and financial year. The Finance Act 2020 governs the rules for the tax year 2020/21 and for financial year 2020 and will be tested in exams from June 2021.

- The tax year runs from 6 April to the following 5 April.
- The tax year 2020/21 runs from 6 April 2020 to 5 April 2021.
- A tax year is the period in respect of which individuals submit returns and pay tax (eg income tax, capital gains tax, national insurance).
- A financial year runs from 1 April to the following 31 March.
- Financial year 2020 runs from 1 April 2020 to 31 March 2021.
- Corporation tax rates and rules are set for financial years

Tax year: A tax year is the period in respect of which **individuals** submit returns and pay tax (eg income tax, capital gains tax, national insurance).

Financial year: A financial year runs from 1 April to the following 31 March and relates to **companies**.

4.2 Sources of revenue law practice

HMRC produces a number of sources setting out how it thinks revenue law works in practice. These do not have legal force but are useful guidance and include:

(a) Statements of practice which set out how HMRC intends to apply the law

(b) Extra statutory concessions which set out circumstances in which HMRC will not apply the law strictly where it would be unfair

(c) Internal manuals used by HMRC staff

5 Tax avoidance and tax evasion

PER alert

One of the competencies you require to fulfil Performance Objective 17 *Tax planning and advice* of the PER is to advise clients responsibly about the differences between tax planning, tax avoidance and tax evasion. You can apply the knowledge you obtain from this section of the Workbook to help to demonstrate this competence.

Tax planning: Tax planning is the reduction in an individual's or company's tax liabilities in accordance with the tax legislation such as claiming capital allowances on machinery.

Tax avoidance: Tax avoidance is the legal minimisation of tax liabilities (including tax planning mentioned above).

Tax evasion: Tax evasion consists of seeking to mislead HMRC by either suppressing information or providing deliberately false information. It is illegal.

Essential reading

See Chapter 1 Section 2 of the Essential reading for more detail on tax avoidance and tax evasion.

The Essential reading is available as an Appendix of the digital edition of the Workbook.

5.1 General Anti-Abuse Rule (GAAR)

There is a General Anti-Abuse Rule (GAAR) enabling HMRC to counteract tax advantages from abusive tax arrangements.

(a) The GAAR provides the means for HMRC to counteract tax advantages from abusive tax arrangements.

(b) Abusive tax arrangements involve obtaining a tax advantage as one of their main purposes.

(c) Arrangements are abusive if they cannot be regarded as a reasonable course of action (for example, involving contrived steps) and result in, for example, significantly less income, profits or gains being taxable.

(d) A tax advantage includes relief from or reduction in tax charged, repayment of tax, deferral of tax payment or acceleration of payment.

(e) HMRC may counteract tax advantages arising by, for example, increasing the tax payer's tax liability.

5.2 Reporting suspicions

The practising accountant often acts for taxpayers in their dealings with HMRC and situations can arise where the accountant has concerns as to whether the taxpayer is being honest in providing information to the accountant for onward transmission. They must use their professional judgement and uphold the standards of the ACCA.

If a client evades tax, for example by making a material error or omission in a tax return, the accountant must first try to make the client change it and disclose the error or omission. If the client does not correct the error, omission or failure when advised, the accountant should cease to act for the client, inform HMRC of this cessation (without informing them of the reason to maintain client confidentiality) and consider making a money laundering report to the accountant's firm's money laundering reporting officer (or the National Crime Agency if the accountant is a sole practitioner).

Accountants who suspect, or are aware of, tax evasion by a client may be committing an offence if they do not report their suspicions. Furthermore, the accountant must not disclose to the client or a third party that a money laundering report has been made. Doing so would constitute a criminal offence of 'tipping-off'.

Exam focus point

Under self-assessment, all taxpayers (whether individuals or companies) are responsible for disclosing their taxable income and gains and the deductions and reliefs they are claiming against them.

Many taxpayers arrange for their accountants to prepare and submit their tax returns. The taxpayer is still the person responsible for submitting the return and for paying whatever tax becomes due; the accountant is only acting as the taxpayer's agent.

Activity 1: Tax avoidance and tax evasion

The following acts have been committed in the course of business of one of your clients.

Action 1: A customer invoice was omitted from accounting records in order to push it into the taxable profits of the following tax year.

Action 2 The client decided to gift an asset to their spouse in order to reduce a capital gains tax liability.

Required

Which of these actions amounts to tax evasion?

O   Action 1 only

O   Action 2 only

○   Both Actions

○   Neither Action

Solution

---

6   Interaction with other tax jurisdictions

6.1   European Union (EU)

There is no general common system of taxation in the EU.

However, value added tax (VAT) is an EU-wide tax and EU countries are obliged to pass laws to conform with the rules laid down in EU legislation.

For TX-UK exams in the period 1 June 2021 to 31 March 2022, all questions will assume that the UK remains in the European Union.

6.2   Other countries

The rules of tax jurisdictions of other countries do not have a direct interaction with UK tax.

6.3   Double taxation agreements

Double taxation agreements are designed to protect against the risk of double taxation where the same income or gains are taxable in two countries.

They give relief from double taxation by, for example:

- Taxing the source only in one country; or
- Giving credit for tax paid in one country against tax in another country

Double taxation agreements may also include non-discrimination provisions which prevent a foreign national from being treated more harshly than a national of a country.

6.4   Exchange of information

There are provisions regarding the exchange of information between the revenue authorities of EU member states.

Double taxation agreements also usually include rules for the exchange of information between revenue authorities.

Chapter summary

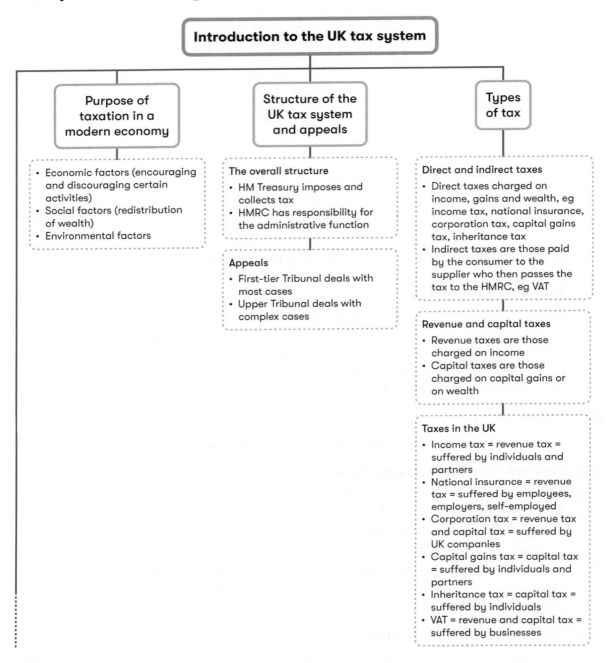

Introduction to the UK tax system

Purpose of taxation in a modern economy

- Economic factors (encouraging and discouraging certain activities)
- Social factors (redistribution of wealth)
- Environmental factors

Structure of the UK tax system and appeals

The overall structure
- HM Treasury imposes and collects tax
- HMRC has responsibility for the administrative function

Appeals
- First-tier Tribunal deals with most cases
- Upper Tribunal deals with complex cases

Types of tax

Direct and indirect taxes
- Direct taxes charged on income, gains and wealth, eg income tax, national insurance, corporation tax, capital gains tax, inheritance tax
- Indirect taxes are those paid by the consumer to the supplier who then passes the tax to the HMRC, eg VAT

Revenue and capital taxes
- Revenue taxes are those charged on income
- Capital taxes are those charged on capital gains or on wealth

Taxes in the UK
- Income tax = revenue tax = suffered by individuals and partners
- National insurance = revenue tax = suffered by employees, employers, self-employed
- Corporation tax = revenue tax and capital tax = suffered by UK companies
- Capital gains tax = capital tax = suffered by individuals and partners
- Inheritance tax = capital tax = suffered by individuals
- VAT = revenue and capital tax = suffered by businesses

Sources of revenue law and practice

Sources of revenue law
- Primary legislation (Acts of Parliament)
- Secondary legislation (Statutory Instruments)
- Case law
- The tax year runs from 6 April to following 5 April
- The financial year runs from 1 April to following 31 March

Sources of revenue law practice
- Statements of practice
- Extra-statutory concessions
- Internal manuals

Tax avoidance and tax evasion

- Tax avoidance = legal minimisation of tax liabilities
- Tax evasion = seeking to mislead HMRC by suppressing information/providing deliberately false information

General Anti-Abuse Rule (GAAR)
- HMRC may counteract tax advantages arising

Reporting suspicions
- Recommend client discloses error to HMRC
- If client does not disclose/correct error, accountant should:
  - Cease to act for client
  - Inform HMRC of cessation (but no details why)
  - Consider making money laundering report
  - Avoid 'tipping-off' the client

Interaction with other tax jurisdictions

European Union (EU)
- VAT is an EU-wide tax and EU countries are obliged to pass laws to conform with the rules laid down in EU legislation

Other countries
- Rules of tax jurisdictions of other countries do not have a direct interaction with UK tax

Double taxation agreements
- Protect against risk of double taxation where same income/gains are taxable in two countries
- Give relief by:
  - Taxing the source only in one country; or
  - Giving credit for tax paid in one country against tax in another country

Exchange of information
- Information agreements between the Revenue authorities of EU member states
- Double taxation agreements usually include exchange of information rules between Revenue authorities

Knowledge diagnostic

1. Purpose of taxation in a modern economy

Taxation can be used to encourage or discourage economic, social and environmental behaviour.

2. Structure of UK tax system and appeals

Taxes are administered by HM Revenue & Customs (HMRC). The Tax Tribunal hears appeals.

3. Types of tax

Taxes may be direct or indirect and revenue or capital.

4. Sources of revenue law and practice

Revenue law consists of legislation (primary and secondary) and case law. HMRC provides guidance on revenue law.

5. Tax avoidance and tax evasion

Tax evasion is illegal. Tax avoidance is legal, although may be challenged by HMRC. Accountants should cease to act for clients who evade tax and should also consider making a money laundering report.

6. Interaction with other tax jurisdictions

There is no general system of taxation within the EU but VAT is an EU-wide tax. Double taxation agreements give relief from where the same revenue source is taxed in both the UK and another country. There are provisions for exchange of information between the UK and other countries.

Further study guidance

Question practice

Now try the following from the Further question practice bank (available in the digital edition of the Workbook):

Section A questions

Q1, Q2, Q3

Activity answers

Activity 1: Tax avoidance and tax evasion

The correct answer is: Action 1 only

Action 1 is tax evasion as it involves misleading HMRC to delay a legitimate tax charge.

Action 2 is tax planning.

Computing taxable income and the income tax liability

Learning objectives

On completion of this chapter, you should be able to:

	Syllabus reference no.
Explain how the residence of an individual is determined.	B1(a)
Compute the tax payable on savings and dividends income.	B4(g)
Recognise the treatment of individual savings accounts (ISAs) and other tax exempt investments.	B4(h)
Understand how the accrued income scheme applies to UK Government securities (gilts).	B4(i)
Prepare a basic income tax computation involving different types of income.	B5(a)
Calculate the amount of personal allowance available.	B5(b)
Understand the impact of the transferable amount of personal allowance for spouses and civil partners.	B5(c)
Compute the amount of income tax payable.	B5(d)
Understand the treatment of interest paid for a qualifying purpose.	B5(e)
Understand the treatment of gift aid donations and charitable giving.	B5(f)
Explain and compute the child benefit tax charge.	B5(g)
Understand the treatment of property owned jointly by a married couple, or by a couple in a civil partnership.	B5(h)
Understand how a married couple or a couple in a civil partnership can minimise their tax liabilities.	B7(b)
Basic income tax planning.	B7(c)

Exam context

Section A questions on the topics in this chapter may include identification of different types of income or calculation of the personal allowance. They could also include a simple computation of income tax liability on one type of income, or a computation of the child benefit income tax charge. Section B questions on the topics in this chapter could focus on tax implications of various types of income and the treatment of married couples/civil partners.

It is likely that you will have to prepare a full computation of income tax liability (and possibly income tax payable) in a Section C question, in a 15-mark question or a 10-mark question. You should familiarise yourself with the layout of the computation, and the three types of income: non-savings, savings and dividends. It is then a simple matter of slotting the final figures into the computation from supporting workings for the different types of income.

Gift aid donations could feature in a question in any section. You will come across the technique of increasing the basic rate and higher rate limits again when you deal with pensions later in this Workbook.

Throughout this chapter, you should be aware of basic income tax planning such as investing in sources of exempt income. We will also deal with some tax planning for spouses/civil partners.

Chapter overview

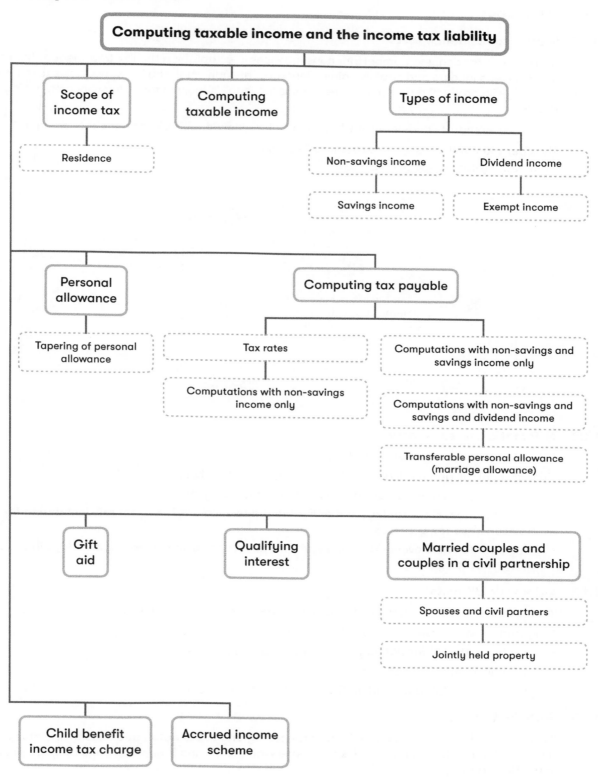

Computing taxable income and the income tax liability

- Scope of income tax
  - Residence
- Computing taxable income
- Types of income
  - Non-savings income
    - Savings income
  - Dividend income
    - Exempt income

- Personal allowance
  - Tapering of personal allowance
- Computing tax payable
  - Tax rates
    - Computations with non-savings income only
  - Computations with non-savings and savings income only
    - Computations with non-savings and savings and dividend income
    - Transferable personal allowance (marriage allowance)

- Gift aid
- Qualifying interest
- Married couples and couples in a civil partnership
  - Spouses and civil partners
    - Jointly held property

- Child benefit income tax charge
- Accrued income scheme

1 Scope of income tax

1.1 Residence

1.1.1 Statutory residence tests

A taxpayer's **residence** has important consequences in establishing the **tax treatment of their UK and overseas income and capital gains**. Generally, an individual who is UK resident is taxed on worldwide income whereas a non-UK resident is liable to UK income tax only on income arising in the UK.

Statute sets out tests to determine whether or not an **individual is UK resident in a tax year.**

The **operation of the tests** can be summarised as follows:

Figure 2.1: Statutory test of residence

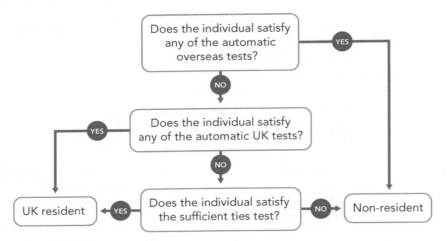

1.1.2 Automatic overseas tests

The automatic overseas tests must be considered first.

An individual will automatically **not** be UK resident for the whole tax year if:

- They spend **less than 16 days in the UK** during that tax year; or
- They spend **less than 46 days in the UK** during a tax year and were **not resident during the previous three tax years**; or
- They **work full time overseas** throughout that tax year and **spend less than 91 days in the UK during that tax year.**

1.1.3 Automatic UK tests

If none of the automatic overseas test are met, then the automatic UK tests are considered.

An individual will automatically be UK resident if:

- They are **in the UK for 183 days or more** during a tax year; or
- Their **only home** is in the UK; or
- They carry out **full-time work in the UK** during that tax year

1.1.4 Sufficient ties test

If an individual's residence **cannot be determined by any of the automatic tests** their status will be determined by the **number of ties they have with the UK** and how **many days they are present in the UK** in a tax year.

There are **five ties**:

- Having **close family in the UK** (spouse/civil partner or minor child)
- Having accommodation **in the UK** in which the individual spends at least one night during the tax year
- Doing **substantive work in the UK** (at least 40 days working at least 3 hours a day)

- Being in the UK for **more than 90 days** during **either of the two previous tax years**
- **Spending more time in the UK** than in **any other country** in the tax year (only relevant if **individual was UK resident in any of the previous three tax years**).

The **following table**, showing the **number of ties** by reference to the **number of days in the UK**, will be **provided in the Tax rates and allowances in the exam**.

Days in UK	Previously resident	Not previously resident
Less than 16	Automatically **not** resident	Automatically **not** resident
16 to 45	Resident if 4 UK ties (or more)	Automatically **not** resident
46 to 90	Resident if 3 UK ties (or more)	Resident if 4 UK ties
91 to 120	Resident if 2 UK ties (or more)	Resident if 3 UK ties (or more)
121 to 182	Resident if 1 UK tie (or more)	Resident if 2 UK ties (or more)
183 or more	Automatically resident	Automatically resident

1.1.5 Days spent in the UK

A **day in the UK** is **any day** in which an individual is **present in the UK at midnight**.

Activity 1: UK resident or not UK resident

In one tax year, Sally spent 15 days in the UK.

Required

State with reasons, whether Sally would be UK resident in that tax year.

Solution

Activity 2: UK resident?

Jimmy has lived in Tokyo all of his life where he owned a house. He came to the UK on 1 May 2020 having sold his house in Tokyo the month before. He decided to buy a flat in London which he uses as his only home.

Jimmy lived in the London property until 30 September 2020 and then went on a backpacking holiday for a year.

Required

State with reasons, whether Jimmy would be UK resident in the tax year 2020/21.

Solution

Activity 3: Sufficient ties test

Andy was UK resident in the tax year 2019/20, but was only present in the UK for 80 days in that tax year. He does not satisfy either the automatic overseas test or the automatic UK test in the tax year 2020/21.

In the tax year 2020/21, Andy spent 48 days working five hours a day in the UK where he was present at midnight. Andy's wife lives in the UK in their joint home and Andy lives in this home when he is in the UK. Andy spent the rest of the tax year 2020/21 in Spain.

Required

State with reasons, whether Andy is UK resident in the tax year 2020/21.

Solution

2 Computing taxable income

An individual's income from all sources is brought together (aggregated) in a personal tax computation for each tax year.

Tax year: The **tax year**, or **fiscal year**, or **year of assessment** runs from 6 April to 5 April. For example, the tax year 2020/21 runs from 6 April 2020 to 5 April 2021.

Income tax is charged on **taxable income**. Here is a proforma computation of taxable income:

	Non-savings income	Savings income	Dividend income
	£	£	£
Trading income	X		
Less loss relief	(X)		
	X		
Employment income	X		
Property income	X		
UK dividends			X
Building society/bank interest		X	
Other interest		X	
Total income	X	X	X
Less qualifying interest	(X)		
Less loss relief	(X)		
Net income	X	X	X
Less personal allowance (PA)	(X)		
Taxable income	X	X	X

Total income: Total income is all income subject to income tax. Each of the amounts that make up total income is called a component.

Net income: Net income is total income after qualifying interest and trade losses.

Taxable income: Taxable income is net income less the personal allowance.

3 Types of income

Income must be classified according to the nature of the income as different computational rules apply to different types of income.

PER alert

One of the competencies you require to fulfil Performance Objective 15 *Tax computations and assessments* of the PER is to extract and analyse data from financial records and filing information relevant to the preparation of tax computations and related supporting documents. You can apply the knowledge you obtain from this section of the Workbook to help to demonstrate this competence.

3.1 Non-savings income

Non-savings income consists of:

- Trading income
- Employment income
- Property income
- Pension income

3.2 Savings income

Savings income is interest income, including:

- Bank interest
- Building society interest
- Interest from company loan stock
- Interest from government stocks (gilts)
- Interest from National Savings & Investments accounts

3.3 Dividend income

Dividend income is the dividends received from owning shares in companies.

3.4 Exempt income

Income from certain investments is exempt from income tax. They are therefore useful for tax planning to minimise tax from investments.

PER alert

One of the competencies you require to fulfil Performance Objective 17 *Tax planning and advice* of the PER is to mitigate and/or defer tax liabilities through the use of standard reliefs, exemptions and incentives. You can apply the knowledge you obtain from this section of the Workbook to help to demonstrate this competence.

Exempt income:

- Income from National Savings Certificates
- Statutory redundancy money
- Winnings (including premium bond prizes)
- Scholarships
- Interest on damages for personal injuries
- Local authority grants
- Income from investments made through individual savings accounts (ISAs)

3.4.1 Individual savings accounts (ISAs)

There are two types of ISA:

- Cash ISA (which only has a cash component)
- Stocks and shares ISA (which only has a stocks and shares component unless the provider allows some cash to be held in this type of ISA)

The annual subscription limit for ISAs is £20,000 per tax year (2020/21). It is possible to withdraw funds from a flexible cash ISA and reinvest them without that reinvestment using up any of the annual limit.

Dividend income and interest income received from investments held in an ISA are exempt from income tax. Likewise, gains on disposal of such investments are free from capital gains tax.

Note that **additional rate taxpayers** and individuals who have already **used their savings income nil band will benefit from using a cash ISA** (see savings income nil band later in this Workbook).

4 Personal allowance

The personal allowance is £12,500. It is deducted from net income to arrive at taxable income, firstly against non-savings income, then savings income and finally against dividend income. It is given to all individuals (subject to tapering – see next paragraph) including children.

4.1 Tapering of the personal allowance

If an individual's **adjusted net income** (ANI) exceeds £100,000, the personal allowance is reduced by £1 for every £2 excess income. Once an individual's 'adjusted net income' reaches £125,000 or over, the personal allowance will be reduced to nil.

Adjusted net income: Adjusted net income is net income less the gross amounts of personal pension contributions and gift aid donations.

Exam focus point

The limit of £125,000 will be given to you in the Tax Rates and Allowances available in the exam.

The examining team has stated that, if adjusted net income clearly exceeds £125,000, there is no need to perform the calculations to restrict the personal allowance. A simple statement that no personal allowance is available because adjusted net income exceeds £125,000 is sufficient.

Illustration 1: Personal allowance

In 2020/21, Clare receives employment income of £95,000, bank interest of £8,000 and dividends of £7,500.

Required

Calculate Clare's taxable income for 2020/21.

Solution

	Non-savings income £	Savings income £	Dividend income £	Total £
Employment income	95,000			
Bank interest		8,000		

	Non-savings income £	Savings income £	Dividend income £	Total £
Dividends			7,500	
Net income	95,000	8,000	7,500	110,500
Less PA (see below)	(7,250)			(7,250)
Taxable income	87,750	8,000	7,500	103,250

Net income	110,500
Less income limit	(100,000)
Excess	10,500

PA	12,500
Less half excess (£10,500/2)	(5,250)
	7,250

Note. Where there is no qualifying interest, so that total income is the same as net income, it is acceptable just to state the net income at this stage of the computation.

Activity 4: Personal allowance

Jesse has net income of £105,000.

Required

What is his personal allowance for the tax year 2020/21?

£ [   ]

Solution

5 Computing tax payable

PER alert

One of the competencies you require to fulfil Performance Objective 15 *Tax computations and assessments* of the PER is to prepare or contribute to the computation or assessment of tax computations for individuals. You can apply the knowledge you obtain from this section of the Workbook to help to demonstrate this competence.

Having calculated the taxable income, an exam question could ask for one of two things:

* Tax liability
* Tax payable

Income tax liability: the amount of tax charged on the individual's taxable income.

Income tax payable: the balance of the income tax liability still to be settled in cash.

Income tax payable is computed on an individual's taxable income. The tax rates are applied to taxable income first to non-savings income, then to savings income and finally to dividend income.

5.1 Tax rates

When calculating the income tax liability the tax bands are:

	NSI	SI	DI
Additional-rate band (>£150,000)	45%	45%	38.1%
Higher-rate band (>£37,500)	40%	40%	32.5%
Basic-rate band	20%	20% 0% *	7.5%

*The 0% savings starting rate applies to savings income only in the first £5,000 of taxable income. If non-savings income after the personal allowance is greater than £5,000 then the starting rate does not apply.

Exam focus point

Certain aspects of income tax are devolved. However, since none of the devolved taxes for Scotland, Wales and Northern Ireland are, or will be, examinable, all questions will require application of the income tax rates as shown in the Tax Rates and Allowances available in the exam. Therefore, questions will not state in which part of the UK taxpayers live.

5.2 Computations with non-savings income only

Illustration 2: All rates of tax on non-savings income

In 2020/21 Milo has employment income of £145,000 and property income of £10,800.

Required

Calculate Milo's tax liability for 2020/21.

Solution

	Non-savings income £
Employment income	145,000
Property income	10,800
Net income/taxable income (no PA available as net income exceeds £125,000)	155,800

Income tax

	£
Non-savings income	
£37,500 × 20%	7,500
£112,500 (150,000 – 37,500) × 40%	45,000
£5,800 (155,800 – 150,000) × 45%	2,610
Tax lability	55,110

5.3 Computations with non-savings and savings income only

5.3.1 Savings income starting rate

There is a **tax rate of 0% for savings income up to £5,000 (the savings income starting rate limit)**. This rate is called the **savings income starting rate**. The savings income starting rate only applies where the **savings income falls in the first £5,000 of taxable income.**

Remember that income tax is charged first on non-savings income. So, in most cases, an individual's non-savings income will exceed the savings income starting rate limit and the savings income starting rate will not be available on savings income.

The savings income starting rate counts towards the basic rate limit of £37,500 and the higher rate limit of £150,000.

5.3.2 Savings income nil rate band

There is a **tax rate of 0%** for **savings income** within the **savings income nil rate band.** The savings income nil rate band for 2020/21 is **£1,000** if the individual is a **basic rate taxpayer** and **£500** if the individual is a **higher rate taxpayer**. There is **no savings income nil rate band** for **additional rate taxpayers.**

The savings income nil rate band counts towards the basic rate limit of £37,500 and the higher rate limit of £150,000.

Illustration 3: Savings income starting rate and savings income nil rate band

In 2020/21 Alicia has trading income of £15,100 and bank interest of £8,000.

Required

Calculate Alicia's tax liability for 2020/21.

Solution

	Non-savings income £	Savings income £	Total £
Trading income	15,100		
Bank interest		8,000	
Net income	15,100	8,000	23,100
Less PA	(12,500)		(12,500)
Taxable income	2,600	8,000	10,600

Income tax

	£
Non-savings income	
£2,600 × 20%	520
Savings income	
£2,400 (5,000 - 2,600) × 0% (savings starting rate)	0
£1,000 × 0% (savings income nil rate band)	0
£4,600 (8,000 - 2,400 - 1,000) × 20%	920
Tax liability	1,440

Illustration 4: Savings nil rate, basic rate and higher rate with savings income

In 2020/21, Joe has employment income of £46,450 and bank interest of £5,550.

Required

Calculate Joe's tax liability for 2020/21.

Solution

	Non-savings income £	Savings income £	Total £
Employment income	46,450		
Bank interest		5,550	
Net income	46,450	5,550	52,000
Less PA	(12,500)		(12,500)
Taxable income	33,950	5,550	39,500

Income tax

	£
Non-savings income	
£33,950 × 20%	6,790
Savings income	
£500 × 0% (savings income nil rate band – higher rate taxpayer)	0
£3,050 (37,500 - 33,950 - 500) × 20%	610
£2,000 (5,550 - 500 - 3,050) × 40%	800
Tax liability	8,200

The savings income nil rate band of £500 counts towards the basic rate limit. Therefore, the limit of £37,500 is reduced by both the non-savings income taxed at the basic rate, and the savings income taxed at 0%, to calculate how much of the remaining savings income is taxed at 20% rather than 40%.

Illustration 5: All rates of tax with savings income

In 2020/21 Maddie has trading income of £146,800 and building society interest of £6,700.

Required

Calculate Maddie's tax liability for 2020/21.

Solution

	Non-savings income Total £	Savings income Total £	Total £
Trading income	146,800		
Building society interest		6,700	
Net income/taxable income (no PA available)	146,800	6,700	153,500

Maddie is not entitled to the PA as her net income exceeds £125,000.

Income tax

	£
Non-savings income	
£37,500 × 20%	7,500
£109,300 (146,800 – 37,500) × 40%	43,720
Savings income	
£3,200 (150,000 – 146,800) × 40%	1,280
£3,500 (6,700 – 3,200) × 45%	1,575

	£
Tax liability	54,075

No savings income nil rate band is available because Maddie is an additional rate taxpayer.

5.4 Computations with non-savings, savings and dividend income

5.4.1 Dividend nil rate band

There is a **tax rate of 0%** for **dividend income** within the **dividend nil rate band.** The dividend nil rate band is **£2,000** for **all taxpayers.**

The dividend nil rate band counts towards the basic rate limit of £37,500 and the higher rate limit of £150,000.

 ## Illustration 6: Dividend nil rate, basic rate and higher rate with dividend income

In 2020/21 Margery has employment income of £60,450, building society interest of £1,600 and dividends of £12,000.

Required

Calculate Margery's tax liability for 2020/21.

Solution

	Non-savings income £	Savings income £	Dividend income £	Total £
Employment income	60,450			
Building society interest		1,600		
Dividends			12,000	
Net income	60,450	1,600	12,000	74,050
Less PA	(12,500)			(12,500)
Taxable income	47,950	1,600	12,000	61,550

Income tax

	£
Non-savings income	
£37,500 × 20%	7,500
£10,450 (47,950 - 37,500) × 40%	4,180
Savings income	
£500 × 0% (savings income nil rate band – higher rate taxpayer)	0
£1,100 (1,600 - 500) × 40%	440
Dividend income	
£2,000 × 0% (dividend nil rate band)	0

	£
£10,000 (12,000 – 2,000) × 32.5%	3,250
Tax liability	15,370

Activity 5: Income tax calculations

Holly receives a salary of £45,150 (PAYE deducted in the year was £6,530) and £8,000 of bank deposit interest in the tax year.

Marella has property income of £13,500 and interest income of £15,000 in the tax year.

Fabian has interest income of £163,650 in the tax year.

Required

1 What is Holly's income tax payable for the year?

   ○ £8,660

   ○ £2,130

   ○ £2,030

   ○ £7,030

2 What is Marella's income tax liability for the tax year?

   ○ £3,200

   ○ £2,300

   ○ £3,000

   ○ £2,200

3 What is Fabian's income tax liability for the tax year?

   £ ⬚

Solution

BPP
LEARNING
MEDIA

Activity 6: Income tax payable

Faryl has the following income in the tax year:

	£
Salary	11,100 (PAYE £75)
Building society interest	10,000
Dividends	54,500

Required

What is Faryl's income tax payable?

Solution

Activity 7: Non-savings income, savings income and dividend income

Rajesh has trading income of £130,000 in the tax year. He also received building society interest of £3,750 and dividends of £40,000.

Required

Calculate Rajesh's income tax liability.

Solution

Essential reading

See Chapter 2 Section 1 of the Essential reading for a summary of the steps in the income tax liability and some examples of calculating additional tax due by working at the margin.

The Essential reading is available as an Appendix of the digital edition of the Workbook.

5.5 Transferable personal allowance (marriage allowance)

An individual can elect to transfer £1,250 of their PA to their spouse/civil partner if certain conditions are met. This is sometimes known as the marriage allowance.

Exam focus point

The transferable amount of PA will be given to you in the Tax Rates and Allowances available in the exam.

Neither the spouse/civil partner making the transfer nor the spouse/civil partner receiving the transfer can be a higher rate or additional rate taxpayer.

The spouse/civil partner receiving the transfer does not have an increased PA. **Instead, they are entitled to a tax reducer of £1,250 × 20% = £250. The tax reducer reduces the individual's tax liability.** If the individual has a tax liability of less than £250, the tax reducer reduces the tax liability to nil.

Illustration 7: Transferable personal allowance

Alec and Bertha are a married couple. In the tax year 2020/21, Alec has net income of £11,150 and Bertha has net income of £26,500. All their income is non-savings income. Alec has made an election to transfer part of his PA to Bertha.

Required

Show Alec and Bertha's taxable income for 2020/21 and compute Bertha's income tax liability.

Solution

Alec

	Non-savings income
	£
Net income	11,150
Less PA £(12,500 − 1,250)	(11,250)
Taxable income	0

Bertha

	Non-savings income
	£
Net income	26,500
Less PA	(12,500)
Taxable income	14,000
Income tax	
£14,000 × 20%	2,800
Less transferable personal allowance tax reducer £1,250 × 20%	(250)
Income tax liability	2,550

Activity 8: Transferable amount of personal allowance

Ash and Den are married. Ash has trading income of £10,090 and Den has employment income of £43,550.

Required

1   How will the transferable personal allowance work for Ash and Den?

   ○ It is not allowed as Den is a higher rate taxpayer

   ○ It is not allowed as Ash is using some of this year's personal allowance

   ○ Ash transfers £1,250 of his personal allowance to Den

   ○ Den transfers £1,250 of his personal allowance to Ash

2   What is Den's income tax liability for the tax year 2020/21?

   ○ £3,710

   ○ £250

   ○ £5,960

   ○ £6,210

Solution

6 Gift aid

KEY
TERM

> **Gift aid:** One-off and regular charitable gifts of money qualify for tax relief under the **gift aid scheme** provided the donor gives the charity a gift aid declaration.

(a) **Basic rate**

A gift aid donation is treated as though it is paid **net of basic rate tax** (20%). This gives basic rate tax relief when the payment is made. For example, if the taxpayer wants the charity to receive a donation of £1,000, they would only need to make a payment to the charity of £800. The charity reclaims the 20% tax relief that the taxpayer has received, resulting in a gross gift of £1,000.

(b) **Higher and additional rate**

Additional tax relief for higher rate and additional rate taxpayers is **given in the personal tax computation by increasing the donor's basic rate limit and higher rate limit by the gross amount of the gift.** To arrive at the gross amount of the gift you must multiply the amount paid (the net amount) by 100/80. In the above example, the gross amount would be the amount paid of £800 × 100/80 = £1,000. The effect of increasing the basic rate limit is to increase the amount on which basic rate tax is payable. This is sometimes called 'extending the basic rate band'.

The effect of increasing the higher rate limit is simply to preserve the amount of taxable income on which higher rate tax is payable.

No additional relief is due for basic rate taxpayers. Increasing the basic rate limit is irrelevant as taxable income is below this limit.

The gross gift aid donation is also deducted from adjusted net income (ANI) for the purposes of tapering the personal allowance.

Illustration 8: Gift aid, basic rate band and adjusted net income

Margaretta earns a salary of £112,000 in 2020/21. In January 2021, she made a gift aid donation of £5,000 (net).

Required

Compute Margaretta's income tax liability for 2020/21.

Solution

		Non-savings income
		£
Employment income/Net income		112,000
Less PA (W1)		(9,625)
Taxable income		102,375
Income tax		
Basic rate (W2)	£43,750 × 20%	8,750
Higher rate	£58,625 × 40%	23,450

BPP
LEARNING
MEDIA

		Non-savings income
		£
	102,375	32,200

Workings

1   **Personal allowance**

	£
Net income	112,000
Less: gift aid donation £5,000 × 100/80	(6,250)
Adjusted net income	105,750
Less income limit	(100,000)
Excess	5,750
PA	12,500
Less half excess £5,750 × 1/2	(2,875)
	9,625

2   **Basic rate limit**

£37,500 + (£5,000 × 100/80) = £43,750

Activity 9: Gift aid

Gloria has employment income of £120,000. She made a gift aid donation of £7,200 (net) to a charity.

Required

1   What is Gloria's personal allowance for this tax year?

O   £2,500

O   £5,500

O   £6,100

O   £7,000

2   What is the basic rate limit for Gloria for this tax year?

O   £37,500

O   £28,500

O   £46,500

O   £44,700

Solution

7 Qualifying interest/qualifying loan

Interest paid gross on the following can be deducted from total income:

(a) Loan to buy plant and machinery for use in a partnership or employment

(b) Loan to invest in partnership

(c) Loan to buy interest in employee-controlled company

(d) Loan to invest in a co-operative

For the purposes of TX, qualifying interest is deducted from non-savings income first, then from savings income and lastly from dividend income.

Essential reading

For more detail on qualifying interest and an example, see Chapter 2 Section 2 of the Essential reading.

The Essential reading is available as an Appendix of the digital edition of the Workbook.

8 Married couples and couples in a civil partnership

PER alert

One of the competencies you require to fulfil Performance Objective 17 *Tax planning and advice* of the PER is to review the situation of an individual or entity advising on any potential tax risks and/or additional tax minimisation measures. You can apply the knowledge you obtain from this section of the Workbook to help to demonstrate this competence.

8.1 Spouses and civil partners

Spouses and civil partners are taxed as two separate people. Each spouse/civil partner is entitled to a personal allowance depending on their income.

Spouses and civil partners should ensure, where possible, that **each spouse/civil partner uses their main nil rate band, savings income nil rate band and dividend nil rate band** (eg by transferring assets, bank accounts or shares).

8.2 Jointly held property

Income from jointly held property is split 50:50 unless the couple make a joint declaration to HMRC specifying the actual proportions they are each entitled to.

Essential reading

See Chapter 2 Section 3 of the Essential reading for some examples of tax planning for spouses/civil partners.

The Essential reading is available as an Appendix of the digital edition of the Workbook.

9 Child benefit income tax charge

An income tax charge applies if a taxpayer receives child benefit (or their partner receives child benefit) and the taxpayer has **adjusted net income over £50,000 in a tax year**. Adjusted net income is defined in the same way as for the restriction of the PA described earlier in this chapter. The effect of the charge is to recover child benefit from taxpayers who have higher incomes.

A 'partner' is a **spouse**, a **civil partner,** or an **unmarried partner** where the couple are **living together as though they were married or were civil partners.**

If the taxpayer has **adjusted net income over £60,000,** the charge is equal to the **full amount of child benefit received**.

If the taxpayer has **adjusted net income between £50,000 and £60,000**, the charge is **1% of the child benefit amount for each £100 of adjusted net income in excess of £50,000**. The calculation, at all stages, is rounded down to the nearest whole number.

> ### Exam focus point
>
> This information will be given in the Tax Rates and Allowances available in the exam.

If **both partners have adjusted net income in excess of £50,000,** the **partner with the higher adjusted net income** is liable for the charge.

Illustration 9: Child benefit income tax charge

Samantha is divorced and has two children aged ten and six. She has net income of £56,000 in 2020/21. Samantha made personal pension contributions of £4,500 (gross) during 2020/21. She receives child benefit of £1,788 in 2020/21.

Required

Calculate Samantha's child benefit income tax charge for 2020/21.

Solution

	£
Net income	56,000
Less personal pension contributions (gross)	(4,500)
Adjusted net income	51,500
Less threshold	(50,000)

		£
Excess		1,500
÷ £100		15
Child benefit income tax charge:		
1% × £1,788 × 15		268

> **Tutorial note.** If Samantha had made an extra gross personal pension contribution of £1,500 during 2020/21, her adjusted net income would not have exceeded £50,000 and she would not have been subject to the child benefit income tax charge.

Activity 10: Child benefit

Ralph has a salary of £54,000. He received child benefit of £2,500.

Required

Calculate the child benefit income tax charge.

£ [   ]

Solution

10 Accrued income scheme

Gilts are securities issued by the UK Government as a way of borrowing money. Interest is paid to the holder of the gilt (the investor) in fixed amounts on fixed dates.

The accrued income scheme ensures that a taxpayer who **sells a gilt** is **taxed on any interest income** included in the proceeds. Similarly, **relief** is given to the **purchaser** of the gilt for the **interest included in the price** paid.

As a forthcoming interest payment approaches the price of the gilt will start to increase. This is because a purchaser of the gilt will be entitled to the next interest payment, so the closer to the interest date we get the more expensive the gilt becomes as investors are willing to pay more for the gilt.

Usual income tax rules state that interest is taxable on individuals when it is received. However, where an individual holds gilts with a total nominal (face) value of more than £5,000 and they sell the gilts for a price which includes interest then the amount of interest which has **accrued** since the last interest payment up to the date of the sale is taxed as savings income on the seller.

When the interest is paid to the buyer of the gilt, they are given tax relief by deducting the seller's accrued income.

Illustration 10: Accrued income scheme

Owen owned £10,000 (nominal value) 5% UK Government Loan Stock. Interest was payable on 30 June and 31 December each year. Owen sold the loan stock to Yvonne on 30 November 2020 for sale proceeds of £11,208 including accrued interest of £208 for the period between 1 July 2020 and 30 November 2020 (£10,000 × 5% × 5/12).

Required

What are the amounts taxable on Owen and Yvonne as savings income in respect of the loan stock for 2020/21?

Solution

	£
Owen	
Interest received 30.6.20	
£10,000 × 5% × 6/12	250
Accrued interest deemed received 31.12.20	
£10,000 × 5% × 5/12	208
Total taxable as savings income	458
Yvonne	
Interest received 31.12.20	
£10,000 × 5% × 6/12	250
Less relief for accrued interest (amount taxable on Owen)	
£10,000 × 5% × 5/12	(208)
Total taxable as savings income (ie 1 month of interest £10,000 × 5% × 1/12)	42

Exam focus point

The accrued income scheme rules may seem complicated but remember that the aim is to tax each taxpayer on the interest which relates to their period of ownership, regardless of whether it was actually received by the buyer or the seller.

Activity 11: Interest assessable

On 1 August 2020 Caroline bought some 4% gilts from Jamie. They have a nominal value of £50,000 and pay interest on 30 June and 31 December each year. She paid £52,000 (including interest) on 1 August 2020 and sold them for £54,500 (including interest) on 31 March 2021 to Tyrone.

Required

How much interest is assessable on Caroline in the tax year 2020/21 in relation to these gilts?

£ [ ]

Solution

Chapter summary

Computing taxable income and the income tax liability

Scope of income tax

Residence
- UK residents taxed on worldwide income
- Non UK residents taxed on UK income only
- Statutory test of residence

Computing taxable income

- Tax/fiscal year runs from 6 April to 5 April
- Total income = all income subject to income tax
- Taxable income = net income less the personal allowance
- Net income = total income after qualifying interest and trade losses

Types of income

Non-savings income
- Trading income
- Employment income
- Property income
- Pension income

Savings income
- Building society/bank interest
- Received gross

Dividend income
- Received gross from UK companies

Exempt income
- Individual savings accounts (ISAs), limit £20,000 per year
- Income from National Savings Certificates
- Statutory redundancy
- Winnings

Personal allowance

- £12,500 deducted from net income

Tapering of personal allowance
- Taper if 'adjusted net income' ANI exceeds £100,000
- ANI = Net income less trading losses, qualifying interest, gross gift aid donations and gross personal pension contributions

Computing tax payable

- Tax liability = income tax on taxable income
- Tax payable = tax liability less tax already deducted at source

Tax rates
- NSI – Tax @ 20%, 40%, 45%
- SI – Tax @ 0% if in the starting rate band or savings income nil rate band (£1,000 for BR taxpayers, £500 for HR taxpayers) then 20%, 40%, 45%
- DI – Tax @ 0% if in the dividend nil rate band (£2,000) then 7.5%, 32.5%, 37.5%

Computations with non-savings income only
- Add up income, deduct qualifying interest and trade losses to compute net income
- Deduct PA to compute taxable income
- Tax @ 20% up to BR limit, between BR and HR @ 40%, above HR @ 45%

Computations with non-savings and savings income only
- Savings income starting rate – 0% for savings income up to £5,000
  - Where savings income falls wholly or partly below the starting rate limit
- Savings income nil rate band – £1,000 for BR taxpayers, £500 for HR taxpayers
- Tax @ 20% up to BR limit, between BR and HR @ 40%, above HR @ 45%

Computations with non-savings and savings and dividend income
- Dividend nil rate band = £2,000
- Tax @ 7.5% up to BR limit, between BR and HR @ 32.5%, above HR @ 37.5%

Transferable personal allowance (marriage allowance)
- Spouses/CPs
- Fixed amount of £1,250 (2020/21)
- Tax reducer @ 20% ie reduction in transferee's IT liability of £250
- Cannot trigger a repayment
- Not available if either spouse/CP is HR or AR taxpayer

Gift aid

- Paid net of 20%
- HR and AR taxpayers extend bands by payment × 100/80

Qualifying interest

- Loan to buy plant or machinery for use in partnership/employment
- Loan to invest in partnership
- Loan to buy interest in employee controlled company
- Loan to invest in a cooperative

Married couples and couples in a civil partnership

Spouses and civil partners
- Married couples/civil partners to minimise tax: using personal allowance and nil rate bands

Jointly held property
- Jointly owned property, assumed to be held 50:50 unless actual proportions declared

Child benefit income tax charge

- Charge if ANI >£50,000, entire benefit clawed back if ANI reaches £60,000

Accrued income scheme

- Interest included in the selling price of a government security is taxed as income on accruals basis
- Only if nominal value exceeds £5,000

Knowledge diagnostic

1. Scope of income tax

UK resident individuals are liable to income tax on all income.

Non-UK resident individuals are only liable to UK income tax on UK income only.

There is a statutory test of residence.

2. Income tax computation

Make sure you learn the proforma.

3. Types of income

Income is categorised into three sections – non-savings, savings and dividend income.

4. Personal allowance

Everyone receives a personal allowance. However, if adjusted net income > £100,000 it is reduced by £1 for every £2 excess income.

5. Computing tax payable

Non-savings income is taxed at 20%/40%/45%.

Savings income is taxed at 0%/20%/40%/45%.

Dividend income is taxed at 0%/7.5%/32.5%/38.1%.

6. Gift aid

Gift aid donations enable the taxpayer to save tax at their marginal rate. For higher and additional rate taxpayers this is achieved by extending the basic rate and higher rate limits by the gross donation.

7. Qualifying interest

Interest on certain loans can be deducted from total income.

8. Married couples/civil partners

Split property income 50:50 for spouses/civil partners unless election for actual entitlements.

Each spouse/civil partner should use their personal allowance, savings income nil rate band and dividend nil rate band.

9. Child benefit charge

If ANI is between £50,000 and £60,000 charge will be 1% of amount received for every £100 of income over £50,000.

10. Accrued income scheme

Seller taxed on accrued interest received on sale. Buyer given tax relief against interest received of seller's accrued interest.

Further study guidance

Question practice

Now try the following from the Further question practice bank (available in the digital edition of the Workbook):

Section A questions:

Q4, Q5, Q6, Q7, Q8

Section C questions:

Q9 Sandeep, Harriet and Romelu

Q10 John and Helen

Q11 Michael and Josie

Activity answers

Activity 1: UK resident or not UK resident

Sally has spent fewer than 16 days in the UK in the tax year.

Sally is therefore automatically not UK resident for that tax year.

Activity 2: UK resident?

Jimmy does not satisfy the automatic overseas test because he is present in the UK ≥ 46 days in the tax year and does not work overseas full time.

Jimmy satisfies the automatic UK resident test; he only has a UK home.

Jimmy is therefore UK resident in the tax year.

Activity 3: Sufficient ties test

Andy has:

- Been present in the UK for 46–90 days (48 days)
- Three UK ties (close family, available accommodation, and substantive UK work)

Andy is therefore UK resident in the tax year 2020/21

Activity 4: Personal allowance

£ 10,000

	£	£
Basic personal allowance		12,500
Less reduction		
ANI	105,000	
Less limit	(100,000)	
	5,000	
× 0.5		(2,500)
Personal allowance		10,000

Activity 5: Income tax calculations

1   The correct answer is: £2,130

	Non-savings income £	Savings income £	Total £
Employment income	45,150		
Bank interest		8,000	
Net income	45,150	8,000	
Less PA	(12,500)		
Taxable income	32,650	8,000	40,650

Income tax

	£
Non-savings income	
£32,650 × 20%	6,530
Savings income	
£500 × 0%	0
£4,350 × 20%	870
£3,150 × 40%	1,260
Tax liability	8,660
PAYE	(6,530)
Tax payable	2,130

The answer £8,660 is the tax liability. The answer £2,030 uses a savings income nil rate band of £1,000. The answer £7,030 does not deduct the personal allowance.

2 The correct answer is: £2,200

	Non-savings income £	Savings income £	Total £
Property income	13,500		
Interest income		15,000	
Net income	13,500	15,000	
Less PA	(12,500)		
Taxable income	1,000	15,000	16,000

Income tax

	£
Non-savings income	
£1,000 × 20%	200
Savings income	
£4,000 (£5,000 - £1,000 NSI) × 0% (starting rate)	0
£1,000 × 0% (NRB for basic rate payer)	0
£10,000 × 20%	2,000
Tax liability	2,200

3 £ 57,643

	Savings income £	Total £
Interest income	163,650	
Net income	163,650	
Less PA*	(–)	
Taxable income		

	Savings income	Total
	£	£
	163,650	163,650

*No personal allowance as ANI exceeds £125,000.

Income tax

	£
Savings income	
0% (starting rate)	0
32,500 × 20%	6,500
112,500 × 40%	45,000
13,650 × 45%	6,142
Tax liability	57,642

Activity 6: Income tax payable

	Non-savings income £	Savings income £	Dividend income £	Total £
Employment income	11,100			
Building society interest		10,000		
Dividends			54,500	
Net income	11,100	10,000	54,500	75,600
Less PA	(11,100)	(1,400)		(12,500)
Taxable income	–	8,600	54,500	63,100

Income tax

	£
Savings income	
5,000 × 0%	0
500 × 0% (NRB - higher rate taxpayer)	0
3,100 (8,600 - 5,000 - 500) × 20%	620
Dividend income	
2,000 × 0% (NRB)	0
26,900 (37,500 - 8,600 - 2,000) × 7.5%	2,017
25,600 (54,500 - 2,000 - 26,900) × 32.5%	8,320
Income tax liability	10,957
Less PAYE	(75)
Income tax payable	10,882

Activity 7: Non-savings income, savings income and dividend income

	Non-savings income £	Savings income £	Dividend income £
Trading profit	130,000		
Building society interest		3,750	
Dividend income			40,000
Less PA	(0)*		
Taxable income	130,000	3,750	40,000

*No personal allowance as Rajesh's ANI of £173,750 (£130,000 + £3,750 + £40,000) exceeds £125,000.

Income tax

	£
Non-savings income	
37,500 × 20%	7,500
92,500 × 40%	37,000
130,000	
Savings income	
£3,750 × 40% (No NRB as Rajesh is an additional rate taxpayer)	1,500
Dividend income	
2,000 × 0%	0
£14,250 (150,000 - 2,000 - 3,750 - 130,000) × 32.5%	4,631
150,000	
23,750 (40,000 – 2,000 – 14,250) × 38.1%	9,049
Income tax liability	59,680

Activity 8: Transferable amount of personal allowance

1   The correct answer is: Ash transfers £1,250 of his personal allowance to Den

   Den is not a higher rate taxpayer. After his personal allowance, his taxable income is £43,550 – £12,500 = £31,050. Ash is using some of his personal allowance but that does not prevent the transfer. It is still beneficial if some of Ash's personal allowance is unused. The transfer would be from Ash to Den.

2   The correct answer is: £5,960

	£
Employment income	43,550
Personal allowance	(12,500)
	31,050
Income tax at 20%	6,210
Tax reducer (20% × £1,250)	(250)

The answer £3,710 assumes that the whole of Ash's personal allowance can be transferred to Den. The answer £250 is the tax reducer. The answer £6,210 is the income tax before the tax reducer is applied.

Activity 9: Gift aid

1   The correct answer is: £7,000

Personal allowance

	£
Employment income	120,000
Less gift aid donation 7,200 × 100/80	(9,000)
ANI	111,000
Less limit	(100,000)
	11,000
Personal allowance	12,500
Less 1/2 × 11,000	(5,500)
	7,000

The answer £2,500 does not adjust for the gift aid donation. The answer £5,500 is the restriction on the personal allowance. The answer £6,100 does not gross up the gift aid donation.

2   The correct answer is: £46,500

Increase basic rate limit by gross gift donation

£37,500 + £7,200 × 100/80 = £46,500

The answer £37,500 is the unadjusted basic rate limit. The answer £28,500 decreases the basic rate band limit by the gross gift aid donation. The answer £44,700 does not gross up the gift aid donation.

Activity 10: Child benefit

£ 1,000

The child benefit income tax charge is £1,000 (£2,500 × 1% × 40 (54,000 − 50,000/100)).

Activity 11: Interest assessable

£ 1,333

	£
Interest actually received 31.12.20	
(½ × 4% × £50,000)	1,000
Less interest accrued to Jamie (July 2020)	
(1/12 × 4% × £50,000)	(167)

	£
Add interest accrued up to sale (Jan–Mar 2021)	
(3/12 × 4% × £50,000)	500
	1,333

Sense check: eight months' ownership, therefore 8/12 × 4% × £50,000 = £1,333

3

Employment income

Learning objectives

On completion of this chapter, you should be able to:

	Syllabus reference no.
Recognise the factors that determine whether an engagement is treated as employment or self-employment.	B2(a)
Recognise the basis of assessment for employment income.	B2(b)
Recognise the income assessable.	B2(c)
Recognise the allowable deductions, including travelling expenses.	B2(d)
Discuss the use of the statutory approved mileage allowances.	B2(e)
Understand the treatment of gift aid donations and charitable giving.	B5(f)

Exam context

You are very likely to be asked a question concerning at least one aspect of employment taxation in your exam. This could range from identifying the date on which earnings are received in Section A or Section B to a discussion of the distinction between employment and self-employment in Section C, either as part of a 15-mark question or a 10-mark question.

Chapter overview

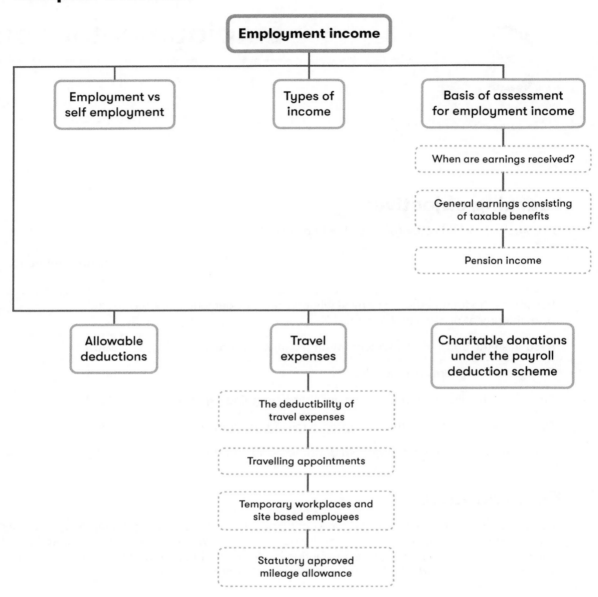

1 Employment vs self-employment

It can be difficult to distinguish between employment (receipts taxable as earnings) and self-employment (profits taxable as trading income). Taxpayers tend to prefer self-employment, because the rules on deductions for expenses are more generous.

(a) The advantages of being self-employed are many:

    (i) For the client:

        (1) No national insurance contribution (NIC) liability

        (2) No need to apply Pay As You Earn (PAYE)

    (ii) For the worker:

        (1) Income received gross with a delay before having to pay a tax bill

        (2) Better deductibility of expenses (see later in this chapter)

(b) It has been held that employment is a **contract of service**, whereas self-employment is a **contract for services.**

(c) Factors which might lead to a presumption of employment rather than self-employment would include the following:

    (i) If the client provides any equipment necessary for the work, this is likely to indicate employment.

    (ii) Whether the individual can choose the place of their work, the hours of work and method of working (ie the degree of control). If they are subject to the direction of another person in these matters, they are likely to be employed.

    (iii) If the individual can choose whether they perform the work, they are likely to be self-employed. If they are subject to another person's instructions and cannot decline work they are offered, they are likely to be employed.

    (iv) If the individual holds an integral position within an organisation (eg manager), they are likely to be employed.

    (v) Where the individual bears individual risk in respect of the work performed, this would be a sign of self-employment. If they suffer no financial or personal risk in respect of the duties performed, they are likely to be employed.

    (vi) If the individual has rights under employment legislation, or has the right to receive regular remuneration, holiday pay, redundancy pay or benefits, this is likely to indicate employment rather than self-employment.

    (vii) If the individual can hire other people rather than having to perform the duties themselves, they are likely to be self-employed.

    (viii) If the individual works for multiple clients, they are likely to be self-employed.

2 Types of income

Any amounts deriving from an office or employment:

Salary	X
Bonus	X
Commission/tips	X
Benefits	X̲
	X
Allowable deductions (later in this chapter)	(X̲)
Employment income	X̲

3 Basis of assessment for employment income

Employment income includes income arising from an employment under a contract of service and the income of office holders, such as directors. The term 'employee' is used in this Workbook to mean anyone who receives employment income (ie both employees and directors).

General earnings are an employee's earnings (see the following key term) plus the 'cash equivalent' of any taxable non-monetary benefits.

KEY TERM

> **Earnings:** Any salary, wage or fee, any gratuity or other profit or incidental benefit obtained by the employee if it is money or money's worth (something of direct monetary value or convertible into direct monetary value) or anything else which constitutes a reward of the employment.

3.1 When are earnings received?

Employees are assessed on amounts received in the current tax year. An amount is treated as received on the earlier of either:

- Cash receipt; or
- When the employee becomes entitled to payment

If the employee is a **director** of a company, earnings from the company are deemed to be received on the earliest of:

- The earlier of the two alternatives given in the general rule (above)
- The time when the amount is credited in the company's accounting records
- The end of the company's period of account (if the amount was determined by then)
- The time the amount is determined (if after the end of the company's period of account)

3.1.1 General earnings consisting of taxable benefits

Taxable benefits (see next chapter) are generally treated as received when they are provided to the employee.

3.1.2 Pension income

The receipts basis does not apply to pension income. Pension income is taxed on the amount accruing in the tax year, whether or not it has actually been received in that year.

 ## Illustration 1: Receipt of money earnings

Josephine and Vincent are employed by Diamond plc. Josephine is a director of Diamond plc. Vincent is not a director of Diamond plc. Diamond plc makes up its accounts to 31 March each year.

Bonuses were awarded by Diamond plc as follows:

Josephine

£5,000. This amount was determined by the directors on 28 February 2021 and credited to Josephine's director's account on 10 March 2021, subject to a condition that she was could not draw down the bonus until 15 April 2021, on which date she became entitled to payment of the bonus. Josephine was actually paid the bonus on 28 April 2021.

Vincent

£3,000. Vincent became entitled to be paid this bonus on 31 March 2020, but agreed that payment should be delayed due to Diamond plc's cash flow problems. He was actually paid the bonus on 30 April 2020.

Required

Explain when each of the bonuses is received for the purposes of employment income, and determine the tax year in which each bonus will be taxed.

Solution

Josephine

Josephine is a director and so her bonus is received for the purposes of employment income on the earliest of:

Time payment made: 28 April 2021

Time of entitlement: 15 April 2021

Credited in records: 10 March 2021

End of period of account: 31 March 2021 (amount determined before end of period)

The earliest of these dates is 10 March 2021 and so this is the date of receipt of the bonus. The tax year in which the bonus is taxed is therefore 2020/21.

Vincent

Vincent is not a director so his bonus is received for the purposes of employment income on the earlier of:

Time payment made: 30 April 2020

Time of entitlement: 31 March 2020

The earlier of these dates is 31 March 2020 and so this is the date of receipt of the bonus. The tax year in which the bonus is taxed is therefore 2019/20.

Tax on earnings from employment income is collected through the **PAYE system** (covered in the next chapter).

4 Allowable deductions

> **Exam focus point**
>
> The general rule for allowable deductions states that expenses must be incurred **wholly, exclusively** and **necessarily** in the performance of duties.

The following are allowable deductions:

(a) Contributions by the individual to a registered occupational pension scheme (see Chapter 5)

(b) Fees and subscriptions to relevant professional bodies

(c) Travelling expenses incurred in the performance of duties (see next)

(d) Capital allowances on plant and machinery necessarily provided by the employee

(e) Donations to charity under payroll giving scheme

(f) Insurance premiums to cover directors' and employees' liabilities and payments to meet those liabilities (eg liability for negligence and related legal proceedings cost)

An employee required to work at home may be able to claim a deduction for the additional costs of working from home. Employers can pay up to £6 per week without the need for supporting evidence of the costs.

Note that the **cost of clothes** for work is **not deductible,** except for certain trades requiring protective clothing where there are annual deductions on a set scale.

5 Travel expenses

5.1 The deductibility of travel expenses

A deduction will be available for:

• Any amount **necessarily** expended on travelling and subsistence in the performance of duties

- Any amount attributable to the necessary attendance at any place in the performance of duties
- Any other expenses wholly, exclusively and necessarily incurred in the performance of duties
- Any travel to a temporary workplace

A deduction from employment income is **not available** for the cost of the **employee's normal commute to work.**

5.2 Travelling appointments

Where an individual has a **travelling appointment** (ie where travelling is an integral part of the job such as for a service engineer), it is accepted that duties commence on leaving home and it will still be possible to obtain a deduction for travelling expenses, even for those legs of a journey which start or finish at home, provided the employee lives within their normal work area. Otherwise, travel from home to the work area is ordinary commuting, as is travel from home to a regular depot or base.

5.3 Temporary workplaces and site-based employees

The cost of travel to a temporary workplace is allowable, whether direct from home or from another (permanent or temporary) workplace. Tax relief is also available for accommodation and subsistence expenses incurred by an employee who is working at a temporary workplace on a secondment expected to last up to 24 months.

Site-based employees are those individuals who have no permanent workplace and do not hold a travelling appointment but work at successive places spending a few days, weeks or months at each place, eg computer consultant.

A workplace is permanent if the employee:

(a) Spends at least 40% of their working time at the workplace; or

(b) The period they expect to work at the workplace exceeds 24 months.

If the employee initially expects to spend less than 24 months at the workplace but subsequently plans change (eg if the posting is extended) then travel expenses will be denied at that point (and *vice versa*).

Activity 1: Relief for travelling costs

Judi is an accountant. She often travels to meetings at the firm's offices in Scotland, returning to her office in Leeds after the meetings.

Required

What tax relief is available for Judi's travel costs?

Solution

5.4 Statutory approved mileage allowances

Amounts up to the statutory approved mileage allowance (given in the tax rates and allowances in the exam) are received tax free. If less than statutory approved mileage allowance is given, a deduction for the shortfall may be claimed. If an amount greater than the statutory approved allowance is received, then the excess is a taxable benefit. This is instead of claiming a proportion of the car running expenses and capital allowances.

Authorised mileage allowances: cars

Up to 10,000 miles	45p
Over 10,000 miles	25p

Activity 2: Mileage allowance

Fred owns a car and travels 11,000 business miles in the car in a tax year. He is paid 35p per mile by his employer.

Required

What is the impact on Fred's assessable employment income for the tax year?

- O Deduction of £1,100
- O Deduction of £900
- O Increase of £1,100
- O Increase of £900

Solution

6 Charitable donations under the payroll deduction scheme

Employees can make charitable donations under the payroll deduction scheme by asking their employer to make deductions from their gross earnings. The deductions are then passed to a charitable agency which will either distribute the funds to the employees' chosen charities on receipt of their instructions or provide the employee with vouchers that can be redeemed by the recipient charities.

The donation is an allowable deduction from the employee's earnings for tax purposes. Tax relief is given at source as the employer must deduct the donation from gross pay before calculating PAYE.

Exam focus point

Make sure you understand the difference between how tax relief is given for gift aid donations and how tax relief is given through the payroll deduction scheme.

Chapter summary

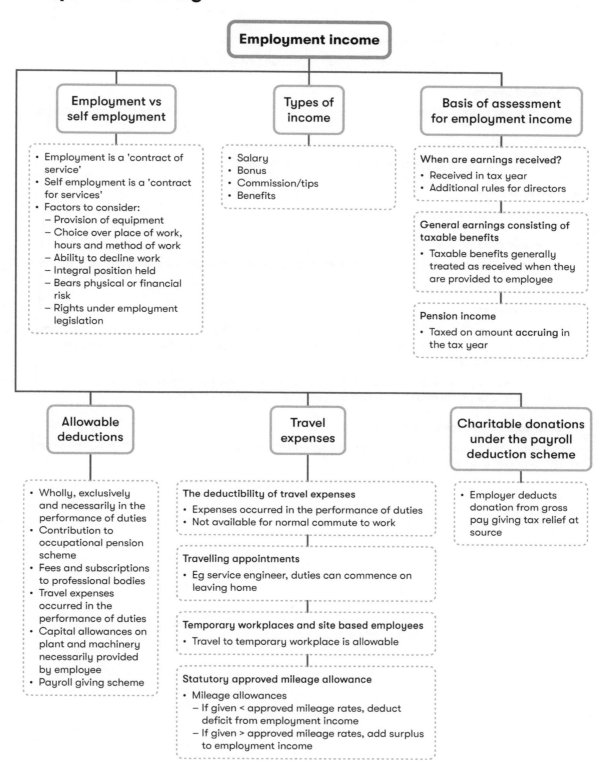

Employment income

Employment vs self employment

- Employment is a 'contract of service'
- Self employment is a 'contract for services'
- Factors to consider:
  - Provision of equipment
  - Choice over place of work, hours and method of work
  - Ability to decline work
  - Integral position held
  - Bears physical or financial risk
  - Rights under employment legislation

Types of income

- Salary
- Bonus
- Commission/tips
- Benefits

Basis of assessment for employment income

When are earnings received?
- Received in tax year
- Additional rules for directors

General earnings consisting of taxable benefits
- Taxable benefits generally treated as received when they are provided to employee

Pension income
- Taxed on amount accruing in the tax year

Allowable deductions

- Wholly, exclusively and necessarily in the performance of duties
- Contribution to occupational pension scheme
- Fees and subscriptions to professional bodies
- Travel expenses occurred in the performance of duties
- Capital allowances on plant and machinery necessarily provided by employee
- Payroll giving scheme

Travel expenses

The deductibility of travel expenses
- Expenses occurred in the performance of duties
- Not available for normal commute to work

Travelling appointments
- Eg service engineer, duties can commence on leaving home

Temporary workplaces and site based employees
- Travel to temporary workplace is allowable

Statutory approved mileage allowance
- Mileage allowances
  - If given < approved mileage rates, deduct deficit from employment income
  - If given > approved mileage rates, add surplus to employment income

Charitable donations under the payroll deduction scheme

- Employer deducts donation from gross pay giving tax relief at source

Knowledge diagnostic

1. Employment vs self-employment

Employment is a 'contract of service'. Self-employment is a 'contract for services'.

2. Types of income

Any amount received from an office or employment is assessed under employment income.

3. Basis of assessment

Basis of assessment is the amount received in a tax year.

4. Administration

Tax is collected through the PAYE system.

5. Allowable deductions

Deductions can be made but only if **wholly, exclusively and necessarily** in the performance of duties.

6. Travel expenses

Normal commuting costs are not deductible. Cost of getting to and from work is allowable as a deduction against employment income for site-based employees, those with travelling appointments or those who travel to temporary workplaces.

Business mileage allowance up to statutory approved mileage allowance is received tax free. Any shortfall is a deductible expense but any excess is a taxable benefit.

7. Charitable donations via payroll

Employees can make tax deductible donations to charity under the payroll deduction scheme. The amount paid is deducted from gross pay.

Further study guidance

Question practice

Now try the following from the Further question practice bank (available in the digital edition of the Workbook):

Section A questions:

Q12, Q13, Q14

Activity answers

Activity 1: Relief for travelling costs

Relief is available for the full cost of these journeys as the travel is undertaken in the performance of Judi's duties.

To prevent manipulation of the basic rule normal commuting will not become a business journey just because the employee stops during the journey to perform a business task (eg to send an email). Nor will relief be available if the journey is essentially the same as the employee's normal journey to work.

Activity 2: Mileage allowance

The correct answer is: Deduction of £900

Fred's employment income will decrease by £900 as a result of the payment of the mileage allowance.

	£	£
Actually paid 35p × 11,000 miles		3,850
Allowed:		
10,000 × 45p	4,500	
1,000 × 25p	250	
11,000		(4,750)
Allowable deduction		(900)

A deduction of £1,100 assumes relief is given at 45p per mile. Fred is being paid less for his mileage than is allowed under the statutory rates so he is entitled to an additional deduction.

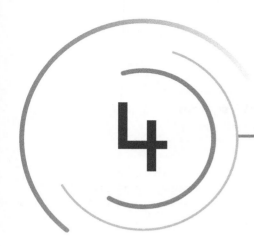

4

Taxable and exempt benefits. The PAYE system

Learning objectives

On completion of this chapter, you should be able to:

	Syllabus reference no.
Explain the PAYE system, how benefits can be payrolled, and the purpose of form P11D.	B2(f)
Explain and compute the amount of benefits assessable.	B2(g)
Recognise the circumstances in which real time reporting late filing penalties will be imposed on an employer and the amount of penalty which is charged.	B2(h)

Exam context

Benefits are a very important part of employment income and you are likely to come across them in your exam in any of Sections A, B or Section C, in a 15-mark question or a 10-mark question. If you come across exempt benefits in a Section C question, note this in your answer to show that you have considered each item.

The Pay As You Earn (PAYE) system is a system of deduction of tax at source. You should be able to explain how it collects tax. The forms for the PAYE system are important, as are the dates for submission.

Chapter overview

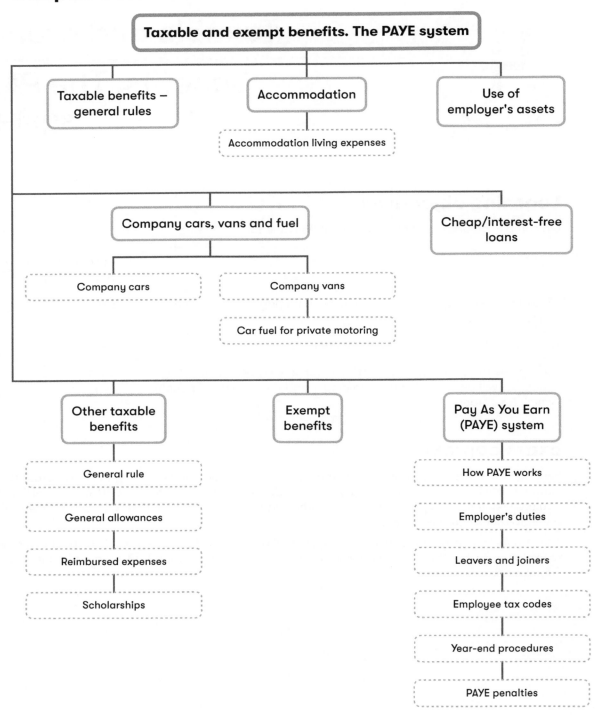

Taxable and exempt benefits. The PAYE system

- Taxable benefits – general rules
- Accommodation
  - Accommodation living expenses
- Use of employer's assets
- Company cars, vans and fuel
  - Company cars
  - Company vans
    - Car fuel for private motoring
- Cheap/interest-free loans
- Other taxable benefits
  - General rule
  - General allowances
  - Reimbursed expenses
  - Scholarships
- Exempt benefits
- Pay As You Earn (PAYE) system
  - How PAYE works
  - Employer's duties
  - Leavers and joiners
  - Employee tax codes
  - Year-end procedures
  - PAYE penalties

1 Taxable benefits - general rules

Certain benefits provided by employers are taxable on employees. They must be valued using rules set out in tax legislation and included in the taxpayer's employment income in their income tax computation for the tax year.

(a) **Time apportionment.** Time apportion the benefit if it is only available for part of the year by multiplying it by number of months (n)/12.

(b) **Employee contributions.** Any contributions made on or before 6 July following the end of the tax year, to the employer by employees for benefits provided by their employers, are deductible from the taxable benefit, with the exception of car and fuel benefit (see later in this chapter).

2 Accommodation

(a) An employee who is provided with job-related accommodation is not taxed on it under the benefit rules.

(b) Accommodation is job-related if it is:

   (i) Provided for security reasons;

   (ii) Necessary for the proper performance of duties; or

   (iii) Customary and ensures better performance of duties.

(c) If the accommodation is not job-related then a taxable benefit arises. The taxable value of accommodation provided to an employee is the rent that would have been payable if the premises had been let at their annual value (sometimes called 'rateable value'). There is an additional benefit if the property cost over £75,000. The benefit is calculated as follows:

   (i) Greater of:

     ◦ Annual value

     ◦ Rent paid by employer

   (ii) Additional charge if the original cost of the property is greater than £75,000: (Cost - £75,000) × official rate of interest

     The official rate of interest is 2.25% in the tax year 2020/21 (given in the Tax Rates and Allowances table)

(d) The cost used in the calculation is the cost of purchase plus any improvements to the property made before the start of the tax year for which the benefit is being calculated.

(e) If the property is first made available to the employee more than six years after the employer purchased it, use market value (MV) when made available instead of cost.

(f) Any contribution paid by the employee can be deducted in arriving at the taxable benefit.

Illustration 1: Accommodation

Quinton was provided with a company flat in January 2020. The rateable value of the flat is £1,200. The property cost his employer £125,000, but was valued at £150,000 in January 2020. Quinton paid rent of £500 in each tax year.

Required

What is the taxable benefit for 2020/21, assuming:

(a) His employer purchased the property in 2018?

(b) His employer purchased the property in 2012?

(c) Quinton was required to live in the flat as he was employed as the caretaker for the company premises (of which the flat was part)?

Solution

(a)

	£
Annual value	1,200
Less rent paid	(500)
	700
Additional amount (£125,000 − £75,000) × 2.25%	1,125
Taxable benefit	1,825

(b)

	£
Annual value	1,200
Less rent paid	(500)
	700
Additional amount (£150,000 − £75,000) × 2.25%	1,688
Taxable benefit	2,388

As Quinton first moved in more than six years after the company bought the flat, the value at the date he moved in is used.

(c) Job related accommodation: taxable benefit   £ nil

Activity 1: Taxable benefit

Ralph has the use of a house belonging to his employer, for which he pays a notional rent of £2,000. It is not job-related accommodation. The annual value is £8,000.

Ralph has lived in the house since October 2010. It had cost the company £175,000 in October 2007.

Required

Calculate the taxable benefit for the current tax year.

Solution

2.1 Accommodation living expenses

A benefit arises on employees if living expenses are paid for by the employer. For example, heating, lighting, cleaning, repairing or decorating.

The benefit depends on the accommodation provided:

(a) Job-related accommodation
- Taxable benefit = cost to employer
- But cannot exceed 10% of employee's net earnings (not including expenses)

(b) Not job-related accommodation
- Taxable benefit = cost to employer

Activity 2: Accommodation and living expenses

Maggie lives in accommodation provided by her employer and her salary is £7,000 each tax year.

The accommodation was made available to her on 6 August 2020. It has an annual value of £8,000 and it cost her employer £225,000 in 2010. Its market value in August 2020 was £375,000.

Household expenses of £1,800 are paid by her employer and she has other benefits totalling £2,000.

Required

Calculate the taxable benefit for accommodation and the living expenses assuming:

(a) The accommodation is job-related

(b) The accommodation is not job-related

Solution

BPP LEARNING MEDIA

4: Taxable and exempt benefits. The PAYE system   **65**

3 Private use of employer's assets

(a) When an employee is provided with employer's assets for private purposes this gives rise to a taxable benefit. The employee is taxed on the higher of:

   (i)   20% of the value when first made available to employee

   (ii) Rental paid by employer

(b) The 20% charge is time-apportioned when the asset is provided for only part of the year and is reduced by any contribution made by the employee.

(c) If the asset is subsequently given to the employee, the assessment would be the higher of:

   (i)   Market value when given

   (ii) Market value when first used less amounts taxed as taxable benefits up to date of gift

(d) Furniture in accommodation provided by an employer is also taxed in this way.

(e) Mobile phones (including smartphones) are exempt, but this exemption is limited to one mobile phone per employee. An additional mobile phone is taxed at 20% of the cost plus any running costs paid by the employer.

(f) Bicycles provided for journeys to work, as well as being available for private use, are exempt from the private use benefit rules.

 Illustration 2: Assets made available for private use

A suit costing £400 is purchased by an employer for use by an employee on 6 April 2019. On 6 April 2020, the suit is purchased by the employee for £30, its market value then being £50.

Required

1   What is the benefit in 2019/20?

2   What is the benefit in 2020/21?

Solution

1   The benefit in 2019/20 is £400 × 20% = £80.

2   The benefit in 2020/21 is £290, being the **greater** of:

(1)

	£
Market value at acquisition by employee	50
Less price paid	(30)
	20

(2)

	£
Original market value	400
Less taxed in respect of use	(80)
	320
Less price paid	(30)
	290

Activity 3: Private use of asset

Gustav was given the use of some video equipment on 6 October 2018 when it had a value of £1,000. On 1 January 2021, the company gave the equipment to Gustav when its market value was £600.

Required

What is the taxable benefit for Gustav of the gift in January 2021?

O   £600

O   £550

O   £450

O   £1,000

Solution

BPP
LEARNING
MEDIA

4: Taxable and exempt benefits. The PAYE system   **67**

4 Company cars, vans and fuel

4.1 Company cars

(a) Employees are taxed on company cars provided for private use, but not on pool cars (cars kept at employer's premises, not exclusively for use by one employee and with no more than incidental private use).

(b) Private use includes home to work travel, ie commuting.

(c) The annual benefit = CO_2 % × the list price of the car.

A zero percentage applies to electric-powered motor cars with zero CO_2 emissions.

For hybrid-electric cars with emissions between 1 and 50g/km the CO_2 percentage is as follows:

Electric range	
130 miles or more	0%
70 to 129 miles	3%
40 to 69 miles	6%
30 to 39 miles	10%
Less than 30 miles	12%

For petrol cars with emissions of up to 55g/km (and diesel cars meeting RDE2 standard) the CO_2 percentage is as follows:

Petrol range	
51 grams to 54 grams per kilometre	13%
55 grams per kilometre	14%

Note that the percentages will be given to you in the tax rates and allowances table.

(d) For cars with CO_2 emissions higher than these levels the percentage starts at 14% as above and builds up in 1% steps for every 5g/km of carbon dioxide emitted in excess of 55g/km. To calculate, round the CO_2 emissions down to the nearest 5g/km then use the following calculation: taxable % = 14% + (CO_2 - 55)/5.

(e) Diesel cars (including the low emission cars) have a supplement of 4%. The supplement does not apply to cars meeting the RDE2 standard.

(f) The maximum percentage is 37% for both petrol and diesel cars.

(g) The price of the car is usually the list price as published by its manufacturer (including delivery charges, standard accessories and all customs duties, value added tax (VAT), car tax and the list price of any additional fitting costs of optional accessories). Any optional accessories fitted later which cost at least £100 are also included.

(h) Any capital contribution made by the director/employee is deducted from the list price up to a maximum deduction of £5,000. Any contribution for the use of the car is deducted from the value of the benefit.

(i) The benefit is pro-rated if the car is not available for use throughout the tax year.

Illustration 3: Company cars

Florrie was provided with a hybrid-electric company car throughout the tax year 2020/21. The car has a list price of £29,000 with CO_2 emissions of 30g/km and an electric range of 41 miles.

Jasper was provided with a petrol company car throughout the tax year 2020/21. The car has a list price of £15,000 with CO_2 emissions of 54g/km. Jasper contributes £500 annually towards the use of the car.

Nigel was provided with a diesel car on 6 July 2020 which did not meet the RDE2 standard. It had a list price of £22,000 when it was first registered. The car has CO_2 emissions of 118g/km.

Robyn is provided with a diesel car throughout the tax year 2020/21 which meets the RDE2 standard. The car had a list price of £18,000 when it was first registered. The car has CO_2 emissions of 90g/km.

Vicky starts her employment on 6 January 2021 and is immediately provided with a new petrol car with a list price of £25,000. The car was more expensive than her employer would have provided and she therefore made a capital contribution of £6,200. The employer was able to buy the car at a discount and paid only £23,000. Vicky contributed £100 a month for being able to use the car privately. CO_2 emissions are 218g/km.

Required

Calculate the car benefit for Florrie, Jasper, Nigel, Robyn and Vicky for 2020/21.

Solution

Florrie

The CO_2 emissions are between 1g and 50g so we need to use the electric range for the CO_2 percentage. The percentage for 41 miles is 6%.

Car benefit = £29,000 x 6% = £1,740

Jasper

Car benefit = (£15,000 x 13%) - £500 = £1,450

Nigel

The emissions are above 55g/km so we need to calculate the relevant percentage to apply to the list price.

Step 1 Round down to the nearest 5g/km

118g/km rounds down to 115g/km.

Step 2 Deduct 55g/km (from tax tables)

115g/km - 55g/km = 60g/km

Step 3 Divide by 5

60g/km/5 = 12

Step 4 Add the base % of 14%

12 + 14 = 26%

As the car is a diesel car that does not meet the RDE2 standard, we need to add the 4% surcharge.

26 + 4 = 30%

Car benefit = list price x CO_2% x 9 months of benefit = £22,000 x 30% x 9/12 = £4,950

Robyn

Car benefit = £18,000 x 21% (14% + (90 - 55)/5) = £3,780

Vicky

	£
List price*	25,000

BPP LEARNING MEDIA

4: Taxable and exempt benefits. The PAYE system **69**

	£
Less capital contribution (maximum)	(5,000)
	20,000
£20,000 x 37%** x 3/12***	1,850
Less contribution to running costs (£100 x 3)	(300)
Car benefit	1,550

* The discounted price is not relevant.

**14% + (215 - 55)/5 = 46% restricted to 37% max.

***Only available for three months in 2020/21.

Activity 4: Car benefit

Stuart has the use of a company car. The motor car has a list price of £16,500 and an official CO_2 emission rate of 98g/km.

Required

(a) Calculate Stuart's taxable benefit.

(b) Recalculate your answer in (a) assuming that Stuart had made a capital contribution of £5,500.

(c) Recalculate your answer in (a) assuming the car was a diesel (not meeting the RDE2 standard) rather than a petrol car.

(d) Recalculate your answer in (c) assuming Stuart only had use of the car from 6 October until the end of the tax year and he contributed £1,000 to his company for use of the car.

(e) If Stuart's car had an official emission rate of 54g/km, was petrol-fuelled and was available for the entire tax year, what would the taxable benefit be?

(f) If Stuart's car was a hybrid electric with an electric range of 39 miles, an emission rate of 45g/km and was available for the entire year, what would the taxable benefit be?

Solution

4.2 Car fuel for private motoring

(a) For fuel provided to users of company cars, the taxable benefit is a percentage of £24,500.

(b) The percentage is the same as the percentage used to calculate the car benefit. As with the car benefit, the fuel benefit is pro-rated if not provided throughout the tax year.

(c) There is no reduction in taxable benefit for **partial** refunds made for private cost of fuel by the employee. The charge is cancelled if full refunds are made.

4.3 Company vans

There is a standard benefit of £3,490 a year for employees with private use of a company van. Unlike cars, there is no taxable benefit where an employee takes a van home (ie uses the van for commuting). Where private fuel is provided, there is an additional charge of £666.

 Essential reading

See Chapter 4 Section 1 of the Essential reading for an example on car and fuel benefits.

The Essential reading is available as an Appendix of the digital edition of the Workbook.

5 Cheap/interest-free loans

Employment related loans to employees and their relatives give rise to a benefit equal to:

(a) Any amounts written off (unless the employee has died)

 BPP LEARNING MEDIA

(b)   The excess of the interest based on an official rate prescribed by the Treasury, over any interest actually charged ('taxable cheap loan'). Interest payable during the tax year but paid after the end of the tax year is taken into account.

Only loans greater than £10,000 give rise to a benefit. However, if a loan is greater than £10,000, the entirety of the loan will be treated as a benefit, ie rather than the excess.

The taxable benefit is:

	£
Average loan × 2.25% (official rate of interest)	X
Less interest paid	(X)
	X

There are two methods of calculating the 'average loans': the 'average method' (using only the balance of the loan at the start and end of the period) and the 'strict method' (using the loan balance at the end of every month within the period). The default method is the average method but the taxpayer or HMRC can choose to use the strict method. HMRC will usually only choose to use the strict method if the average method is being deliberately exploited.

Essential reading

See Chapter 4 Section 2 of the Essential reading for an example and more detail on beneficial loans.

The Essential reading is available as an Appendix of the digital edition of the Workbook.

Activity 5: Interest-free loan

Laura was provided with an interest-free loan of £100,000 on 6 April 2020. She repaid £20,000 of the loan on 6 January 2021.

Required

What is Laura's taxable benefit in respect of the loan for 2020/21 under the:

(a)   Average method?

(b)   Strict method?

Comment on whether the strict method will be chosen by either Laura or HMRC.

Solution

6 Other taxable benefits

6.1 General rule

Generally, the taxable amount is the cost to the employer of providing the benefit eg medical insurance, vouchers, or the use of a credit card.

6.2 General allowances

General (or round sum) allowances are taxable but a deduction is available if the expenses paid out of the allowance would have been allowable had the employer paid them directly.

6.3 Reimbursed expenses

The general principle is that reimbursement by an employer of expenses incurred by an employee is a taxable benefit for the employee, but the employee may be able to claim a deduction if the expense is incurred wholly, exclusively and necessarily for their job eg business travel costs.

There is automatic exemption for the reimbursement of expenses if the amount of the deduction is at least equal to the amount of the expense. This can apply to actual expenses and also allowances, eg for travel and meals.

Essential reading

See Chapter 4 Section 3 of the Essential reading for more detail on reimbursed expenses.

The Essential reading is available as an Appendix of the digital edition of the Workbook.

6.4 Scholarships

If scholarships are given to members of an employee's family, the **employee is taxable on the cost** unless the scholarship fund's or scheme's payments by reason of people's employments are not more than 25% of its total payments.

7 Exempt benefits

(a) Free/subsidised canteen meals (if same facilities provided to all employees on similar terms)

(b) Medical treatment not taxable up to £500 for each employee if employer pays for medical treatment to assist the employee in their return to work after ill-health or injury lasting at least 28 days

(c) Workplace childcare (creches, nurseries)

(d) Qualifying removal expenses up to £8,000

(e) Car parking spaces at or near place of work

(f) Contributions by an employer to a registered pension scheme

(g) Staff parties, generally provided that the cost per head per year is £150 or less

(h) Sport and recreational facilities available generally for the staff

(i) Outplacement counselling services to employees made redundant who have been employed full time for at least two years; the services can include counselling to help adjust to the loss of the job and to help in finding other work

(j) Weekly tax-free allowance of £6 can be paid by an employer to an employee who works from home

BPP LEARNING MEDIA

4: Taxable and exempt benefits. The PAYE system   **73**

(k) Trivial benefits – cost ≤ £50 and not cash or cash vouchers

(l) Pension advice – cost ≤ £500 per employee per tax year, if exceeds £500, first £500 is exempt

(m) Workplace charging points for electric or hybrid cars

(n) Mobile phone

Essential reading

See Chapter 4 Section 4 of the Essential reading for more detail on exempt benefits.

The Essential reading is available as an Appendix of the digital edition of the Workbook.

8 Pay As You Earn (PAYE) system

> **Pay as you earn (PAYE):** PAYE is a system of deducting income tax and national insurance from salary before the salary is received.

The objective of the PAYE system is to deduct the correct amount of income tax and national insurance contributions from employees over the year. Its scope is very wide. It applies to most cash payments, other than reimbursed business expenses, and to certain non-cash payments.

In addition to wages and salaries, PAYE applies to round sum expense allowances and payments instead of benefits. It also applies to any readily convertible asset.

A readily convertible asset is any asset which can effectively be exchanged for cash. The amount subject to PAYE is the amount that would be taxed as employment income. This is usually the cost to the employer of providing the asset.

The following count as pay:

(a) Salaries, wages, overtime, bonuses

(b) Pensions

(c) Commissions

(d) Benefits

(e) Statutory sick pay/maternity pay

(f) Tips

Tips paid direct to an employee are normally outside the PAYE system (although still assessable as employment income).

Benefits may be included within the payroll if the employer chooses to do so. Otherwise they will be reported on Form P11D and the employee's PAYE code will be adjusted to collect the income tax due on these benefits.

8.1 How PAYE works

Employers must report their PAYE information in real time (RTI = real time information). Every time an employee is paid, the employer must electronically send a 'full payment submission' (FPS) on or before the day the employee is paid which includes:

- Amount paid to each employee

- Deductions of income tax and NIC

- Starter and leaver information

The software used to submit the RTI to HMRC will calculate the amount of deductions that must be made from the payment. This is done on a cumulative basis.

8.2 Employer's duties

Under RTI, **an employer is required to submit information to HMRC electronically.** This can be done by:

(a) Using commercial payroll software;

(b) Using HMRC's Basic PAYE Tools software (designed for use by an employer who has up to nine employees); or

(c) Using a payroll provider (such as an accountant or payroll bureau) to do the reporting on behalf of the employer.

The employer has a duty to:

(a) Deduct the correct income tax and NIC from employees' pay

(b) Keep a record of pay and deductions

(c) Pay tax/NIC over on the due date which is 14 days from the end of the tax month

(d) Send relevant income tax and NIC information electronically every time employees are paid

8.3 Leavers and joiners

When an employee **leaves** employment the employer must:

(a) Fill in the relevant parts of the deductions working sheet

(b) Complete P45, send part 1 to HMRC and give parts 1A (which the employee keeps for their own records), 2 and 3 to the employee

When an employee **joins** and has a P45 they give it to their new employer who fills in part 3 and sends it to HMRC. The employer keeps part 2 for their own records.

The employer will usually use the tax code on the P45 to compute income tax for the joiner when the next payroll is run.

8.4 Employee tax codes

(a) An employee's tax code indicates the amount of tax-free pay that they are entitled to.

(b) In working out the coding, HMRC uses the following calculation:

	£	£
Allowances:		
Personal allowances	X	
Personal pension contributions – higher rate relief	X	
Expense deductions	X	
		X
Less deductions (reducing tax-free pay):		
Benefits	X	
Untaxed income	X	
Tax under payments b/f (grossed up) (x 100/20 or 100/40 or 100/45)	X	
		(X)
Allowance to set against pay		X

(c) To obtain the code number, the last figure is removed and replaced with a letter:

L	For people entitled to the full personal allowance
M	For people who are receiving the transferable personal allowance
N	For people who have elected to give the transferable personal allowance to their spouse/civil partner

BPP LEARNING MEDIA

4: Taxable and exempt benefits. The PAYE system   **75**

BR	Basic rate tax deducted without allowances
DO	Higher rate tax deducted without allowances
OT	Personal allowance has been used up or started a new job and do not have a P45 form

Activity 6: Tax code

Finzi earns £15,000. In 2018/19, he underpaid income tax by £50. He has a company car with a taxable benefit of £3,905.

Required

What is Finzi's tax code for 2020/21? (Assume tax rates for 2020/21 apply throughout.)

O 1615L

O 1665L

O 834L

O 884L

Solution

8.5 Year-end procedures

The employer must send to HMRC the following items for each employee:

Date	Form/information
19 May	Final real-time submission
31 May	P60 provided to employees showing total taxable earnings for the tax year, tax deducted, code number and NI number
6 July	Form P11D – benefits for employees Form P11D(b) Class1A NIC return

8.6 PAYE penalties

Daily interest is charged on late payments of income tax and NICs under PAYE by taking the number of days by which a payment is late and applying the relevant late payment interest rate. HMRC make the charge after the end of the tax year.

Late payment penalties may be charged on PAYE amounts that are not paid in full and on time. Employers are not charged a penalty for the first late PAYE payment in a tax year, unless that payment is over six months late. The amounts of the penalties on subsequent late payments in the tax year depend on how much is late each time and the number of times payments are late in a tax year. The maximum penalty is 4% of the amount that is late in the relevant tax month and applies to the 11th (or more) late payment that tax year. **Where the tax remains unpaid at six**

months, the further penalty is 5% of tax unpaid, with a further 5% if tax remains unpaid at 12 months, even if there is only one late payment in the year.

There are also penalties for making late returns under RTI which are imposed on a monthly basis. The first late submission of the tax year is ignored. Further late submissions will attract penalties based on the **number of employees** as follows:

Number of employees	Monthly penalty
1 to 9	£100
10 to 49	£200
50 to 249	£300
250 or more	£400

If the return is more than three months late, there is an additional penalty due of 5% of the tax and NIC due.

Exam focus point

HMRC allows a return to be up to three days late before imposing a penalty. However, the examining team has specifically stated this aspect is **not examinable** in Taxation (TX – UK). There are also various other relaxations to the penalty rules which may apply but you should assume that the rules set out above apply when answering a Taxation (TX – UK) examination question.

Penalties for inaccurate returns are subject to the common penalty regime for errors (see later in this Workbook).

Chapter summary

Taxable and exempt benefits. The PAYE system

Taxable benefits – general rules

- Cost to employer
- Pro-rate if benefit only available for part of year
- Deduct employee contributions if paid by 6 July following end of tax year, except for private fuel

Accommodation

- Job related - exempt
- Not job related - higher of
  – Rent paid by employer
  – Annual value
- and Additional charge = Official rate of interest 2.25% × (cost - £75,000)

Accommodation living expenses
- Job related: Cost to employer limited to 10% of net earnings
- Not job related: Cost to employer

Use of employer's assets

- 20% x MV (not cars, not mobile phones)
- Gifts of employer's asset, higher of
  – MV when given
  – MV when first used less amounts already assessed

Company cars, vans and fuel

Company cars
- CO_2% x list price
- Hybrid electric cars 1 – 50g/km, % depends on miles
- Petrol cars to 51-54g/km and diesel meeting RDE2 std, % = 13%
- Petrol cars 55g/km and diesel meeting RDE2 std, % = 14%
- Petrol cars > 55g/km and diesel meeting RDE2 std, 14% builds up 1% for every 5g of CO_2% emitted per km in excess of 55g/km
- Maximum 37% × list price
- Diesel cars 4% supplement added to CO_2% (maximum still 37%)
- Deduct capital contribution from list price (max deduction £5,000)

Company vans
- £3,490 plus an additional £666 if fuel provided
- No benefit if private use is only for home to work commute

Car fuel for private motoring
- £24,500 × CO_2%

Cheap/interest-free loans

- ORI x average loan or strict basis
- £10,000 *de minimis* limit

Other taxable benefits

General rule
- Taxable amount = cost to employer eg insurance, vouchers, use of credit card

General allowances
- Taxable but allowable deduction is available if necessarily incurred

Reimbursed expenses
- Not taxable

Scholarships
- If given to members of employee's family, employee is taxable on cost
- Unless the scholarship fund's or scheme's payments by reason of people's employments are not more than 25% of its total payments

Exempt benefits

- Free/subsidised canteen meals if available to all employees on similar terms
- Medical treatment exempt up to £500 paid by employer to assist return to work
- Workplace childcare
- Pension advice up to £500
- Relocation (max £8,000)
- Car parking near work and electric car charging points
- Employer's pension contribution
- Mobile phone
- Sports and recreational facilities
- £150 per head – annual parties
- Outplacement counselling services
- Weekly allowance of £6 for employees working from home
- Trivial benefits £50 or less, not cash or cash vouchers

Pay As You Earn (PAYE) system

How PAYE works
- System used for calculating and collecting income tax and NIC

Employer's duties
- Deduct correct amounts from employee's pay and keep records
- Pay tax/NIC over 14 days from end of tax month
- Send information electronically every time employees are paid

Leavers and joiners
- Complete P45 for leavers
- Joiners give employer their P45

Employee tax codes
- Tax code indicates tax free pay
- Penalties apply for both late payments and late returns

Year-end procedures
- 19 May – final real-time submission
- 31 May – P60
- 6 July – P11D – benefits for employees and P11D(b) Class 1A NIC return

PAYE penalties
- Interest and late payment penalties
- Penalties for late returns based on number of employees

BPP
LEARNING
MEDIA

4: Taxable and exempt benefits. The PAYE system   **79**

Knowledge diagnostic

1. Taxable benefits

Specific rules apply to determine the taxable amount of benefits but remember:

- Employee contributions are deductible (except private fuel); and
- Pro-rate if the benefit is only available for part of a tax year

2. Exempt benefits

Certain benefits are tax free so make sure you know which ones.

3. PAYE system

This system imposes the collection of tax of employees onto the employer. There are penalties for making late payments and late returns.

Further study guidance

Question practice

Now try the following from the Further question practice bank (available in the digital edition of the Workbook):

Section A questions:

Q15, Q16, Q17

Section B questions:

Q18 Clara

Section C questions:

Q19 Azure plc

Further reading

There is a technical article available on ACCA's website, called *Benefits*, which covers topics included in this chapter. There is also an article called *Motor cars* that explains the implications of acquiring, running, or having the use of a motor car for income tax, corporation tax, value added tax (VAT) and national insurance contributions (NIC).

You are strongly advised to read these articles in full as part of your preparation for the TX exam.

Activity answers

Activity 1: Taxable benefit

Accommodation

	£
Annual value	8,000
Additional charge	
(£175,000 – £75,000) × 2.25%	2,250
Employee contribution	(2,000)
Taxable benefit	8,250

Activity 2: Accommodation and living expenses

(a) If the accommodation is job-related, there is no charge for the accommodation.

Accommodation expenses – employee taxed on lower of:

		£
(1)	Expenses	1,800
(2)	10% net earnings	
	= 10% (£7,000 + £2,000)	900

Therefore, taxable benefit = £900 (lower amount)

(b) If the accommodation is not job-related, there is a charge for both the accommodation and the living expenses.

Accommodation

	£
Annual value	8,000
Additional charge	
[(£375,000 – £75,000) × 2.25%]	
NB more than six years since the property acquired so use MV	6,750
	14,750
Taxable benefit time apportioned (× 8/12)	9,833

Taxable benefit in relation to the expenses (unrestricted) = 1,800

Total benefit = £9,833 + £1,800 = £11,633

Activity 3: Private use of asset

The correct answer is: £600

Use of asset:

		£
2018/19	1,000 × 20% × 6/12 =	100
2019/20	1,000 × 20% =	200
2020/21	1,000 × 20% × 9/12 =	150
		450

Gift of asset:

2020/21   Higher of:

		£
(1)	MV of asset at date of gift =	600
(2)	MV when first provided minus the values already taxed:	
	= £1,000 − £450 =	550
	Therefore:	600 (higher amount)

The answer £550 is the lower amount. The answer £450 is the use benefit. The answer £1,000 is the market value when first provided.

Activity 4: Car benefit

(a) **Car benefit**

Company car g/km (round down) = 95

Therefore percentage = 14 + (95 - 55)/5 = 22%

Benefit = 16,500 × 22% = £3,630

(b)

	£
List price	16,500
Less capital contribution (maximum £5,000)	(5,000)
	11,500

Benefit = £11,500 × 22% = £2,530

(c) If car was diesel

Benefit = 22% + 4% = 26% × 16,500 = £4,290

(d) Basic benefit (above) × 6/12 - contribution = £4,290 × 6/12 - £1,000 = £1,145

(e) 16,500 × 13% = £2,145

(f) 16,500 x 10% = £1,650

Activity 5: Interest-free loan

(a) **Average method**

(a) $\dfrac{100,000 + 80,000}{2} \times 2.25\% = £2,025$

(b) **Strict method**

BPP
LEARNING MEDIA

4: Taxable and exempt benefits. The PAYE system   **83**

		£
£100,000 × 2.25% × 9/12	=	1,688
£80,000 × 2.25% × 3/12	=	450
		2,138

Laura will not choose to use the strict method as it produces a higher benefit, and HMRC will also not choose to use the strict method as the average method is not being deliberately exploited.

Activity 6: Tax code

The correct answer is: 834L

	£
PA	12,500
Car benefit	(3,905)
Tax underpaid £50 x (100/20)	(250)
	8,345
Tax code	834L

The answer 1615L adds the company car instead of deducting it. The answer 1665L adds both deductions. The answer 884L adds the adjustment for underpaid tax instead of deducting it.

Skills checkpoint 1

Approach to objective test (OT) questions

Chapter overview

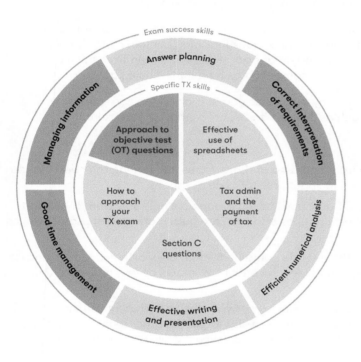

Introduction

Sections A and B of the TX exam will contain OTs worth 60 marks (ie 60% of your exam) and, therefore, being able to answer OT questions effectively is extremely important.

Section A - Single OT questions

OT questions are single, short questions that are auto marked and worth two marks each. You must answer the whole question correctly to earn their two marks. There are no partial marks.

The OT questions in Section A aim for a broad coverage of the syllabus, and so all areas of the syllabus need to be carefully studied. You need to work through as many practice OT questions as possible, reviewing carefully to see how correct answers are derived.

The following types of OT questions commonly appear in the TX exam:

Question type	Explanation
Multiple choice questions (MCQ)	You need to choose one correct answer from four given response options.

Question type	Explanation
Multiple response options (MRO)	These are a type of multiple-choice question where you need to select more than one answer from a number of given options. The question will specify how many answers need to be selected. It is important to read the requirement carefully.
Fill-in-the-blank (FIB)	This question type requires you to type a numerical answer into a box. The unit of measurement (eg £) will sit outside the box. For TX, calculations and workings need only be made to the nearest £ and all apportionments should be made to the nearest month.
Drag and drop	Drag and drop questions involve you dragging an answer and dropping it into place. Some questions could involve matching more than one answer to a response area and some questions may have more answer choices than response areas, which means not all available answer choices need to be used.
Drop down list	This question type requires you to select one answer from a drop-down list. Some of these questions may contain more than one drop down list and an answer must be selected from each one. This requires the same skills as a multiple-choice question.
Hot area	This question type requires you to click on the correct area or words, such as 'true' or 'false', or 'exempt' or 'not exempt'.

Section B – OT Case questions

As with Section A, questions can come from any area of the syllabus, reinforcing the need for you to study the whole syllabus. Section B will include three OT case questions.

Each OT Case contains a group of five OT questions based around a single scenario. These can be any combination of the single OT question types and they are auto marked in the same way as the single OT questions.

OT Cases are worth ten marks (each of the five OTs contained within are worth two marks, and as with the OT questions described above, you will receive either two marks or zero marks for those individual questions).

OT cases are written so that there are no dependencies between the individual questions. Therefore, if you did get the first question wrong, your ability to get the other four correct is not affected. The OT Case scenario remains on screen so you can see it while answering the questions.

Each OT case normally consists of several numerical questions and at least one knowledge style question, such as tax due dates or true or false statements. It is often quicker to tackle the knowledge questions first, leaving some additional time to tackle calculations.

Note that the exam software contains a 'flag' functionality, meaning that you can flag any questions that you want to return to and review, if you have spare time at the end.

Approach to OT questions

TX Skill: Approach to OT questions

A step-by-step technique for approaching OT questions is outlined below. Each step will be explained in more detail in the following sections as the OT case question, 'Danni' is answered in stages.

> **General guidance for approaching OT questions**
>
> **STEP 1: Answer the questions you know first.**
>
> If you're having difficulty answering a question, move on and come back to tackle it once you've answered all the questions you know.
>
> It is often quicker to answer discursive style OT questions first, leaving more time for calculations.

> **General guidance for approaching OT questions**
>
> **STEP 2: Answer all questions.**
>
> There is no penalty for an incorrect answer in ACCA exams; there is nothing to be gained by leaving an OT question unanswered. If you are stuck on a question, as a last resort, it is worth selecting the option you consider most likely to be correct and moving on. Make a note of the question, so if you have time after you have answered the rest of the questions, you can revisit it.

> **Guidance for answering specific OT questions**
>
> **STEP 3: Read the requirement first!**
>
> The requirement will be stated in bold text in the exam. Identify what you are being asked to do, any technical knowledge required and **what type of OT question** you are dealing with. Look for key words in the requirement such as "which **TWO** of the following," "which of the following is **NOT**"

> **Guidance for answering specific OT questions**
>
> **STEP 4: Apply your technical knowledge to the data presented in the question.**
>
> Take your time working through questions, and make sure to read through each answer option with care. OT questions are designed so that each answer option is plausible. Work through each response option and eliminate those you know are incorrect.

Exam success skills

The following question is a Section B OT case question worth ten marks.

For this question, we will also focus on the following **exam success skills**:

- **Managing information.** It is easy for the amount of information contained in an OT case question in Section B to feel a little overwhelming. **Active reading** is a useful technique to avoid this. This involves focusing on each of the five requirements first on the basis that, until you have done this, the detail in the question will have little meaning and will seem more intimidating.

Focus on the requirements, noting key verbs to ensure you understand the requirement properly, and correctly identify what type of OT question you are dealing with. Then read the rest of the scenario, making a note of important and relevant information and technical information you think you will need. (Note that you can highlight and strikethrough text in the question scenario in the CBE.)

Remember that Sections A and B are computer marked and so your answer will be either right or wrong. If you misread the information, you could be wasting valuable time as well as choosing the wrong answer.

- **Correct interpretation of requirements.** Identify from the requirement the different types of OT question. This is especially important with multiple response options (MRO) to ensure you select the correct number of response options.

- **Good time management.** Complete all OTs in the time available. Each OT is worth two marks and a whole Section B question should take 18 minutes.

Skills activity

The following scenario relates to Questions (a) to (e).

Danni joined a UK company, Clifton plc, as purchasing director on 1 July 2020, based at their Nottingham office.

Salary and bonus

Until 31 December 2020, Danni's monthly salary as a director was £6,000. From 1 January 2021, her salary increased by 2.5%.

Clifton plc awarded Danni a bonus of £10,000 in relation to a special purchasing project during Clifton plc's period of account ended 31 March 2021. This bonus was determined by the board of directors on 15 March 2021, credited in the company's accounts on 10 April 2021, which was also the date when Danni became entitled to payment of the bonus. The bonus was paid to Danni on 31 May 2021.

Travel to Clifton plc's offices

From 1 July 2020, Danni travelled to Clifton plc's office in Nottingham from home using the Nottingham Tram Network. Danni bought a monthly tram season ticket for each of the months from July 2020 to December 2020.

From 1 January 2021, Danni was seconded to Clifton plc's office in Manchester for a period of six months. Danni bought a monthly rail season ticket for each month of her secondment.

Travel to clients

Danni also used her own car for journeys to meet clients in Leicester, which is 24 miles from Nottingham. She made five return journeys between 1 July 2020 and 5 April 2021. Clifton plc paid Danni 30p per mile for these journeys.

Subscriptions

Danni is a member of the Chartered Institute of Purchasing and Supply (MCIP) and paid her annual membership fee on 31 December 2020. Danni is also a member of her local tennis club at which she sometimes meets potential suppliers for Clifton plc and paid her annual membership fee on 1 September 2020.

Payroll giving

Clifton plc has a payroll giving scheme. Danni made monthly contributions through the scheme from 31 December 2020.

Required

(a) **What is the amount of Danni's employment income from her salary and bonus taxable in the tax year 2020/21?**

£_____

(2 marks)

Note. This is a FIB question and so you need to enter your answer carefully, to the nearest pound. This particular question does not require rounding because the numbers are whole pounds. It tests your ability to recognise that Danni is a director and therefore this may affect the date and tax year in which the bonus is deemed to have been received.

(b) **Indicate, by selecting the relevant boxes below, whether Danni's travel to Clifton plc's offices will be qualifying or non-qualifying travel expenses?**

Travel from home to Clifton plc's office in Nottingham	QUALIFYING	NON-QUALIFYING
Travel from home to Clifton plc's office in Manchester	QUALIFYING	NON-QUALIFYING

(2 marks)

Note. This is a hot area question. Read the scenario and the question carefully and do not assume that if one option is qualifying then the other one must be non-qualifying. They could both be qualifying or they could both be non-qualifying.

(c) **What are the employment income consequences of Danni using her own car for journeys to meet clients in Leicester?**

- £72 taxable benefit
- £108 allowable deduction
- £12 taxable benefit
- £36 allowable deduction

(2 marks)

Note. This is an MCQ requiring one correct answer to be selected. Remember that the distractors (incorrect answer options) contain numbers that you will obtain if you make a particular mistake. Do not look at the options until you have finished your calculation as it is possible that a 'part finished calculation' is one of the incorrect distracters.

(d) **Indicate, by selecting the relevant boxes below, whether the following subscriptions will be deductible in computing Danni's employment income?**

Chartered Institute of Purchasing and Supply (MCIP)	DEDUCTIBLE	NON-DEDUCTIBLE
Tennis club	DEDUCTIBLE	NON-DEDUCTIBLE

(2 marks)

Note. This is another hot area question.

(e) **How is tax relief given for Danni's contributions through the payroll giving scheme?**

By whom	How tax relief given
• Clifton plc	Deducting the donation from Danni's gross pay before calculating PAYE
• Clifton plc	Increasing the basic rate limit when computing PAYE on Danni's gross pay
• Danni	Making contributions net of basic rate tax
• Danni	Making a claim in her self-assessment tax return

(2 marks)
(Total = 10 marks)

Note. This is another MCQ requiring one correct answer to be selected.

STEP 1 **Answer the questions you know first.**

If you are having difficulty answering a question, move on and come back to tackle it once you have answered all the questions you know. It is often quicker to answer discursive style OT questions first, leaving more time for calculations.

Questions (b), (d) and (e) are discursive style questions. It would make sense to answer these two questions first as it is likely that you will be able to complete them comfortably within the 1.8 minutes allocated to them. Any time saved could then be spent on the more complex calculations required to answer the remaining questions.

STEP 2 **Answer all questions.**

There is no penalty for an incorrect answer in ACCA exams so there is nothing to be gained by leaving an OT question unanswered. If you are stuck on a question, as a last resort, it is worth selecting the option you consider most likely to be correct and moving on. Make a note of the question, so if you have time after you have answered the rest of the questions, you can revisit it.

Two of the five questions in the OT case are MCQs. With these types of questions, you have a 25% chance of getting the question correct so do not leave any unanswered. It is obviously more difficult to get a fill in the blank question correct by guessing.

STEP 3 **Read the requirement first!**

The requirement will be stated in bold text in the exam. Identify what you are being asked to do, any technical knowledge required and **what type of OT question** you are dealing with. Look for key words in the requirement such as 'Which TWO of the following…' or 'Which of the following is NOT…'

Question (a) is a FIB question and so you need to read the question carefully and insert your answer to the carefully. Questions (b) and (d) require you to select a correct answer for each option. Each question is worth two marks but there is no partial marking. So, if you correctly select 'deductible' for one subscription but select the wrong answer for the other subscription, you will gain no marks for that question.

STEP 4 **Apply your technical knowledge to the data presented in the question.**

Take your time working through calculations and be sure to read through each answer option with care. OT questions are designed so that each answer option is plausible.

Let's look at a few of the questions in detail.

Question (a) asks for a calculation of Danni's employment income and bonus taxable in 2020/21.

To answer this, you need to read the scenario carefully.

Danni joined a UK company, Clifton plc, as purchasing director on 1 July 2020, based at their Nottingham office.

Notes.

1   As Danni is a director, this means that the rules relating to directors regarding the date of earnings will apply.

2   As Danni joined part way through the year, she has not worked a full 12 months.

Salary and bonus

Until 31 December 2020, Danni's monthly salary as a director was £6,000. From 1 January 2021, her salary increased by 2.5%.

Note. A calculation of Danni's monthly salary from January is required.

Clifton plc awarded Danni a bonus of £10,000 in relation to a special purchasing project during Clifton plc's period of account ended 31 March 2021. This bonus was determined by the board of directors on 15 March 2021, credited in the company's accounts on 10 April 2021, which was also the date when Danni became entitled to payment of the bonus. The bonus was paid to Danni on 31 May 2021.

Note. These dates need to be read carefully, applying the rules for directors in order to establish the tax year that the bonus should fall into.

The correct answer is £64,450.

	£
Salary	
1.7.20 – 31.12.20	
£6,000 × 6	36,000
1.1.21 – 31.3.21	
(£6,000 × 102.5%) × 3	18,450
Bonus	
31 March 2021 (receipts basis)	10,000
Taxable in tax year 2020/21	64,450

As Danni is a director of Clifton plc, bonus is received on the earliest of:

- The time when payment is made (31 May 2021)
- The time when she becomes entitled to payment of the bonus (10 April 2021)
- The time when the amount is credited in the company's accounting records (10 April 2021)
- The end of the company's period of account (as the amount was determined on 15 March 2021 which is within the period of account) (31 March 2021)

The earliest of these dates is provided by the last test and so the date of receipt is 31 March 2021.

Question (e) is an MCQ asking how tax relief is given for Danni's contributions through the payroll giving scheme. The scenario says:

Payroll giving

Clifton plc has a payroll giving scheme. Danni made monthly contributions through the scheme from 31 December 2020.

You will notice that this question is much quicker to answer than Question (a). If you have remembered the rules about charitable donations under the payroll deduction scheme, this is an easy question.

The correct answer is: By Clifton plc deducting the donation from Danni's gross pay before calculating PAYE. Note that you could answer this question before attempting the more time-consuming numerical questions.

Exam success skills diagnostic

Every time you complete a question, use the diagnostic below to assess how effectively you demonstrated the exam success skills in answering the question. The table has been completed below for the Danni activity to give you an idea of how to complete the diagnostic.

Exam success skills	Your reflections/observations
Managing information	• Did you read each of the five requirements first? • Did you actively read the scenario making a note of relevant points such as the fact that Danni is a director?
Correct interpretation of requirements	• Did you identify the correct technical knowledge needed to answer each requirement? For example, using the information in the scenario about Danni being seconded to Manchester for six months and your technical knowledge about qualifying travel expenses to a temporary workplace, to answer Question (b). • Did you identify what type of OT question you were dealing with? For example, knowing that only one correct answer is required for a multiple-choice question.
Good time management	• Did you manage to answer all five questions within 18 mins? • Did you manage your time well by answering Questions (b), (d) and (e) first?
Most important action points to apply to your next question	

Summary

60% of the TX exam consists of OT questions. Key skills to focus on throughout your studies will therefore include:

- Always reading the requirements first to identify what you are being asked to do and what type of OT question you are dealing with
- Actively reading the scenario, making a note of key data needed to answer each requirement
- Answering OT questions in a sensible order, dealing with any easier discursive style questions first

5

Pensions

Learning objectives

On completion of this chapter, you should be able to:

	Syllabus reference no.
Explain and compute the relief given for contributions to personal pension schemes and to occupational pension schemes.	B7(a)

Exam context

Pension contributions can be paid by all individuals and you may come across these contributions as part of an income tax question in Section C. In Section C, you may also be required to discuss the types of pension schemes available and the limits on the tax relief due, or you may have to deal with them in an income tax computation. Pensions may be tested in a 15 mark question or a 10 mark question. Section A or B questions might test a specific aspect of pensions such as the amount of the annual allowance.

You must be sure that you know how to deal with the two ways of giving relief – contributions to occupational schemes are deducted from earnings whilst contributions to personal pensions are paid net of basic rate tax and further tax relief is given by increasing the basic rate and higher rate limits.

Chapter overview

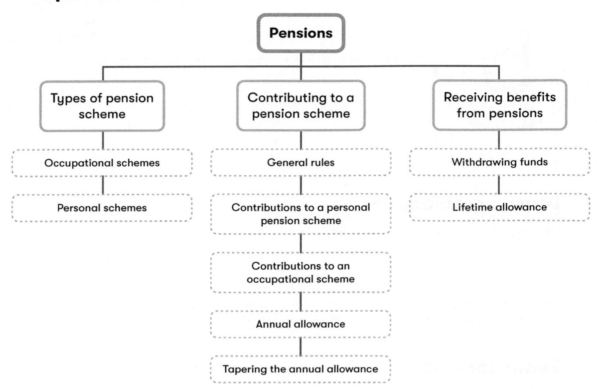

1 Introduction

Individuals are encouraged by the government to make financial provision to cover their needs when they reach a certain age. There are state pension arrangements which provide some financial support, but the government are keen for individuals to make their own pension provision to supplement their state pensions.

Under **automatic enrolment**, employers must automatically enrol most employees into a **workplace pension scheme** (although employees can then **opt out** of the scheme). There are **minimum contributions** to the workplace pension scheme required by law (usually equal to 8% of earnings of which a minimum amount equal to 3% of earnings must be contributed by the employer, as of April 2019).

Alternatively, individuals (employees, self-employed and those who are not working) may make their **own pension provision** through a personal pension provider.

Tax relief is given for both employer pension provision and personal pension provision. This includes both relief for contributions paid into pension schemes during an individual's working life and an exemption from tax on income and gains arising in the pension fund itself.

2 Types of pension scheme

2.1 Occupational schemes

> **Occupational pension scheme:** Employers may set up an occupational pension scheme. The employer may use the services of an insurance company (an insured scheme) or may set up a totally self-administered pension fund.

There are two kinds of occupational pension scheme – earnings-related (**defined benefits arrangements**) and investment-related (**money purchase arrangements**). In a **defined benefits arrangement** the pension is generally based on employees' earnings either at retirement (a **final salary** scheme) or throughout their employment (a **career average** scheme) and linked to the number of years they have worked for the employer.

A **money purchase pension** – also known as a **defined contribution scheme** – does not provide any guarantee regarding the level of pension which will be available. The individual invests in the pension scheme and the amount invested is used to build up a pension.

An individual has to be employed to have access to an occupational scheme.

2.2 Personal schemes

> **Personal pension scheme:** Personal pensions are money purchase (defined contribution) schemes, which are provided by banks, insurance companies and other financial institutions.

Any individual (whether employed or not) may join a personal pension scheme.

Stakeholder pensions are a particular type of personal pension scheme. They must satisfy certain rules, such as a maximum level of charges, ease of transfer and so on.

3 Contributing to a pension scheme

3.1 General rules

Employer contributions are a tax-free benefit for the employee and a deductible trading expense in the employer's tax computation.

Employer contributions are not limited but they will use up part of the annual allowance (see later in this chapter).

The maximum gross tax relievable contributions made by the individual are the higher of:

- £3,600; and
- An individual's relevant earnings chargeable to income tax in that year.

Relevant earnings are broadly employment income, trading income and income from furnished holiday lettings (see Chapter 6).

Exam focus point

£3,600 will be given to you in the Tax Rates and Allowances available in the exam.

Essential reading

Individuals can make contributions to their pensions which do not attract tax relief. These are covered briefly in the Essential reading for this chapter.

The Essential reading is available as an Appendix of the digital edition of the Workbook.

3.2 Contributions to a personal pension scheme

Any individual **under the age of 75 can make tax relievable pension contributions** in a tax year.

Payments into personal pension schemes are made net of basic rate tax of 20%, ie to end up with £1,000 in a personal pension fund the individual only needs to pay £800.

In this way, basic rate relief is given at source, as we have seen already with gift aid. Higher rate and additional rate taxpayers obtain additional relief by making a claim to increase the basic rate limit (and, if relevant, the higher rate limit) by the gross amount of the pension contribution.

Adjusted basic rate limit = £37,500 + (cash contribution × 100/80)

Adjusted higher rate limit = £150,000 + (cash contribution × 100/80)

Exam focus point

Make sure your workings show clearly how you have increased the basic rate and higher rate limits. Note the difference between this method and that used for net pay arrangements (see below).

Illustration 1: Personal pension contributions (1)

Joe has earnings of £68,650 in 2020/21. He pays a personal pension contribution of £7,200 (net). He has no other taxable income.

Required

Show Joe's tax liability for 2020/21.

Solution

	Non-savings income £
Earnings/Net income	68,650
Less PA	(12,500)
Taxable income	56,150

Tax

	£
£46,500 (W) × 20%	9,300
£9,650 × 40%	3,860
£56,150	13,160

Working

Basic rate limit

£37,500 + (£7,200 × 100/80) = £46,500

Remember that **gross personal pension contributions** are also used to compute **adjusted net income** and that **the restriction on the personal allowance** is calculated in relation to adjusted net income (see Chapter 2).

Activity 1: Personal pension contributions (2)

John earned £132,500 in the tax year. He made a cash contribution to a personal pension scheme of £20,000.

Required

1   What is John's personal allowance in the tax year?

O   £nil

O   £5,000

O   £6,250

O   £8,750

2   What are John's basic rate band and higher rate band limits?

O   BRB: £62,500 and HRB: £175,000

O   BRB: £57,500 and HRB: £175,000

O   BRB: £62,500 and HRB: £170,000

O   BRB: £57,500 and HRB: £170,000

Solution

3.3 Contributions to an occupational pension scheme

Employee contributions get tax relief under 'net pay arrangements' where the employer deducts the employee's gross pension contribution before applying Pay As You Earn (PAYE). This gives the employee tax relief at the correct marginal rate (ie starting with highest rate) of tax without the need to make any additional claims.

Illustration 2: Occupational pension scheme (1)

Maxine has taxable earnings of £68,650 in 2020/21. Her employer deducts a pension contribution of £9,000 from these earnings before operating PAYE. She has no other taxable income.

Required

Show Maxine's tax liability for 2020/21.

Solution

	Non-savings Income £
Earnings/Total income	68,650
Less pension contribution	(9,000)
Net income	59,650
Less PA	(12,500)
Taxable income	47,150

Tax

	£
£37,500 × 20%	7,500
£9,650 × 40%	3,860
£47,150	11,360

This is the same result as Joe in the earlier illustration. Joe had received basic rate tax relief of £9,000 − £7,200 = £1,800 at source, so his overall tax position was £13,160 − £1,800 = £11,360.

Activity 2: Occupational pension scheme (2)

Wendy is paid a salary of £50,000.

She pays 10% of this salary into her employer's occupational pension scheme. The employer matches this contribution. Wendy also receives benefits of £8,000 in the tax year.

Required

1   What is Wendy's employment income for the tax year?
    ○ £45,000
    ○ £51,750
    ○ £53,000
    ○ £58,000

2   What is Wendy's basic rate band for the tax year?
    ○ £37,500
    ○ £42,500
    ○ £43,750
    ○ £47,500

Solution

3.4 Annual allowance

The 'annual allowance' effectively restricts the amount of tax relievable contributions that can be paid into an individual's pension scheme each year. The annual allowance is £40,000. It applies to gross contributions to both personal pension and occupational pension schemes, including any contributions made by an employer.

If the annual allowance is not fully used in any tax year, the unused allowance can be carried forward for up to three years, but only if the individual is a member of a pension scheme in the year the allowance relates to. If the individual is not a member of a pension scheme in any year, then the annual allowance for that year is wasted and cannot be carried forward.

The current year annual allowance is utilised first and then the earliest of the years brought forward.

Illustration 3: Annual allowance (1)

Jess made the following gross personal pension contributions:

2017/18 – £23,600

2018/19 – Nil (Not a member of a pension scheme in this year)

2019/20 – £30,400

Required

What is Jess's annual allowance for 2020/21?

Solution

	Unused allowance	£
2017/18	£40,000 – £23,600	= 16,400
2018/19		Nil
2019/20	£40,000 – £30,400	= 9,600
		26,000
2020/21		= 40,000
		66,000

As Jess was not a member of a pension scheme in 2018/19, the annual allowance for that year is lost.

Activity 3: Annual allowance (2)

Ted is a sole trader. His gross contributions to his personal pension scheme have been as follows:

2017/18	£16,000
2018/19	£36,000
2019/20	£25,000

In 2020/21, Ted will have taxable trading profits of about £100,000 and wishes to make a large pension contribution in January 2021. He has no other sources of income.

Required

1 What is the maximum gross tax relievable pension contribution Ted can make in January 2021, taking into consideration any brought forward annual allowance?

2 If Ted makes a gross personal pension contribution of £43,000 in January 2021, what are the unused annual allowances he could carry forward to 2021/22?

Solution

3.5 Tapering the annual allowance

Individuals who have adjusted income in excess of £240,000 have a reduced annual allowance.

The annual allowance is reduced by £1 for every £2 that the individual's adjusted income exceeds £240,000, subject to a minimum annual allowance of £4,000. The minimum annual allowance will apply where the individual has adjusted income of £312,000 or more.

Adjusted income is **net income** plus any **employee contributions** to **occupational** pension schemes plus any **employer contributions** to **any pension schemes** for the employee. For self-employed people, adjusted income is simply their net income for the tax year.

Exam focus point

There is a threshold level of income below which tapering does not apply but this is **not examinable** in Taxation (TX – UK).

Exam focus point

The £40,000 annual allowance, £4,000 minimum allowance and £240,000 income limit will be given to you in the Tax Rates and Allowances available in the exam.

Activity 4: Tapered annual allowance

Peter is a member of a partnership and his share of the trading income is £265,000 in the tax year 2020/21. During the tax year, Peter paid interest of £12,500 on a loan to invest in the partnership.

Peter's wife, Catherine, is employed by Peter's partnership. She is paid an annual salary of £290,000 in the tax year 2020/21. She pays 10% of her salary into her employer's occupational pension scheme and her employer (the partnership) pays a further 5% into the same scheme. Catherine also made a gross contribution into a personal pension scheme in the tax year of £10,000.

The couple jointly own an investment property which is let out to tenants and has generated profits of £67,000 in the tax year 2020/21.

Required

1   What is Peter's annual allowance for 2020/21?

    O £nil

    O £4,000

    O £27,500

    O £33,750

    O £17,000

2   What is Catherine's annual allowance for 2020/21?

    O £nil

    O £4,000

    O £12,750

    O £7,750

Solution

If gross contributions exceed the annual allowance available, the excess contributions will be taxed as an annual allowance charge for the tax year in which the contribution is paid. This charge is subject to income tax at the individual's marginal rates. In effect, the tax relief given for the contribution is clawed back.

 ## Illustration 4: Annual allowance charge (1)

Jaida had employment income of £315,000 in 2020/21. She made a gross personal pension contribution of £70,000 in December 2020. She does not have any unused annual allowance brought forward.

Required

What is Jaida's income tax liability for 2020/21?

Solution

	Non-savings income
	£
Taxable income (no personal allowance available)	315,000
Tax	
£107,500 (W1) × 20%	21,500
£112,500 × 40%	45,000
£220,000 (W2)	
£95,000 × 45%	42,750
£315,000	
£66,000 (W3) × 45%	29,700
Tax liability	138,950

Workings

1 **Basic rate limit**

   £37,500 + £70,000 = £107,500

2 **Higher rate limit**

   £150,000 + £70,000 = £220,000

3 **Excess pension contribution**

   (£70,000 – £4,000 minimum as adjusted income exceeds £312,000) = £66,000

Activity 5: Annual allowance charge (2)

Shirley has employment income of £126,000 for the tax year and made a personal pension contribution of £46,000. She does not have any brought forward unused annual allowance.

Required

Calculate Shirley's income tax liability for 2020/21.

Solution

---

4 Receiving benefits from pensions

PER alert

One of the competencies you require to fulfil Performance Objective 17 *Tax planning and advice* of the PER is to assess the tax implications of proposed activities or plans of an individual or entity with reference to relevant and up to date legislation. You can apply the knowledge you obtain from this section of the Workbook to help demonstrate this competence.

Individuals with personal pensions have complete flexibility as to how they can access their pension fund once they reach the minimum pension age of 55.

25% of the pension fund can be withdrawn as a tax-free lump sum. The balance of the pension fund can be reinvested to provide taxable pension income whenever the individual wishes. The withdrawals are taxed as non-savings income in the tax years of withdrawal and subject to the normal rates of tax.

> ### Exam focus point
>
> There is an anti-avoidance annual allowance limit which applies when an individual starts to receive pension benefits flexibly but is also entitled to make further contributions to the pension fund. This annual allowance limit is **not examinable** in Taxation (TX – UK).

A lifetime allowance of £1,073,100 applies to the total value of a person's pension schemes when they start to make withdrawals from the schemes. If the pension fund **exceeds the lifetime allowance**, this will give rise to an **income tax charge** on the **excess value of the fund** when the individual receives pension benefits from the fund. The rate of the charge is 55% if the excess value is taken as a lump sum, or 25% if the funds are used to provide a pension income.

Chapter summary

Pensions

Types of pension scheme

Occupational schemes
- Set up by employer
- Defined benefit arrangements – based on employee's earnings
- Defined contribution – provides no guarantee of level of pension

Personal schemes
- Only defined contribution schemes
- Available to any individual (whether employed or not)

Contributing to a pension scheme

General rules
- Employer contributions
  - Exempt benefit
  - Deductible for employer
  - Not limited but use up annual allowance
- Maximum tax-relievable individual contributions are higher of:
  - £3,600
  - Relevant earnings (employment, self-employment, FHL income)

Contributions to a personal pension scheme
- Must be < 75 years of age
- Contributions made net of basic rate of income tax
- Higher and additional rate relief given by adjusting higher and additional rate thresholds
- Gross personal pension contributions deducted in calculation of adjusted net income for restriction of personal allowance

Contributions to an occupational scheme
- Contributions made under "net pay arrangements"

Annual allowance
- Restricts the amount of tax-relievable contributions each year
- £40,000 plus unused AA from previous three years, FIFO (as long as individual was a member of a scheme in that year)

Tapering the annual allowance
- If adjusted income > £240,000
- Reduce by £1 for every £2 adjusted income exceeds £240,000
- Minimum AA £4,000
- Adjusted income = net income + employee contributions to occupational schemes plus employer contributions to any pension schemes for the employee
- If gross contributions > available AA, excess taxed at marginal rate as AA charge

Receiving benefits from pensions

Flexibility with personal schemes once 55 years of age

Withdrawing funds
- 25% as tax free lump sum
- Balance of fund reinvested and taxed as non-savings income as and when withdrawn

Lifetime allowance
- Applies to total value of pension fund
- £1,073,100
- Income tax charge on withdrawal if fund exceeds lifetime allowance

Knowledge diagnostic

1. Occupational pension schemes

Occupational schemes are run by an employer and can be defined benefit or defined contribution schemes.

2. Personal pension schemes

Any individual may invest in a personal pension scheme. These schemes are defined contribution schemes.

3. Employer contributions

Contributions made by an employer into an occupational or a personal pension are an exempt benefit and are tax deductible for the employer.

4. Tax relief

For personal pension schemes basic rate relief is given at source. Higher and additional rate relief is given by increasing the higher and additional rate thresholds by the gross contribution.

For occupational schemes under net pay arrangements the employer deducts the employee's contributions from their gross pay, thereby achieving tax relief at their marginal rate.

Maximum tax relievable contributions are restricted to the higher of £3,600, and the individual's relevant earnings (broadly employment, trading and furnished holiday lettings income).

5. Annual allowance

The annual allowance is an overriding restriction to the amount of contributions getting tax relief each year. The annual allowance is £40,000 per tax year and unused annual allowance can be carried forwards three years, as long as the individual is a member of a pension scheme that year.

The annual allowance is tapered if adjusted net income is in excess of £240,000. There is a minimum annual allowance of £4,000.

If gross contributions are greater than the annual allowance, then the excess contributions are taxed at the marginal rate as an annual allowance charge.

6. Drawing benefits from a pension fund

25% of a pension fund can be withdrawn as a tax free lump sum. The rest is reinvested to be withdrawn as taxable non-savings income as the individual wishes.

If the total pension fund exceeds the lifetime allowance, which is £1,073,100, at the point when funds are withdrawn, there is an income tax charge on the excess.

Further study guidance

Question practice

Now try the following from the Further question practice bank (available in the digital edition of the Workbook):

Section A: Q20, 21, 22

Section B: Q23

Activity answers

Activity 1: Personal pension contributions (2)

1   The correct answer is: £8,750

	£
Net income	132,500
Less pension contribution £20,000 × 100/80	(25,000)
ANI	107,500
Personal allowance	12,500
Less 1/2 × £(107,500 - 100,000)	(3,750)
	8,750

The answer £Nil does not adjust for the pension contribution. The answer £5,000 deducts the full excess of £7,500. The answer £6,250 does not gross up the pension contribution.

2   The correct answer is: BRB: £62,500 and HRB: £175,000

Extend BR and HR bands by gross pension contribution
BR band £37,500 + (20,000 × 100/80) = 62,500
HR band £150,000 + (20,000 × 100/80) = 175,000

The answers BRB £57,500 and HRB £170,000 do not gross up the pension contribution.

Activity 2: Occupational pension scheme (2)

1   The correct answer is: £53,000

	£
Salary	50,000
Less pension contribution (10%)	(5,000)
Add benefits	8,000
	53,000

Note. Employer's contribution is tax free.

The answer £45,000 does not add the taxable benefits. The answer £51,750 grosses up Wendy's occupational pension contribution as if it were a personal pension contribution. £58,000 treats the employer's contribution as a taxable benefit.

2   The correct answer is: £37,500

The basic rate band is not adjusted for occupational pension contributions.

The answer £42,500 adds Wendy's occupational pension contribution to the basic rate limit. The answer £43,750 grosses up Wendy's occupational pension contribution and adds it to the basic rate limit as if it were a personal pension contribution. The answer £47,500 adds both Wendy's contribution and her employer's contribution to the basic rate limit.

Activity 3: Annual allowance (2)

1

	£
Annual allowance 2020/21	40,000
Annual allowance unused in 2017/18 (£40,000 – £16,000)	24,000
Annual allowance unused in 2018/19 (£40,000 – £36,000)	4,000
Annual allowance unused in 2019/20 (£40,000 – £25,000)	15,000
Maximum gross pension contribution in 2020/21	83,000

2

	£
Annual allowance 2020/21 used in 2020/21	40,000
Annual allowance unused in 2017/18 used in 2020/21	3,000
Contribution in 2020/21	43,000

The remaining £24,000 – £3,000 = £21,000 of the 2017/18 annual allowance cannot be carried forward to 2021/22 since this is more than three years after 2017/18. The unused annual allowances are therefore £4,000 from 2018/19 and £15,000 from 2019/20 and these are carried forward to 2021/22.

Activity 4: Tapered annual allowance

1 The correct answer is: £17,000

	£
Trading income from partnership	265,000
Property business income	33,500
Less qualifying interest paid	(12,500)
Net income = adjusted income	286,000

Then compute the reduced annual allowance:

	£
Adjusted income	286,000
Less threshold	(240,000)
Excess	46,000
Annual allowance	40,000
Less half excess £46,000 × ½	(23,000)
Reduced annual allowance	17,000

The answer £nil assumes fully tapered and does not include the minimum allowance. The answer £4,000 does not halve the excess of £46,000 so the minimum allowance of £4,000 applies. The answer £27,500 ignores the property income and does not halve the excess. The answer £33,750 ignores the property income.

2 The correct answer is: £4,000

BPP
LEARNING
MEDIA

		£
Employment income (£290,000 − 10% × £290,000)		261,000
Property business income		33,500
Net income		294,500
Catherine's and employer's contribution to occupational pension (10% + 5%) × £290,000		43,500
Contribution to the personal pension scheme (not relevant)		0
Adjusted income		338,000

Then compute the reduced annual allowance:

	£
Adjusted income	338,000
Less threshold	(240,000)
Excess	98,000
Annual allowance	40,000
Less half excess £98,000 × ½	(49,000)
	(9,000)
Minimum allowance applies	4,000

The answer £nil does not apply the minimum allowance. The answer £12,750 ignores the contributions to the occupational scheme. The answer £7,750 ignores the joint income.

Activity 5: Annual allowance charge (2)

		Non-savings income
		£
Employment income		126,000
Personal allowance (W1)		(12,500)
Taxable income		113,500
Income tax		
	95,000 × 20% (W2)	19,000
	18,500 × 40%	7,400
Annual allowance charge	17,500 (W3) × 40%	7,000
Income tax liability		33,400

Workings

1 **Personal allowance**

Adjusted net income (ANI)	£

Employment income		126,000
Less gross pension contribution		(57,500)
ANI		68,500

∴ Personal allowance is £12,500

2 **BR band limit**

£37,500 + £57,500 = <u>95,000</u>

3 **Excess annual allowance**

Annual allowance charge	£
Gross pension contribution	
£46,000 × 100/80	57,500
Annual allowance	(40,000)
	17,500

6

Property income

Learning objectives

On completion of this chapter, you should be able to:

	Syllabus reference no.
Compute property business profits.	B4(a)
Explain the treatment of furnished holiday lettings.	B4(b)
Understand rent-a-room relief.	B4(c)
Compute the amount assessable when a premium is received for the grant of a short lease.	B4(d)
Understand and apply the restriction on property income finance costs.	B4(e)
Understand how relief for a property business loss is given.	B4(f)

Exam context

You are likely to be required to compute property income as part of a 10- or 15-mark question in Section C. You may find it tested in the context of income tax or corporation tax (see later in this Workbook). Specific aspects of property income such as lease premiums may be tested in Section A or Section B questions. Rent-a-room relief is an important relief for individuals (it does not apply to companies), and the special rules for furnished holiday lettings will only be examined in an income tax context. Remember that property income is non-savings income even though a property portfolio is usually regarded as an investment.

Chapter overview

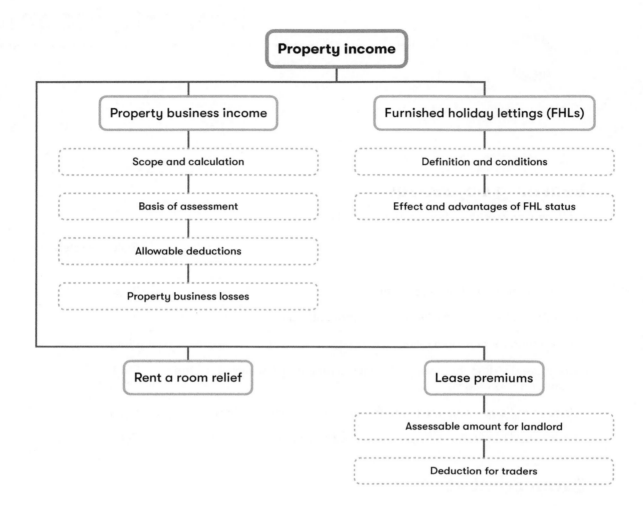

1 Property business income

1.1 Scope and calculation

1.1.1 Scope of charge

Income from land and buildings in the UK is taxed as non-savings income. The profit or loss of the UK property business operated by an individual is computed for a tax year.

1.1.2 Computation of property business profit/loss

A taxpayer with UK rental income is treated as running a business, their 'UK property business'. All the receipts and expenses for all properties are pooled to give a single profit or loss.

The main taxable receipt for a property business is **rent paid by the tenant to the landlord taxpayer**, which is usually in the form of money. If the tenant is required to pay a security deposit to cover costs such as unpaid rent, cleaning or making good damage by the tenant at the end of the tenancy, this is not treated as a receipt unless and until the landlord becomes legally entitled to use it under the terms of the deposit.

	£
Rental income	X
Less allowable expenses including:	
Advertising	(X)
Agent's fees	(X)
Repairs/ replacement domestic items	(X)
Property income profit/(loss)	X/(X)

1.2 Basis of assessment

1.2.1 Cash basis

> **Cash basis:** A landlord who is an individual is by default assessed on rent received less expenses paid in the current tax year (cash basis).

> ### Exam focus point
>
> The examining team has stated that in any examination question involving property income for individuals and partnerships (since the individual partners are taxed on their share of the partnership property business income), it should be assumed that the cash basis is to be used unless specifically stated to the contrary.

1.2.2 Accruals basis

> **Accruals basis:** Property income can alternatively be assessed on rent receivable less expenses payable in the current tax year (accruals basis).

An individual **must** use the accruals basis if cash basis receipts for the tax year exceed £150,000 (reduced proportionately if the property business is not carried on for a full tax year).

An individual can **elect** to use the accruals basis. The election must be made by the 31 January which is 22 months from the end of the tax year.

Companies must use the accruals basis to compute property business income (see Chapter 19).

Activity 1: Assessable property income

Len owns a flat which he lets out from 1 March 2020. Rent is payable quarterly in advance. Payments are made by the tenant as follows:

Payment date	£
1 March 2020	3,000
1 June 2020	3,000
1 September 2020	3,000
1 December 2020	3,600
1 March 2021	3,600

All the payments were made on time apart from the 1 March 2021 payment which was not paid until 10 April 2021.

Required

1   What is the assessable property income for 2020/21?

£ [   ]

2   What is the assessable property income for 2020/21 if Len makes an election to use the accruals basis?

- O £10,800
- O £11,600
- O £12,800
- O £13,200

Solution

1.3 Allowable deductions

1.3.1 General conditions

The general rule is that all expenses incurred wholly and exclusively for the purpose of the letting business are allowable in computing the property business profit or loss. Deductible expenses include repairs to the property, agent's fees, insurance, and rent payable where a landlord is renting the property which they in turn let to others. Capital expenditure (for example mortgage capital repayments, construction of an extension or boundary wall) is not usually deductible.

A landlord can choose to use either actual motoring expenses incurred, or the approved mileage allowances (same as for employment income) for motoring expenses incurred in their property business.

1.3.2 Finance costs

Special rules apply to interest and other finance costs (including incidental costs incurred in obtaining loans such as fees or commission payments) for property businesses carried on by individuals (not companies). The effect of the rule is to restrict tax relief on these costs to the basic rate. The tax liability of basic rate taxpayers will not be affected by the rule but higher and additional rate taxpayers will have an increased tax liability.

The rule applies to **loans taken out for a residential property business**. It is not necessary for the loan to be for the purchase of the property, for example it could be taken out to pay for repairs to the property. Loans relating to commercial properties or for furnished holiday letting business (see later in this chapter) do not fall within the rule.

Instead of being given relief by deducting finance costs from property income, they are instead given as a tax reducer at 20% (ie, deductible from the individual's income tax liability).

 ## Illustration 1: Finance costs tax reducer

Millicent bought a house on 6 April 2020 and let it out throughout the tax year 2020/21 at a monthly rental of £1,500 which she received in full by 5 April 2021. She bought the house with a mortgage loan and in 2020/21 she made capital repayments of £1,000 and paid interest of £4,000. Millicent had other property business expenses (all deductible) of £2,500 for 2020/21. Millicent had other taxable income (after deduction of her personal allowance) of £60,000 in 2020/21.

Required

Compute Millicent's income tax liability in respect of her property income for the tax year 2020/21.

Solution

	£
Rental income £1,500 × 12	18,000
Less deductible expenses	(2,500)
Property income 2020/21	15,500

Note that the mortgage capital repayments are not deductible.

Income tax on property income	£
£15,500 × 40% (higher rate taxpayer)	6,200
Less property business finance costs tax reducer	
£4,000 × 20%	(800)
Property income tax liability 2020/21	5,400

1.3.3 Replacement of furniture and other domestic items

No relief is given for the initial cost of providing furniture in a let property. Relief is however given if an item of furniture is replaced. This is known as 'Replacement of domestic items relief'.

This relief is for a range of domestic items including furniture, furnishings, household appliances and kitchenware, but does not apply to fixtures which become part of a property such as radiators.

The amount of the relief is the expenditure on the new replacement asset less any proceeds from selling the old asset which has been replaced plus any incidental costs of disposal of the old asset or acquisition of the new asset. If the new asset is not the same, or substantially the same, as the old asset, only the cost of an equivalent asset is given relief. For example, if a single bed is replaced with a double bed, only the cost of an equivalent single bed is given relief.

1.4 Property business losses

Generally, there is no difference between the treatment of a property business loss calculated under the cash basis or one calculated under the accruals basis.

If the result is a profit – taxable in the current tax year

If the result is a loss – carry forward to deduct from first available property profits in the future

Activity 2: Computation of property business profits

Fiona owns a property that she has let furnished on a short-term basis for a number of years. The following information relates to the tax year 2020/21:

(1)   Fiona's total property income (after deduction of allowable expenses) amounted to £9,900. This was before taking account of her mortgage repayments which amounted to £2,500 (consisting of £2,000 of interest and £500 capital repayments).

(2)   The property was let out at a monthly rental of £1,000 payable on the 6th of each month. The rent due on 6th March 2020 was not received until 6 April 2020.

(3)   Fiona had received a security deposit of £500 from a tenant when she let the property in January 2020. That tenant left the property on 5 January 2021 at the end of the letting period. On that date, Fiona used £200 of the deposit to pay for cleaning the property and repaid the remaining £300 to the departing tenant. She then let the property again on 6 January 2021 and received a security deposit of £600 from the incoming tenant. This amount was still held as a deposit by Fiona at 5 April 2021.

(4)   Fiona disposed of an old washing machine for £25 and replaced it with a new washer-dryer at a cost of £550. The cost of a new washing machine equivalent to the one she disposed of would have been £330.

(5)   Fiona travelled 1,000 miles in her car in relation to letting the property.

Fiona wants to know what the income tax liability on her property income is for the tax year 2020/21 that is in addition to her income tax liability on her other income. Fiona has other taxable income (all non-savings) of £50,000.

For the tax year 2021/22, Fiona is considering using the accruals basis.

Fiona may incur substantial allowable expenditure on refurbishing the property in the tax year 2021/22 which could result in a property business loss. The property will then generate a profit in subsequent tax years. Fiona wants to know how the loss could be used.

Required

1   What is Fiona's additional income tax liability for 2020/21 on her property income?

   O   £3,960

   O   £3,460

   O   £3,560

   O   £3,160

2   What was the amount of income received when Fiona computed her property income for 2020/21?

   £ [   ]

3   What was the total amount of expenditure paid in respect of the new washer-dryer in (4) and the use of Fiona's car in (5) that was deducted when Fiona computed her property income for 2020/21?

   O   £555

   O   £755

○ £780

○ £975

4   Which **TWO** of the following statements about the use of the accruals basis by Fiona in the tax year 2021/22 are correct?

☐ Under the accruals basis, Fiona will compute property income using rent receivable less expenses payable

☐ Under the accruals basis, Fiona will be able to deduct the whole of her finance costs from her property profit

☐ Fiona must use the accruals basis if her property income under the cash basis exceeds £150,000 in that tax year

☐ Fiona can elect to use the accruals basis and must so elect by 31 January 2023

5   Complete the following sentence about how Fiona could use a property business loss for 2021/22.

Fiona can use a property business loss for 2021/22 against ⬚ (1)   income in

the tax year ⬚ (2)   .

Pull down list 1

* general
* property

Pull down list 2

* 2020/21
* 2021/22
* 2022/23

Solution

2 Furnished Holiday Lettings (FHLs)

2.1 Definition and conditions

Accommodation counts as a furnished holiday letting (FHL) if all of the following apply:

- It is available for commercial letting to the public for no less than 210 days each tax year.
- It is actually let for at least 105 days in each tax year. If a taxpayer owns more than one FHL, this condition can be satisfied based on the average number of days that each property is let.
- Tenants do not stay for a period of more than 31 days. However, the property can be let to the same tenant for periods longer than this provided these long lets do not take up more than 155 days per tax year.
- It is located in the European Economic Area.

> **Exam focus point**
>
> An FHL must be situated in the UK or in another state within the European Economic Area. However, only FHLs situated within the UK are within the Taxation (TX – UK) syllabus.
>
> It is possible to make an election so that a rental property continues to qualify as an FHL for up to two years after the 105-day test ceases to be met. This election is **not examinable** in Taxation (TX – UK).

2.2 Effect and advantages of FHL status

FHL accommodation income is taxable as property income but it is treated as a business.

Landlord needs to keep details of income and expenses separate to other properties. This is so that the profits and losses can be identified for the special rules which apply to FHLs.

Losses can only be offset against future profits from FHLs.

The advantages of having an FHL are that:

- Finance costs are not restricted, ie they are fully deductible from FHL business income.

- Capital expenditure on furniture is deductible when incurred (or under the accruals basis, capital allowances are available), instead of on replacement basis.
- Income is treated as earned income and so qualifies as part of relevant earnings for pension contributions (see Chapter 5).
- Capital gains tax rollover relief, business asset disposal relief and gift relief are available on any subsequent sale of the property (see Chapter 15).

3 Rent-a-room relief

The first £7,500 each tax year collected from a tenant renting a room in the taxpayer's main residence is tax-free. This limit is halved if any other person (eg spouse/civil partner) also received income from renting accommodation in the property. The taxpayer can elect to ignore the exemption, for example to generate a loss by taking into account both rent and expenses.

If the rent received exceeds £7,500 the taxpayer is by default taxable on total rents received less normal rental expenses, but can elect to be taxed on the excess rentals over £7,500 with no deduction for expenses.

An election to ignore the exemption (if gross rents are below £7,500), or an election for the alternative basis (if gross rents exceed £7,500) must be made by the 31 January which is 22 months from the end of the tax year concerned.

Illustration 2: Rent a room relief

Sylvia owns and lives in a house near the sea in the UK. She has a spare bedroom and, during 2020/21, this was let to a lodger who paid her £148 per week which includes the cost of heating and electricity.

Sylvia estimates that her lodger costs her an extra £150 on gas, £125 on electricity, and £50 on buildings insurance each year.

Required

What is Sylvia's property income for 2020/21 assuming that she makes any beneficial election?

Solution

Sylvia's gross rents are above the rent-a-room limit. Therefore, she has the following choices:

(1) Under the normal method (no election needed), she can be taxed on her actual profit:

	£
Rental income £148 × 52	7,696
Less expenses (150 + 125 + 50)	(325)
	7,371

(2) Under the 'alternative basis' (elect for rent-a-room relief):

Total rental income of £7,696 exceeds £7,500 limit, so taxable income is £196 (ie £7,696 – £7,500) if rent-a-room relief claimed.

Sylvia should elect for rent-a-room relief and so be taxed on the 'alternative basis'.

4 Lease premiums

4.1 Assessable amount for landlord

A new tenant often pays both annual rental and a one-off premium. If the lease granted is for 50 years or less, part of the premium is treated as **rent received in advance** and increases the landlord's property income assessment for the year in which the premium falls due.

The property income assessment is calculated as:

	£
Premium	A
Less 2% × (n − 1) × A	(a)
	X
	−

(Where n is the length of the lease)

This treatment applies irrespective of whether the landlord uses the cash or accruals basis.

Illustration 3: Income element of a premium

Janet granted a lease to Jack on 1 March 2021 for a period of 40 years. Jack paid a premium of £16,000.

Required

How much of the premium received by Janet is taxed as property income?

Solution

	£
Premium received	16,000
Less 2% × (40 − 1) × £16,000	(12,480)
Taxable as property income	3,520

4.2 Deduction for traders

Where a trader has **paid** a premium for the granting of a short lease, they may deduct the following amount against their trading income, in addition to any rent paid:

Amount deductible (per annum) = Property income assessment on lessor/Life of lease (in years).

Activity 3: Lease premiums

Denise grants Timothy a lease to a shop on 30 June 2020.

Annual rental	£8,000 due on 1.7.20
Term	15 years
Premium	£60,000

Denise uses the accruals basis to calculate her property business profits.

Required

1   Calculate the property income assessment on Denise for 2020/21.

2 Timothy prepares accounts to 31 December every year.

Required

Show the relief available to Timothy for the premium paid for his year ended 31 December 2020.

Solution

Chapter summary

Property income

Property business income

Scope and calculation
- Profit/loss computed for tax year
- Results from all properties are pooled

Basis of assessment
- Cash basis: rent received less expenses paid in current tax year (use unless told otherwise in question)
- Accruals basis: rent receivable less expenses payable in current tax year (use if cash basis property business income exceeds £150,000 or if election made)

Allowable deductions
- Expenses incurred wholly and exclusively for letting business
- Finance costs relief given as tax reducer at 20%
- No relief for capital items, except
- Cost of replacement furniture and appliances

Property business losses
- Offset vs current and future property income

Furnished holiday lettings (FHLs)

Definition and conditions
- Available for letting for > 210 days per year
- Let for > 105 days
- Lets > 31 days add up to ≤ 155 days in total

Effect and advantages of FHL status
- Treated as a business
- Loss relief only against income from FHL business
- Advantages:
  – Finance costs are not restricted
  – Relevant earnings for pension contributions
  – Business asset for CGT so gift relief, business asset disposal relief and rollover relief available
  – Capital expenditure on furniture deductible when incurred

Rent a room relief

- First £7,500 pa tax free income from lodger

Lease premiums

Assessable amount for landlord

Premium	A
Less 2% × (n – 1) × A	(a)
Rental assessment	X

Deduction for traders
- Trader paying lease premium gets trading profit deduction for rental assessment, spread over lease term

Knowledge diagnostic

1. Property business profits

Income for individuals is usually assessed on a cash basis.

Revenue expenses are deductible (but finance costs are given relief via a tax reducer at 20%) and there is a deduction for the cost of replacement furniture.

A loss on a property letting business is carried forward to set against future property business profits.

2. Furnished holiday lettings (FHLs)

FHLs are seen as a business activity so attract certain advantages. Finance costs are offset against FHL income, purchase of furniture is deductible when incurred and income is relevant earnings for pension purposes. Carry forward loss relief is available against FHL income.

3. Rent-a-room relief

£7,500 each tax year collected from renting a room in a main residence is tax-free. If the rent exceeds £7,500, full amount less expenses is taxable as property business profits. Taxpayer can elect for the excess over £7,500 to be taxable, but with no deduction for expenses.

4. Lease premiums

Lease premiums on the grant of a short lease lead to an element of the premium being treated as rent received in advance. If the premium is paid by a trader, a deduction can be made in computing taxable trading profits.

Further study guidance

Question practice

Now try the following from the Further question practice bank (available in the digital edition of the Workbook):

Section A: Q24, Q25 and Q26

Section C: Q27 Rafe

Activity answers

Activity 1: Assessable property income

1   £ 9,600

		£
1.6.20		3,000
1.9.20		3,000
1.12.20		3,600
		9,600

The payment due on 1.3.21 paid on 10.4.21 will be taxed in 2021/22.

Use the cash basis unless specifically told otherwise in the question.

2   The correct answer is: £12,800

		£
1.3.20 payment:	3,000 × 2/3	2,000
1.6.20		3,000
1.9.20		3,000
1.12.20		3,600
1.3.21	3,600 × 1/3	1,200
		12,800

The answer £10,800 omits the accrual for April and May. The answer £11,600 omits the accrual for March – under the accruals basis it is not relevant that this is not received until April. The answer £13,200 is all the rent from June 2020 to March 2021.

Activity 2: Computation of property business profits

1   The correct answer is: £3,560

	£
Property income (no deduction for any mortgage repayments)	9,900
Tax	
£9,900 × 40%	3,960
Less: finance costs tax reducer £2,000 × 20%	(400)
Tax liability	3,560

Fiona's other taxable income uses up her basic rate band so the additional income tax is computed at the higher rate.

The answer £3,960 does not deduct the tax reducer. The answer £3,460 incorrectly includes capital repayments in the tax reducer. The answer £3,160 deducts the whole of the finance costs in computing the property income, ie gives relief on finance costs at 40% instead of 20%.

2   £ 13,200

	£
Rent received 2020/21 (including late paid rent due 6 March 2020) £1,000 × 13	13,000
Security deposit retained 5 January 2021	200
Tax liability	13,200

The security deposit paid by the incoming tenant is not treated as income unless and until Fiona becomes legally entitled to use it under the terms of the deposit.

3   The correct answer is: £755

	£
Washer-dryer (£330 – £25)	305
Landlord's mileage allowance 1,000 × 45p	450
Total deduction	755

Only the cost of an equivalent asset is allowable, less the proceeds from selling the old washing machine. The mileage allowance is computed using the approved mileage rates.

The answer £555 uses the 25p rate for the mileage allowance. The answer £780 does not deduct the disposal proceeds of the old washing machine. The answer £975 allows the full cost of the new washer-dryer.

4   The correct answers are:

- Under the accruals basis, Fiona will compute property income using rent receivable less expenses payable
- Fiona must use the accruals basis if her property income under the cash basis exceeds £150,000 in that tax year

Finance costs are not deductible from property income, irrespective of whether the cash or the accruals basis is used. Fiona can elect to use the accruals basis but must so elect by 31 January 2024 for the tax year 2021/22.

5   Fiona can use a property business loss for 2021/22 against ⬚ property ⬚ income in the tax year ⬚ 2022/23 ⬚.

Property business losses cannot be carried back and cannot be set against general income.

Activity 3: Lease premiums

1

	£
Premium	60,000
Less 2% × (15 − 1) × 60,000	(16,800)
	43,200
Rent (9/12 × 8,000)	6,000
Property income assessment	49,200

2   Relief available = £43,200/15 = £2,880 for 12-month period of account.

Lease commenced 1 July 2020, so relief available in the year ended 31 December 2020: 6/12 × £2,880 = £1,440.

7

Computing trading income

Learning objectives

On completion of this chapter, you should be able to:

	Syllabus reference no.
Describe and apply the badges of trade.	B3(b)
Recognise the expenditure that is allowable in calculating the tax-adjusted trading profit.	B3(c)
Explain and compute the assessable profits using the cash basis for small businesses.	B3(d)
Recognise the relief that can be obtained for pre-trading expenditure.	B3(e)

Exam context

The final figure to slot into the income tax computation is income from self-employment (trading income).

We are therefore going to look at the computation of profits of unincorporated businesses. We work out a business's profit as if it were a separate entity (the separate entity concept familiar to you from basic bookkeeping) but, as an unincorporated business has no legal existence apart from its trader, we cannot tax it separately. We have to feed its profit into the owner's personal tax computation.

Section A questions on computing taxable trading income may test two or three particular adjustments such as the restriction for motor cars with high carbon dioxide (CO_2) emissions. You may also be required to deal with a number of adjustments in a Section B question. You may be required to compute trading profits in a Section C question. The computation may be for an individual, a partnership or a company. In each case, the same principles are applied. You must however watch out for the adjustments which only apply to individuals, such as private use expenses. You may also be asked to explain the badges of trade in a Section C question. These topics may be tested as part of a 15-mark or a 10-mark question.

Chapter overview

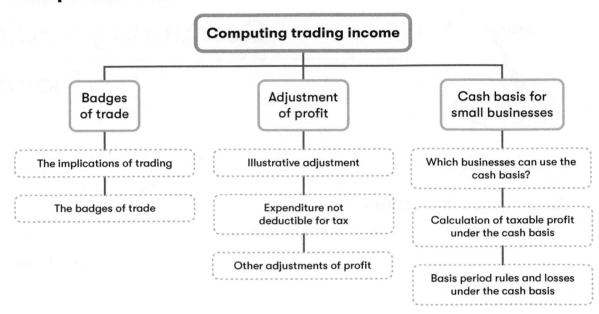

Computing trading income

- Badges of trade
  - The implications of trading
  - The badges of trade
- Adjustment of profit
  - Illustrative adjustment
  - Expenditure not deductible for tax
  - Other adjustments of profit
- Cash basis for small businesses
  - Which businesses can use the cash basis?
  - Calculation of taxable profit under the cash basis
  - Basis period rules and losses under the cash basis

1 The badges of trade

The badges of trade are used to decide whether or not a trade exists. If one does exist, the accounting profits need to be adjusted in order to establish the taxable trading profits.

A trade is defined by the Income Tax Act 2007 as any venture in the nature of trade. Further guidance about the scope of this definition is found in a number of cases which have been decided by the courts. This guidance is summarised in a collection of principles known as the 'badges of trade'. These are set out below. They apply to both corporate and unincorporated businesses.

> **Badges of trade:** A number of principles based on previous court decisions which indicate whether an activity is trading in nature

1.1 The implications of trading

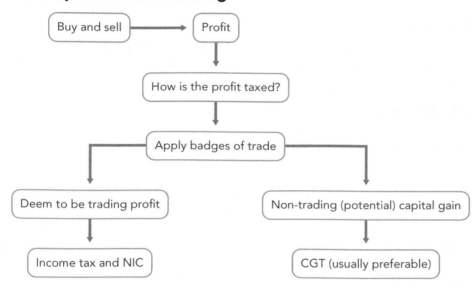

1.2 The badges of trade

It is important to know when an individual's income should be assessed under the trading income rules. The following main tests are used:

1.2.1 Subject matter

Whether a person is trading or not may sometimes be decided by examining the subject matter of the transaction.

1.2.2 Frequency of transactions

Transactions which may, in isolation, be of a capital nature will be interpreted as trading transactions where their frequency indicates the carrying on of a trade.

1.2.3 Length of ownership

Although this is not always the case, the courts may infer adventures in the nature of trade where items purchased are sold soon afterwards.

1.2.4 Profit motive

The presence of a profit motive will be a strong indication that a person is trading.

1.2.5 Supplementary work and marketing

When work is done to make a property more marketable, or steps are taken to find purchasers, the courts will be more ready to ascribe the trading motive.

1.2.6 Manner in which assets were acquired

If acquired unintentionally (eg by inheritance) and then sold, it is unlikely that trading has taken place.

Essential reading

There are certain other relevant factors which may be considered, depending on the facts of the case. These include the existence of similar transactions, the source of finance used, and the organisation of the activity as a trade. These, along with facts relating to relevant case law supporting the above badges of trade, are examined in more detail in the Essential Reading section of your Workbook.

The Essential reading is available as an Appendix of the digital edition of the Workbook.

2 Adjustment of profit

Taxable trading profits are not the same as accounting profits. Accounting profits need to be adjusted to take account of tax legislation and to ensure only trading income and expenditure are included within the 'Trading income' figure.

2.1 Illustrative adjustment

The following proforma should be used to adjust a statement of profit or loss to arrive at the taxable trading profit or loss for the accounting period:

	£	£
Net profit in accounts		X
Add back:		
Expenditure not deductible for tax	X	
Any non-trading expenditure	X	
		X
Deduct:		
Income assessable under other categories	X	
Non-taxable income	X	
Deductible expenditure not shown in accounts	X	
		(X)
Adjusted profits		X
Less: capital allowances on plant and machinery		(X)
Adjusted trading income/(loss)		X

You may refer to deductible and non-deductible expenditure as allowable and disallowable expenditure respectively. The two sets of terms are interchangeable.

Exam focus point

An examination question requiring adjustment to profit will direct you to start the adjustment with the net profit of £X and to deal with all the items listed, indicating with a zero (0) any items which do not require adjustment. Marks will not be given for relevant items unless this approach is used. Therefore, students who attempt to rewrite the statement of profit or loss will be penalised.

2.2 Accounting policies

The fundamental concept is that the profits of the business must be calculated in accordance with generally accepted accounting principles using the accruals basis (but see later in this chapter for details of when the cash basis can be used). These profits are subject to any adjustment specifically required for income tax purposes.

2.3 Expenditure not deductible for tax

Disallowable (ie non-deductible) expenditure must be added back to the net profit in the computation of the taxable trading profit. Any item not incurred wholly and exclusively for trade purposes is disallowable expenditure. Certain other items, such as depreciation, are specifically disallowable.

2.3.1 Capital expenditure

Capital expenditure is not deductible. This means that depreciation is non-deductible, as are legal and professional fees in relation to capital acquisitions and disposals.

Profits and losses on the sale of non-current assets must be deducted or added back respectively.

Chargeable gains or allowable losses may be dealt with under capital gains tax for individuals or separately for corporation tax for companies (see later in this Workbook).

The most contentious items of expenditure will often be repairs (revenue expenditure) and improvements (capital expenditure).

Essential reading

Further detail in relation to the definition of repairs for tax purposes can be found in your Essential Reading.

The Essential reading is available as an Appendix of the digital edition of the Workbook.

There are exceptions to the 'capital rule'; the following three items are all deductible:

- Fees incurred in the renewal of short leases (less than 50 years) of land and buildings
- Incidental costs of obtaining loan finance
- Costs of registering patents and trademarks

2.3.2 Payments contrary to public policy and illegal payments

Fines and penalties are not deductible. However, HMRC usually allow employees' parking fines incurred in parking their employer's cars while on their employer's business. Fines relating to traders, however, are never allowed. A payment is not deductible if making it constitutes an offence by the payer. This covers protection money paid to terrorists, and also bribes. Statute also prevents any deduction for payments made in response to blackmail or extortion.

2.3.3 General provisions and bad debts (impairment losses)

Only impairment losses where the liability was incurred wholly and exclusively for the purposes of the trade are deductible for taxation purposes. For example, loans to employees written off are not deductible.

General provisions (ie those calculated as a percentage of total trade receivables, without reference to specific receivables) will now rarely be seen. In the event that they do arise, increases or decreases in a general provision are not allowable/taxable and an adjustment will need to be made.

2.3.4 Unpaid remuneration

If earnings for employees are charged in the accounts but are not paid within nine months of the end of the period of account, the cost is only deductible for the period of account in which the earnings are paid.

2.3.5 Entertaining and gifts

The general rule is that expenditure on entertaining and gifts is non-deductible. However, the following are allowable:

- Staff entertaining and gifts (note however that a charge to tax may arise on the employee under benefits legislation)
- Gifts to third parties which meet all of the following criteria:
  - Cost <£50 per recipient per annum
  - Bear a conspicuous company logo
  - Are not food, drink, tobacco or vouchers

2.3.6 Appropriations of profit

Private expenditure of the owner (including the private proportion of 'mixed' expenses such as rent, motor expenses and telephone bills) and appropriations of the trade profit (eg proprietor's salary, drawings or tax/NIC) are disallowed. A salary paid to a member of the trader's family is allowed as long as it is not excessive in respect of the work performed by that family member.

2.3.7 Subscriptions and donations

The general 'wholly and exclusively' rule determines the deductibility of expenses. Subscriptions and donations are not deductible unless the expenditure is for the benefit of the trade. Charitable and politicaldonations are disallowed (unless small donations to local charities).

2.3.8 Legal and professional fees

Legal and professional charges relating to capital or non-trading items are not deductible. These include charges incurred in acquiring new capital assets or legal rights, issuing shares, drawing up partnership agreements and litigating disputes over the terms of a partnership agreement.

Professional charges are deductible if they relate directly to trading. Deductible items include:

- Legal and professional charges incurred defending the taxpayer's title to non-current assets
- Charges connected with an action for breach of contract
- Expenses of the renewal (not the original grant) of a short lease for less than 50 years
- Charges for trade debt collection
- Normal charges for preparing accounts/assisting with the self-assessment of tax liabilities

Accountancy fees for tax appeals and assisting with enquiries are allowable provided no adjustments arise that relate to negligence or fraud by the taxpayer.

2.3.9 Leased cars

There is a restriction on the leasing costs of a car with CO_2 emissions exceeding 110g/km. 15% of the leasing costs will be disallowed in the adjustment of profits calculation.

2.3.10 Interest payable

Interest paid by an individual on borrowings for trade purposes is deductible as a trading expense on an accruals basis, so no adjustment to the accounts figure is needed. Individuals cannot deduct interest on overdue tax. Interest that qualifies for relief under the 'qualifying interest' rules seen in Chapter 3 must be disallowed if it has been charged as an expense in the statement of profit or loss (to prevent double relief).

2.3.11 Expenditure not wholly and exclusively for the purpose of the trade

Expenditure is not deductible if it is not for trade purposes (the remoteness test), or if it reflects more than one purpose (the duality test). The private proportion of payments for motoring expenses, rent, heat and light and telephone expenses of a trader is non-deductible. If an exact apportionment is possible, relief is given on the business element.

Essential reading

Further detail and case law relating to the remoteness test and the duality test can be found in your essential reading.

The Essential reading is available as an Appendix of the digital edition of the Workbook.

2.3.12 Other allowable and disallowable expenses

Essential reading

A table summarising other allowable and disallowable items can be found in your essential reading.

The Essential reading is available as an Appendix of the digital edition of the Workbook.

Activity 1: Disallowed expenses

Lulu has the following expenses in her statement of profit or loss.

Required

Indicate in the table below, which of these expenses must be added back to work out her tax-adjusted trading profit before capital allowances.

Expenses	Add back/Do not add back
Legal fees in connection with the acquisition of a freehold building	
Legal fees in connection with the renewal of a 15-year lease on some land	
Motor insurance on a van used in her trade	
The gift of 25 identical pens bearing Lulu's business to clients (total cost = £1,375)	

Solution

2.4 Other adjustments of profit

2.4.1 Trading income excluded from accounts

If any trading income is omitted from the accounts, it must be added back in the adjustment of profits in order for it to be taxed.

The usual example is when a trader takes goods for their own use.

In such circumstances, the selling price of the goods if sold in the open market (less any amount the trader actually paid for the goods) is added to the accounting profit. In other words, the trader is treated for tax purposes as having made a sale to themselves.

2.4.2 Accounting profits not taxable as trading income

There are three types of receipts which may be found in the accounting profits but which must be excluded from the taxable trading profit computation (and are therefore deducted from net profit as shown in the proforma). These are:

(a) Capital receipts (eg profit on disposal of fixed assets)

(b) Income taxed in another way (at source or as another type of income), eg bank interest received taxable as savings income for individuals or rental income is taxed as property income

(c) Income specifically exempt from tax

It is important that items deducted in this way are correctly taxed where necessary - for example, a capital receipt may require the calculation of a chargeable gain, or items such as rental income or interest will be included elsewhere in the trader's income tax computation.

 Illustration 1: Adjustment of profits (1)

Here is the statement of profit or loss of Steven, a trader, for the year ended 5 April 2021.

	£	£
Gross profit		90,000
Other income		
Bank interest received		860
		90,860
Expenses		
Wages and salaries	59,000	
Rent and rates	8,000	
Depreciation	1,500	
Impairment losses (trade)	150	
Entertainment expenses for customers	750	
Patent royalties paid	3,200	
Legal expenses on acquisition of new factory	250	
		(72,850)
Finance costs		
Bank interest paid		(300)
Net profit		17,710

Salaries include £15,000 paid to Steven's wife, Melanie, who works full time in the business.

Required

Compute the adjusted taxable trade profit. You should start with the net profit figure of £17,710 and indicate by the use of zero (0) any items which do not require adjustment.

Solution

STEVEN

Adjusted taxable trading profit for the year ended 5 April 2021

	£	£
Net profit		17,710
Add: Wages and salaries (Melanie's salary not excessive for full-time work)	0	
Rent and rates	0	
Depreciation	1,500	
Impairment losses (trade)	0	
Entertainment expenses for customers	750	
Patent royalties	0	
Legal expenses (capital)	250	
Bank interest paid	0	
		2,500
		20,210
Less: Bank interest received		(860)
Profit adjusted for tax purposes		19,350

Bank interest will be taxed as savings income on Steven.

Activity 2: Adjustment of profits (2)

John's summarised statement of profit or loss for the year ended 31 December 2020 is as follows:

		£
Gross profit		30,000
Less:	depreciation	(2,000)
	entertaining (Additional information 1)	(3,000)
	wages and salaries (Additional information 2)	(15,000)
	car expenses (Additional information 3)	(1,500)
	rent and rates	(1,000)
	bank interest paid	(800)
Plus:	bank interest received	500
	profit on sale of assets	700
Net profit		7,900

Additional information

(1) Entertaining comprised £2,500 for customer entertaining and £500 for staff entertaining

(2) Wages and salaries comprised £10,000 for John and £5,000 for John's wife, Penny. Penny worked part-time in John's business and the same salary would have been payable to an unconnected employee.

(3) John uses the car 20% privately.

Required

Calculate John's adjusted trading profit.

Your computation should commence with net profit of £7,900 and should list all of the items referred to in the statement of profit or loss, indicating by the use of a zero (0) any items that do not require adjustment.

	£
Net profit	[ ]
Add: depreciation	[ ]
customer entertaining	[ ]
John's salary	[ ]
car private expenses	[ ]
rent and rates	[ ]
bank interest paid	[ ]
Less: bank interest received	[ ]
profit on sale	[ ]
Adjusted trading profit	[ ]

Solution

2.4.3 Deductible expenditure not charged in the accounts

Amounts not charged in the accounts that are deductible from trading profits must be deducted when computing the taxable trading income.

Examples of these are:

- Capital allowances (see next chapter)
- Annual sum which can be deducted by a trader that has paid a lease premium to a landlord who is taxable on the premium as property income (see chapter 6 on property income)
- Pre-trading expenditure (see below)

2.4.4 Pre-trading expenditure

Pre-trading expenditure is treated as a trading expense incurred on the first day of trading providing the following conditions are met:

- The expense was incurred in the seven years prior to the commencement of trading; and
- It would have been a deductible expense had the trade already started.

3 Cash basis for small businesses

An election can be made for an unincorporated business to calculate trading profits on the cash basis (instead of in accordance with generally accepted accounting principles) in certain circumstances.

> **Exam focus point**
>
> The detailed cash basis rules are quite complex. These more complex aspects are **not examinable** in Taxation (TX – UK). In any examination question involving an unincorporated business, it should be assumed that the cash basis is not relevant unless it is specifically mentioned.

3.1 Which businesses can use the cash basis?

If an unincorporated business has revenue which does not exceed £150,000 (given in tax rates and allowances in exam), it has the option to compute its trading profit using the cash basis. The cash basis will then apply to the current, and all subsequent eligible tax years.

The business would continue to use this basis until either:

- Its receipts in the previous tax year exceed £300,000 **and** receipts for the current year exceed £150,000; or
- Its 'commercial circumstances' change such that the cash basis is no longer appropriate and an election is made to use accruals accounting.

3.2 Calculation of taxable profits under the cash basis

The taxable trading profits under the cash basis are calculated as cash receipts less deductible business expenses actually paid in the period.

3.2.1 Cash receipts

This includes both cash and card receipts, including amounts received from the sale of plant and machinery (other than cars).

3.2.2 Deductible business expenses

Business expenses for the cash basis of accounting include capital expenditure on plant and machinery (except motor cars). Other capital expenses are not business expenses, eg purchase of land and buildings.

The majority of the specific tax rules covered earlier in this chapter concerning the deductibility of business expenses (for example, personal expenses of the owner) also apply when the cash basis is used.

Fixed rate expenses for private use of motor cars and business premises used for private purposes may be used instead (see further below).

3.2.3 Fixed rate expenses

When using the cash basis, certain expenses can be computed on a flat rate basis as follows:

(a) Use the statutory approved mileage allowance to compute the deduction for business miles (given in tax rates and allowances in exam).

(b) If a business premises are used partly for private purposes the private use adjustment can be made on the number of occupants (this will be given in an exam question).

BPP
LEARNING
MEDIA

Where a business elects to use the cash basis, for Taxation (TX – UK) purposes, it will be assumed to use fixed rate expenses rather than make deductions on the usual basis of actual expenditure incurred.

Essential reading

Further detail regarding fixed rate expenses and a numerical example of the cash basis can be found in your essential reading.

The Essential reading is available as an Appendix of the digital edition of the Workbook.

3.3 Basis period rules and losses under the cash basis

3.3.1 Basis period rules

A trader using the cash basis can, like any other trader, prepare their accounts to any date in the year. The basis of assessment rules which determine in which tax year the profits of an accounting period are taxed apply in the same way for accruals accounting and cash basis traders (see Chapter 9 of this Workbook).

3.3.2 Cash basis losses

If the cash basis produces a trading loss the only relief available is to carry the loss forward against future trading profits. The rules regarding loss relief for accruals basis traders are covered in Chapter 10 of this Workbook.

Chapter summary

Computing trading income

Badges of trade

The implications of trading

- Trading – profits liable to income tax and NIC. Losses used flexibly
- Not trading – could be capital gains tax or not taxable. Usually lower tax liabilities

The badges of trade

- Tests developed from case law to establish whether trading exists:
  - Subject matter
  - Frequency of transactions
  - Length of ownership
  - Profit motive
  - Supplementary work
  - Manner acquired/reason for sale

Adjustment of profit

Illustrative adjustment

	£
Net profit	X
Add back	
Disallowable expenditure	X
Deduct	
Income assessable elsewhere	(X)
Non taxable income	(X)
Deduct	
Capital allowances	(X)
Trading income	X

- In the exam, you will be asked to begin with net profit and to list all items including a zero if no adjustment is needed

Expenditure not deductible for tax

- Add back to net profit
- General rule = expenditure must be wholly and exclusively for trade
- Many disallowable items, eg capital items, third party entertaining and gifts

Other adjustments of profit

- Ensure any trading income omitted from accounts is taxed (add back)
- Deduct income that isn't taxable or is not taxed as trading income, eg interest
- Deduct any allowable expenses not recorded in accounts, including pre-trading expenditure in last seven years

Cash basis for small businesses

Which businesses can use the cash basis?

- Revenue <£150,000 to start using CB
- When revenue exceeds £300,000 in prior year must usually stop using CB (accruals must apply)

Calculation of taxable profit under the cash basis

- Cash receipts less deductible expenses paid
- Can use fixed rate expenses instead of actual, eg for business mileage

Basis period rules and losses under the cash basis

- Basis period rules = as per accruals accounting
- Losses can only be carried forward

Knowledge diagnostic

1. Badges of trade

The badges of trade are used to decide whether or not a trade exists. If one does exist, the accounts profits need to be adjusted in order to establish the taxable profits.

2. Adjustment of profits

The net profit in the statement of profit or loss must be adjusted to find the taxable trading profit.

Disallowable (ie non-deductible) expenditure must be added back to the net profit in the computation of the taxable trading profit. Any item not incurred wholly and exclusively for trade purposes is disallowable expenditure. Certain other items, such as depreciation, are specifically disallowable.

Receipts not taxable as trading profit must be deducted from the net profit. For example, rental income and interest received are not taxable as trading profit. The rental income is taxed instead as property business income, whilst the interest is taxed as savings income.

Amounts not charged in the accounts that are deductible from trading profits must be deducted when computing the taxable trading income. An example is capital allowances. Amounts not charged in the accounts that are deductible from trading profits must be deducted when computing the taxable trading income. An example is capital allowances.

3. The cash basis

An election can be made for an unincorporated business to calculate trading profits on the cash basis (instead of in accordance with generally accepted accounting principles) in certain circumstances.

Fixed rate expenses can be used in relation to expenditure on motor cars and business premises partly used as the trader's home.

Further study guidance

Question practice

Now try the following from the Further question practice bank (available in the digital edition of the Workbook):

Section A: Q28, Q29, Q30

Section B: Q31 Margaret

Section C: Q32 Archie

Further reading

ACCA's article *Adjustment of profit*, written by a member of the Taxation (TX – UK) examining team, gives advice on attempting exam questions on adjustment of profit, with a working example of a question in a recent Taxation (TX – UK) exam.

ACCA's article *Motor cars*, written by a member of the Taxation (TX – UK) examining team, explains the implications of acquiring, running, or having the use of a motor car for income tax, corporation tax, value added tax (VAT) and national insurance contributions (NIC).

Activity answers

Activity 1: Disallowed expenses

Expenses	Add back/Do not add back
Legal fees in connection with the acquisition of a freehold building	Add back
Legal fees in connection with the renewal of a 15-year lease on some land	Do not add back
Motor insurance on a van used in her trade	Do not add back
The gift of 25 identical pens bearing Lulu's business to clients (total cost = £1,375)	Add back

Legal fees incurred on the acquisition of capital assets are not allowable, whereas those incurred on the renewal of a short lease are allowed. Motor insurance is a normal business expense incurred wholly and exclusively for the purpose of the trade. The pens are not allowed because, despite bearing a business logo and not being food, drink, tobacco or vouchers, the cost is in excess of £50 per recipient.

Activity 2: Adjustment of profits (2)

		£
Net profit		7,900
Add:	depreciation	2,000
	customer entertaining	2,500
	John's salary	10,000
	car private expenses 20% × 1,500	300
	rent and rates	0
	bank interest paid	0
Less:	bank interest received	(500)
	profit on sale	(700)
Adjusted trading profit		21,500

The bank interest received will be taxed on John as savings income and the profit on disposal is a capital, not a trading receipt.

8

Capital allowances

Learning objectives

On completion of this chapter, you should be able to:

	Syllabus reference no.
Define plant and machinery for capital allowances purposes.	B3(h)(i)
Compute writing down allowances, first year allowances and the annual investment allowance.	B3(h)(ii)
Compute capital allowances for motor cars.	B3(h)(iii)
Compute balancing allowances and balancing charges.	B3(h)(iv)
Compute structures and buildings allowances	B3(h)(v)
Recognise the treatment of short life assets.	B3(h)(vi)
Recognise the treatment of assets included in the special rate pool.	B3(h)(vii)

Exam context

Section A questions on capital allowances may focus on one particular type of asset such as a motor car. You may also be asked to compute capital allowances on a variety of assets in a Section B question. In Section C, you may have to answer a whole question on capital allowances, or a capital allowances computation may be included as a working in a computation of taxable trading profits. This may be as part of a 15-mark question or a 10-mark question.

The computations may be for either income tax or corporation tax purposes; the principles are basically the same. Look out for private use assets; only restrict the capital allowances if there is private use by **traders**, never restrict capital allowances for private use by **employees**. This means that when you calculate capital allowances for a company there will never be any private use adjustments. Also watch out for the length of the period of account; you may need to scale writing down allowances (WDAs) and the annual investment allowance (AIA) up (income tax only) or down (income tax or corporation tax).

Chapter overview

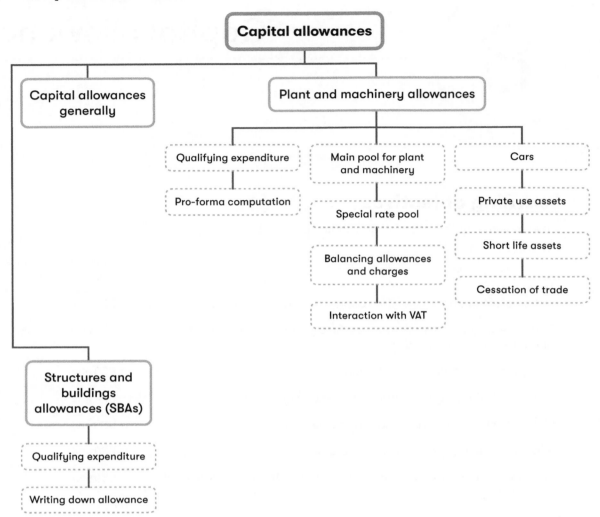

1 Capital allowances generally

Allowances are given against adjusted trading profits in respect of the fall in value, due to business use, of qualifying assets. This replaces depreciation which is disallowed in the adjustment of profits.

Capital allowances are calculated for periods of account (or accounting periods for companies). They are treated as allowable trading expenses in arriving at trading income for the period of account. Balancing charges are treated as trading receipts.

Both unincorporated businesses (sole traders and partnerships) and companies are entitled to capital allowances. For completeness, in this chapter, we will look at the rules for companies alongside those for unincorporated businesses.

Essential reading

Information relating to the date expenditure is deemed to be incurred for capital allowances purposes can be found in your Essential reading.

The Essential reading is available as an Appendix of the digital edition of the Workbook.

PER alert

One of the competencies you require to fulfil Performance Objective 17 *Tax planning and advice* of the PER is to identify when to refer matters to someone with more specialist knowledge. You can apply the knowledge you obtain from this chapter to help to demonstrate this competence.

2 Plant and machinery allowances

2.1 Qualifying expenditure

Include all additions and disposals occurring in the relevant period of account. It does not matter at what point during the period the additions and disposals are made.

Plant and machinery allowances are only available for expenditure on plant and machinery which performs a function in the trade rather than provide a setting within which the trade is carried on. For that reason, capital allowances are available on cars, most factory and office machinery and equipment. They are not available to relieve expenditure on buildings or structures (including doors, floors, windows, bridges, waste disposal and drainage systems). Some integral features of structures, however, do qualify as plant and machinery (see later in this chapter).

Essential reading

Further information on the definition of plant and machinery, including relevant case law, can be found in your Essential reading.

The Essential reading is available as an Appendix of the digital edition of the Workbook.

2.2 Proforma plant and machinery allowances computation

The following format is recommended for use in the exams, for each period of account. As you work through this section of the chapter, you will learn how the content of each column is determined.

	AIA	FYA	Main pool	Special rate pool	Short life assets	Private used asset (40%)	Allowances
	£	£	£	£	£	£	£
TWDV b/fwd			X	X		X	
Additions	X	X	X	X	X		
Disposals (proceeds limited to cost)			(X)			(X)	
			X	X	X	X	
AIA	(X)						X
Tfr to MP/SRP	(X)		X	X	X		
			X	X	X		
FYA 100%		(X)					X
WDA 18%/6%			(X)	(X)	(X)	(X)	X
							(× 60% for private use asset)
TWDV c/fwd			X	X	X	X	X

2.3 Main pool for plant and machinery

2.3.1 Qualifying expenditure

Most expenditure on plant and machinery, including expenditure on cars with CO_2 emissions of 110g/km or less, is put into a pool of expenditure (the main pool) on which capital allowances may be claimed. An addition increases the pool whilst a disposal decreases it.

Exceptionally the following items are not put into the main pool:

- Assets dealt with in the special rate pool
- Assets with private use by the trader
- Short life assets where an election has been made

These exceptions are dealt with later in this chapter.

2.3.2 Writing down allowances (WDAs)

Allowances called writing down allowances (WDA) are given at a rate of 18% for a 12-month period of account on the tax written down value (TWDV) after adding the current period's additions and taking out the current period's disposals.

When plant is sold, **proceeds**, limited to a **maximum of the original cost**, are taken **out of the pool.**

2.3.3 Annual Investment Allowance (AIA)

An allowance of 100% is available for the first £1,000,000 of expenditure on plant and machinery for a 12-month period of account.

There is no AIA on purchase of cars.

AIA should be first allocated to additions qualifying for WDA at lower rate (see later in this chapter).

Exam focus point

The AIA limit changed from £1 million to £200,000 on 1 January 2021. However, for the purposes of the TX-UK examinations in June 2021, September 2021, December 2021 and March 2022, it will be assumed that the £1 million limit continues to apply. This will be the case regardless of the period covered by an exam question so, for example, the AIA limit for a year ended 31 March 2021 will be assumed to be £1 million.

Illustration 1: Plant and machinery main pool

Julia is a sole trader preparing accounts to 5 April each year. At 5 April 2020, the tax written down value on her main pool is £12,500.

In the year to 5 April 2021, Julia bought the following assets:

1 June 2020	Machinery	£990,000
12 November 2020	Van	£17,500
10 February 2021	Car for salesman (CO_2 emissions 100g/km)	£9,000

She disposed of plant on 15 December 2020 for £12,000 (original cost £16,000).

Required

Calculate the maximum capital allowances claim that Julia can make for the year ended 5 April 2021.

Solution

	AIA	Main pool	Allowances
	£	£	£
y/e 5 April 2021			
TWDV b/f		12,500	
Additions qualifying for AIA			
1.6.20 Machinery	990,000		
12.11.20 Van	17,500		
	1,007,500		
AIA	(1,000,000)		1,000,000
	7,500		
Transfer balance to pool	(7,500)	7,500	
Additions not qualifying for AIA			
10.2.21 Car		9,000	
Disposal			
15.12.20 Plant		(12,000)	
		17,000	

	AIA	Main pool	Allowances
	£	£	£
WDA @ 18%		(3,060)	3,060
TWDV c/f		13,940	
Maximum capital allowances			1,003,060

Activity 1: Main pool allowances

Mr Foxtrot, a sole trader, draws up accounts to 31 December and incurred the following transactions in the year ended 31 December 2020.

28 April – Bought factory equipment for £155,000

1 May – Sold machine (original cost £6,000) for £2,000

1 August – Bought some forklift trucks for £70,000

The TWDV of the main pool at 1 January 2020 was £28,000

Required

Calculate the allowances to be claimed for the year ended 31 December 2020.

Solution

2.3.4 Small balance on main pool

Where the balance of unrelieved expenditure on the main pool (after additions and disposals) is £1,000 or less, then this balance can all be claimed as a writing down allowance leaving the relevant pool with a nil balance.

2.3.5 Accounting periods longer or shorter than twelve months

The following are pro-rated in accounting periods that are longer or shorter than 12 months:

- Writing down allowances
- The AIA limit of £1 million
- The small pool threshold of £1,000

The allowances and limits are apportioned by multiplying by n/12, where n is the length of the accounting period in months.

Note that for companies, an accounting period can never be longer than 12 months for tax purposes (and therefore the allowances and limits could only ever be scaled down, and not up for a company). We will look at the rules governing long periods of account for companies in Chapter 19 of this Workbook.

2.4 Special rate pool

2.4.1 Qualifying expenditure

Certain items of expenditure are not dealt with in the main pool, but are required to be allocated to the special rate pool. These are:

- **Long life assets:** Assets with an expected working life of 25 years or more, where a business has incurred expenditure of more than £100,000 on such assets in a 12-month period. The £100,000 limit is pro-rated for period of accounts longer or shorter than 12 months. Plant and machinery in dwelling houses, retail shops, showrooms, hotels and offices, and cars, are not treated as long-life assets.
- **Cars** with CO_2 emissions of **over 110g/km**
- Expenditure on plant and machinery that is integral to a building **(integral features).** The following items are integral features:
  - Electrical and lighting systems
  - Cold water systems
  - Space or water heating systems
  - Powered systems of ventilation, cooling or air purification
  - Lifts or escalators

2.4.2 Writing down allowances

The WDA applicable to the SR pool is 6% for a 12-month period of account. This is pro-rated for accounting periods longer or shorter than 12 months.

A small balance on the special rate pool can be claimed as a writing down allowance in a similar way to the main pool.

2.4.3 Allocation of the AIA

The AIA can apply to expenditure on SR pool assets (except cars).

The taxpayer can decide how to allocate the AIA. It will be more tax efficient to set it against the SR pool expenditure rather than main pool expenditure where there is expenditure on assets in both pools in the period.

Activity 2: Special rate pool and AIA allocation

1   The TWDV in Enrique's main pool on 1 April 2020 was £80,000. In May 2020, he spent £1,020,000 on integral features and £5,800 on furniture.

    Required

    What is the maximum claim for capital allowances for the year ended 31 March 2021?

    ○ £1,019,044

    ○ £1,015,948

    ○ £1,025,800

    ○ £1,016,644

2   What are the maximum allowances that would have been available if Enrique's accounts had instead been prepared for the six months to 30 September 2020?

    £ [   ]

Solution

Exam focus point

Note the tax planning opportunities available. If plant is bought just before an accounting date, allowances become available as soon as possible. Alternatively, it may be desirable to claim less than the maximum allowances to even out annual taxable profits and avoid a higher rate of tax in later years. In the exam, you should always claim the maximum available capital allowances unless you are told otherwise.

2.5 Balancing allowances and charges

When an asset that qualified for capital allowances is disposed of, the proceeds on disposal (limited to purchase cost) are deducted from the TWDV of the pool to which the asset was originally allocated.

If proceeds from the disposal > TWDV of any pool, a balancing charge arises. This is effectively a negative capital allowance and increases taxable profits.

A balancing allowance, where proceeds on disposal are less than the balance on a pool, can only arise on the main and special rate pools on cessation of trade. However, for assets in single pools (see later in this chapter), a balancing allowance may arise when that asset is sold.

2.6 Interaction with VAT

We deal with value added tax (VAT) in Chapters 24 and 25. You may want to make a note to re-read this section when you study VAT.

Qualifying expenditure includes irrecoverable VAT. The VAT may be irrecoverable because the trader is not VAT registered, or because it is the type of expenditure on which the VAT is not recoverable (eg the acquisition of a car not used wholly for business purposes).

If the trader is VAT registered and can reclaim VAT on a purchase, only the expenditure net of VAT will be qualifying expenditure. Similarly, on a disposal of an asset on which capital allowances have been claimed, if VAT is charged by the trader on the disposal, only the disposal proceeds net of VAT will be deducted.

2.7 Cars

The treatment depends on the CO_2 emission of the car. There are three categories:

- Motor cars with CO_2 emissions of 50g/km or less receive 100% first year allowances (FYA). To qualify for FYA, the car must be new (ie unused and not second hand). FYAs are **not** pro-rated for non 12-month accounting periods.
- Motor cars with CO_2 emissions of between 51 and 110g/km (and second-hand low emission cars) go into main pool (no AIA) and receive WDA of 18% pa.
- Motor cars with CO_2 emissions of >110g/km go into SR pool (no AIA) and receive WDA of 6% pa.

Activity 3: Capital allowances on cars

Myles prepares accounts to 31 December each year and incurred the following transactions for the two years to 31 December 2021.

12.2.20 – Bought car for £26,000 with CO_2 emissions of 112g/km

15.2.20 – Sold a car with CO_2 emissions of 132g/km for £2,000 (original cost £12,000)

1.7.20 – Bought car for £19,000, CO_2 emissions of 100g/km

30.7.20 – Sold a car with CO_2 emissions of 84g/km for £1,000 (original cost £15,000)

1.10.21 – Bought car for £8,000, CO_2 emissions of 45g/km

Myles also bought some plant and machinery at a cost of £10,000 in each period of account.

On 1 January 2020, the TWDV of plant and machinery were as follows:

	£
Main pool	25,000
SR pool	8,000

Required

Calculate the capital allowances for the y/e 31 December 2020 and y/e 31 December 2021.

Note. Assume tax rates for the tax year 2020/21 apply throughout.

Solution

2.8 Private use assets

Special rules apply to any asset which is used partly for private purposes by a sole trader or a partner:

(a) Separate calculation for each asset, ie the asset is put into its own pool

(b) Deduct the whole WDA for the period from the TWDV of the asset

(c) Only claim the business proportion of the WDA, by copying only the business proportion into the allowances column

(d) This restriction applies to the AIA, FYAs, WDAs, balancing allowances and balancing charges.

(e) The restriction is not relevant for employee's private use – it applies to a proprietor's private use only. The employee may be taxed under the benefits code (see earlier in this Workbook) so the business receives capital allowances on the full cost of the asset.

Illustration 2: Private use assets

Jacinth has been in business as a sole trader for many years, preparing accounts to 31 March. On 1 November 2020, she bought computer equipment for £2,700 which she uses 75% in her business and 25% privately. She has already used the AIA against other expenditure in the year to 31 March 2021.

Required

Calculate the maximum capital allowance that Jacinth can claim in respect to the computer equipment in the year to 31 March 2021.

Solution

	Computer equipment		Allowances
	£		£
y/e 31 March 2021			
Acquisition	2,700		
WDA @ 18%	(486)	× 75%	365
TWDV c/f	2,214		
Maximum capital allowance on computer equipment			365

Activity 4: Private use assets and balancing adjustments

Felipe starts to trade on 1 April 2019 and prepares accounts to 31 March each year. Felipe buys two cars for his business on 30 June 2019.

Car 1 was bought for £18,000, has CO_2 emissions of 120g/km, and is used by Felipe privately 20% of the time.

Car 2 was bought for £15,000, has CO_2 emissions of 105g/km and is used privately by an employee, Juan Carlos, 50% of the time.

On 1 September 2020, both cars were sold for £10,000.

Required

Calculate his capital allowances for the years ending 31 March 2020 and 31 March 2021.

Note. Assume tax rates for the tax year 2020/21 apply throughout.

Solution

2.9 Short life assets

Short life assets are assets which normally go in the main pool and have an expected life of less than eight years.

As we have seen, balancing allowances cannot normally be claimed on assets in the main pool. However, plant and machinery (except cars) may be 'depooled' on election by the taxpayer. Any asset subject to this election is known as a **'short life asset' (SLA)**, and the election is known as a 'de-pooling election'.

Calculate allowances on each SLA in a separate column. If the SLA is sold **within eight years of the end of the accounting period** in which it was bought, a balancing allowance or charge arises on disposal.

Special treatment is lost on eighth anniversary of the end of the period of account in which the asset was acquired. The asset then automatically returns to the main pool at TWDV.

The election should therefore be made for assets likely to be sold for less than their tax written down values within eight years.

Activity 5: Capital allowance computation - main pool and short-life asset

Guy prepares accounts to 31 March each year. At 1 April 2020, the TWDV values of plant and machinery were as follows:

	£
Main pool	15,000
Short life asset	4,000

The following transactions took place during the year ended 31 March 2021:

		£
15.4.20	Purchased equipment	123,000
31.8.20	Purchased motor car [1]. CO_2 emissions 49g/km	17,000
31.8.20	Purchased motor car [2], CO_2 emissions 112g/km	20,000

| 2.9.20 | Sold a lorry (original cost £9,800) | (12,000) |
| 1.2.21 | Sold short life asset (original cost £8,000) | (800) |

Required

Calculate Guy's capital allowances for year ended 31 March 2021.

Solution

---

3 Cessation of trade

When a business ceases to trade, no WDAs, FYAs or AIAs are given in the final period of account.

Additions in the relevant period are brought in and then the disposal proceeds (limited to purchase cost) are deducted from the balance of qualifying expenditure. If the assets are not sold (for example, a trader decides to keep certain items of plant and machinery), each such asset is deemed to be disposed of on the date the trade ceased (usually at the then market value).

Each pool must be 'closed', and so a balancing adjustment must arise on every pool. If the proceeds exceed the TWDV at disposal then a balancing charge arises. If proceeds are less, a balancing allowance is given.

Activity 6: Cessation of trade

Mezan ceased to trade on 31 December 2020 after several years in business. His last period of account was the nine-month period to 31 December 2020. On 1 April 2020 the TWDVs of plant and machinery are as follows:

	£
Main pool	12,000
SR pool (integral features)	18,000

The following transactions took place during the period ended 31 December 2020:

| 15.4.20 | Purchased a van | 5,000 |
| 31.8.20 | Purchased motor car, CO_2 emissions 112g/km | 22,000 |

| 2.9.20 | Sold a van (original cost £18,000) | (9,800) |

Mezan kept the car for himself when the market value was £17,500. He scrapped the integral features for no consideration and he sold the other assets for £10,000.

Required

Calculate Mezan's capital allowances for the period ended 31 December 2020.

Solution

4 Structures and buildings allowances

4.1 Qualifying expenditure

A structures and buildings allowance (SBA) is available for qualifying expenditure on **new commercial** structures and buildings for contracts entered into on/after 29 October 2018. For the purpose of the TX-UK exam, all expenditure will have been incurred on or after 6 April 2020 (or 1 April 2020 for companies).

Qualifying expenditure is expenditure on the construction of the building or structure itself (or the acquisition cost if bought from a developer), but **not** the cost of **land**, nor the cost of planning permission, fees and stamp taxes.

Where an existing building is renovated or converted, this expenditure may qualify (even if the underlying property was constructed prior to 29 October 2018).

Commercial structures and buildings include:

- Offices
- Retail and wholesale premises
- Factories
- Warehouses
- Walls
- Bridges
- Tunnels

Residential property or any part of a building which functions as a dwelling does not qualify for SBAs.

> **Exam focus point**
>
> You should assume that for any question involving the purchase (as opposed to a new construction) of a building, the SBA is not available unless stated otherwise.

4.2 Writing down allowance

The allowance is given at 3% **straight line**, over a 33 1/3 year period.

Each building or structure is treated separately, and enhancement expenditure is treated separately to the underlying building.

For SBAs to be claimed, the relevant asset must be in qualifying use, for example used in a trade or property letting business.

The allowance is pro-rated for accounting periods which are not 12 months in length, or where the structure or building is **brought into use or sold during the period**. This is in contrast to plant and machinery allowances which are given in full in the period of acquisition (with no WDA at all in the period of disposal).

There is no balancing adjustment on sale of an SBA asset; however, an adjustment is made to the chargeable gain or capital loss arising, by adding the SBA claimed to the seller's disposal proceeds. You will see chargeable gains for both individuals and companies later in this Workbook.

The new purchaser takes over the remaining allowances (based on the original cost) over the remainder of the 33 1/3 year period. The seller time apportions relief up to the date of the disposal.

Activity 7: SBAs

1   Dumpling Ltd purchases a newly-constructed office building from a developer for £2,050,000 on 1 July 2020 and brought it into use immediately. The purchase price of £2,050,000 includes £50,000 relating to solicitor's fees and other acquisition costs.

Dumpling Ltd prepares accounts to December each year.

Required

What are the maximum SBAs available to Dumpling Ltd in the year ended 31 December 2020?

O   £30,000

O   £30,750

O   £60,000

O   £61,500

2   Dumpling Ltd continued to use the office building for its trade until 30 June 2023, when it was sold to Suet plc for £2,500,000 (excluding land). Suet immediately started using the office for trading purposes.

Suet plc prepares its accounts to March each year.

Required

Which **TWO** of the following statements are correct regarding the implications of the disposal?

☐   Dumpling Ltd will not be entitled to any WDA on the building for its year ended 31 December 2023

☐   Dumpling Ltd's chargeable gain will increase by £180,000 due to the SBAs claimed

☐   Suet plc will claim £75,000 pa writing down allowances on the office

☐   Suet plc will time apportion its writing down allowance by 9/12ths in its year ended 31 March 2024

Solution

Chapter summary

Capital allowances

Capital allowances generally

- Relief against trading profits for the fall in value of qualifying assets
- Calculated for periods of account
- Available to all businesses

Structures and buildings allowances (SBAs)

Qualifying expenditure
- Construction/ acquisition from builder of qualifying assets
- Qualifying property includes offices, shops, factories, bridges
- Cost of land and acquisition expenses excluded
- Enhancing/renovating existing property can qualify

Writing down allowance
- 3% straight line
- Apportioned in periods of acquisition and disposal
- SBAs claimed are added to seller's sale proceeds in gain computation

Plant and machinery allowances

Qualifying expenditure
- Function ("with which") vs setting ("within which")
- If asset performs an active function for the trade, it is plant and machinery
- If part of setting, not P&M (may qualify for SBAs)

Pro-forma computation
- Column for each pool/ depooled asset
- Bring in additions, remove assets disposed of, then compute allowances
- Memorandum CA column to sum the allowances available for the AP

Main pool for plant and machinery
- 18% WDA
- AIA max £1m pa (not cars)
- If balance < £1k can claim 100% WDA
- Allowances pro-rated for non-12m APs

Special rate pool
- 6% WDA
- Expected working life > 25 years, P&M integral to a building, and cars with CO_2 emissions > 110g/km
- Allocate AIA to SRP assets in priority (not cars)
- If balance < £1k can claim 100% WDA

Balancing allowances and charges
- BC arises any time a pool is negative after disposals
- BA can only arise on a pool if trade ceases, but can arise at any time on a depooled asset

Interaction with VAT
- If VAT can be reclaimed, CAs are available on net (VAT-exclusive) cost
- If VAT irrecoverable, claim CAs on gross (VAT-inclusive) cost

Cars
- Low emission cars CO_2 of 50g/km or less = 100% FYA
- CO_2 emissions of between 51-110g/km = main pool = 18% WDA
- CO_2 emissions over 110g/km = special rate pool = 6% WDA

Private use assets
- Separate column for each asset
- Reduce TWDV by full WDA
- Only claim business use percentage of WDA
- Balancing adjustment on sale is business use percentage only

Short life assets
- Election on asset by asset basis (not cars)
- Separate column for each asset
- Allows balancing allowance on sale
- Once 8 × WDAs claimed reverts to main pool

Cessation of trade
- No WDA in final period
- Calculate balancing allowances and charges on everything
- Assets removed by trader deemed sale at MV

Knowledge diagnostic

1. Capital allowances

These are deductible in computing trading income and are given to compensate for the wear and tear of qualifying assets.

2. Writing down allowances

Most expenditure on plant and machinery qualifies for a WDA at 18% for a 12-month period. A WDA of 6% applies for special rate pool expenditure. Small pool balances up to £1,000 can be written off in full.

3. Annual investment allowance

An annual investment allowance of 100% is available for the first £1,000,000 of expenditure on plant and machinery (not cars) for a 12-month period of account.

4. Balancing allowances and charges

Balancing charges arise at any time when proceeds exceed TWDV of the pool. Balancing allowances on the main and special rate pools can only arise on cessation.

5. Depooled assets

Assets with private use by the proprietor are not pooled. Only the business proportion of WDAs and balancing adjustments can be claimed.

Short life assets can be 'depooled'. A balancing allowance may be claimed if proceeds from the disposal are less than the TWDV of the pool.

6. Cessation of trade

When a business ceases to trade no WDAs, FYAs or AIAs are given in the final period of account. Assets removed by the trader are deemed to be sold at market value. Balancing adjustments will arise.

7. Structures and buildings allowances

Qualifying buildings constructed since October 2018 are entitled to a 3% straight-line writing down allowance on cost.

Further study guidance

Question practice

Now try the following from the Further question practice bank (available in the digital edition of the Workbook):

Section A: Q33, Q34 and Q35

Section B: Q36 Sylvester

Section C: Q37 Tom

Further reading

ACCA's article *Motor cars*, written by a member of the Taxation (TX – UK) examining team, explains the implications of acquiring, running, or having the use of a motor car for income tax, corporation tax, value added tax (VAT) and national insurance contribution (NIC).

Activity answers

Activity 1: Main pool allowances

Year ended 31 December 2020		AIA £	Main pool £	Allowances £
TWDV b/fwd			28,000	
Additions: 28 April	– factory equipment	155,000		
1 August	– forklift trucks	70,000		
Disposal: 1 May	– machinery		(2,000)	
		225,000	26,000	
AIA		(225,000)		225,000
			26,000	
WDA 18%			(4,680)	4,680
TWDV c/fwd			21,320	229,680

Activity 2: Special rate pool and AIA allocation

1 The correct answer is: £1,016,644

Year ended 31 March 2021	AIA £	Main pool £	Special rate pool £	Allowances £
TWDV b/f		80,000		
Additions:				
Integral features	1,020,000			
Furniture		5,800		
		85,800		
AIA (best use)	(1,000,000)			1,000,000
Transferred to SR pool	(20,000)		20,000	
			20,000	
WDA 18%/6%		(15,444)	(1,200)	16,644
TWDV c/f		70,356	18,800	1,016,644

The answer £1,019,044 gives WDA @ 18% on the special rate pool. The answer £1,015,948 sets the AIA against the furniture and then the balance against the integral features. The answer £1,025,800 is 100% relief on the additions.

2 £ 523,322

Period ended 30 September 2020	AIA	Main pool	Special rate pool	Allowances
	£	£	£	£
TWDV b/f		80,000		
Additions:				
Integral features	1,020,000			
Furniture		5,800		
		85,800		
AIA (best use): £1m × 6/12	(500,000)			500,000
Transferred to SR pool	(520,000)		520,000	
			520,000	
WDA 18%/6% × 6/12		(7,722)	(15,600)	23,322
TWDV c/f		78,078	504,400	523,322

Note that both the limit of the AIA and the WDAs are time apportioned to take account of the short accounting period.

Activity 3: Capital allowances on cars

	AIA	FYA	Main pool	Special rate pool	Allowances
	£	£	£	£	£
Y/e 31.12.20					
TWDV b/f			25,000	8,000	
Additions	10,000		19,000	26,000	
Disposals			(1,000)	(2,000)	
			43,000	32,000	
AIA	(10,000)		-	-	10,000
WDA 18%/ 6%			(7,740)	(1,920)	9,660
c/f			35,260	30,080	19,660
Y/e 31.12.21					
TWDV b/f			35,260	30,080	
Additions	10,000	8,000			
AIA/FYA 100%	(10,000)	(8,000)	–	–	18,000
		–	35,260	30,080	
WDA 18%/6%			(6,347)	(1,805)	8,152
c/f			28,913	28,275	26,152

Activity 4: Private use assets and balancing adjustments

	Main pool	Privately used asset (80%)		Allowances
	£	£		£
Y/e 31.3.20				
Addition	15,000	18,000		
WDA 18%/6%	(2,700)	(1,080)	× 80%	3,564
Allowances				3,564
TWDV c/f	12,300	16,920		
Y/e 31.3.21				
TWDV b/f	12,300	16,920		
Disposal	(10,000)	(10,000)		
	2,300			
WDA 18%	(414)			414
Balancing allowance		6,920	× 80%	5,536
Allowances				5,950
TWDV c/f	1,886	–		–

Remember, no balancing allowance is available on the main pool unless the business has ceased.

Activity 5: Capital allowance computation - main pool and short-life asset

	AIA	FYA	Main pool	Special Rate pool	SLA	Allowances
	£	£	£	£	£	£
Y/e 31.3.21						
TWDV b/fwd			15,000		4,000	
Addition – equipment	123,000					
– car [1]		17,000				
– car [2]				20,000		
Disposal						
– lorry (cost)			(9,800)			
– SLA					(800)	
			–			
	123,000					
AIA @ 100%	(123,000)					123,000
	–					
FYA @ 100%		(17,000)				17,000
		–	5,200	20,000	3,200	
WDA @ 18%/6%			(936)	(1,200)		2,136

	AIA	FYA	Main pool	Special Rate pool	SLA	Allowances
	£	£	£	£	£	£
Balancing allowance			–	–	(3,200)	3,200
TWDV c/fwd			4,264	18,800	–	
						145,336

Activity 6: Cessation of trade

	M pool	SR pool	Allowances
	£	£	£
9 m/e 31.12.20			
TWDV b/fwd	12,000	18,000	
Addition – van	5,000		
– car		22,000	
Disposal – van	(9,800)		
Cessation	(10,000)	(17,500)	
	(2,800)	22,500	
Balancing allowance	–	(22,500)	22,500
Balancing charge	2,800	–	(2,800)
	Nil	Nil	19,700

Activity 7: SBAs

1   The correct answer is: £30,000

£2,000,000 × 3% × 6/12 = £30,000

The cost of acquisition excludes acquisition fees. The SBA must be time-apportioned in the year of acquisition.

2   The correct answers are:

- Dumpling Ltd's chargeable gain will increase by £180,000 due to the SBAs claimed
- Suet plc will time apportion its writing down allowance by 9/12ths in its year ended 31 March 2024

Statement 1 is incorrect as the seller may claim a time-apportioned WDA in the year of disposal.

Statement 2 is correct, as Dumpling Ltd would have claimed (3 × 3% × £2,000,000) = £180,000 of SBAs at the date of disposal, which are added to the proceeds in its chargeable gain computation.

Statement 3 is incorrect, as SBAs are based on the original qualifying cost of £2 million.

Statement 4 is correct, as the building was brought into qualifying use by Suet plc on 1 July 2023, and therefore the WDA must be multiplied by 9/12.

9

Assessable trading income

Learning objectives

On completion of this chapter, you should be able to:

	Syllabus reference no.
Recognise the basis of assessment for self-employment income.	B3(a)
Compute the assessable profits on commencement and on cessation.	B3(f)
Recognise the factors that will influence the choice of accounting date.	B3(g)

Exam context

You are likely to have to deal with a tax computation for an unincorporated business in any of Sections A, B or C. It may be a simple computation for a continuing business, or you may have to deal with a business in its opening or closing years, including computing taxable trading profits and allocating them to tax years. You must be totally familiar with the rules and be able to apply them in the exam. These topics may be tested in a 15-mark question or a 10-mark question in Section C. A specific point, such as computing an amount of overlap profits, may be tested in Sections A or B.

Chapter overview

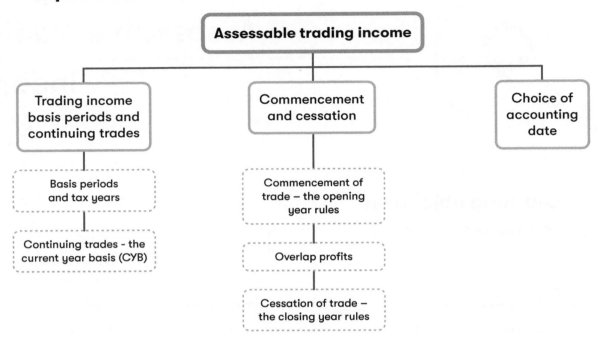

Assessable trading income

- Trading income basis periods and continuing trades
  - Basis periods and tax years
  - Continuing trades - the current year basis (CYB)

- Commencement and cessation
  - Commencement of trade – the opening year rules
  - Overlap profits
  - Cessation of trade – the closing year rules

- Choice of accounting date

1 Trading income basis periods and continuing trades

1.1 Basis periods and tax years

A tax year runs from 6 April to 5 April, but most businesses do not have periods of account ending on 5 April. Thus, there must be a link between a period of account of a business and a tax year. The procedure is to find a period to act as the **basis period** for a tax year.

> **Basis period:** The profits for a basis period are taxed in the corresponding tax year.

If a basis period is not identical to a period of account, the profits of periods of account are time-apportioned as required (on a **monthly basis for exam purposes**) on the assumption that profits accrue evenly over a period of account.

1.2 Continuing trades – the current year basis (CYB)

The general rule is that the basis period is the year of account ending in the tax year. This is known as the **current year basis** of assessment. For example, if a trader prepares accounts to 31 December each year, the profits of the year to 31 December 2020 will be taxed in the tax year 2020/21.

Activity 1: Current year basis

A business which has been trading for many years has a year end of 31 March.

Recent adjusted profits are:

Year ended	£
31 March 2020	22,000
31 March 2021	18,000
31 March 2022	30,000

Required

1   What profits will be assessed in 2020/21?

2   What profits would be assessed if instead the year end was 30 April?

Solution

2 Commencement and cessation

The current year basis does not apply in the opening or closing years of a business. This is because in the first few years the business has not normally established a pattern of annual accounts, and very few businesses cease trading on the annual accounting date.

Apart from the first tax year of trade and the last tax year of trade, HM Revenue & Customs (HMRC) will expect to see 12 months of profits showing in the income tax computation each year. As the periods of account may not be 12 months long in the opening and closing years, special rules are needed to establish which 12 months should be allocated to which tax year.

2.1 Commencement of trade - the opening year rules

The following diagram shows the method of determining the basis period for the first three tax years of trading:

First tax year = Tax year in which trade starts

Tax the profits of the actual tax year (from date trade starts – 5 April)

Second tax year = Ask the question

Is there a period of account ending the second tax year?

YES

NO

How long is the period of account ending in the second tax year?

Tax the profits of the second tax year (6 April – 5 April)

12 MONTHS

< 12 MONTHS

> 12 MONTHS

Tax the 12 months ending in tax Year 2 (current year basis)

Tax the first 12 months of trade

Tax the 12 months up to the end of the long accounting period ending in second tax year

Third and subsequent tax years:

Keep asking 'Is there an accounting period ending in this tax year?'– once you have a 12 month accounting period ending in the tax year you are in the current year basis and will stay in it year on year until you cease to trade (see next section).

2.2 Overlap profits

Overlap profits: Profits which have been taxed more than once are called **overlap profits**.

When a business starts, some profits may be taxed twice because the basis period for the second year includes some or all of the period of trading in the first year or because the basis period for the third year overlaps with that for the second year, or both.

Overlap profits are relieved when the trade ceases by being deducted from the final year's taxable profits.

Illustration 1: Opening year rules (1)

Jonathan commences business on 1 January 2019 and makes up his first accounts to 30 June 2019 and then 30 June annually thereafter. The tax-adjusted trade profits after capital allowances are as follows:

Period		
6 months	to 30 June 2019	£10,000
Year	to 30 June 2020	£18,000
Year	to 30 June 2021	£26,000

Required

Apply the opening year basis period rules to work out what profits are taxed in which tax years. Determine the date(s) and amount(s) of overlap profits.

Solution

1st tax year: 2018/19 – tax profits 1.1.19 – 5.4.19

2nd tax year: 2019/20

- Is there a period of account ending in 2019/20? (Yes, the period ended 30.6.19)
- How long is the period of account?
  - Less than 12 months, ie six months long.
- So, in 2019/20, tax the profits of the first 12 months of trade (1.1.19–31.12.19), ie:
  - pe 30.6.19 profits; plus
  - 6/12 of y/e 30.6.20 profits.

3rd tax year: 2020/21 - CYB, ie profits of year ended 30 June 2020

Overlap periods:

- The period 1.1.19 - 5.4.19 is taxed in both 2018/19 and 2019/20
- The period 1.7.19 - 31.12.19 is taxed in both 2019/20 and 2020/21

Tax year	Calculation		£
	Actual (1.1.19 – 5.4.19)		
2018/19			5,000
	First 12 months (1.1.19 – 31.12.19)		
	1.1.19 – 30.6.19	10,000	
	1.7.19 – 31.12.19 (6/12 × £18,000)		
2019/20		9,000	19,000
2020/21	CYB (year to 30.6.20)		18,000
2021/22	CYB (year to 30.6.21)		26,000
	1.1.19 – 5.4.19	5,000	
Overlap profits	1.7.19 – 31.12.19	9,000	14,000

Activity 2: Opening year rules (2)

Scott commences trading on 1 January 2019 and makes up his first accounts to 30 June 2020 and then 30 June annually thereafter.

	£
18 months to 30 June 2020	27,600
Year ended 30 June 2021	26,000

Required

What are his assessments based on these profits and what are his overlap profits?

Solution

Activity 3: Opening year rules (3)

Peter begins trading on 1 July 2019. He decides on a December year end but draws up his first accounts to 31 December 2020.

He made £18,000 profit in the 18 months to 31 December 2020 and £15,000 in the year ended 31 December 2021.

Required

What are his assessments based on these profits and what are his overlap profits?

Solution

Exam focus point

A business with a 31 March year end will have no overlap profits as its accounting year coincides with the tax year. A business with a 31 December year end, for example, will have three months of overlap profit as its accounting year ends three months before the end of the tax year. Use this rule of thumb to check your calculation of overlap profits.

2.3 Cessation of trade - the closing year rules

If the final year is the third year or a later year, the basis period runs from the end of the basis period for the previous year (which will have been assessed under the current year basis) to the date of cessation. This rule overrides the rules that normally apply in the third and later years.

Remember, overlap profits are deducted from the final tax year's taxable profits. Any deduction of overlap profits may create or increase a loss (see next chapter).

Essential reading

Your Essential reading contains details of the basis period rules where cessation happens in the first two tax years of trading.

The Essential reading is available as an Appendix of the digital edition of the Workbook.

Activity 4: Closing year rules

1 Albert, who has been trading for some years making up his accounts to 31 December, ceases to trade on 31 March 2021 with profits as follows:

	Adjusted profits
	£
Year to 31 December 2019	19,000
Year to 31 December 2020	22,000
3 months to 31 March 2021	12,000

The overlap profits arising in the opening years of his trade were £3,500.

Required

What is Albert's trading income assessment in the tax year 2019/20?

- ○ £19,000
- ○ £22,000
- ○ £19,750
- ○ £15,500

2 What is Albert's trading income assessment in the tax year 2020/21?

- ○ £18,500
- ○ £22,000
- ○ £30,500
- ○ £34,000

Solution

Essential reading

Your Essential reading contains an example illustrating the basis periods over the full life of a business, from commencement to cessation.

The Essential reading is available as an Appendix of the digital edition of the Workbook.

3 Choice of accounting date

The choice of an accounting date may affect when tax is payable on trading profits. It may also create overlap profits and help or hinder tax planning.

A new trader should consider which accounting date would be best. There are a number of factors to consider from the point of view of taxation.

- If profits are expected to rise, a date early in the tax year (such as 30 April) will delay the time when rising accounts profits feed through into rising taxable profits.
- An accounting date of 30 April gives the greatest time between earning the profits and paying the tax.
- Knowing profits well in advance of the end of the tax year makes tax planning easier.
- A 31 March/5 April year end is more straightforward and avoids overlap profits.
- The choice of an accounting date affects the profits shown in each set of accounts, and this may affect the taxable profits (especially for heavily seasonal businesses).

Essential reading

These points are examined in more detail in your Essential reading, along with a numerical example comparing the assessable profits with three different accounting date choices.

The Essential reading is available as an Appendix of the digital edition of the Workbook.

Chapter summary

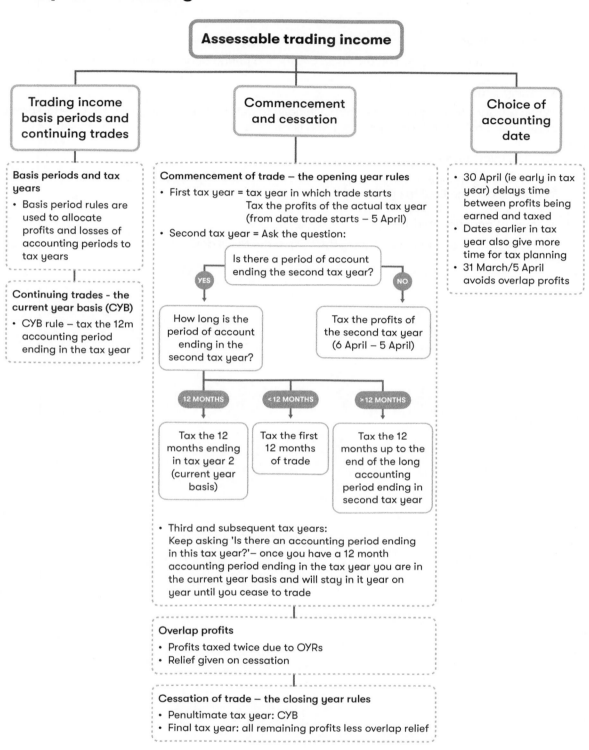

Assessable trading income

Trading income basis periods and continuing trades

Commencement and cessation

Choice of accounting date

Basis periods and tax years
- Basis period rules are used to allocate profits and losses of accounting periods to tax years

Continuing trades - the current year basis (CYB)
- CYB rule – tax the 12m accounting period ending in the tax year

---

Commencement of trade – the opening year rules
- First tax year = tax year in which trade starts
  Tax the profits of the actual tax year (from date trade starts – 5 April)
- Second tax year = Ask the question:

Is there a period of account ending the second tax year?

YES

NO

How long is the period of account ending in the second tax year?

Tax the profits of the second tax year (6 April – 5 April)

12 MONTHS | **<12 MONTHS** | **>12 MONTHS**

Tax the 12 months ending in tax year 2 (current year basis)

Tax the first 12 months of trade

Tax the 12 months up to the end of the long accounting period ending in second tax year

- Third and subsequent tax years:
  Keep asking 'Is there an accounting period ending in this tax year?'– once you have a 12 month accounting period ending in the tax year you are in the current year basis and will stay in it year on year until you cease to trade

Overlap profits
- Profits taxed twice due to OYRs
- Relief given on cessation

Cessation of trade – the closing year rules
- Penultimate tax year: CYB
- Final tax year: all remaining profits less overlap relief

Choice of accounting date
- 30 April (ie early in tax year) delays time between profits being earned and taxed
- Dates earlier in tax year also give more time for tax planning
- 31 March/5 April avoids overlap profits

Knowledge diagnostic

1. Current year basis

Trading income is assessed on a CYB, ie profits of a period of account ending in that tax year.

2. Opening year rules

When a trade starts, special rules apply initially to get the trader onto the CYB. Overlap profits will arise unless a 31 March or 5 April year end is selected.

3. Closing year rules

On cessation, special rules apply to make sure all the trade profits are taxed. Any overlap profits are relieved in the final tax year.

4. Choice of accounting date

The choice of accounting date can affect when the tax is paid and the amount of any overlap profits.

Further study guidance

Question practice

Now try the following from the Further question practice bank (available in the digital edition of the Workbook):

Section A: Q38, Q39, Q40

Section C: Q41 Clive, Q42 Fiona

Activity answers

Activity 1: Current year basis

1   Profits assessed on a current year basis

   2020/21 - year ended 31 March 2021: £18,000

2   2020/21 - year ended 30 April 2020: £22,000

Activity 2: Opening year rules (2)

Tax year	Calculation	£
	Actual (1.1.19 – 5.4.19) 3/18 × £27,600	
2018/19		4,600
	Actual (6.4.19 – 5.4.20) 12/18 × £27,600	
2019/20		18,400
	12m to a/c date (1.7.19 – 30.6.20)	
2020/21	12/18 × £27,600	18,400
2021/22	CYB (year to 30.6.21)	26,000
	1.7.19 – 5.4.20	
Overlap profits	9/18 × £27,600	13,800

Activity 3: Opening year rules (3)

Tax year	Calculation	£
	Actual (1.7.19 – 5.4.20) 9/18 × £18,000	
2019/20		9,000
	12 months to 31.12.20 12/18 × £18,000	
2020/21		12,000
2021/22	CYB (year to 31.12.21)	15,000
	1.1.20 – 5.4.20	
Overlap profits	3/18 × £18,000	3,000

Activity 4: Closing year rules

1   The correct answer is: £19,000

		£
2019/20	CYB (y/e 31.12.19)	19,000

The answer £22,000 is profit for the y/e 31.12.20. The answer £19,750 uses the actual basis for 2019/20. The answer £15,500 deducts the overlap profits.

2   The correct answer is: £30,500

		£
2020/21	Year ended 31.12.20	22,000
	3 months to 31.3.21	12,000
	Less 'overlap' relief	(3,500)
		30,500

The answer £18,500 is the profits for the year ended 31.12.20 less overlap profits. The answer £22,000 is the profits for the year ended 31.12.20. The answer £34,000 does not deduct the overlap profits.

10

Trading losses

Learning objectives

On completion of this chapter, you should be able to:

	Syllabus reference no.
Understand how trading losses can be carried forward	B3(i)(i)
Understand how trading losses can be claimed against total income and chargeable gains, and the restriction that can apply	B3(i)(ii)
Explain and compute the relief for trading losses in the early years of a trade	B3(i)(iii)
Explain and compute terminal loss relief	B3(i)(iv)
Recognise the factors that will influence the choice of loss relief claim	B3(i)(v)

Exam context

Section A questions on loss relief may deal with a specific aspect such as the cap on loss relief against general income. You may also have to deal with a number of aspects of loss relief in a Section B question. Section C could have a detailed computational question involving the carry back and carry forward of losses for a sole trader. Ensure you know the rules for ongoing trades and the additional relief in the early years of trading. On cessation, terminal loss relief may be used. Once you have established the reliefs available look to see which is most beneficial.

Business context

If a trader generates losses, it may well be that they are in financial difficulty (especially if they do not have significant other source of income). A tax adviser's role can then be important, to give appropriate advice as to the use of the loss to optimise the individual's cash flow position.

Chapter overview

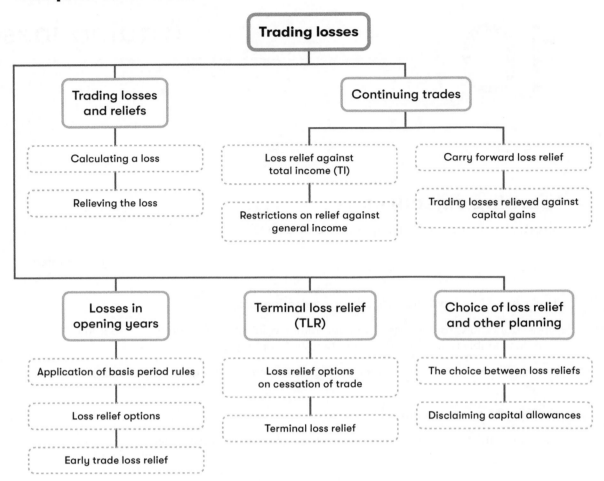

Trading losses

- **Trading losses and reliefs**
  - Calculating a loss
  - Relieving the loss

- **Continuing trades**
  - Loss relief against total income (TI)
    - Restrictions on relief against general income
  - Carry forward loss relief
    - Trading losses relieved against capital gains

- **Losses in opening years**
  - Application of basis period rules
  - Loss relief options
  - Early trade loss relief

- **Terminal loss relief (TLR)**
  - Loss relief options on cessation of trade
  - Terminal loss relief

- **Choice of loss relief and other planning**
  - The choice between loss reliefs
  - Disclaiming capital allowances

1 Trading losses and reliefs

1.1 Calculating a loss

A tax loss is computed in exactly the same way as a taxable profit, making the same adjustments to the accounts profit or loss. The loss is the (negative) adjusted figure after capital allowances for an accounting period.

If there is a loss in a basis period, the taxable trade profits for the tax year based on that basis period are nil. Never put in a negative assessment.

1.2 Relieving the loss

The taxpayer will be able to claim relief for the loss by setting it against income in accordance with legislation. This will involve deducting the loss from either total income, chargeable gains, or future trading income, depending on which form of loss relief is used.

> ### PER alert
>
> One of the competencies you require to fulfil Performance Objective 17 *Tax planning and advice* of the PER is to mitigate and/or defer tax liabilities through the use of standard reliefs, exemptions and incentives. You can apply the knowledge you obtain from this chapter of the Workbook to help to demonstrate this competence.

2 Continuing trades

2.1 Loss relief against total income

A claim may be made by a taxpayer to offset a trading loss against their general income.

- The loss available for relief is the loss in the basis period for that tax year.
- Loss relief is against total income of:
  - The tax year in which the loss was suffered (known as a 'current year claim'); and/or
  - The preceding tax year (known as a 'carry back claim').
- If claims against both current and prior year income are made, the taxpayer can specify in which order the loss is used (ie current year and then prior year, or *vice versa*)
- The loss is offset against non-savings income as far as possible, and then against savings income and finally dividends.
- If a claim is made, the maximum possible loss must be set off (ie the loss may have to be set against income part of which would have been covered by the personal allowance or taxed at 0% in the savings income nil rate band or the dividend nil rate band).

Illustration 1: Loss relief against total income (1)

Janet has a loss in her period of account ending 31 December 2020 of £38,500. Her other income is dividend income of £31,500 a year, and she wishes to claim loss relief against general income for the year of loss and then for the preceding year. Her trading income in the previous year was £1,500.

Required

Show her taxable income for each year, and comment on the effectiveness of the loss relief. Assume that tax rates and allowances for 2020/21 have always applied.

Solution

The loss-making period ends in 2020/21, so the year of the loss is 2020/21.

	2019/20	2020/21
	£	£
Total income (£31,500 + £1,500)/£31,500	33,000	31,500
Less loss relief against general income	(7,000)	(31,500)
Net income	26,000	0
Less personal allowance	(12,500)	(12,500)
Taxable income	13,500	0

In 2020/21, (£2,000 + £12,500) = £14,500 of the loss has been wasted because that amount of income would have been covered by the personal allowance and the dividend nil rate band and the remainder of the loss will attract tax relief at the relatively low rate of 7.5%. If Janet claims loss relief against general income in that tax year, there is nothing she can do about this inefficient use of loss relief.

Activity 1: Relief against total income

Feng runs a market stall. Accounts for the year ended 30 June 2019 show a trading profit of £16,000. For the year ended 30 June 2020 there is a trading loss of £34,000. In the year ended 30 June 2021, he made a trading profit of £6,000. His only other income was property income of £15,000 each tax year.

Required

Show how the loss is relieved if he makes the earliest claim(s) to set his trading loss against total income.

Solution

2.2 Restrictions on relief against general income

There are two circumstances where loss relief against general income is either not permitted or is restricted.

2.2.1 Commercial basis

Relief cannot be claimed against general income unless the loss-making business is conducted on a commercial basis with a view to the realisation of profits throughout the basis period for the tax year.

2.2.2 Cap on income tax relief

If loss relief is claimed against total income the maximum that can be relieved is the **higher** of:
(a)   £50,000
(b)   25% of person's total income (after deducting gross personal pension contributions)

The cap is applied separately to the total income for each year for which relief is claimed.

This restriction does not apply where a loss is relieved against profits of the same trade for the preceding tax year. The restriction only applies to the offset of losses against other income in that year.

Activity 2: Cap on income tax relief - high income

Paul has traded for many years. Recent results are as follows:

Year ended	£
30.6.19	40,000
30.6.20	(200,000)

He has other income of £100,000 per annum.

Required

Calculate Paul's taxable income for 2019/20 and 2020/21 assuming the largest and earliest claim against total income is made. Assume the personal allowance is £12,500 in both tax years.

Solution

2.3 Carry forward loss relief

If no claim is made to set loss against total income, or some of the loss is left after such a claim, then the balance will be carried forward indefinitely.

A carried forward loss is relieved against the first available future profits from the same trade.

Set-off is automatic and compulsory.

Activity 3: Carry forward loss relief

Bert Gown has traded for many years. Recent results are as follows:

	£
31.12.18	20,000

	£
31.12.19	(46,000)
31.12.20	(30,000)
31.12.21	8,000

He has other income of £13,000 per annum.

Required

Calculate the net income for 2018/19 to 2021/22 assuming that the largest and earliest possible claims against total income are made, and show the losses to be carried forward against future trading profits.

Solution

2.4 Trading losses relieved against capital gains

If a claim is made against total income, the taxpayer can make a further claim to offset any remaining loss against the chargeable gains for the year. Offset must be made against total income in that year first.

Essential reading

Further detail and an example of this relief is contained in your Essential reading. You will study chargeable gains later in this Workbook and we suggest that you come back to this section at that point.

The Essential reading is available as an Appendix of the digital edition of the Workbook.

---

3 Losses in opening years

3.1 Application of basis period rules

Under the rules determining the basis period for the first three tax years of trading, there may be periods where the basis periods overlap (as seen in Chapter 9). If profits arise in these periods, they are taxed twice but are relieved later, usually on cessation. However, a loss in an overlap period can only be relieved once. It must not be double counted.

Therefore If basis periods overlap, the opening year rules are modified such that a loss in the overlap period is treated as a loss for the earlier tax year only.

3.2 Loss relief options

The taxpayer has the following reliefs available:

- Loss relief against total income
- Carry forward relief
- Early trade loss relief

3.3 Early trade loss relief

This relief is available in respect of trading losses incurred in the first four tax years of trade.

The relief enables the loss to be carried back three tax years on a first in, first out basis (FIFO) ie applying the loss to the earliest year first. The loss is deducted from the taxpayer's total income.

A claim applies to all three carryback years automatically provided that the loss is large enough. The taxpayer cannot choose to relieve the loss against just one or two of the years, or to relieve only part of the loss.

The advantage of early trade losses relief is that it enables losses to be carried back for three years and so gives relief earlier than the other loss reliefs.

Activity 4: Early trade loss relief

Bob Fisher commenced trading on 1 July 2017. Results are as follows:

Year ended		£
30.6.18	Loss	(40,000)
30.6.19	Profit	24,000
30.6.20	Profit	30,000
30.6.21	Profit	36,000

Bob's total income prior to 2017/18 was £68,000 in each tax year. Bob has no other income.

Required

1 Determine Bob's trading income assessments based on the above results, and to which year(s) Bob's trading loss is attributed under the opening year rules.

2 Explain what loss reliefs are available to Bob for his trading losses of 2017/18 and 2018/19. Advise Bob on the best use of his losses.

Solution

Essential reading

A further illustration of the rules regarding overlapping losses can be found in the Essential reading.

The Essential reading is available as an Appendix of the digital edition of the Workbook.

4 Terminal loss relief (TLR)

4.1 Loss relief options on cessation of trade

Carry forward relief is no longer available when a trade has ceased. A loss arising in the final tax year of assessment (after closing year rules are applied) may be relieved by loss relief against general income in the normal way.

However, trade loss relief against general income will often be insufficient on its own to deal with a loss incurred in the last months of trading. For this reason there is a special relief, terminal trade loss relief, which allows a loss on cessation to be carried back for relief against taxable trading profits in previous years.

4.2 Terminal loss relief

4.2.1 Operation of the relief

Terminal loss relief (TLR) allows relief against **trading** profits of the tax year of cessation and the three preceding years, on a last in, first out (LIFO) basis

4.2.2 Calculation of the terminal loss

The loss of the last period of account is increased by any overlap profits.

The loss available for relief under TLR is the actual loss in the last 12 months of trading, constructed as follows:

(a) **Final tax year**

	£
Unrelieved trading loss from 6 April to date of cessation (increased by overlap profits)	X

(b) **Penultimatetax year**

	£
Unrelieved trading loss (if any) arising from a date 12 months before cessation to 5 April	X
	X

If either (a) or (b) above yields a profit as opposed to a loss, the profit is regarded as zero for this purpose.

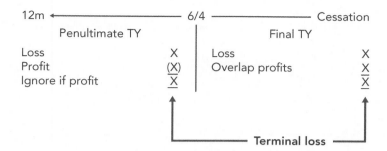

Activity 5: Terminal loss relief

Ali commenced trading on 1 May 2011 making up accounts to 30 September each year. She ceased trading on 30 June 2020. The most recent results were:

Year 30 September 2016	£10,000 profit
Year 30 September 2017	£8,000 profit
Year 30 September 2018	£10,000 profit
Year 30 September 2019	£4,000 profit
Period to 30 June 2020	£27,000 loss

Ali had overlap profits from the commencement of trade of £3,000.

Required

1   What is Ali's maximum claim for terminal loss relief?

£ [   ]

2   Identify, by clicking on the relevant boxes in the table below, the amount of terminal loss relief that can be utilised in the tax years 2016/17 and 2017/18

2016/17: [   ]   (1)

2017/18: £ [   ]   (2)

Pull down list 1
- nil
- £10,000
- £7,000

Pull down list 2
- 8,000
- £4,000
- £nil

Solution

5 Choice of loss relief and other planning

5.1 The choice between loss reliefs

To decide on whether a loss should be relieved in the current year, carried back or carried forward will involve consideration of:

(a) Marginal rates of tax - offsetting a loss against income of a year where the taxpayer is being taxed at the higher rate is more tax-efficient than a year where the taxpayer pays basic rate tax

(b) Timing of tax payments/repayments: The carry back of a loss results in a refund of the relevant amount of income tax already paid

(c) The possibility of personal allowance, savings nil rate band and dividend nil rate band being wasted, due to the fact that a taxpayer cannot specify the amount of loss they wish to use

 Illustration 2: Choice of loss relief

Felicity's trading results are as follows.

Year ended 30 September	Trading profit/(loss)
	£
2019	3,900
2020	(21,000)
2021	14,000

Her other income (all non-savings income) is as follows.

	£
2019/20	8,300
2020/21	35,000

Required

Show the most efficient use of Felicity's trading loss. Assume that the personal allowance has been £12,500 throughout.

Solution

Relief could be claimed against general income for 2020/21 and/or 2019/20, with any unused loss being carried forward. Relief in 2019/20 would be against general income of £(3,900 + 8,300) = £12,200, all of which would be covered by the personal allowance anyway, so this claim should not be made.

A claim against general income should be made for 2020/21 as this saves tax more quickly than carry forward loss relief would in 2021/22.

The final results will be as follows:

	2019/20	2020/21	2021/22
	£	£	£
Trading income	3,900	0	14,000
Less carry forward loss relief	(0)	(0)	(0)
	3,900	0	14,000
Other income	8,300	35,000	19,500
	12,200	35,000	33,500
Less loss relief against general income	(0)	(21,000)	(0)
Net income	12,200	14,000	33,500
Less personal allowance	(12,500)	(12,500)	(12,500)
Taxable income	0	1,500	21,000

5.2 Disclaiming capital allowances

 Essential reading

Your Essential reading shows you another planning tool that can be used to minimise the wastage of a loss: adjusting a capital allowances claim.

The Essential reading is available as an Appendix of the digital edition of the Workbook.

Chapter summary

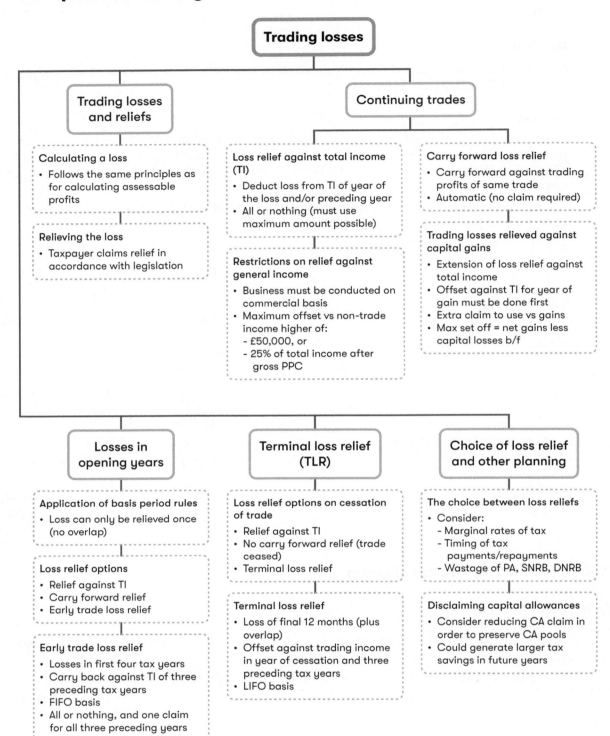

Trading losses

Trading losses and reliefs

Calculating a loss
- Follows the same principles as for calculating assessable profits

Relieving the loss
- Taxpayer claims relief in accordance with legislation

Continuing trades

Loss relief against total income (TI)
- Deduct loss from TI of year of the loss and/or preceding year
- All or nothing (must use maximum amount possible)

Restrictions on relief against general income
- Business must be conducted on commercial basis
- Maximum offset vs non-trade income higher of:
  - £50,000, or
  - 25% of total income after gross PPC

Carry forward loss relief
- Carry forward against trading profits of same trade
- Automatic (no claim required)

Trading losses relieved against capital gains
- Extension of loss relief against total income
- Offset against TI for year of gain must be done first
- Extra claim to use vs gains
- Max set off = net gains less capital losses b/f

Losses in opening years

Application of basis period rules
- Loss can only be relieved once (no overlap)

Loss relief options
- Relief against TI
- Carry forward relief
- Early trade loss relief

Early trade loss relief
- Losses in first four tax years
- Carry back against TI of three preceding tax years
- FIFO basis
- All or nothing, and one claim for all three preceding years

Terminal loss relief (TLR)

Loss relief options on cessation of trade
- Relief against TI
- No carry forward relief (trade ceased)
- Terminal loss relief

Terminal loss relief
- Loss of final 12 months (plus overlap)
- Offset against trading income in year of cessation and three preceding tax years
- LIFO basis

Choice of loss relief and other planning

The choice between loss reliefs
- Consider:
  - Marginal rates of tax
  - Timing of tax payments/repayments
  - Wastage of PA, SNRB, DNRB

Disclaiming capital allowances
- Consider reducing CA claim in order to preserve CA pools
- Could generate larger tax savings in future years

Knowledge diagnostic

1. What to do with trading losses

Trading losses are computed in exactly the same way as trading income (although there are no overlap losses).

It is then up to the taxpayer to decide how to relieve the loss.

2. Continuing trades

Trading losses can be relieved against total income (and then subsequently gains) in the year of loss and/or preceding year. The amount being offset against non-trading income is restricted to the higher of £50,000 or 25% of an individual's total income.

Any remaining loss is then carried forward against future trading income of the same trade.

3. Losses in opening years

On commencement an additional loss relief is available allowing trading losses to be carried back against the total income of the preceding three tax years.

4. Terminal loss relief

On cessation to compensate for no carry forward relief, traders can use TLR to carry back trading losses against the trading income of the three previous tax years.

5. Choice of loss relief

It is important for a trader to choose the right loss relief, so as to save tax at the highest possible rate and so as to obtain relief reasonably quickly.

Further study guidance

Question practice

Now try the following from the Further question practice bank (available in the digital edition of the Workbook):

Section A: Q43, Q44, Q45

Section C: Q46 Morgan

Activity answers

Activity 1: Relief against total income

	2019/20	2020/21	2021/22
	£	£	£
Trading income	16,000	–	6,000
Other income	15,000	15,000	15,000
Total income	31,000	15,000	21,000
Loss relief against total income	(31,000) (i)	(3,000) (ii)	–
Net income	–	12,000	21,000

Loss memo:

		£
Y/e 30.6.20		34,000
	– 19/20	(31,000) (i)
	– 20/21	(3,000) (ii)
		–

Note. It is possible to claim relief in 2020/21 in priority to 2019/20; however here it is not beneficial as the carry back results in a refund of income tax paid.

Activity 2: Cap on income tax relief - high income

	2019/20	2020/21
	£	£
Trading profit	40,000	–
Other income	100,000	100,000
	140,000	100,000
Loss relief	(90,000)	(50,000)
	50,000	50,000
Less PA	(12,500)	(12,500)
Taxable income	37,500	37,500

Loss memo

		£
Y/e 30.6.20		200,000
Loss relief	– 19/20 (£40,000 + £50,000) (Note 1)	(90,000)
	– 20/21 (Note 2)	(50,000)
	Loss remaining	60,000

Notes.

1. In 2019/20 the relief against trading income of £40,000 is not capped. Relief against other income is capped at the higher of £50,000 or 25% × £140,000 = £35,000. So claim is £90,000 (£40,000 + £50,000).

2. In 2020/21, loss relief is capped at the higher of £50,000 or 25% × 100,000 = £25,000, ie £50,000.

Activity 3: Carry forward loss relief

	2018/19	2019/20	2020/21	2021/22
	£	£	£	£
Trading income	20,000	–	–	8,000
Carry forward relief	–	–	–	(8,000) (iv)
	20,000	–	–	–
Other income	13,000	13,000	13,000	13,000
Total income	33,000	13,000	13,000	13,000
Relief against total income	(33,000) (i)	(13,000) (ii)	(13,000) (iii)	–
Net income	–	–	–	13,000

Loss memo:

	£	£
Y/e 31.12.19	46,000	
Relief vs income – 2018/19	(33,000) (i)	
– 2019/20	(13,000) (ii)	
		–
Y/e 31.12.20	30,000	
Relief vs income – 2019/20	–	
– 2020/21	(13,000) (iii)	
c/fwd		17,000
		17,000
Automatic relief vs income – 2021/22		(8,000) (iv)
C/fwd		9,000

Activity 4: Early trade loss relief

1

Trading assessments		£
2017/18	Actual (1.7.17–5.4.18)	Nil
2018/19	12m to permanent accounting date (y/e 30.6.18)	Nil
2019/20	CYB (y/e 30.6.19)	24,000
2020/21	CYB (y/e 30.6.20)	30,000

Trading assessments		£
2021/22	CYB (y/e 30.6.21)	36,000

Bob's trading losses are attributed as follows:

		£
2017/18	9/12 × £40,000	30,000
2018/19	12m to permanent accounting date (y/e 30.6.18)	40,000
	Less used in 2017/18	(30,000)
		10,000

2 **2017/18 loss of £30,000:**

Relief available against total income of 2017/18 (£nil) and/or 2016/17 (£68,000) under normal loss relief against total income.

Relief against total income of 2014/15, 2015/16 and 2016/17 (£68,000 pa) in that order under early trade loss relief - the loss would be offset fully against 2014/15 income.

Carry forward relief against the first available trading profits of the same trade - £24,000 would be relieved in 2019/20 and the remainder in 2020/21.

2018/19 loss of £10,000:

Relief available against total income of 2018/19 (£nil) and/or 2017/18 (£nil) under normal loss relief against total income.

Relief against total income of 2015/16, 2016/17 and 2017/18 (£68,000 pa) in that order under early trade loss relief - the loss would be offset fully against 2015/16 income.

Carry forward relief against the first available trading profits of the same trade - depending on the relief used for the 2017/18 loss, relief would be obtained against 2019/20 or 2020/21 income.

Advice

Early years loss relief is the most beneficial claim for both losses - relief is obtained at the earliest point, generating repayments, and furthermore Bob was a higher rate taxpayer in the years prior to starting his trade and so relief for his losses will be mainly obtained at 40%.

Activity 5: Terminal loss relief

1 £ 29,000

Calculation of the terminal loss: Final year 2020/21

			Losses
			£
(a)	6.4.20 – 30.6.20 = 3/9 × (27,000) =		(9,000)
(b)	Overlap profits		(3,000)
(c)	1.10.19 – 5.4.20		
	6/9 × (27,000) =	(18,000)	
	1.7.19 – 30.9.19		
	3/12 × £4,000 profit	1,000	
			(17,000)
Total terminal loss claim			(29,000)

2   2016/17: nil

2017/18: £ 8,000

Response Option	Explanation
£7,000	This answer assumes the loss can be carried back further than three years
£10,000	This assumes that relief can be carried back further than three years, and either relief on a FIFO basis, or a larger terminal loss.
£nil	This answer ignores the possibility of terminal loss relief
£4,000	This is the amount relieved in 2019/20

Since there is no assessment for 2020/21 the £29,000 will be carried back and set against the assessments for:

	£
Terminal loss	29,000
2019/20	(4,000)
2018/19	(10,000)
2017/18	(8,000)
Unrelieved terminal loss	7,000

This amount cannot be carried back any further (ie to 2016/17) and is lost.

Skills checkpoint 2

Effective use of spreadsheets

Chapter overview

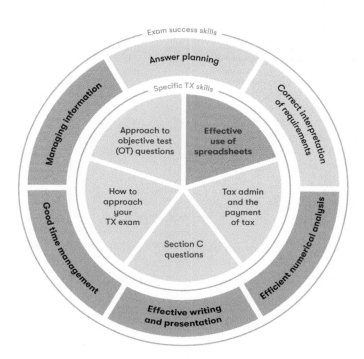

Introduction

It is very likely that you will be required to use the spreadsheet response option in the constructed workspace for Section C questions. It is imperative that you know how to use the spreadsheet functions to prepare accurate and easy to follow calculations. Efficient use of the spreadsheets will save valuable time, which you can then use to address any difficult or discursive elements. Using spreadsheets correctly can also help to show the marker your calculations and reduce calculation errors.

Effective use of spreadsheets

The key steps are outlined below and will be demonstrated in the following section as the question 'Florrie' is answered.

STEP 1 **Start by setting up the spreadsheet.**

The examining team would like to see negative numbers as negative numbers, in brackets and in a red font.

This is quick to do before you start to enter your answer. Click on the blue triangle left of the A cell, then right click, format cells, All, scroll down and click on #,##0_);[Red](#,##0), OK

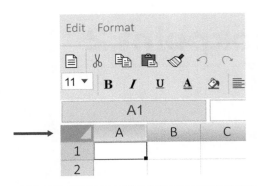

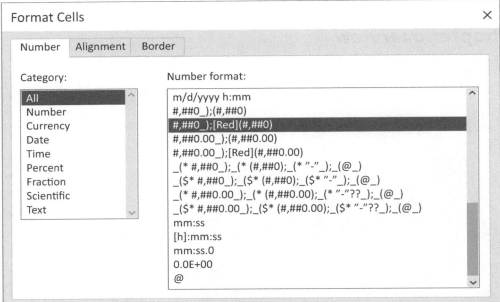

Alternatively, you can click on the blue triangle, click on the 'format as currency' icon (left of the % icon) and select #,##0;[Red](#,##0)

Now, whenever you type a minus number, (eg -200), it will appear in brackets in red font.

B4		=-180*12
	A	B
1	**Taxable income**	
2	Employment income	74,400
3	Mileage allowance	345
4	Leasing costs	(2,160)

STEP 2 Ensure the numbers are in a separate cell from the label.

This makes the numbers easier to mark for the examiner as well as making it possible to use spreadsheet formulae for any necessary calculations.

	A	B
1	**Taxable income**	
2	Employment income	
3	Salary	74,400
4	Mileage allowance	345
5	Leasing costs	(2,160)

	A	B
1	**Taxable income**	
2	Employment income	
3	Salary 74400	
4	Mileage allowance 345	
5	Leasing costs (2160)	

STEP 3 Always use formulae to perform calculations.

Do not write out your working, eg 800-700+400=600 in a single cell because it wastes time and you may make a mistake. Use the spreadsheet functions instead! You can always double check your answer on your calculator. Remember to use * for multiplying and / for dividing. Percentages can be entered using a percentage symbol or as a fraction, eg 20% or 0.2.

◢	A	B
1	**Taxable income**	
2	Employment income	
3	Salary	=6200*12
4	Mileage allowance	=2300*(0.6-0.45)
5	Leasing costs	=-180*12

◢	A	B	C
1	**Taxable income**		
2	Employment income		
3	Salary = 6200x12=74400		
4	Mileage allowance 2300x15p=345		
5	Leasing costs 180x12=(21600)		

The leasing cost is showing as (21,600) and when the marker clicks on the cell B5, they can see the formula as shown above.

The student here has not used the spreadsheet formula and has wasted time typing 180x12. They have then made a mistake writing down the answer and have added an extra zero.

STEP 4 Make efficient use of the SUM function.

Remember, if some of the numbers in a list need to be deducted, enter a minus sign for these and then use the 'SUM' formula to add all of the numbers together. Type =sum(then select the cells you want to add together with your mouse and press return. This is quicker than entering = A1-A2+A3 and so on, and you are less likely to make a mistake.

◢	A	B
1	**Taxable income**	
2	Employment income	
3	Salary	=6200*12
4	Mileage allowance	=2300*(0.6-0.45)
5	Leasing costs	=-180*12
6		=SUM(B3:B5)

◢	A	B
1	**Taxable income**	
2	Employment income	
3	Salary	=6200*12
4	Mileage allowance	=2300*(0.6-0.45)
5	Leasing costs	=-180*12
6		=B3+B4-B5

Here, the student has wasted time trying to add and deduct each cell instead of using the SUM function. They have also made a mistake and deducted B5. Since B5 was already a negative number, it should have been added instead.

STEP 5 Only use separate workings for longer calculations and cross reference any workings using '=' rather than re-typing the numbers

Basic calculations, for example the salary, should be done within the cell (ie =6,200*12). Only longer workings, such as property income, should be shown separately.

	A	B
1	**Taxable income**	
2	Employment income	
3	Salary	74,400
4	Mileage allowance	345
5	Leasing costs	(2,160)
6	Property income	=B19
7		
8		
9	**Working**	
10	**Property income**	
11	Rent received	10,080
12	Mortgage interest	(2,100)
13	Replacement furniture relief	
14	Washing machine	(380)
15	Dishwasher	0
16	Other expenses	(1,110)
17		6,490
18	Furnished room	1,080
19		7,570

	A	B
1	**Taxable income**	
2	Employment income	
3	Salary	74,400
4	Mileage allowance	345
5	Leasing costs	(2,160)
6	Property income	7,550
7		
8		
9	**Working**	
10	**Property income**	
11	Rent received	10,080
12	Mortgage interest	(2,100)
13	Replacement furniture relief	
14	Washing machine	(380)
15	Dishwasher	0
16	Other expenses	(1,110)
17		6,490
18	Furnished room	1,080
19		7,570

Here, the student has worked out the property income in a separate working. Then, instead of typing 7,570 into cell B6, they have used the spreadsheet function '=' to pick up the number. This ensures that the marker can see exactly where the number has come from, and also reduces the chances of making a mistake.

Here, the student has typed property income into cell B6 and has made a mistake.

STEP 6 Does your answer look reasonable?

Take a moment to look at your answers and see whether any of the numbers look odd. If they do, re-check your calculations. You cannot insert or delete rows on the CBE spreadsheet software but you can copy and paste or cut and paste. For example, if you have left too many rows between a computation and the workings, you can cut and paste the workings so that they appear higher up. This sort of adjustment requires plenty of practice at using the CBE spreadsheet software. You need to feel confident using the software before you sit the exam.

Exam success skills

The following question is worth 15 marks.

For this question, we will also focus on the following exam success skills:

- **Managing information.** It is easy for the amount of information contained in a Section C question to feel overwhelming. Read the requirement first before you set up your spreadsheet and go through the detail in the scenario.

- **Efficient numerical analysis.** Use the spreadsheet functionality. Do not waste time doing calculations manually when the spreadsheet can do them for you. Cross reference your workings using '=' rather than re-typing the numbers.
- **Effective writing and presentation.** The markers want to see a clear layout with workings directly underneath. You can use the cut and paste functions to ensure that your answer looks neat.
- **Good time management.** Using the spreadsheet functions will save you time.

Skills activity

Florrie is employed by Shelford Ltd. The following information is available for the tax year 2020/21:

Employment

- Florrie was paid a gross annual salary of £63,730 by Shelford Ltd.
- In addition to her salary, Florrie received a bonus payment of £10,325 from Shelford Ltd. Florrie became entitled to this bonus on 31 March 2021 but it was not paid until 25 April 2021.
- Shelford Ltd has provided Florrie with living accommodation since 1 January 2018. The company had purchased the property in 2016 for £195,000, and it was valued at £210,000 on 1 January 2018. Improvements costing £10,000 were made to the property during June 2019. The annual value of the property is £8,570.
- In July 2020, Florrie paid a train fare of £150 for a business journey. This was reimbursed by Shelford Ltd in August 2020.
- In September 2020, Shelford Ltd gave each of its employees a one-day gym membership pass worth £45 as part of a healthy living promotion.
- During February 2021, Florrie spent four nights overseas on company business. Shelford Ltd paid Florrie a daily allowance of £20 to cover the cost of personal expenses such as telephone calls to her family.
- Income tax of £12,150 was deducted under PAYE.

Property income

- Florrie owns two houses which are let out.
- The first house was let from 6 May 2020 to 5 September 2020 at a monthly rent of £450, payable in advance.
- During March 2021, Florrie spent £1,130 repairing the roof of the house.
- The second house was purchased on 6 July 2020 and was let immediately to 5 April 2021 at a monthly rent of £750, payable in advance. The rent due on 6 March 2021 was not paid until 6 April 2021.
- During June 2020, Florrie spent £675 on advertising for tenants and she bought furniture at a cost of £3,500.
- Florrie bought a new three-seat sofa in March 2021 at a cost of £750. This replaced a two-seat sofa that she bought in June 2020. If Florrie had bought another two-seat sofa in March 2021 it would have cost £550. Florrie sold the original two-seat sofa for £170.
- Florrie had a property income loss of £2,100 brought forward from 2019/20.

Other information

- During the tax year 2020/21 Florrie received dividends of £2,850.
- During the tax year 2020/21 Florrie made Gift Aid donations totalling £2,000 (net) to national charities.

Required

Calculate the income tax payable by Florrie for the tax year 2020/21. You should indicate by the use of zero any items that are non-taxable/exempt from tax.

(15 marks)

STEP 1 **Start by setting up the spreadsheet.**

Note. The requirement asks you to calculate the income tax payable so once you have formatted the cells, you can start to draw up a proforma to calculate the taxable income, the tax liability and the income tax payable.

STEP 2   **Ensure the numbers are in a separate cell from the label.**

Note. Enter the labels into column A, enter a header for non-savings income in column B, dividend income on column C and a total in column D.

STEP 3   **Always use the formulae to perform calculations.**

Note. For example, use the SUM function to add up the living accommodation additional benefit, improvements and deduction of the £75,000 limit. Then use the spreadsheet to calculate the benefit at 2.25% (eg =B36*2.25%).

STEP 4   **Make efficient use of the SUM function.**

Note. For example, use the SUM function to add up the net income, the taxable income, the income tax liability, the income tax payable and the employment income.

STEP 5   **Only use separate workings for longer calculations and cross reference any workings using '=' rather than retyping the numbers.**

Note. For example, the basic rate tax on the non-savings income can be entered into cell B12 as =A52*20%.

STEP 6   **Does your answer look reasonable?**

Note. The figure should sound reasonable and the answer should be well presented.

This answer should look like this:

	A	B	C	D
1	**Florrie – income tax payable 2020/21**			
2		Non-savings income	Dividend income	Total
3		£	£	£
4	Employment income	85,630		
5	Property income	3,515		
6	Dividends		2,850	
7	Net income	89,145	2,850	91,995
8	Less PA	(12,500)		
9	Taxable income	76,645	2,850	79,495
10		£		
11	*Non savings income*			
12	Basic rate	8,000		
13	Higher rate	14,658		
14	*Dividend income*			
15	2,000@0%	0		
16	Higher rate	276		
17	Income tax liability	22,934		
18	Less PAYE	(12,150)		
19	Income tax payable	10,784		
20				
21	**Workings**			
22	**Employment income**	£		
23	Salary	63,730		
24	Bonus	10,325		
25	Living accommodation	11,495		
26	Reimbursed expenses	0		
27	Gym membership < £50	0		
28	Overseas allowance	80		
29	Employment income	85,630		
30				
31	**Living accommodation**	£	£	
32	Annual benefit		8,570	
33	Additional benefit	195,000		
34	Improvements	10,000		
35	Less limit	(75,000)		
36		130,000		
37	Benefit		2,925	
38			11,495	
39				
40	**Property income**	£	£	
41	Property 1 – rent received		1,800	
42	Property 2 – rent received, not March		6,000	
43	Repairs to roof	(1,130)		
44	Advertising	(675)		
45	Furniture – June 2020	0		
46	Replacement furniture	(380)	(2,185)	
47			5,615	
48	Less loss b/f 2019/20		(2,100)	
49			3,515	
50				
51	**Basic rate limit**			
52		40,000		

Exam success skills diagnostic

Every time you complete a question, use the diagnostic below to assess how effectively you demonstrated the exam success skills in answering the question. The table has been completed below for the 'Florrie' activity to give you an idea of how to complete the diagnostic.

Exam success skills	Your relections/observations
Managing information	Did you remember to extend the basic rate band because of the gift aid donation? Did you remember to deduct the PAYE?

Exam success skills	Your relections/observations
Efficient numerical analysis	Did you use the functions in the spreadsheet to help with numerical accuracy?
Effective writing and presentation	Did you present a neat set of figures with appropriate workings that would have been easy for a marker to follow?
Good time management	Did you manage your time to ensure you completed the question in the time available?
Most important action points to apply to your next question	

Summary

Section C of the TX exam is worth 40 marks, most of which will need to be answered using a spreadsheet.

The best way to score well in Section C questions is to practise them frequently using the CBE software. You need to know how to get the best out the spreadsheet functions. You therefore need to ensure that you:

- Always enter negative figures as negatives (best practice is in brackets in red font).
- Always use the spreadsheet functions to perform your calculations, eg the SUM function and calculations involving percentages.
- Only use separate workings for longer calculations and cross reference any workings using '=' rather than retyping the figures.

11

Partnerships

Learning objectives

On completion of this chapter, you should be able to:

	Syllabus reference no.
Explain and compute how a partnership is assessed to tax.	B3(j)(i)
Explain and compute the assessable profits for each partner following a change in the profit-sharing ratio.	B3(j)(ii)
Explain and compute the assessable profits for each partner following a change in the membership of the partnership	B3(j)(iii)
Describe the alternative loss relief claims that are available to partners.	B3(j)(iv)

Exam context

Section A questions on partnerships may involve allocation of profits to partners, possibly involving salaries and/or interest on capital. You may also have to deal with a number of partners in a Section B question. A Section C question, which may be for 15 marks or 10 marks, may involve changes in partnerships such as a partner joining or leaving. As long as you remember to allocate the profits between the partners according to their profit-sharing arrangements for the period of account, you should be able to cope with any aspect of partnership tax. Remember that each partner is taxed as a sole trader, and you should apply the opening and closing year rules and loss reliefs as appropriate to that partner.

Chapter overview

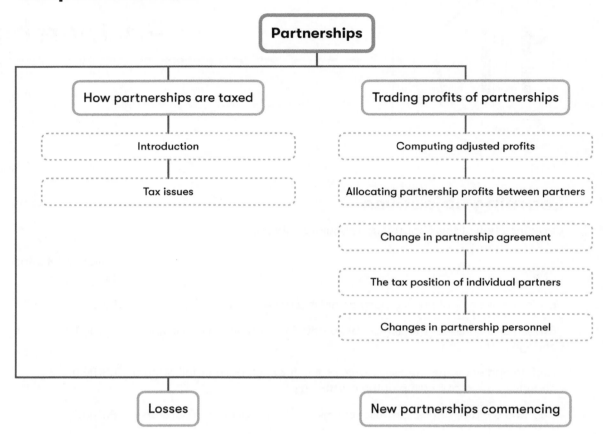

1 How partnerships are taxed

1.1 Introduction

A partnership is a group of individuals who are trading together. All partnerships, including LLPs, are not treated as separate entities from the partners for tax purposes (in contrast to companies). Therefore, a business run as a partnership will, for tax purposes, need to have its taxable income split among the partners.

1.2 Tax issues

For tax purposes, you need to be able to deal with the following:
- Computation of adjusted trading profits
- Allocation of trading profits between partners
- The effect of a change in the profit share ratio
- The effect of a change in the membership of a partnership
- The treatment of losses for partners

2 Trading profits

2.1 Computing adjusted profits

A business partnership is treated like a sole trader for the purposes of computing its profits. Partners' salaries and interest on capital are not deductible expenses and must be added back in computing profits, because they are a form of drawings.

Where the partners own assets (such as their cars) individually, capital allowances must be calculated in respect of such assets (not forgetting any adjustment for private use). The capital allowances must go into the partnership's tax computation as they must be claimed by the partnership, not by the individual partner.

2.2 Allocating partnership profits between partners

Profits or losses are divided between the partners according to the profit-sharing arrangements in the period of account concerned. If any of the partners are entitled to a salary or interest on capital, apportion this first, not forgetting to pro-rate in periods of less than 12 months.

The residue of profit is then split according to the agreed profit-sharing ratio (PSR).

Illustration 1: Allocation of partnership profits

Gustav and Melanie have been in partnership for many years, preparing accounts to 31 March each year. They share profits in the ratio 3:2. In the year to 31 March 2021, the partnership's trading profit is £60,000. The partnership does not own any assets which qualify for capital allowances but Gustav owns a car (which he acquired for £22,000 in May 2020) which he uses 75% for the business of the partnership. The car has CO_2 emissions of 150 g/km.

Required

Show the trade profits allocated to each partner for the period of account to 31 March 2021, assuming that the partnership makes the maximum capital allowances claim.

Solution

	Total	Gustav	Melanie
	£	£	£
Partnership profit	60,000		
Less capital allowance on car £22,000 × 6% × 75%	(990)		

	Total £	Gustav £	Melanie £
Trade profits allocated to partners (3:2)	59,010	35,406	23,604

2.3 Change in partnership agreement

If the profit sharing agreement changes mid-way through the accounting period, first pro-rate the adjusted profit, then allocate the apportioned amounts in accordance with the applicable agreement for each part of the accounting period separately.

Activity 1: Change in partnership agreement

Ron and Steve have been in partnership since 1 July 2003 sharing profits and losses as follows:

	Ron	Steve
Salary	£5,000	£nil
Balance – profit share ratio	3	2

On 1 April 2021, the agreement was changed such that profits and losses are shared equally, with no further salary payments.

During y/e 30 June 2021 the partnership made a taxable trading profit of £60,000.

Required

Show how this is split between the partners.

Note. Remember, any salaries or interest on capital are allocated first, then the balance is split according to the profit-share ratio. In this case, the salary needs to be pro-rated as it ceased on 31 March.

Solution

2.4 The tax position of individual partners

Each partner is taxed like a sole trader who runs a business which:

- Starts when they join the partnership
- Finishes when they leave the partnership
- Has the same periods of account as the partnership (except that a partner who joins or leaves during a period will have a period which starts and/or ends part way through the partnership's period)
- Makes profits or losses equal to the partner's share of the partnership's profits or losses

Activity 2: Taxation of partners

You are responsible for the personal tax affairs of Ron and Steve (see the previous activity)

Required

In which tax year(s) will their allocated profit shares for the year ended 30 June 2021 be taxed?

- ○ 2020/21 only
- ○ 2021/22 only
- ○ 9/12 in 2020/21 and 3/12 in 2021/22
- ○ Both 2020/21 and 2021/22, creating overlap profits

Solution

2.5 Changes in partnership personnel

The partnership is always treated as continuing, but:

- Outgoing partner: Use cessation rules for evaluating their share of profits
- Existing partners: Continue on current year basis (CYB) rules
- New partner: Use opening year rules to evaluate their share of profits deemed to commence from date of joining, preparing accounts to the partnership's year end

Illustration 2: New partner (1)

Daniel and Ashley have been in partnership for many years preparing accounts to 31 December each year and sharing profits in the ratio 2:1.

On 1 June 2020, Kate joined the partnership. From that date, profits were shared Daniel 50% and Ashley and Kate 25% each.

The partnership profits for the year ended 31 December 2020 were £72,000 and for the year ended 31 December 2021 were £90,000.

Required

Compute the partnership profits taxable on Kate for 2020/21 and 2021/22 and her overlap profits on commencement.

Solution

Allocation of partnership profits

	Total	Daniel	Ashley	Kate
	£	£	£	£
y/e 31.12.20				
1.1.20–31.5.20				

	Total	Daniel	Ashley	Kate
	£	£	£	£
Profits (5/12) 2:1	30,000	20,000	10,000	n/a
1.6.20–31.2.20				
Profits (7/12) 50:25:25	42,000	21,000	10,500	10,500
Profit allocation	72,000	41,000	20,500	10,500
y/e 31.12.21	–			
Profits 50:25:25	90,000	45,000	22,500	22,500

Taxable partnership profits for Kate for 2020/21 and 2021/22

	Kate
	£
First year – actual basis	
1.6.20–31.12.20	10,500
1.1.21–5.4.21	
3/12 × £22,500	5,625
	16,125
2021/22	
Second year – 12 months to 31.12.21	22,500

Activity 3: New partner (2)

Meg and Gina began a partnership on 1 June 2008, sharing profits and losses equally. On 1 December 2018, Brett joined them, the new arrangement being 2:2:1. Results have been as follows:

Y/e 31.5.18	£33,000
Y/e 31.5.19	£51,000
Y/e 31.5.20	£72,000

Required

Show the assessments on the partners for the tax years 2018/19 to 2020/21. Show Brett's overlap profits

Solution

2.6 Summary - taxation of partnership profits

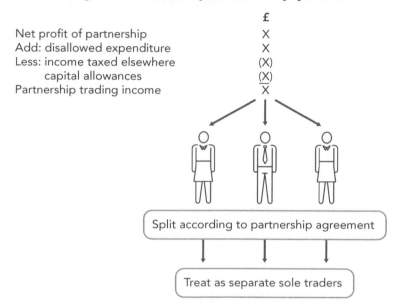

	£
Net profit of partnership	X
Add: disallowed expenditure	X
Less: income taxed elsewhere	(X)
capital allowances	(X)
Partnership trading income	X

Split according to partnership agreement

Treat as separate sole traders

3 Losses

Partners are entitled to the same loss reliefs as sole traders. The reliefs are:

- Carry forward against future trading profits.
- Set off against general income of the same and/or preceding year. This claim can be extended to set off against capital gains. The restriction on loss relief (see earlier in this Workbook) applies.
- For a new partner, losses in the first four tax years of trade, ie joining the partnership, can be set off against general income of the three preceding years. This is so even if the actual trade commenced many years before the partner joined.
- For a ceasing partner, terminal loss relief is available when they are treated as ceasing to trade. This is so even if the partnership continues to trade after they leave.

Different partners may claim loss reliefs in different ways.

> ### Exam focus point
>
> Partnership losses were tested in the December 2017 exam. The examining team commented that when allocating a partner's share of a partnership trading loss, candidates need to be very careful regarding dates and profit share percentages, in order to gain the relatively easy marks. Candidates must also remember that capital allowances are deducted before a profit or loss is allocated.

Activity 4: Partnership losses

James and Keith have been in partnership since 1 September 2002, sharing profits and losses in the ratio 3:2, after allocating a salary of £6,000 to James.

In y/e 31 August 2020, the partnership makes a loss of £30,000.

Required

1   How much of the trading loss will be allocated to James?

     O   £15,600

     O   £18,000

     O   £27,600

     O   £14,400

2   In what ways could James' loss be used?

Solution

Essential reading

Your Essential reading contains a more detailed example of the use of losses for different partners in a partnership.

The Essential reading is available as an Appendix of the digital edition of the Workbook.

---

4   New partnerships commencing

Profits and losses are allocated on the basis of the arrangement in force for the period of account when the profit or loss arose.

- Profits: these will be assessed under opening year rules
- Losses: the following options are available:
    - The loss can be relieved in the tax year in which the period ended and/or the previous tax year.
    - Under opening years loss relief: loss of the period will be carried back to the three tax years prior to the year when the loss-making period ended
    - If neither of the above are claimed or, for any losses remaining, set loss against first available future trading profits from the partnership.

Activity 5: New partnership

Abdul and Blake commence in partnership on 1 July 2019. They produce accounts to 31 December each year and their early results are as follows:

6 months to 31 December 2019 – £16,000 profit

Year ended 31 December 2020 – £20,000 loss

Profits were allocated to Abdul and Blake in the ratio 3:1 until 1 January 2020, from when they were split equally.

Required

Calculate the taxable trading profit for each partner for 2019/20 and 2020/21. Show how the loss incurred can be relieved.

Solution

Chapter summary

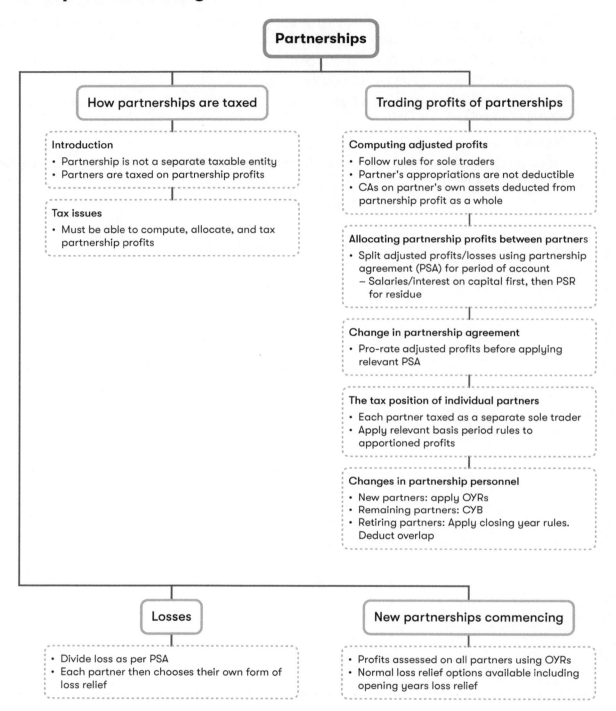

Partnerships

How partnerships are taxed

Introduction
- Partnership is not a separate taxable entity
- Partners are taxed on partnership profits

Tax issues
- Must be able to compute, allocate, and tax partnership profits

Trading profits of partnerships

Computing adjusted profits
- Follow rules for sole traders
- Partner's appropriations are not deductible
- CAs on partner's own assets deducted from partnership profit as a whole

Allocating partnership profits between partners
- Split adjusted profits/losses using partnership agreement (PSA) for period of account
  – Salaries/interest on capital first, then PSR for residue

Change in partnership agreement
- Pro-rate adjusted profits before applying relevant PSA

The tax position of individual partners
- Each partner taxed as a separate sole trader
- Apply relevant basis period rules to apportioned profits

Changes in partnership personnel
- New partners: apply OYRs
- Remaining partners: CYB
- Retiring partners: Apply closing year rules. Deduct overlap

Losses
- Divide loss as per PSA
- Each partner then chooses their own form of loss relief

New partnerships commencing
- Profits assessed on all partners using OYRs
- Normal loss relief options available including opening years loss relief

Knowledge diagnostic

1. How partnerships are taxed

A partnership is simply treated as a source of profits and losses for trades being carried on by the individual partners. Limited liability partnerships (LLPS) are treated in the same way as normal partnerships.

2. Trading profits

Divide adjusted profits or losses between the partners according to the profit-sharing arrangements in the period of account concerned. If any of the partners are entitled to a salary or interest on capital, apportion this first, not forgetting to pro-rate in periods of less than 12 months.

The relevant basis period rules are applied to each partner's share of the profits. Commencement and cessation rules apply to partners individually when they join or leave.

3. Losses

Losses are allocated in the same way as profits. Partners decide individually how to relieve their share of the loss.

4. New partnerships

Each partner is treated as commencing trade.

Further study guidance

Question practice

Now try the following from the Further question practice bank (available in the digital edition of the Workbook):

Section A: Q47, Q48, Q49

Section B: Q50 Anne, Betty and Chloe

Activity answers

Activity 1: Change in partnership agreement

	Ron £	Steve £	Total £
1.7.20–31.3.21			
(£45,000 to allocate (9/12 × £60,000))			
Salary (× 9/12)	3,750	–	3,750
Balance (3:2)	24,750	16,500	41,250 (bal)
	28,500	16,500	45,000
1.4.21–30.6.21			
(£15,000 to allocate (3/12 × £60,000))			
Balance (1:1)	7,500	7,500	15,000
Assessments	36,000	24,000	60,000

Activity 2: Taxation of partners

The correct answer is: 2021/22 only

Profits for an ongoing trader are assessed under the current year basis. The year ended 30 June 2021 ends in the tax year 2021/22.

Activity 3: New partner (2)

Sharing of profits

	Total £	M £	G £	B £
y/e 31.5.18 ie £33,000				
(1:1)	33,000	16,500	16,500	–
y/e 31.5.19 ie £51,000				
Up to 1.12.18 (1:1) 51,000 × 6/12	25,500	12,750	12,750	–
From 1.12.18 (2:2:1 each) 51,000 × 6/12	25,500	10,200	10,200	5,100
	51,000	22,950	22,950	5,100
y/e 31.5.20 ie £72,000				
(2:2:1)	72,000	28,800	28,800	14,400

New partner (B): Trading assessments

Started trading 1.12.18

6 months to 31.5.19:	£5,100
Year ended 31.5.20:	£14,400

2018/19 Actual basis 1.12.18–5.4.19

5,100 × 4/6 =	£3,400

2019/20 (1st 12 months) ie 1.12.18–30.11.19

ie £5,100 + 6/12 × £14,400 =	£12,300
2020/21 (y/e 31.5.20) ie 1.6.19–31.5.20:	£14,400

B's overlap profits

1.12.18–5.4.19 =	3,400
1.6.19–30.11.19 6/12 × £14,400 =	£7,200
Total (£3,400 + £7,200) =	£10,600

Existing partners: Trading assessments

	M	G
	£	£
2018/19 (y/e 31.5.18)	16,500	16,500
2019/20 (y/e 31.5.19)	22,950	22,950
2020/21 (y/e 31.5.20)	28,800	28,800

Activity 4: Partnership losses

1   The correct answer is: £15,600

	J	K	Total	
	£	£	£	
Salary	6,000	–	6,000	
Balance (3:2)	(21,600)	(14,400)	(36,000)	(bal)
Trading loss	(15,600)	(14,400)	(30,000)	

The answer £18,000 does not allocate the salary first so is just 3/5 × £30,000. The answer £27,600 increases the loss by the salary. The answer £14,400 is Kevin's loss.

2   The losses are available for use against total income (and then gains) in 2020/21 and/or 2019/20. Alternatively, the loss can be carried forward against the first available profits from the same trade.

Activity 5: New partnership

	Total	A	B
	£	£	£
Share of profits/losses:			
6m to 31.12.19 (3:1)	16,000	12,000	4,000
Year ended 31.12.20 (1:1)			

	Total	A	B
	£	£	£
	(20,000)	(10,000)	(10,000)

A's assessment

£

2019/20 actual (1.7.19–5.4.20)

£12,000 + 3/12 × (£10,000)   9,500

2020/21 CYB (y/e 31.12.20)   (10,000)

Less used in 19/20   2,500

         (7,500)

B's assessment

2019/20 Actual (1.7.19–5.4.20)

£4,000 + 3/12 × (£10,000)   1,500

2020/21 CYB (y/e 31.12.20)   (10,000)

Less used in 19/20   2,500

         (7,500)

Options:

(1) Current year claim against total income of 2020/21 and/or carry back against total income of 2019/20.

(2) Early year claim against total income of 2017/18, then 2018/19, then 2019/20.

(3) Carry forward against future trading profit from the same trade.

National insurance contributions

Learning objectives

On completion of this chapter, you should be able to:

	Syllabus reference no.
Explain and compute national insurance contributions payable:	
• Class 1 and 1A NIC	B6(a)(i)
• Class 2 and 4 NIC	B6(a)(ii)
Understand the annual employment allowance.	B6(b)

Exam context

National insurance contributions may be tested in Sections A or B or as part of a 15-mark or 10-mark question in Section C. You must be absolutely clear who is liable for which class of contributions; only employers, for example, pay Class 1A.

Chapter overview

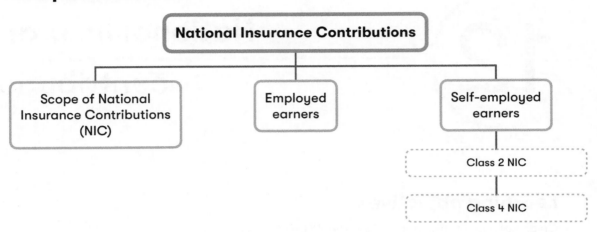

1 Scope of national insurance contributions (NIC)

Four main classes of national insurance contribution (NIC) exist, as set out below.

- **Class 1**. This is divided into:
  - Employee's Class 1, paid by employees
  - Employer's Class 1, Class 1A and Class 1B, paid by employers
- **Class 2**. Paid by the self-employed
- **Class 3**. Voluntary contributions (paid to maintain rights to certain state benefits)
- **Class 4**. Paid by the self-employed

Exam focus point

Class 1B and Class 3 contributions are outside the scope of your syllabus.

The National Insurance Contributions Office (NICO), which is part of HM Revenue & Customs (HMRC), examines employers' records and procedures to ensure that the correct amounts of NICs are collected.

2 Employed earners

Both **employees** and **employers** pay NICs related to the employee's earnings. NICs are not deductible from an employee's gross salary for income tax purposes. However, employers' contributions are deductible trade expenses. Class 1 Employee and Employer contributions are payable via the PAYE system described in Chapter 4 of this Workbook.

2.1 Class 1 Employee contributions

Contributions suffered by employees are calculated on cash earnings above £9,500 per year (the 'employee's threshold') for individuals over 16.

Employee's contributions are paid by the employee as follows:

- 12% on earnings between £9,500 and £50,000 (the 'upper earnings limit') per year
- 2% on earnings above £50,000 per year

Contributions cease when employee reaches state retirement age.

Exam focus point

There are different rules for employer's contributions if the employee is aged under 21 and for apprentices aged under 25. These rules are **not examinable** in Taxation (TX – UK). You should therefore assume that all employees are aged 25 or over in questions.

2.2 Class 1 Employer contributions

2.2.1 Employer contributions for each employee

Where the employee is aged 21 or over, employer contributions are paid on cash earnings above £8,788 per year but there is no upper limit for such earnings.

The rate is 13.8%.

Illustration 1: Class 1 Employee and Employer NIC

Sally works for Red plc. She is paid £4,800 per month.

Required

Show Sally's employee's Class 1 contributions and the employer's Class 1 contributions paid by Red plc for 2020/21. Ignore the employment allowance (see next section).

Solution

Employee's threshold £9,500

Employer's threshold £8,788

Upper earnings limit £50,000

Annual salary £4,800 × 12 = £57,600

	£
Sally	
Employee's contributions	
£50,000 − £9,500 = £40,500 × 12% (main)	4,860
£57,600 − £50,000 = £7,600 × 2% (additional)	152
Total employee's contributions	5,012
Red plc	
Employer's contributions	
£57,600 − £8,788 = £48,812 × 13.8%	6,736

2.2.2 Employment allowance

An employer can make a claim to reduce its total Class 1 employer's contributions by an employment allowance equal to those contributions, subject to a maximum allowance of £4,000 per tax year.

If the employer's Class 1 contribution would otherwise be less than £4,000 then the allowance will reduce the employer's Class 1 contributions to nil.

The employment allowance is not available to companies where a director is the sole employee (or where other employees are paid below the employer threshold), nor to any business whose total employer NIC liability in the previous tax year was over £100,000.

Activity 1: Employment allowance

Stoney Heap Ltd is a trading company which has two employees; one earns £38,000 per year and the other earns £15,000 per year. Each employee is paid in equal monthly amounts.

Required

How much employer's Class 1 contributions are payable by Stoney Heap Ltd for 2020/21?

○ £6,101

○ £4,888

○ £31

○ £888

Solution

2.3 Earnings and earnings periods

2.3.1 Definition of earnings

'Earnings' broadly comprise gross pay, excluding benefits which cannot be turned into cash by surrender (eg holidays).

Essential reading

Further detail on the definition of earnings for the purpose of Class 1 NICs can be found in the Essential reading.

The Essential reading is available as an Appendix of the digital edition of the Workbook.

2.3.2 Earnings periods

NICs are calculated in relation to an earnings period. This is the period to which earnings paid to an employee are deemed to relate. Where earnings are paid at regular intervals, the earnings period will generally be equated with the payment interval, for example a week or a month. An earnings period cannot usually be less than seven days long.

Exam focus point

In the exam NICs will generally be calculated on an annual basis.

Essential reading

An illustrative calculation of NIC for a monthly earnings period and detail relating to earnings periods for directors is contained in the Essential reading.

The Essential reading is available as an Appendix of the digital edition of the Workbook.

2.4 Class 1A contributions

The employer is required to pay Class 1A contributions for employees provided with taxable employment income benefits.

The contribution is calculated as 13.8% of the taxable benefit.

Class 1A contributions must be paid by 19 July (cheque)/22 July (electronically) following the end of the tax year.

Activity 2: Class 1 and 1A NIC

Tyrone is one of 3,000 employees of Taverner plc.

	£
Salary for 2020/21	52,000
Benefits per P11D	6,450

Required

1 What amount of national insurance contributions does Tyrone suffer in the tax year?

○ £4,860

○ £4,900

○ £5,029

○ £5,963

2 What amount of national insurance contributions does Taverner plc pay in relation to Tyrone?

○ £5,727

○ £5,963

○ £6,853

○ £8,066

Solution

3 Self-employed earners

3.1 Class 2 NIC

The self-employed are required to pay:

A flat rate contribution of £3.05 pw for those weeks trading if taxable trading profits exceed a small profits threshold for the tax year of £6,475.

Class 2 NIC is payable under the self-assessment system and is due for payment on 31 January following the tax year. Class 2 for the tax year 2020/21 is therefore due for payment on or before 31 January 2022.

3.2 Class 4 NIC

In addition, the self-employed pay Class 4 contributions which are profit related.

They are calculated as:

- 9% of 'profits' between £9,501 and £50,000
- 2% of 'profits' in excess of £50,000

Profits assessable to Class 4 NIC for a tax year are calculated in the same way as for income tax purposes (see the chapter Assessable trading income).

No contributions are payable if the taxpayer is older than state retirement age at the start of the tax year.

Class 4 NICs are collected by HMRC through the self-assessment system. They are paid at the same time as the associated income tax liability and so are part of payments on account and balancing payments. We look at the self-assessment system in detail later in this Workbook.

Activity 3: Class 2 and 4 NIC

Gunvald, a trader, has trading profits of £14,000 for 2020/21.

Required

1   Complete the following sentence:

Gunvald's Class 2 NIC contributions are £ [   ] and his Class 4 contributions are

£ [   ] for 2020/21.

2   What would Gunvald's Class 4 contributions be if his profits were £52,000 for 2020/21?

   O   £3,645

   O   £3,685

   O   £3,844

   O   £4,900

Solution

Chapter summary

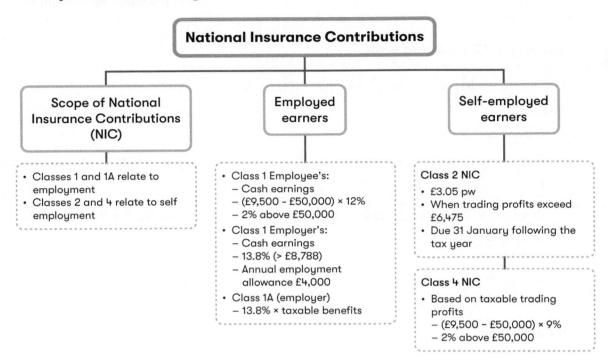

National Insurance Contributions

Scope of National Insurance Contributions (NIC)

- Classes 1 and 1A relate to employment
- Classes 2 and 4 relate to self employment

Employed earners

- Class 1 Employee's:
  - Cash earnings
  - (£9,500 - £50,000) × 12%
  - 2% above £50,000
- Class 1 Employer's:
  - Cash earnings
  - 13.8% (> £8,788)
  - Annual employment allowance £4,000
- Class 1A (employer)
  - 13.8% × taxable benefits

Self-employed earners

Class 2 NIC
- £3.05 pw
- When trading profits exceed £6,475
- Due 31 January following the tax year

Class 4 NIC
- Based on taxable trading profits
  - (£9,500 - £50,000) × 9%
  - 2% above £50,000

Knowledge diagnostic

1. Employed earners

Class 1 is calculated on cash earnings and is suffered by employees and employers. Class 1A is on benefits provided to employees and is payable by employers.

The employment allowance enables an employer to reduce its total Class 1 employer's contributions by up to £4,000 per tax year.

2. Self-employed earners

The self-employed pay Class 2 and Class 4 NICs. Class 2 NICs are paid at a flat weekly rate. Class 4 NICs are based on the level of the individual's profits.

Further study guidance

Question practice

Now try the following from the Further question practice bank (available in the digital edition of the Workbook):

Section A: Q51, Q52 and Q53

Section B: Q54 Derek and Denise

Section C: Q55 Sasha

Further reading

The ACCA article called *Motor cars* explains the implications of acquiring, running, or having the use of a motor car for income tax, corporation tax, value added tax (VAT) and national insurance contribution (NIC).

You are strongly advised to read this article in full as part of your preparation for the TX exam.

Activity answers

Activity 1: Employment allowance

The correct answer is: £888

	£
Employee 1: (£38,000 − £8,788) × 13.8%	4,031
Employee 2: (£15,000 − £8,788) × 13.8%	857
	4,888
Less employment allowance (maximum)	(4,000)
Employer's contributions	888

The answer £6,101 adds the earnings together and then deducts the threshold and does not deduct the employment allowance. The answer £4,888 does not deduct the employment allowance. The answer £31 assumes that an employment allowance is available for each employee.

Activity 2: Class 1 and 1A NIC

1 The correct answer is: £4,900

Tyrone suffers Class 1 employee's contributions on his cash earnings.

Employee's contributions	£
£50,000 − £9,500 = £40,500 × 12% (main)	4,860
£52,000 − £50,000 = £2,000 × 2% (additional)	40
	4,900

The answer £4,860 is the liability up to the upper earnings limit. The answer £5,029 includes the benefits. The answer £5,963 is the employer's Class 1 NIC.

2 The correct answer is: £6,853

Employer's contributions	£
Class 1: (£52,000 − £8,788) × 13.8%	5,963
Class 1A: £6,450 × 13.8%	890
	6,853

The answer £5,727 applies the upper earnings limit and does not include Class 1A. The answer £5,963 does not include Class 1A. The answer £8,066 does not apply the threshold.

Activity 3: Class 2 and 4 NIC

1 Gunvald's Class 2 NIC contributions are £ 159 and his Class 4 contributions are £ 405 for 2020/21.

Class 2: £3.05 × 52 = £159

Class 4: (£14,000 - £9,500) × 9% = £405

2 The correct answer is: £3,685

Class 4 contributions	£
£50,000 − £9,500 = £40,500 × 9%	3,645
£52,000 − £50,000 = £2,000 × 2%	40
	3,685

£3,645 includes only the main rate (9%) NIC. £3,844 is the total NIC payable, including Class 2. £4,900 uses the Class 1 Employee rate of 12% instead of 9%.

13 Computing chargeable gains

Learning objectives

On completion of this chapter, you should be able to:

	Syllabus reference no.
Describe the scope of capital gains tax.	C1(a)
Recognise those assets which are exempt.	C1(b)
Compute and explain the treatment of capital gains.	C2(a)
Compute and explain the treatment of capital losses.	C2(b)
Understand the treatment of transfers between a married couple or between a couple in a civil partnership.	C2(c)
Understand the amount of allowable expenditure for a part disposal.	C2(d)
Recognise the treatment where an asset is damaged, lost or destroyed, and the implications of receiving insurance proceeds and reinvesting such proceeds.	C2(e)
Compute the amount of capital gains tax payable.	C5(a)
Basic capital gains tax planning.	C6(b)

Exam context

Section A questions on the topics in this chapter may include dealing with losses or computing the amount of capital gains tax payable. You may have to deal with a number of disposals in a Section B question. You might have to prepare a detailed capital gains computation for either an individual or company in Section C. Learn the basic layout, so that slotting in the figures becomes automatic. Then in the exam you will be able to turn your attention to the particular points raised in the question. The A/(A+B) formula for part disposals must be learnt.

Chapter overview

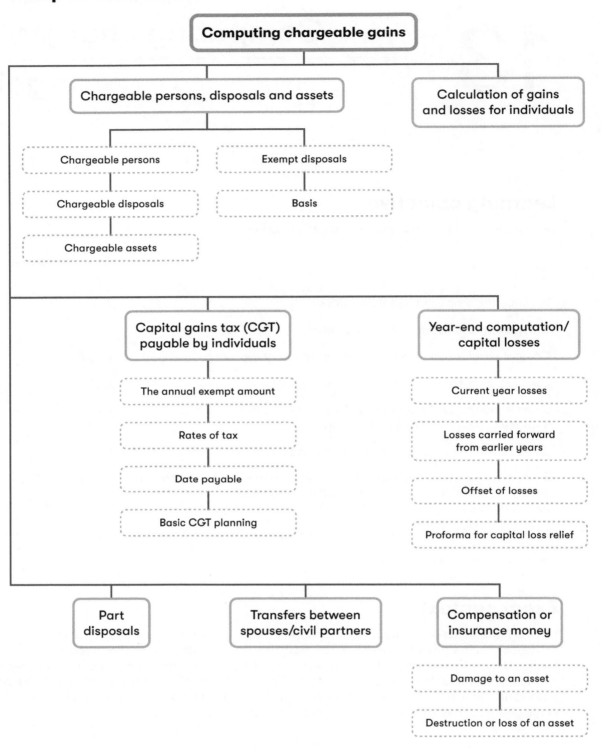

Computing chargeable gains

- Chargeable persons, disposals and assets
  - Chargeable persons
  - Chargeable disposals
  - Chargeable assets
  - Exempt disposals
  - Basis
- Calculation of gains and losses for individuals

- Capital gains tax (CGT) payable by individuals
  - The annual exempt amount
  - Rates of tax
  - Date payable
  - Basic CGT planning
- Year-end computation/ capital losses
  - Current year losses
  - Losses carried forward from earlier years
  - Offset of losses
  - Proforma for capital loss relief

- Part disposals
- Transfers between spouses/civil partners
- Compensation or insurance money
  - Damage to an asset
  - Destruction or loss of an asset

1 Chargeable persons, disposals and assets

> **KEY TERM**
>
> **Chargeable gain:** For a chargeable gain to arise there must be:
> - A **chargeable person**; and
> - A **chargeable disposal**; and
> - A **chargeable asset**
>
> Otherwise no charge to tax occurs.

Chargeable gains arise if there is a **chargeable disposal** of a **chargeable asset** by a **chargeable person.**

1.1 Chargeable persons

Capital gains are chargeable on individuals and companies.

Individuals resident in the UK (see Chapter 2) pay **capital gains tax** on **net chargeable gains** (and are chargeable persons in relation to the disposal of assets situated anywhere in the world).

Companies pay **corporation tax** on **net chargeable gains** (see later in this Workbook).

1.2 Chargeable disposals

These are:
- Sales of assets or parts of assets
- Gifts of assets or parts of assets
- Loss or destruction of assets

1.2.1 Chargeable disposal dates

A chargeable disposal occurs on the date of the contract (where there is one, whether written or oral), or the date of a conditional contract becoming unconditional. This may differ from the date of transfer of the asset. However, when a capital sum is received for example on the loss or destruction of an asset, the disposal takes place on the day the sum is received.

Where a disposal involves an acquisition by someone else, the date of acquisition for that person is the same as the date of disposal.

1.3 Chargeable assets

All assets are chargeable assets, wherever they are in the world, unless they are exempt.

1.4 Exempt disposals

- Transfers of assets on death
- Gifts to charities

The following assets are exempt from capital gains tax:
(a) Cars (suitable for private use)
(b) Gilt-edged securities (treasury stock)
(c) Qualifying corporate bonds (QCB)
(d) Wasting chattels (greyhounds, racehorses)
(e) Currency for personal use
(f) Medals awarded for valour or inherited (not if purchased)
(g) Gold sovereigns minted after 1837
(h) National Savings Certificates and premium bonds
(i) Gambling winnings
(j) Inventory and other current assets
(k) Investments held in individual savings accounts (ISAs)
(l) Damages for personal or professional injury

1.5 Basis

Tax is on **net gains** arising from disposals in the current tax year.

2 Calculation of gains and losses for individuals

Computation of gains and losses:

	£
Gross proceeds	X
Less incidental costs of disposal	(X)
Net proceeds	X
Less: cost	(X)
enhancement expenditure	(X)
Chargeable gain/(allowable loss)	X/(X)

Enhancement expenditure is capital expenditure which enhances the value of the asset and is reflected in the state or nature of the asset at the time of disposal, or expenditure incurred in establishing, preserving or defending title to, or a right over, the asset. Excluded from this category are:

- Costs of repairs and maintenance
- Costs of insurance
- Any expenditure deductible from trading profits
- Any expenditure met by public funds (eg council grants)

Essential reading

See Chapter 13 Section 1 of the Essential reading for more detail on computing a gain or loss.

The Essential reading is available as an Appendix of the digital edition of the Workbook.

Activity 1: Calculating a gain

Goran sold a workshop in July 2020 for £83,000. He had bought it for £15,000 in 2000. Solicitors' fees were 5% of the consideration at both sale and purchase. In 2004, Goran spent £8,000 on an extension to the workshop. In 2006, he spent £4,000 on legal fees while defending his legal title to the land. In 2009, Goran spent £12,000 on a second extension which was subsequently demolished. A total of £2,300 has been spent on repairs to the workshop between 2000 and 2020. Goran never used the workshop himself as it was always let out to a local mechanic.

Required

What is Goran's chargeable gain?

Solution

---

3 Capital gains tax (CGT) payable by individuals

PER alert

One of the competencies you require to fulfil Performance Objective 15 *Tax computations and assessments* of the PER is to prepare or contribute to the computation or assessment of tax computations for individuals. You can apply the knowledge you obtain from this section of the Workbook to help to demonstrate this competence.

3.1 The annual exempt amount

Individuals have an annual exempt amount of £12,300 for 2020/21 which means that the first £12,300 of chargeable gains made by the individual in the tax year are not taxable.

The annual exempt amount is deducted from the **chargeable gains** for the year after the deduction of current year losses and other reliefs. The resulting amount is the individual's **taxable gains.**

3.2 Rates of tax

Gains above the annual exempt amount are taxed at 10% if they fall into any remaining basic rate (BR) band and 20% where they exceed this threshold. The same basic and higher rate limits are used for CGT as for income tax. This includes any increases due to gift aid and/or personal pension contributions.

Taxable gains on residential property are taxed at 18% (basic rate) and 28% (higher/additional rate). As far as possible the annual exempt amount should be used to reduce gains on residential property.

Illustration 1: Rates of CGT

Mo has taxable non-savings income of £28,130 in 2020/21. He made personal pension contributions of £242 (net) per month during 2020/21. In December 2020, he makes a chargeable gain of £29,900 on the disposal of some shares. The gain does not qualify for business asset disposal relief (see Chapter 15 in this Workbook).

Required

Calculate the CGT payable by Mo for 2020/21.

Solution

	£
Chargeable gain	29,900
Less annual exempt amount	

	£
	(12,300)
Taxable gain	17,600

Basic rate limit	37,500
Add personal pension contributions £242 × 12 = £2,904 × 100/80	3,630
Increased basic rate limit	41,130
CGT	
£(41,130 − 28,130) = £13,000 @ 10%	1,300
£(17,600 − 13,000) = £4,600 @ 20%	920
Total CGT payable	2,220

Illustration 2: Rates of CGT on mixture of gains

Fran has taxable income of £28,500 in 2020/21. In August 2020, she makes a chargeable gain of £15,500 on the sale of some shares. In March 2021, she makes a chargeable gain of £19,900 on the disposal of a residential property which is not covered by private residence relief (see Chapter 14 in the Workbook).

Required
Calculate the CGT payable by Fran for 2020/21.

Solution

	Other gain	Residential property
	£	£
Shares	15,500	
Residential property		19,900
Less annual exempt amount (best use)	−	(12,300)
Taxable gains	15,500	7,600
CGT		
If tax residential property gain first		
£7,600 @ 18%		1,368
£1,400 (37,500 − 28,500 − 7,600) @ 10%		140
£14,100 (15,500 − 1,400) @ 20%		2,820
Total CGT		4,328
If tax other gain first		
£9,000 (37,500 − 28,500) @ 10%		900
£6,500 (15,500 − 9,000) @ 20%		1,300
£7,600 @ 28%		2,128

	Other gain	Residential property
Total CGT		4,328

Activity 2: Capital gains tax liability

In the tax year 2020/21, Thomas has net income of £27,350 and realises a chargeable gain of £23,000 on the disposal of a painting and a gain of £55,600 on the disposal of a house which he used to let out to tenants.

Required

Calculate Thomas's capital gains tax liability in 2020/21.

Solution

Exam focus point

In the exam, **you only need to compute the CGT payable one way,** eg residential property gains then other gains. It is **not necessary** to show that the same amount of CGT is payable if the gains are taxed the other way around.

3.3 Date payable

Unless the disposal is a residential property, CGT is payable on 31 January after the end of the tax year of disposal (ie **31 January 2022 for disposals in 2020/21**).

For disposals of **residential property**, a **payment on account** must be made to HMRC **within 30 days of the disposal,** along with **a return**. For example, if the disposal of the residential property is on 31 July, then a payment on account must be made by 30 August.

The payment on account takes account of:

- Annual exempt amount
- Capital losses during same tax year only up to the date of the residential property disposal
- Brought forward capital losses

Illustration 3: Payment on account

Jo is a higher rate tax payer who had the following chargeable gains and capital losses during 2020/21:

1 May 2020	Chargeable gain of £40,000
24 June 2020	Capital loss of £15,000
30 November 2020	Chargeable gain on residential property of £94,000
5 January 2021	Capital loss of £10,000

Required

How much is the payment on account and when will it be due?

Solution

	£
Residential property gain	94,000
Capital loss 24 June 2020	(15,000)
Annual exempt amount	(12,300)
	66,700

Payment on account = £66,700 × 28% = £18,676

Due date: 30 December 2020

Note that the payment on account calculation relies on estimating whether there will be any basic rate band available for the tax year. The residential property gain is included on the self assessment return with a deduction for the payment on account.

Any additional tax is payable on 31 January following the tax year (ie 31 January 2022 for tax year 2020/21). If a refund is due, this is claimed via the self-assessment.

Illustration 4: Additional CGT due

Following on from the illustration above, how much CGT would be payable on 31 January 2022?

Solution

	£
Residential property gain	94,000
Capital losses (£15,000 + £10,000)	(25,000)
Annual exempt amount	(12,300)
	56,700
Other gain	40,000
Capital gains tax: £56,700 × 28%	15,876

	£
£40,000 × 20%	8,000
	23,876
Less payment on account	(18,676)
Amount due on 31 January 2022	5,200

Note that the capital losses and the annual exempt amount have been offset against the residential property as this saves CGT at a higher rate (residential property rate of 28% instead of 20%).

3.4 Basic CGT planning

Basic CGT planning usually involves three considerations.

The first consideration is that an individual should make use of the annual exempt amount. For example, if there is a gain which already uses the annual exempt amount in the tax year, it may be advisable to delay making another gain until the next tax year.

The second consideration is the rate of tax in relation to the individual's taxable income. Where possible, gains should be made in the tax year in which the individual has the lowest amount of taxable income, in particular where they have part of the basic rate band unused.

The third consideration is the timing of the payment of CGT. It may be better to make a gain early in a tax year rather than late in a tax year to give the longest gap between receiving the proceeds and paying the tax due.

4 Year-end computation/capital losses

4.1 Current year losses

Current year losses must be offset against current year gains. The annual exempt amount is then deducted from any remaining gain.

An individual who has gains taxable at more than one rate of tax may deduct any allowable losses in the way that produces the lowest possible tax charge.

4.2 Losses carried forward from earlier years

Where current year losses exceed current year gains the net current loss is carried forward to offset against future capital gains remaining **after** the annual exempt amount.

Where losses are brought forward from earlier years, they need only be used to the extent needed to bring the gains down zero after the application of the annual exempt amount.

4.3 Offset of losses

Losses should be offset against gains on residential property before those relating to other disposals.

4.4 Proforma for capital loss relief

	Total	
Gains	X	
Current year losses	(X)	1
Less annual exempt amount	(12,300)	2
	X	

	Total	
Less brought forward losses *	(X)	3
Taxable gains	X	

* any unutilised brought forward losses will be carried forward to be offset in future years.

Unused annual exempt amounts cannot be carried forward.

4.5 Examples - the use of losses

(a) George has gains for 2020/21 of £13,000 and allowable losses of £6,000. As the losses are current year losses, they must be fully relieved against the £13,000 of gains to produce net gains of £7,000 despite the fact that net gains are below the annual exempt amount.

(b) Bob has gains of £15,900 for 2020/21 and allowable losses brought forward of £6,000. Bob will deduct the annual exempt amount of £12,300 for 2020/21 leaving gains of (£15,900 – £12,300) = £3,600. This amount of the brought forward loss will be set off to reduce the taxable gains to nil. The remaining loss of (£6,000 – £3,600) = £2,400 will be carried forward to 2021/22.

(c) Tom has gains of £11,500 for 2020/21 and losses brought forward from 2019/20 of £4,000. He will not use any of his brought forward losses in 2020/21 and instead will carry forward all of his losses to 2021/22. His gains of £11,500 are covered by his annual exempt amount for 2020/21.

Activity 3: Losses

In 2020/21 Ted makes a gain of £25,000 on some shares he held as an investment and a gain of £10,000 on a residential property, and a capital loss of £12,000 on another. He also has a capital loss brought forward of £31,000.

Required

1   What is Ted's taxable gain for 2020/21 and the capital loss carried forward to 2021/22?

2   What would the answer to requirement 1 have been if the £31,000 loss had been a current year loss and the £12,000 loss had been a brought forward loss?

Solution

5 Part disposals

When only part of an asset is sold, the original cost of the whole asset needs to be split up.

The gain on the part disposed of is calculated as follows:

	£
Proceeds of part disposal	A
Less selling costs	(X)
	X

Less:

$$\text{Original cost of whole asset} \times \frac{A}{A+B} \qquad (C)$$

Chargeable gain	X

A = MV of the part disposed of (ie **gross** proceeds)

B = MV of the remainder of the asset (you will be given in question)

Illustration 5: Part disposal

Hedley owns a four hectare plot of land which originally cost him £150,000. He sold one hectare in July 2020 for £60,000. The incidental costs of sale were £3,000. The market value of the three hectares remaining is estimated to be £180,000.

Required

What is the gain on the sale of the one hectare?

Solution

The amount of the cost attributable to the part sold is:

$$\frac{60,000}{60,000 + 180,000} \times £150,000 = £37,500$$

	£
Proceeds	60,000
Less disposal cost	(3,000)
Net proceeds of sale	57,000
Less cost (see above)	(37,500)
Gain	19,500

Activity 4: Chargeable gain

Fred sells two paintings for £40,000 on 7 September 2020 from a set of four that cost £30,000 eight years ago. He suffers 10% auctioneer's fees. The market value of the remaining two paintings is £35,000.

Required

What is the chargeable gain arising on disposal of the two paintings?

○ £21,000

○ £20,000

○ £24,000

○ £20,789

Solution

---

6 Transfers between spouses/civil partners

Individuals are taxed separately from their spouses/civil partners. Each has an individual annual exempt amount which **cannot** be transferred to the other spouse/civil partner.

Transfers of assets between spouses/civil partners are on a **no gain/no loss basis**.

The base cost of the asset is transferred to the recipient spouse/civil partner.

Since transfers between spouses/civil partners are on a no gain no loss basis, it may be beneficial to transfer the whole or part of an asset to the spouse/civil partner with an unused annual exempt amount or with taxable income below the basic rate limit.

 ### Illustration 6: Inter spouse transfer

Harry is a higher rate taxpayer who always makes gains of at least £20,000 each year on disposals of investments. His wife, Margaret, has taxable income of £7,630 each year and has no chargeable assets.

Harry bought a plot of land for £150,000 in 2016. He gave it to Margaret when it was worth £180,000 on 10 May 2019. Margaret sold it on 27 August 2020 for £190,000. The land does not qualify for business asset disposal relief and is not residential property.

Required

Calculate any chargeable gains arising to Harry and Margaret and show the tax saving arising from the transfer between Harry and Margaret, followed by the disposal by Margaret, instead of a disposal in August 2020 by Harry.

Solution

The disposal from Harry to Margaret in May 2019 is a no gain no loss disposal. Harry has no chargeable gain, and the cost for Margaret is Harry's original cost.

The gain on the sale by Margaret in August 2020 is:

	£
Proceeds of sale	190,000
Less cost	(150,000)

	£
Gain	40,000

If Harry had made the disposal in August 2020, the whole of the gain would have been taxed at 20%.

Margaret's gain will be reduced by her annual exempt amount, saving tax at 20% on that amount compared with the situation where Harry makes the disposal.

Margaret also has £37,500 – £7,630 = £29,870 of her basic rate band remaining. She will be taxed at 10% on the gain within the basic rate band, instead of 20% if Harry makes the disposal.

The tax saving is therefore:

	£
Tax saved on annual exempt amount £12,300 @ 20%	2,460
Tax saved at basic rate £(40,000 – 12,300) = £27,700 @ (20 – 10)%	2,770
Tax saving on disposal by Margaret instead of Harry	5,230

Activity 5: Chargeable gain after spouse transfer

Julie bought an antique table for £8,000 in January 1987. In August 1993, she transferred the table to her husband Joseph when its market value was £10,000.

Joseph subsequently sold the table at the end of October 2020 for £20,000.

Required

What is Joseph's chargeable gain?

Solution

7 Compensation or insurance money

7.1 Damage to an asset

If an asset is damaged and compensation or insurance money is received, this is treated as a part disposal with the compensation as the proceeds.

$\dfrac{A}{(A + B)}$ applies where

A = compensation received

B = unrestored value of asset

If all of the compensation is applied in restoring the asset, the taxpayer can elect to disregard the part disposal. The proceeds are then deducted from the cost of the asset.

Illustration 7: Asset damaged

Frank bought an investment property for £100,000 in May 2020. It was damaged two and a half months later. Insurance proceeds of £20,000 were received in November 2020, and Frank spent a total of £25,000 on restoring the property. Prior to restoration the property was worth £120,000.

Required

Compute the gain immediately chargeable, if any, and the base cost of the restored property assuming Frank elects for there to be no part disposal.

How would your answer differ if no election were made?

Solution

As the proceeds have been applied in restoring the property Frank could elect to disregard the part disposal and there would therefore be no gain chargeable.

The base cost of the restored property is £(100,000 - 20,000 + 25,000) = £105,000.

If no election were made, the receipt of the proceeds would be a part disposal in November 2020:

	£
Proceeds	20,000
Less cost £100,000 × 20,000/(20,000 + 120,000)	(14,286)
Gain	5,714

The base cost of the restored asset is £100,000 – £14,286 + £25,000 = £110,714.

Assuming this is Frank's only disposal in the tax year, the gain is covered by the annual exempt amount. It may therefore be preferable not to make the election so that he has a higher base cost for future disposals.

Activity 6: Damaged property

Amandine bought a holiday cottage for £40,000 in August 1992. In August 2002, the cottage was damaged in a fire. An insurance claim was made and £33,000 was received in September 2002. The cottage was valued at £45,000 after the fire.

In December 2002 Amandine put £37,000 into restoring the cottage. She then sold the cottage for £95,000 in the current tax year.

Required

1   Calculate the gain arising assuming Amandine elects for there to be no part disposal.

2   How would your answer differ if no election were made?

Solution

7.2 Destruction or loss of an asset

- If an asset is completely destroyed, there is a 'full' disposal and compensation monies are wholly charged to CGT.
- If the compensation receipts are reinvested in a replacement asset within 12 months, a form of 'rollover' relief is available. The gain is calculated and the difference between the amount received and amount reinvested is taxable now. The remainder can be rolled over and reduces the base cost of the asset by that amount.
- The 'replacement' asset should be within the scope of CGT and must be of similar function and type to the original asset.

 Illustration 8: Asset destroyed

Fiona bought a painting for £25,000. It was destroyed in July 2020. Insurance proceeds were £34,000, and Fiona spent £30,500 on a replacement painting in January 2021.

Required

Compute the gain immediately chargeable and the base cost of the new painting.

Solution

	£
Proceeds	34,000
Less cost	(25,000)
Gain	9,000
Gain immediately chargeable (£34,000 - £30,500)	(3,500)
Deduction from base cost	5,500

The base cost of the new painting is £30,500 - £5,500 = £25,000.

Activity 7: Chargeable gain and base cost

Jeff bought a painting for £30,000 in 2000. It was completely destroyed in August of the current tax year. Jeff received insurance proceeds of £40,000 a month later and spent £36,000 on a replacement asset a month after that.

Required

Compute the chargeable gain and the base cost of the new asset.

Solution

Chapter summary

Computing chargeable gains

Chargeable persons, disposals and assets

Chargeable persons
- Individuals
- Companies

Chargeable disposals
- Sale of asset
- Gift of asset (@MV)
- Loss or destruction (compensation)

Chargeable assets
- All assets unless exempt

Exempt disposals
- Cars
- Wasting chattels
- National savings certificates
- ISAs
- Gambling winnings
- Gilt-edged securities (treasury stock)
- Qualifying corporate bonds

Basis
- Tax on net gains from disposals during the current tax year

Calculation of gains and losses for individuals

Gross proceeds	X
Less incidental costs of disposal	(X)
Net proceeds	X
Less cost	(X)
Less enhancement expenditure	(X)
Chargeable gain/ (allowable loss)	X

Capital gains tax (CGT) payable by individuals

The annual exempt amount
- £12,300 for 2020/21

Rates of tax
- Tax at 10%/20%
- 18%/28% on residential property
- Tax at 10% gains qualifying for business asset disposal relief
- Annual exempt amount reduces taxable gains. Set off against highest taxed gains first

Date payable
- 31 January 2022 (for disposals in 2020/21)
- Residential property - POA and return due within 30 days of disposal

Basic CGT planning
- Make use of AEA, eg delay second gain
- Make gains in year where individual has lowest amount of taxable income
- Consider timing giving longest gap between receiving proceeds and paying tax due

Year-end computation/ capital losses

Current year losses
- Offset current year losses before annual exempt amount
- Current year losses set against current year gains automatically
- Excess carried forward

Losses carried forward from earlier years
- Set off after annual exempt amount

Offset of losses
- Offset against gains on residential property before those relating to other disposals

Proforma for capital loss relief

Gains	X
Current year losses	(X)
Less annual exempt amount	(12,300)
	X
Less b/f losses	(X)
Taxable gains	X

```
                                    |
    +-------------------------------+-------------------------------+
    |                               |                               |
+----------+              +------------------+           +------------------+
|  Part    |              | Transfers between|           | Compensation or  |
| disposals|              | spouses/civil    |           | insurance money  |
|          |              | partners         |           |                  |
+----------+              +------------------+           +------------------+
```

Part disposals

- Cost × A/(A+B)
- Where
  - A = disposed MV of part
  - B = MV of remainder

Transfers between spouses/civil partners

- Nil gain/Nil loss transfers

Compensation or insurance money

Damage to an asset
- Treat as part disposal using A/(A+B) where
  A = compensation,
  B = unrestored value of asset

Destruction or loss of an asset
- Full disposal – can rollover gain if compensation is reinvested in replacement asset within 12 months

Knowledge diagnostic

1. Chargeable persons, disposals and assets

Chargeable gains arise when there is a chargeable disposal of a chargeable asset by a chargeable person.

2. Calculation of gains and losses

Make sure you can compute an individual's gain or loss using the proforma.

3. CGT payable by individuals

An individual is entitled to an annual exempt amount each tax year.

Rates of tax depend on an individual's taxable income and the type of asset.

Lower rate of 10% if gains fall into any remaining BR band (18% if residential property).

Higher rate of 20% if gains above BR band (28% if residential property).

4. Year-end computation/capital losses

Losses are offset against gains. Brought forward capital losses are deducted after the annual exempt amount.

5. Part disposals

A/(A + B) is used to determine the cost when there is a part disposal.

6. Transfers between married couples and civil partners

Transfers between married couples or members of a civil partnership are made at no gain/no loss.

7. Compensation or insurance money

A damaged asset is treated as a part disposal.

When an asset is destroyed a form of rollover relief is available if a replacement asset is purchased within 12 months.

Further study guidance

Question practice

Now try the following from the Further question practice bank (available in the digital edition of the Workbook):

Section A questions:

Q56 Q57 Q58

Section C question:

Q59 Peter

Further reading

There are two technical articles available on ACCA's website, called *Chargeable gains*, *Parts 1 and 2*. Part 1 looks at chargeable gains in either a personal or corporate context. Part 2 focuses on shares, reliefs, and the way in which gains made by limited companies are taxed.

You are strongly advised to read these articles in full as part of your preparation for the TX exam.

Activity answers

Activity 1: Calculating a gain

	£
Gross sale proceeds:	83,000
solicitor's fee re sale (5%)	(4,150)
cost including solicitor's fee re purchase (5%)	(15,750)
enhancement – first extension	(8,000)
Enhancement (defence of title)	(4,000)
Enhancement (second extension now demolished)	(–)
Repairs (not capital – relievable against property income)	(–)
Chargeable gain	51,100

Activity 2: Capital gains tax liability

	£
Net income	27,350
Personal allowance	(12,500)
Taxable income	14,850

BRB remaining = £37,500 – £14,850 = £22,650.

	Residential property	Painting
	£	£
Chargeable gains	55,600	23,000
Annual exempt amount	(12,300)	(0)
Taxable gain	43,300	23,000

CGT payable		£
£22,650 × 18%		4,077
20,650 × 28%		5,782
£43,300		
£23,000 × 20% =		4,600
		14,459

Alternatively:

CGT payable	£
£22,650 × 10%	2,265
£350 × 20%	70

CGT payable

	£
£23,000	
£43,300 × 28% =	12,124
	14,459

Activity 3: Losses

1

	Property £	Other £
Gain	10,000	25,000
Current year loss (must be deducted in full)	(10,000)	(2,000)
Annual exempt amount	NIL	(12,300)
		10,700
Brought forward losses		(10,700)
Taxable gain		NIL
Capital loss brought forward		31,000
Utilised in 2020/21		(10,700)
Capital loss carried forward		20,300

2

	Property £	Other £
Gain	10,000	25,000
Current year loss	(10,000)	(21,000)
	NIL	4,000
Annual exempt amount		(4,000)
Brought forward loss		(–)
Taxable gain		NIL
Capital loss brought forward		12,000
Utilised in 2020/21		(–)
Capital loss carried forward		12,000

Activity 4: Chargeable gain

The correct answer is: £20,000

	£
Proceeds	40,000
Less selling expenses	(4,000)
	36,000

$$\text{Cost } 30{,}000 \times \frac{40}{40 + 35}$$ (16,000)

| Chargeable gain | 20,000 |

The answer £21,000 apportions the cost by the number of paintings, not their values. The answer £24,000 does not deduct the selling expenses. The answer £20,789 deducts the selling expenses in the part disposal fraction.

Activity 5: Chargeable gain after spouse transfer

Transfer Julie to Joseph = NG/NL

	£
ie cost = Deemed proceeds	8,000

Disposal by Joseph	
Proceeds	20,000
Less cost (deemed proceeds)	(8,000)
Chargeable gain	12,000

Activity 6: Damaged property

1   As all of the compensation received has been used to restore the asset Amandine can elect to disregard the part disposal.

Base cost of restored property is (£40,000 − £33,000 + £37,000) = £44,000

Current tax year	£
Proceeds	95,000
Base cost	(44,000)
Chargeable gain	51,000

2   Tax year 2002/03

	£
Compensation received	33,000

$$\text{Cost } 40{,}000 \times \frac{33{,}000}{33{,}000 + 45{,}000}$$ (16,923)

| | 16,077 |

Current tax year

	£
Proceeds	95,000
Cost (£40,000 − £16,923)	(23,077)
Restoration	(37,000)
Chargeable gain	34,923

Activity 7: Chargeable gain and base cost

Current tax year	£
Proceeds	40,000
Cost	(30,000)
	10,000
Gain chargeable (£40,000 − £36,000)	(4,000)
Deduction from base cost	6,000

Base cost of replacement asset (£36,000 − £6,000) = £30,000

14

Chattels and the private residence relief

Learning objectives

On completion of this chapter, you should be able to:

	Syllabus reference no.
Identify when chattels and wasting assets are exempt.	C3(a)
Compute the chargeable gain when a chattel or a wasting asset is disposed of.	C3(b)
Calculate the chargeable gain when a principal private residence is disposed of.	C3(c)
Basic capital gains tax planning.	C6(b)

Exam context

You are quite likely to come across a question on either chattels or the reliefs available on the disposal of a private residence in any of Sections A, B or C.

With chattels always look for the exemption for wasting chattels, a restriction of the gain if proceeds exceed £6,000, or a restriction of loss relief if proceeds are less than £6,000. The rules for chattels apply to companies as well as individuals, but watch out for assets on which capital allowances have been given.

On the disposal of a private residence, if there has been any non-occupation or business use, make a schedule of the relevant dates before you start to calculate the gain in case it turns out to be wholly exempt.

Chapter overview

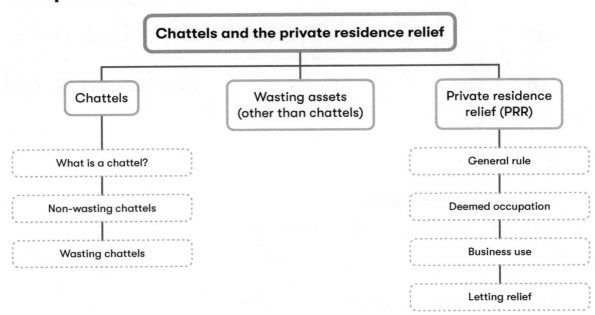

1 Chattels

1.1 What is a chattel?

> **Chattel:** A chattel is tangible moveable property.
>
> **Wasting asset:** A **wasting asset** is an asset with an estimated remaining useful life of 50 years or less.

1.2 Non-wasting chattels

The expected life of non-wasting chattels from date of disposal > 50 years.

Non-wasting chattels are chargeable to capital gains tax (CGT) in the normal way, subject to the following exception/restrictions:

	Original cost £	Gross proceeds £	Treatment	Technique
(a)	< 6,000	< 6,000	Wholly exempt	No need to calculate any gain.
(b)	< 6,000	> 6,000	Any gain restricted to $\frac{5}{3}$(Gross proceeds − £6,000)	Calculate gain, compare to the maximum, take the lower figure.
(c)	> 6,000	< 6,000	Gross proceeds deemed to be £6,000	Do normal calculation but always use £6,000 as proceeds figure.
(d)	> 6,000	> 6,000	Normal disposal	

Illustration 1: Chattels: gains

Adam purchased a Chippendale chair for £1,800. On 10 October of the current tax year, he sold the chair at auction for £6,300 (which was net of the auctioneer's 10% commission).

Required

What is the gain?

Solution

	£
Proceeds (£6,300 × 100/90)	7,000
Less incidental costs of sale	(700)
Net proceeds	6,300
Less cost	(1,800)
Gain	4,500

The maximum gain is 5/3 × £7,000 − £6,000 = £1,667.

The chargeable gain is the lower of £4,500 and £1,667, so it is £1,667.

Illustration 2: Chattels: losses

Eve purchased a rare first edition book for £8,000 which she sold in October of the current tax year at auction for £2,700 (which was net of 10% commission).

Required

Compute the gain or loss.

Solution

	£
Proceeds (assumed)	6,000
Less incidental costs of disposal (£2,700 × 10/90)	(300)
	5,700
Less cost	(8,000)
Allowable loss	(2,300)

Activity 1: Chargeable gain/loss

Orlando purchased a rare manuscript for £500. He sold it several years later for £9,000, before deducting the auctioneer's commission of £1,000.

Edwina purchased an antique table for £7,000. She sold it several years later for £3,000.

Required

1   What is the chargeable gain arising on the disposal of the manuscript?

O £5,000

O £7,500

O £4,500

O £3,333

2   What is the capital loss arising on the disposal of the antique?

O £4,000

O £1,000

O £1,667

O £nil

Solution

1.3 Wasting chattels

Wasting chattels are exempt (so that there are no chargeable gains and no allowable losses).

There is one exception to this: assets used for the purpose of a trade, profession or vocation in respect of which capital allowances have been or could have been claimed. This means that items of plant and machinery used in a trade are not exempt merely on the grounds that they are wasting. However, cars are always exempt.

2 Wasting assets (other than chattels)

A wasting asset is one which has an estimated remaining useful life of 50 years or less and whose original value will depreciate over time (eg copyrights).

The normal capital gains computation is amended to reflect the anticipated depreciation over the life of the asset.

When calculating the gain, the cost is written down on a straight-line basis and it is this depreciated cost which is deducted in the computation.

Thus, if a taxpayer acquires a wasting asset with a remaining life of 40 years and disposes of it after 15 years, so that 25 years of useful life remain, only 25/40 of the cost is deducted in the computation.

Any enhancement expenditure must be separately depreciated.

Illustration 3: Wasting asset

Harry bought a copyright on 1 July 2016 for £20,000. The copyright is due to expire in July 2036. He sold it on 1 July 2020 for £22,000.

Required

What is Harry's gain?

Solution

	£
Proceeds of sale	22,000
Less depreciated cost £20,000 × 16/20	(16,000)
Gain	6,000

Activity 2: Copyright disposal

On 31 March 2021, Nigel sold a copyright for £17,280. It had been purchased on 1 April 2016 for £18,000 when it had an unexpired life of 20 years.

Required

What is Nigel's chargeable gain or allowable loss in respect of the disposal of the copyright?

- ○ £nil
- ○ £12,780 gain
- ○ £3,780 gain
- ○ £720 loss

Solution

---

3 Private residence relief (PRR)

3.1 General rule

The gain arising on individual's only or main residence including a garden of up to half a hectare is reduced by the private residence relief (PRR).

The PRR is calculated as:

> **Formula to learn**
>
> $$PRR = Gain \times \frac{Period\ of\ occupation}{Period\ of\ ownership}$$

Thus, only gains arising in periods of absence will be chargeable. Gains not covered by the PRR exemption (and the letting exemption – see later) will be taxed at 18% and 28% depending on whether the taxpayer has any basic rate band unused and subject to annual exempt amount and capital losses.

3.2 Deemed occupation

(a) The last nine months are always deemed occupation in full provided it was the taxpayer's principal private residence at some point.

(b) Certain periods of absence are deemed occupation, providing that they are preceded and followed (at any time whatsoever) by actual occupation:

  (i) Any period during which the owner was abroad by reason of their employment. The employee is not required to return to the property if this has been prevented by their employment.

  (ii) Any periods (not exceeding four years in total) during which the owner was required to work away from home because of either employment or self-employment. If an employee, the individual is not required to return to the property if this has been prevented by their employment.

  (iii) Any periods for whatever reason not exceeding three years in total.

It does not matter if the residence is let during the absence.

Exempt periods of absence must normally be preceded and followed by periods of actual occupation. This rule is relaxed where an individual who has been required to work abroad or elsewhere – ie (b)(i) and (b)(ii) above – is unable to resume residence in their home because the terms of their employment require them to work elsewhere.

Illustration 4: Private residence relief

Abel purchased a house on 1 April 1995 for £88,200. He lived in the house until 31 December 1996. He then worked abroad for two years before returning to the UK to live in the house again on 1 January 1999. He stayed in the house until 30 June 2015 before retiring and moving out to live with friends in Spain until the house was sold on 31 December 2020 for £175,000.

Required

Calculate Abel's capital gains tax payable for 2020/21, assuming that this is the only disposal that he makes in the tax year and that he is a higher rate taxpayer.

Solution

	£
Proceeds	175,000
Less cost	(88,200)
Gain before PRR exemption	86,800
Less PRR exemption (working)	
252/309 × £86,800	(70,788)
Chargeable gain	16,012
Less annual exempt amount	(12,300)
Taxable gain	3,712
CGT on £3,712 @ 28% (residential property rate)	1,039

Exempt and chargeable periods

	Period	Total months	Exempt months	Charge-able months
(i)	April 1995–December 1996 (occupied)	21	21	0
(ii)	January 1997–December 1998 (working abroad)	24	24	0
(iii)	January 1999–June 2015 (occupied)	198	198	0
(iv)	July 2015–March 2020 (see below)	57	0	57
(v)	April 2020–December 2020 (last 9 months)	9	9	0
		309	252	57

No part of the period from July 2015 to March 2020 can be covered by the exemption for three years of absence for any reason because it is not followed at any time by actual occupation.

Exam focus point

To help you answer questions such as that above it is useful to draw up a table showing the period of ownership, exempt months (actual/deemed occupation) and chargeable months (non-occupation) similar to that in the working.

3.3 Business use

If any part of the residence is not occupied by the owner for residence purposes, the PRR exemption will be proportionately withdrawn, eg if a proportion has been let out or used as a trading premises. The application of the last nine-month rule will depend on whether the property has always been only part occupied or whether it has at some point all been residential.

Essential reading

See Chapter 14 Section 1 of the Essential reading for more detail on business use.

The Essential reading is available as an Appendix of the digital edition of the Workbook.

Activity 3: Chargeable gain

Harry bought his house in London on 1 April 1996 and lived in it until 1 April 1997. From that date until 1 April 2002 he was required by his employer to work overseas. On returning, he moved back into the house until 1 October 2002 when he went to live with his mother. The house remained empty until he sold his house on 30 September 2020 realising a gain of £100,000.

Required

Calculate the chargeable gain on sale of his house.

Solution

3.4 Letting relief

When the owner lets part of the property for residential use while still occupying the rest of it, the PRR is withdrawn on the proportion let (see business use above) but letting relief applies to extend the PRR up to a limit.

The extra exemption is restricted to the lowest of:

(a) The amount equivalent to the total **gain** which is already **exempt under the PRR provisions**

(b) The gain accruing during the letting period (the **letting part of the gain**)

(c) **£40,000** (maximum)

Letting relief cannot convert a gain into an allowable loss.

As noted above, periods covered by the deemed occupation rules where the property has been let qualify for PRR so letting relief is not relevant in this case. Letting relief does **not** apply where the owner moves out and lets the entire property.

 ## Illustration 5: Letting relief

Celia purchased a house on 1 April 2006 for £90,000. She sold it on 31 August 2020 for £340,000. Throughout her ownership, Celia lived on the top floor, renting out the balance of the house (constituting 60% of the total house) to tenants.

Required

What is the gain arising?

Solution

	£
Proceeds	340,000
Less: Cost	(90,000)
Gain before PRR	250,000
Less PRR (working)	
£250,000 × 40%	(100,000)
	150,000
Less letting exemption: Lowest of:	
(1) Gain exempt under PRR rules: £100,000	
(2) Gain attributable to letting: £250,000 × 60% = £150,000	
(3) £40,000 (maximum)	(40,000)
Gain	110,000

Chapter summary

Chattels and the private residence relief

Chattels

What is a chattel?
- Tangible moveable property

Non-wasting chattels
- Remaining useful life > 50 years
- Rules for computing gains/losses

Original cost	Gross proceeds	Treatment
<£6,000	<£6,000	Wholly exempt
<£6,000	>£6,000	Any gain restricted to 5/3 (Gross proceeds – £6,000)
>£6,000	<£6,000	Proceeds deemed to be £6,000
>£6,000	>£6,000	Normal disposal

Wasting chattels
- Exempt

Wasting assets (other than chattels)

- Eg copyright
- Normal capital gains computation is amended to reflect the anticipated depreciation over the life of the asset

Private residence relief (PRR)

General rule
- PRR = gain × (period of occupation/period of ownership)

Deemed occupation
- Last 9 months
- If preceded and followed by genuine occupation
  - Any period abroad due to employment
  - Any period up to four years due to working elsewhere in the UK
  - Any period up to three years for whatever reason

Business use
- PRR proportionally withdrawn if part used for business

Letting relief
- Applies if property part let out while owner occupies the rest
- Lower of:
  - £40,000
  - Letting gain arising
  - PRR

Knowledge diagnostic

1. Chattels

Chattels fall into two categories:

- Wasting – exempt
- Non-wasting – special rules/restrictions apply

2. Wasting assets

Depreciate cost over its estimated useful life.

3. Private residence exemption

Selling your private residence exempts any gain providing you have been in full occupation. Periods of non-occupation or business use may cause some of this exemption to be withdrawn.

Letting exemption exempts a gain on a PRR during a let period up to a maximum of £40,000.

Further study guidance

Question practice

Now try the following from the Further question practice bank (available in the digital edition of the Workbook):

Section A questions:

Q60, Q61, Q62, Q63

Activity answers

Activity 1: Chargeable gain/loss

1   The correct answer is: £5,000

	£
Proceeds	9,000
Less: commission	(1,000)
cost	(500)
	7,500
5/3 (£9,000 – £6,000)	5,000
Therefore take lower gain	5,000

The answer £7,500 is the actual gain. The answer £4,500 uses the loss rule to deem the proceeds to be £6,000. The answer £3,333 deducts the commission before applying the 5/3 fraction.

2   The correct answer is: £1,000

	£
Proceeds (deemed)	6,000
Cost	(7,000)
Allowable loss	(1,000)

The answer £4,000 is the actual loss. The answer £1,667 confuses the gain rule so applies the 5/3 fraction to the excess of cost over £6,000. The answer £nil treats the table as an exempt asset.

Activity 2: Copyright disposal

The correct answer is: £3,780 gain

Copyright	£
Proceeds	17,280
Cost £18,000 × 15/20	(13,500)
	3,780

The answer £nil treats the copyright as an exempt asset. The answer £12,780 gain deducts 5/20 of the cost (ie the expired years, not the remaining years). The answer £720 loss deducts the whole cost.

Activity 3: Chargeable gain

PRR- periods of absence

	Occupied	Non-occupied
1.4.96–31.3.97 (occupation)	12	

	Occupied	Non-occupied
1.4.97–31.3.02 (working overseas)	60	
1.4.02–30.9.02 (occupation)	6	
1.10.02–31.12.19 (no deemed occupation as not reoccupied)		207
1.1.20–30.9.20 (last nine months)	9	
	87	207

	£
Gain	100,000
Less PRR (87/294 × £100,000)	(29,592)
	70,408

15

Business reliefs

Learning objectives

On completion of this chapter, you should be able to:

	Syllabus reference no.
Explain and apply business asset disposal relief.	C5(b)
Explain and apply investors' relief.	C5(c)
Explain and apply capital gains tax reliefs • rollover relief	C6(a)(i)
Explain and apply capital gains tax reliefs • holdover relief for the gift of business assets	C6(a)(ii)
Basic capital gains tax planning.	C6(b)

Exam context

Business reliefs are an important part of the Taxation (TX – UK) exam and may be tested in any of Sections A, B or C. Rollover relief may be met in either an unincorporated business or a company context and, as it is an extremely important relief for all businesses, it is likely to be examined. If you are required to compute a gain on a business asset, look out for the purchase of a new asset but carefully check the date and cost of the acquisition. Do not be caught out by the purchase of an investment property. The relief for gifts of assets is only available to individuals, and effectively passes the gain to the donee. Business asset disposal relief is only available to individuals but is a particularly valuable relief as it reduces the rate of capital gains tax (CGT) to 10%.

Chapter overview

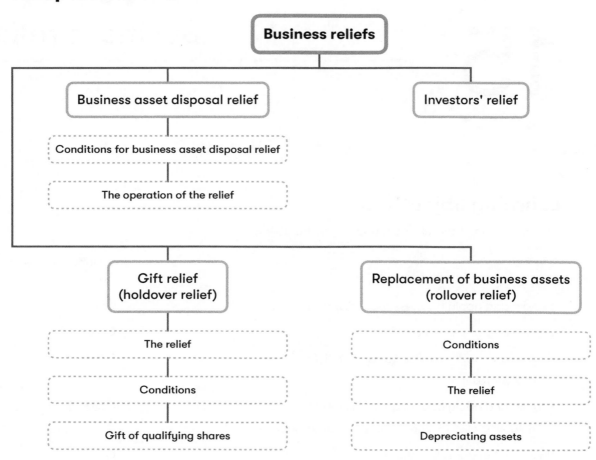

1 Business asset disposal relief

> **PER alert**
>
> One of the competencies you require to fulfil Performance Objective 17 *Tax planning and advice* of the PER is to mitigate and/or defer tax liabilities through the use of standard reliefs, exemptions and incentives. You can apply the knowledge you obtain from this chapter of the Workbook to help to demonstrate this competence.

1.1 Conditions for business asset disposal relief

Individuals can claim this relief when they dispose of the whole of a business or a significant part of a business (not just business assets).

The relief covers the first £1 million of chargeable gains on the disposal of:

- The **whole or a part** of a business. However, relief is only available in respect of gains on the disposal of business assets, therefore there is no relief on gains arising from investments.
- The disposal of **shares** in a trading company where an individual has **at least a 5% shareholding** (personal company) and is **also an employee** of the company.

There is no restriction if the company holds non-trading assets like investments.

Note that the business or shares must have been owned for two years prior to disposal.

You can use the phrase 'For The Tax Win' to help remember when business asset disposal relief can be applied:

F - Five% (an individual has at least a 5% shareholding)

T - Trading company

T - Two-year ownership before disposal

W - Work there (ie employee or director)

1.2 The operation of the relief

Gains on assets qualifying for business asset disposal relief are taxed at **10% regardless of an individual's taxable income**.

Losses and annual exempt amount should initially be deducted from gains that do not qualify for the relief. The most beneficial order is:

(1) Residential property gains

(2) Other gains not qualifying for business asset disposal relief

(3) Business asset disposal relief gains

Gains qualifying for business asset disposal relief **reduce the amount of any unused basic rate band** despite being taxed at a rate of 10%.

> **PER alert**
>
> One of the competencies you require to fulfil Performance Objective 16 *Tax compliance and verification* of the PER is to identify available claims, or the need to object to/appeal an assessment, ensuring that they are submitted within the required time limits. You can apply the knowledge you obtain from this section of the Workbook to help to demonstrate this competence.

An individual must claim business asset disposal relief; it is not automatic. The claim deadline is the first anniversary of 31 January following the end of the tax year of disposal. For a 2020/21 disposal, the taxpayer must claim by 31 January 2023.

The £1 million is a lifetime limit so applies to successive disposals.

Essential reading

See Chapter 15 Section 1 of the Essential reading for an example of the lifetime limit.

The Essential reading is available as an Appendix of the digital edition of the Workbook.

Exam focus point

The business asset disposal relief lifetime limit of £1 million and rate of tax of 10% will be given in the Tax Rates and Allowances available in the exam.

Illustration 1: Business asset disposal relief

Simon sells his business, all the assets of which qualify for business asset disposal relief, in September 2020. The chargeable gain arising is £10,000.

Simon also made a chargeable gain of £25,900 in December 2020 on an asset which did not qualify for business asset disposal relief and is not residential property.

Simon has taxable income of £20,500 in 2020/21.

Required

What is Simon's CGT payable for 2020/21?

Solution

The CGT payable for 2020/21 is calculated as follows:

	Gains £	CGT £
Gain qualifying for business asset disposal relief		
Taxable gain	10,000	
CGT @ 10%		1,000
Gain not qualifying for business asset disposal relief		
Gain	25,900	
Less annual exempt amount (best use)	(12,300)	
Taxable gain	13,600	
CGT on £37,500 – £20,500 – £10,000 = £7,000 @ 10%		700
CGT on £13,600 – £7,000 = £6,600 @ 20%		1,320
CGT 2020/21		3,020

Note that the £10,000 gain qualifying for business asset disposal relief is deducted from the basic rate limit for the purposes of computing the rate of tax on the gain not qualifying for business asset disposal relief.

Activity 1: Business asset disposal

Gerald sold his sole trader business on 3 August 2020. Gains arose on chargeable assets as follows:

	£
Offices	300,000
Goodwill	75,000
Investments	120,700

All assets had been owned for two years prior to disposal.

On 23 March 2021, Gerald sold a 15% shareholding in Puddle Ltd which resulted in a chargeable gain of £600,000. Gerald had acquired these shares on 1 June 2009 and had been an employee of the company ever since.

Gerald has taxable income of £10,000 in 2020/21 and capital losses of £15,000 brought forward.

Required

Calculate Gerald's capital gains tax liability for 2020/21, assuming Gerald has not previously claimed business asset disposal relief.

Solution

2 Investors' relief

Investors' relief is available on the disposal of shares in an **unlisted** trading company.

- Gains on disposal of the shares are taxed at 10%.
- The shares must have been issued direct to the taxpayer (ie subscription) on or after 17 March 2016 and held continuously for at least three years.
- Unlike for business asset disposal relief, the taxpayer does not have to have a minimum percentage of the shareholding and cannot usually be an employee/officer.
- A separate £10 million lifetime allowance is available.

- An individual must claim investors' relief by the first anniversary of 31 January following the end of the tax year of disposal, eg for a 2020/21 disposal, the taxpayer must claim by 31 January 2023.

Exam focus point

The investors' relief lifetime limit of £10 million and rate of tax of 10% will be given in the Tax Rates and Allowances available in the exam.

Illustration 2: Investors' relief

Sarah subscribed for 20,000 £1 ordinary shares in Sinclair Ltd, an unquoted trading company, on 1 July 2016. The shares were issued at par (ie she paid £1 for each £1 share) and they were a 4% shareholding in the company. Sarah was never an officer or employee of Sinclair Ltd. Sarah sold her shares for £5 per share on 10 December 2020. This was the only disposal that Sarah made in 2020/21.

Required

Calculate the CGT payable by Sarah for 2020/21, giving a brief explanation of the rate of tax applicable to the disposal.

Solution

	£
Proceeds £5 × 20,000	100,000
Less cost £1 × 20,000	(20,000)
Chargeable gain	80,000
Less annual exempt amount	(12,300)
Taxable gain	67,700
CGT @ 10%	6,770

Sarah's shareholding in Sinclair Ltd qualifies for investors' relief because she subscribed for new ordinary shares in an unquoted trading company on or after 17 March 2016 which she held for at least three years and she was not an officer nor an employee of the company. The rate of tax on gains qualifying for investors' relief is 10%.

Activity 2: CGT liability - investors' relief

On 8 July 2016 Konstance subscribed for 100,000 £1 ordinary shares (a 1% shareholding) at face value, in BKE Ltd, an unquoted trading company. Konstance has never worked for BKE Ltd.

On 5 December 2020 Konstance sold the 100,000 shares for £500,000.

Required

Calculate Konstance's CGT liability for 2020/21.

Solution

---

3 Gift relief (holdover relief)

3.1 The relief

Gift relief can be claimed on **gifts of business assets**.

If an individual gives away a qualifying asset, the transferor and the transferee can jointly claim within four years of the end of the tax year of the transfer, that the transferor's gain be reduced to nil. The transferee is then deemed to acquire the asset for market value at the date of transfer less the transferor's deferred gain.

3.2 Conditions

- Disposal is made to an individual who is UK resident
- Disposal is of
    - A business asset used in donor's trade; or
    - Unquoted shares in a trading company; or
    - Quoted shares in a personal trading company (ie at least 5% shareholding).

There is a restriction on a gift relief claim if the asset is sold at less than market value (sale at undervalue). Disposals by way of sale at undervalue are chargeable to capital gains tax (CGT), with proceeds deemed to be market value.

- The excess of actual proceeds received over the original cost is taxed immediately.
- The rest of the gain is held over into the base cost for a subsequent disposal of the asset.
- If the transferee moves abroad within six years of the disposal, the deferred gain becomes taxable on the transferee immediately before they leave the country.

Illustration 3: Gift relief

On 6 May 2020, Angelo sold to his son Michael a freehold shop valued at £200,000 for £50,000, and claimed gift relief. Angelo had originally purchased the shop from which he had run his business for £30,000. Michael continued to run a business from the shop premises but decided to sell the shop in March 2021 for £195,000.

Required

Compute any chargeable gains arising.

Solution

Angelo's gain:

	£
Proceeds (market value)	200,000
Less cost	(30,000)

		£
Gain		170,000
Less gain deferred (balance)		(150,000)
Chargeable gain (£50,000 – £30,000) (actual proceeds less actual cost)		20,000

Michael's gain:

		£
Proceeds		195,000
Less cost (£200,000 - £150,000) (MV less deferred gain)		(50,000)
Gain		145,000

Activity 3: Chargeable gain

Maxwell bought a workshop used in his trade several years ago for £50,000. A few years later he sold it to his son for £95,000 (when its market value was £210,000) and, along with his son, made a joint claim for gift relief.

The son subsequently sold the workshop for £250,000.

Required

Calculate the chargeable gain on disposal of the workshop by Maxwell and his son.

Solution

3.3 Gift of qualifying shares

- Gain on gift of shares may not all be eligible for relief.
- Where the taxpayer's **personal** company has investments in its net assets, the gift relief is restricted.
- Gain eligible for relief will be:

$$\text{Total gain} \times \frac{\text{MV of CBA}}{\text{MV of CA}}$$

MV = market value

CBA = chargeable business asset (chargeable assets except investments)

CA = chargeable asset (assets not exempt from CGT)

Illustration 4: CBA/CA restriction

Morris gifts shares in his personal company to his son Minor realising a gain of £100,000. The market values of the assets owned by the company at the date of the gift are:

	£
Freehold factory and offices	150,000
Leasehold warehouse	80,000
Investments	120,000
Current assets	200,000

Required

Show the gain qualifying for hold-over relief and the chargeable gain.

Solution

Gain qualifying for hold-over relief:

$$£100,000 \times \frac{CBA}{CA} = £100,000 \times \frac{150,000 + 80,000}{150,000 + 80,000 + 120,000}$$

$$= £100,000 \times \frac{230}{350} = £65,714$$

The gain which is not held-over (ie chargeable in current year) is £100,000 − £65,714 = £34,286

Activity 4: Gain arising and base cost

James gave 40% of his holding in Corn Ltd to his son when its market value was £200,000. The cost of the 40% holding was £100,000.

The assets of Corn Ltd comprised the following at the date of the gift:

	£
Freehold property	270,000
Leasehold property	130,000
Inventory	30,000
Debtors	25,000
Investments	20,000
Plant (cost and proceeds < £6,000)	40,000
Creditors	(8,000)
	507,000

Required

What is the chargeable gain arising and the base cost of the shares to James's son?

Solution

4 Replacement of business assets (rollover relief)

4.1 Conditions

A gain may be 'rolled over' (deferred) where it arises on the disposal of a business asset which is replaced.

All of the following conditions must be met:

- The old asset sold and the new asset bought are both used only in the trade carried on by the person claiming rollover relief. Where part of a building is in non-trade use for all or a substantial part of the period of ownership, the building (and the land on which it stands) is treated as two separate assets, the trade part (qualifying) and the non-trade part (non-qualifying). This split cannot be made for other assets.
- The old asset and the new asset both fall within one (but not necessarily the same one) of the following classes:
  - Land and buildings (including parts of buildings) occupied as well as used only for the purpose of the trade
  - Fixed (that is, immovable) plant and machinery
  - Goodwill (for individuals only)
- Reinvestment of the proceeds received on the disposal of the old asset takes place in a period beginning one year before and ending three years after the date of the disposal.
- The new asset is brought into use in the trade on its acquisition (not necessarily immediately, but not after any significant and unnecessary delay).

The new asset can be used in a different trade from the old asset.

A claim for the relief must be made by the later of four years of the end of the tax year in which the disposal of the old asset takes place and four years of the end of the tax year in which the new asset is acquired.

4.2 The relief

- The relief is available to both companies (see later) and individuals.
- It allows the taxpayer to delay the tax liability on the capital gain to the extent that proceeds from sale of a business asset are reinvested in new business assets.
- Any proceeds not reinvested in a qualifying asset are deducted from the gain to be rolled over and are taxed immediately.

 Illustration 5: Rollover relief

A freehold factory was purchased by Zoë for business use in August 2010. It was sold in December 2020 for £70,000, giving rise to a gain of £17,950. A replacement factory was purchased in June 2021 for £60,000.

Required

Compute the base cost of the replacement factory, taking into account any possible rollover of the gain from the disposal in December 2020.

Solution

	£
Gain	17,950
Less rollover relief (balancing figure)	(7,950)
Chargeable gain: Amount not reinvested (£70,000 − £60,000)	10,000
Cost of new factory	60,000
Less rolled over gain	(7,950)
Base cost of new factory	52,050

Activity 5: Chargeable gain and base cost - rollover relief

In June 1997, John bought some land for £140,000 for use in his trade. In August 2020, he sold it for £250,000, immediately reinvesting £230,000 of the proceeds in freehold property for use in his trade.

Required

What is John's chargeable gain in respect of the land and the base cost of the new freehold property?

O   Gain of £Nil, Base cost of £120,000

O   Gain of £Nil, Base cost of £140,000

O   Gain of £20,000, Base cost of £120,000

O   Gain of £20,000, Base cost of £140,000

Solution

Essential reading

See Chapter 15 Section 2 of the Essential reading for an example of rollover relief with assets with non-business use.

The Essential reading is available as an Appendix of the digital edition of the Workbook.

4.3 Depreciating assets

KEY TERM

Depreciating asset: An asset is a depreciating asset if it is or, within the next ten years, will become a wasting asset. Thus, any asset with an expected life of 60 years or less is covered by this definition. Plant and machinery is always treated as depreciating.

If the new asset is a depreciating asset:

- Gain deferred is not deducted from cost of new asset
- Instead it is postponed until the earliest of:
  - Disposal of new asset
  - Date new asset ceases to be used in the trade
  - Ten years after the new asset was acquired

Illustration 6: Gain deferred into depreciating asset

Norma bought a freehold shop for use in her business in June 2019 for £125,000. She sold it for £140,000 on 1 August 2020. On 10 July 2020, Norma bought some fixed plant and machinery to use in her business, costing £150,000. She then sells the plant and machinery for £167,000 on 19 November 2022.

Required

Show Norma's gains in relation to these transactions.

Solution

2020/21 – Gain deferred

	£
Proceeds of shop	140,000
Less cost	(125,000)
Gain	15,000

This gain is deferred in relation to the purchase of the plant and machinery as all the proceeds have been reinvested.

2022/23 – Sale of plant and machinery

	£
Proceeds	167,000
Less cost	(150,000)
Gain	17,000

Total gain chargeable on sale in 2022/23 (gain on plant and machinery plus deferred gain)

£15,000 + £17,000 = £32,000

Activity 6: Chargeable gain or allowable loss

Neil bought a factory for use in his business in November 2003 for £75,000. The factory was sold for £125,000 on 10 August 2011. On 1 June 2012, Neil bought some fixed plant and machinery for use in his business, costing £160,000.

Neil sold the plant and machinery for £140,000 on 7 December 2020

Required

What is Neil's chargeable gain or allowance loss in 2020/21?

O   Loss of £20,000

O   Loss of £70,000

O   Gain of £30,000

O   Gain of £50,000

Solution

Where a gain on disposal is deferred against a replacement depreciating asset it is possible to transfer the deferred gain to a non-depreciating asset provided the non-depreciating asset is bought before the deferred gain has crystallised.

Chapter summary

```
                        ┌──────────────────────┐
                        │   Business reliefs    │
                        └──────────────────────┘
```

Business asset disposal relief

Conditions for business asset disposal relief

- Assets qualifying
  - Disposal of whole or part of business (No relief on gains from investments)
  - Disposal of shares in a trading company, where individual has 5% shareholding and is an employee of the company
- Assets must be owned for two years prior to disposal

The operation of the relief

- £1 million lifetime limit
- Gains taxed at 10%
- These gains use up any unused basic rate band

Investors' relief

- 10% tax on disposals of shares in unquoted trading companies
- No need to have 5% or be an employee
- Separate £10 million lifetime limit
- Newly issued shares only
- Minimum holding period of three years from 17.3.16

Gift relief (holdover relief)

The relief

- Defers gain
- Reduces base cost for donee

Conditions

- Donee must be UK resident
- Assets qualifying
  - Business assets
  - Unquoted shares in a trading company
  - Quoted shares in a personal trading company (at least 5%)

Gift of qualifying shares

- Gain eligible for relief: Total gain x (MV of CBA/MV of CA) where
  - CBA = chargeable business assets (chargeable assets except investments)
  - CA = chargeable assets (assets not exempt from CGT)

Replacement of business assets (rollover relief)

Conditions

- Old and new asset both used only in the trade of taxpayer
- Old and new asset are:
  - Land and buildings
  - Fixed plant and machinery
  - Goodwill (individuals)
- Purchase of replacement asset takes place 12m before to 36m after sale
- The new asset is brought into use in the trade on its acquisition

The relief

- Defers gain by reducing base cost of replacement asset
- Any proceeds not reinvested are immediately taxable

Depreciating assets

- Depreciating asset < 60 years, fixed plant and machinery
- Gain is held over if investment is in a depreciating asset until earliest of:
  - Disposal of new asset
  - New asset ceases to be used in trade
  - Ten years after acquisition

Knowledge diagnostic

1. Business asset disposal relief

Business asset disposal relief has a lifetime limit of £1 million. It applies to the disposal of a business or certain trading company shares. Gains qualifying for business asset disposal relief are taxed at 10%.

2. Investors' relief

This is similar to business asset disposal relief. Gains on unquoted shares in trading companies are taxed at 10% as long as the shares were subscribed for on/after 17 March 2016, a minimum three-year holding period is satisfied, and the taxpayer is not an employee of the company.

3. Gift relief

Gift relief allows an individual to defer a gain arising on gifts of business assets.

4. Replacement of business assets

Rollover relief allows the gain on a qualifying asset to be deferred if the proceeds are reinvested in a replacement qualifying asset purchased 12 months before and 36 months after disposal.

When the replacement asset is a depreciating asset the gain on the old asset is frozen rather than rolled over into the replacement asset.

Further study guidance

Question practice

Now try the following from the Further question practice bank (available in the digital edition of the Workbook):

Section A:

Q64, Q65, Q66

Section B:

Q67 Roy and Graham

Section C:

Q68 Kai

Activity answers

Activity 1: Business asset disposal

Capital gains qualifying for business asset disposal relief:

	£
Offices	300,000
Goodwill	75,000
Shares	600,000
	975,000

Other capital gains:

	£
Investments	120,700
Annual exempt amount	(12,300)
Capital losses b/f	(15,000)
	93,400

CGT payable

	£
£975,000 × 10% =	97,500
(Note) £93,400 × 20% =	18,680
	116,180

Note. BR band is unused but this is set against gains qualifying for business asset disposal relief first.

Activity 2: CGT liability - investors' relief

	£
Proceeds	500,000
Less cost	(100,000)
Gain	400,000
Annual exempt amount	(12,300)
Chargeable gain	387,700

CGT payable: £387,700 × 10% = £38,770

Activity 3: Chargeable gain

Disposal by Maxwell

	£
Deemed proceeds (MV)	210,000

	£
Less cost	(50,000)
Gain	160,000
Gain held over under gift relief	(115,000)
Taxed now (£95,000 – £50,000)	45,000

Acquisition by son

	£
Market value	210,000
Less gain held over under gift relief	(115,000)
Cost for son	95,000

Disposal by son

	£
Proceeds	250,000
Less cost	(95,000)
Gain	155,000

Activity 4: Gain arising and base cost

Disposal by James

	£
Deemed proceeds (MV)	200,000
Less cost	(100,000)
Gain	100,000
Gain eligible for gift relief:	
£100,000 × [(270+130)/(270+130+20)]	(95,238)
Taxed now	4,762

Acquisition by son

	£
MV	200,000
Less gain held over under gift relief	(95,238)
Cost for son	104,762

Activity 5: Chargeable gain and base cost - rollover relief

The correct answer is: Gain of £20,000, Base cost of £140,000

	£
Proceeds	250,000
Less cost	(140,000)

	£
Gain	110,000
Less rollover relief	(90,000)
Taxed now	20,000

Proceeds not reinvested = £250,000 − £230,000 = £20,000

Therefore this will be taxed now.

Rest of gain = 110,000 − 20,000 = £90,000

This can be deferred.

Base cost of new asset:

	£
Cost	230,000
Gain deferred	(90,000)
	140,000

Activity 6: Chargeable gain or allowable loss

The correct answer is: Gain of £50,000

The gain of £125,000 − £75,000 = £50,000 is deferred until the sale of the plant and machinery on 7 December 2020. The fall in value on plant and machinery has been relieved through capital allowances so is not an allowable capital loss.

16

Shares and securities

Learning objectives

On completion of this chapter, you should be able to:

	Syllabus reference no.
Recognise the value of quoted shares where they are disposed of by way of a gift.	C4(a)
Explain and apply the identification rules as they apply to individuals including the same day and 30-day matching rules.	C4(b)
Explain and apply the pooling provisions.	C4(c)
Explain and apply the treatment of bonus issues, rights issues, takeovers and reorganisations.	C4(d)
Identify the exemption available for gilt-edged securities and qualifying corporate bonds.	C4(e)

Exam context

The valuation rules for gifts of quoted shares may be tested in either Section A or B. The disposal of shares and securities are likely to form at least part of a question on capital gains in Section C. You must learn the identification rules as they are crucial in calculating the gain correctly. The identification rules for companies are covered later in this Workbook. Takeovers and reorganisations are important; remember to apportion the cost across the new holding.

Chapter overview

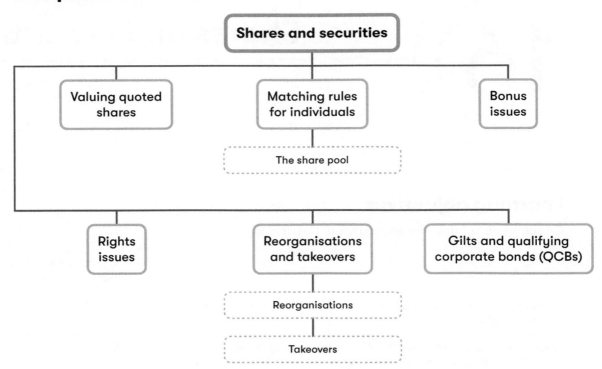

1 Valuing quoted shares

Quoted shares disposed of by way of a gift (including sales at undervalue) are valued at the **mid-price** based on the **quoted price on the disposal day**. This value is needed as 'proceeds' in order to calculate the chargeable gain or loss.

Illustration 1: CGT value of shares

Shares in Abacus plc are quoted at 100p–110p.

Required

What is the market value for CGT purposes?

Solution

The value is 100p + ½ × (110p − 100p) = 105p

Activity 1: Chargeable gain

Nadia bought 20,000 shares in YES plc in 2005 for £5,000. In the current tax year, Nadia transferred all of the shares in YES plc to her sister in law, Brynhilda, who paid £20,000 for them. On the day of the transfer, the shares in YES plc were quoted at £4.44–£4.50.

Required

What is Nadia's chargeable gain as a result of the transfer to Brynhilda?

○ £15,000

○ £83,800

○ £84,400

○ £85,000

Solution

---

2 Matching rules for individuals

Quoted and unquoted shares and securities present special problems when attempting to compute gains or losses on disposal. For instance, suppose that Ivy buys some quoted shares in X plc as follows.

Date	Number of shares	Cost £
5 May 2016	220	150
17 August 2020	100	375

On 25 August 2020, Ivy sells 120 of the shares for £1,450. To determine the chargeable gain, we need to be able to work out which shares out of the two original holdings were actually sold.

We therefore need **matching rules**. These allow us to decide which shares have been sold and so work out what the allowable cost on disposal should be.

Below, 'shares' refers to both shares and securities.

Matching rules

Disposals of shares sold by individuals should be matched in the following order:

(1) Acquisitions on the same day

(2) Acquisition in the next 30 days – first in, first out (FIFO) basis

(3) Shares in the share pool

Exam focus point

Learn the 'matching rules' because a crucial first step to getting a shares question right is to correctly match the shares sold to the original shares purchased.

2.1 The share pool

The share pool aggregates all purchases except those made on the same day as the disposal or within the following 30 days.

In making computations which use the share pool, we must keep track of:

- The **number** of shares
- The **cost** of the shares

Proforma share pool

	Number of shares	Cost £
Additions	X	X
Disposals	(X)	(X)
	X	X

Illustration 2: The share pool

In August 2006 Oliver acquired 4,000 shares in Twist plc at a cost of £10,000. Oliver sold 3,000 shares on 10 July 2020 for £17,000.

Required

Compute the gain and the value of the share pool following the disposal.

Solution

The gain is computed as follows:

	£
Proceeds	17,000
Less cost (working)	(7,500)
Gain	9,500

Working

Share pool

	No of shares	Cost £
Acquisition – August 2006	4,000	10,000
Disposal – July 2020	(3,000)	
	—	
Cost (3,000/4,000) × £10,000	—	(7,500)
	1,000	2,500

Illustration 3: Matching rules

Anita acquired shares in Kent Ltd as follows:

1 July 1996	1,000 shares for £2,000
11 April 2001	2,500 shares for £7,500
17 July 2020	500 shares for £2,000
10 August 2020	400 shares for £1,680

Anita sold 4,000 shares for £16,400 on 17 July 2020.

Required

Calculate Anita's net gain on sale.

Solution

First match the disposal with the acquisition on the same day:

	£
Proceeds (500/4,000) × £16,400	2,050
Less cost	(2,000)
Gain	50

Next match the disposal with the acquisition in the next thirty days:

	£
Proceeds (400/4,000) × £16,400	1,640
Less cost	(1,680)
Loss	(40)

Finally, match the disposal with the shares in the share pool:

	£
Proceeds (3,100/4,000) × £16,400	12,710

		£
Less cost (working)		(8,414)
Gain		4,296
Net gain £(50 + 4,296 − 40)		4,306

Working

	No of shares	Cost £
1.7.96 Acquisition	1,000	2,000
11.4.01 Acquisition	2,500	7,500
	3,500	9,500
17.7.20 Disposal	(3,100)	(8,414)
c/f	400	1,086

Activity 2: Shares - chargeable gains

James acquired the following shares in Rio Grande plc:

Date of acquisition	No of shares	Cost £
10.12.99	10,000	25,000
7.10.08	3,000	12,000
12.8.20	6,000	30,000

James disposed of 12,000 of his shares on 7 August 2020 for £58,000.

Required
Calculate the chargeable gains arising.

Solution

3 Bonus issues

Bonus shares are shares issued by a company in proportion to each shareholder's existing holding. For example, a shareholder may have 1,000 shares. If the company makes two shares for each share held bonus issue (called a 'two for one bonus issue'), the shareholder will receive two bonus shares for each share held. So, the shareholder will end up with 1,000 original shares and 2,000 bonus shares making 3,000 shares in total.

When a company issues bonus shares all that happens is that the size of the original holding is increased. Since bonus shares are issued at no cost there is no need to adjust the original cost.

4 Rights issues

This is an issue for cash, to existing shareholders, given in proportion to their existing shareholdings. The right shares must be allocated to the pool in the same way as bonus shares but there will be an adjustment to the cost of the pool.

 Illustration 4: Rights issue

Sarah had the following transactions in Kat Ltd.

1.10.97	Bought 10,000 shares for £15,000
1.2.10	Took up rights issue 1 for 2 at £2.75 per share
14.10.20	Sold 2,000 shares for £6,000

Required

Compute the gain arising in October 2020.

Solution

Share pool

	Number	Cost £
1.10.97 Acquisition	10,000	15,000
1.2.10 Rights issue (1 for 2)	5,000	13,750
	15,000	28,750
14.10.20 Sale	(2,000)	(3,833)
c/f	13,000	24,917

Gain

	£
Proceeds	6,000
Less cost	(3,833)
Gain	2,167

Illustration 5: Bonus and rights issues

Richard had the following transactions in S plc:

1.10.95	Bought 10,000 shares for £15,000
11.9.99	Bought 2,000 shares for £5,000
1.2.00	Took up rights issue 1 for 2 at £2.75 per share
5.9.05	2 for 1 bonus issue
14.10.20	Sold 15,000 shares for £15,000

Required

Calculate the gain or loss made on these shares.

Solution

Matching rules: All bought prior to date of disposal so all from share pool.

Gain

	£
Proceeds	15,000
Less cost (Working)	(10,139)
Gain	4,861

Working

Share pool

	Number of shares	Cost £
1.10.95	10,000	15,000
11.9.99 acquisition	2,000	5,000
	12,000	20,000
1.2.00 1:2 rights @ £2.75	6,000	16,500
	18,000	36,500
5.9.05 2:1 bonus	36,000	–
	54,000	36,500
14.10.20 sale 15,000/54,000 × £36,500	(15,000)	(10,139)
	39,000	26,361

Activity 3: Rights issue - gain arising

Ross had the following transactions in GH Ltd.

1.10.99	Bought 10,000 shares (10% holding) for £15,000
11.9.03	Bought 2,000 shares for £5,000
1.2.04	Took up rights issue 1 for 2 at £2.75 per share
14.10.20	Sold 5,000 shares for £15,000

Required

Compute the gain arising in October 2020.

Solution

---

5 Reorganisations and takeovers

5.1 Reorganisations

A reorganisation takes place where new shares or a mixture of new shares and debentures are issued in exchange for the original shareholdings. The new shares take the place of the old shares. The problem is how to apportion the original cost between the different types of capital issued on the reorganisation.

If the new shares and securities are quoted, the cost is apportioned by reference to the market values of the new types of capital on the first day of quotation after the reorganisation.

Illustration 6: Reorganisations

Devon has an original quoted shareholding of 3,000 shares which is held in a share pool with a cost of £13,250.

In 2020 there is a reorganisation whereby each ordinary share is exchanged for two ordinary shares (quoted at £2 each) and one preference share (quoted at £1 each).

Required

Show how the original cost will be apportioned.

Solution

Share pool

	New holding	MV £	Cost £
Ords 2 new shares	6,000	12,000	10,600 (W)
Prefs 1 new share	3,000	3,000	2,650 (W)
Total		15,000	13,250

Working

(12/15) × £13,250 = cost of ordinary shares

(3/15) × £13,250 = cost of preference shares

5.2 Takeovers

A chargeable gain does not arise on a 'paper for paper' takeover as the new shares acquired take the place of the original shares.

The cost of the original shares therefore becomes the cost of the new shares.

If there is a cash element then this represents a disposal for capital gains tax (CGT) purposes and the original cost needs to be apportioned between the cash and new shares received.

Cash element treated as proceeds of a part disposal and A/(A+B) rule applied to cost where:

- A = cash element; and
- B = value of non-cash element ie market value at date of takeover.

Illustration 7: Takeover (1)

Simon held 20,000 £1 shares in Duke plc out of a total number of issued shares of one million. They were bought in 2002 for £2 each. In 2020 the board of Duke plc agreed to a takeover bid by Spire plc under which shareholders in Duke plc received three ordinary Spire plc shares plus one preference share for every four shares held in Duke plc. Immediately following the takeover, the ordinary shares in Spire plc were quoted at £5 each and the preferences shares at 90p.

Required

Show the base costs of the ordinary shares and the preference shares in Spire plc.

Solution

The total value due to Simon on the takeover is as follows:

		£
Ordinary	20,000 × 3/4 × £5	75,000
Preference	20,000 × 1/4 × 90p	4,500
		79,500

The base costs of the shares in Spire plc are therefore:

	£
Ordinary shares: 75,000/79,500 × 20,000 × £2	37,736
Preference shares: 4,500/79,500 × 20,000 × £2	2,264
	40,000

Illustration 8: Takeover (2)

In May 2005, Rosanna bought 50,000 £1 shares in Poppit plc (a 1% holding) for £2.10 each. In 2020, Poppit plc was taken over by Lemon plc and shareholders in Poppit plc received two ordinary shares in Lemon plc plus £2 in cash for each five shares held in Poppit plc. Immediately following the takeover, the ordinary shares in Lemon plc were quoted at £6 each.

Required

Calculate the gain arising on the takeover and show the base cost of the ordinary shares in Lemon plc.

Solution

The total value due to Rosanna on the takeover is as follows:

		£
Ordinary	50,000 × 2/5 × £6	120,000
Cash	50,000 × 1/5 × £2	20,000
		140,000

The cost of the original shares is therefore apportioned between the ordinary shares and the cash as follows.

	£
Ordinary shares: 120,000/140,000 × 50,000 × £2.10	90,000
Cash: 20,000/140,000 × 50,000 × £2.10	15,000
	105,000

The base cost of the shares in Lemon plc is therefore £90,000.

The gain on the takeover relates to the cash received.

	£
Proceeds	20,000
Less cost	(15,000)
Gain	5,000

Activity 4: Takeover - gain arising

Ursula acquired 10,000 £1 shares in F plc in June 1987 for £15,000. F plc was taken over by G plc in July 2020 and for each £1 share in F plc Ursula received:

- 2 £1 ordinary shares in G plc valued at £1.10 each; and
- 40p in cash.

Required

Calculate the gain arising at takeover.

6 Gilts and qualifying corporate bonds (QCBs)

Disposals of gilt edged securities (gilts) and qualifying corporate bonds by individuals are exempt from CGT.

Gilts: Gilts are UK Government securities issued by HM Treasury as shown on the Treasury list. You may assume that the list includes all issues of Treasury Loan, Treasury Stock, Exchequer Loan, Exchequer Stock and War Loan.

Qualifying corporate bond (QCB): A **qualifying corporate bond (QCB)** is a security (whether or not secured on assets) which satisfies all of the following conditions:

(a) Represents a **'normal commercial loan'**. This excludes any bonds which are convertible into shares (although bonds convertible into other bonds which would be QCBs are not excluded), or which carry the right to excessive interest or interest which depends on the results of the issuer's business.

(b) Is **expressed in £** and for which no provision is made for conversion into or redemption in another currency.

(c) Was **acquired** by the person now disposing of it **after 13 March 1984**.

(d) Does not have a redemption value which depends on a published index of share prices on a stock exchange.

Exam focus point

The definitions of gilts and QCBs given above are given as background information and are **not examinable** in the TX-UK exam.

Chapter summary

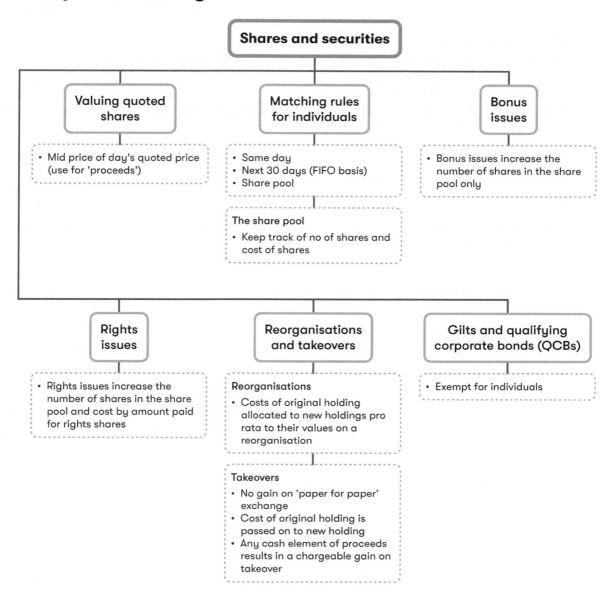

Shares and securities

Valuing quoted shares
- Mid price of day's quoted price (use for 'proceeds')

Matching rules for individuals
- Same day
- Next 30 days (FIFO basis)
- Share pool

The share pool
- Keep track of no of shares and cost of shares

Bonus issues
- Bonus issues increase the number of shares in the share pool only

Rights issues
- Rights issues increase the number of shares in the share pool and cost by amount paid for rights shares

Reorganisations and takeovers

Reorganisations
- Costs of original holding allocated to new holdings pro rata to their values on a reorganisation

Takeovers
- No gain on 'paper for paper' exchange
- Cost of original holding is passed on to new holding
- Any cash element of proceeds results in a chargeable gain on takeover

Gilts and qualifying corporate bonds (QCBs)
- Exempt for individuals

Knowledge diagnostic

1. Valuing quoted shares

Gifted quoted shares are valued at the mid-price quoted on the day of the disposal.

2. Matching rules for individuals

There are special rules for matching shares sold with shares purchased. These rules enable the cost to be determined when shares are sold.

3. Bonus and rights issues

Bonus and rights issues are attached to the holdings to which they relate.

4. Takeovers

On a paper for paper takeover the new shares replace the original shares. Only the receipt of cash will cause a gain to arise.

5. Gilts and QCBs

Gilts and QCBs are exempt for individuals.

Further study guidance

Question practice

Now try the following from the Further question practice bank (available in the digital edition of the Workbook):

Section A:

Q69, Q70, Q71

Section C:

Q72 Melissa

Activity answers

Activity 1: Chargeable gain

The correct answer is: £84,400

	£
Proceeds 20,000 × (£4.44 + ½ × (£4.50 − £4.44))	89,400
Less cost	(5,000)
Gain	84,400

The answer £15,000 uses the actual proceeds to compute the gain. The answer £83,800 uses £4.44 per share for the proceeds. The answer £85,000 uses £4.50 per share for the proceeds.

Activity 2: Shares - chargeable gains

Matching of shares

Acquisition in 30 days after disposal:

	£
Proceeds	
(6,000/12,000) × £58,000 =	29,000
Less cost	(30,000)
Loss	(1,000)

Share pool

	No of shares	Cost £
At 10.12.99	10,000	25,000
7.10.08	3,000	12,000
	13,000	37,000
Disposal	(6,000)	(17,077)
	7,000	19,923

	£
Proceeds	
(6,000/12,000) × £58,000 =	29,000
Less cost	(17,077)
Gain	11,923

Total gain = £10,923 (loss of £1,000 offset against gain of £11,923)

Activity 3: Rights issue - gain arising

Share pool

	No of shares	Cost £
1.10.99	10,000	15,000

	No of shares	Cost £
11.9.03	2,000	5,000
	12,000	20,000
Rights issue 1.2.04 (12,000/2)	6,000	16,500
	18,000	36,500
14.10.20 Sale	(5,000)	(10,139)
	13,000	26,361

	£
Proceeds	15,000
Less cost	(10,139)
Gain	4,861

Activity 4: Takeover - gain arising

Receipt of cash at takeover gives rise to a part disposal

	£
Proceeds 40p × 10,000	4,000
Less cost (W)	(2,308)
Gain	1,692

Working

	MV at takeover £	Cost £
G plc ordinary shares		
20,000 × £1.10	22,000	12,692
Cash	4,000	2,308
	26,000	15,000

17

Self-assessment and payment of tax by individuals

Learning objectives

On completion of this chapter, you should be able to:

	Syllabus reference no.
Explain and apply the features of the self-assessment system as it applies to individuals.	A3(a)
Recognise the time limits that apply to the filing of returns and the making of claims.	A4(a)
Recognise the due dates for the payment of tax under the self-assessment system and compute payments on account and balancing payments/repayments for individuals.	A4(b)
List the information and records that taxpayers need to retain for tax purposes.	A4(d)
Explain the circumstances in which HM Revenue & Customs can make a compliance check into a self-assessment tax return.	A5(a)
Explain the procedures for dealing with appeals and First and Upper Tier Tribunals.	A5(b)
Calculate late payment interest and state the penalties that can be charged.	A6(a)

Exam context

Section A or B questions on the topics in this chapter might relate to the dates for filing returns or the amount of interest or penalties. In Section C, you might be asked to explain an aspect of the self-assessment system, such as the filing of a return, the payment of tax or compliance checks by HMRC. Your knowledge should include the penalties used to enforce the self-assessment system.

Chapter overview

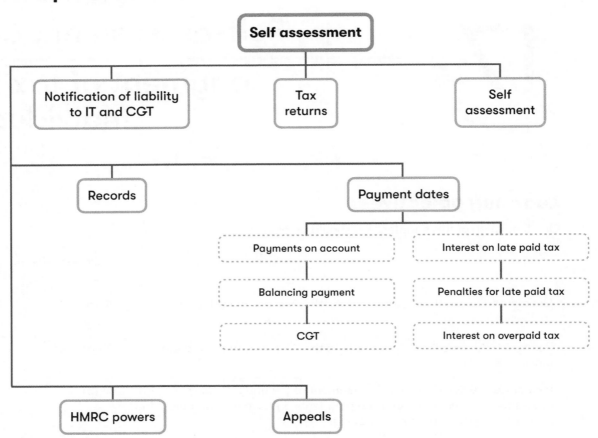

1 Notification of liability to income tax and capital gains tax (CGT)

1.1 Duty to notify

The taxpayer has a duty to notify liability to income tax and/or CGT to HM Revenue & Customs (HMRC) by 5 October following end of tax year, unless they have received a notice from HMRC to file a return.

A taxpayer who has no chargeable gains and who is not liable to higher rate tax does not have to give notice of chargeability if all their income:

- Is taken into account under PAYE;
- Is from a source of income not subject to tax under a self-assessment;
- Has had (or is treated as having had) income tax deducted at source; or
- Is savings income and/or dividend income falling within the savings income nil rate band and the dividend nil rate band.

1.2 Penalties for failure to notify liability

A common penalty regime applies for failure to notify chargeability to, or liability to register for income tax, national insurance contributions (NICs), CGT, corporation tax and VAT. Penalties are behaviour related, increasing for more serious failures, and are based on the 'potential lost revenue' (PLR):

- Up to 30% of PLR if non-deliberate failure to notify
- Up to 70% of PLR if deliberate failure to notify, increased to 100% if also concealment

Penalties can be reduced if taxpayer makes disclosure and are more generous if disclosure is unprompted (can be reduced to 0% for a non-deliberate failure if unprompted disclosure within 12 months).

Essential reading

See the Essential reading for more details on penalties for failure to notify.

The Essential reading is available as an Appendix of the digital edition of the Workbook.

2 Tax returns

PER alert

One of the competencies you require to fulfil Performance Objective 16 *Tax compliance and verification* of the PER is to verify and question client submissions and ensure timely submission of all relevant information to the tax authorities by the due date. You can apply the knowledge you obtain from this section of the Workbook to help to demonstrate this competence.

2.1 Filing dates

HMRC usually issues a notice to the taxpayer requiring them to file a tax return.

Paper returns must usually be filed by **31 October following the end of the tax year.**

Electronically delivered returns must usually be filed by **31 January following the end of the tax year,** or three months from HMRC issuing the taxpayer with a notice to file a tax return if that is later than the 31 October/January deadlines.

The return requires information relating to the taxpayer's:

- Income and gains
- Personal allowances and reliefs

The tax return comprises a basic return form with supplementary pages for particular sources of income (eg employment income) and for chargeable gains.

Activity 1: Filing deadlines

HMRC issued a notice to file a tax return for the tax year 2020/21 to Anna on 16 May 2021.

A similar notice was issued to her husband Franko on 14 December 2021.

Required

What are the deadlines for Anna and Franko's tax returns for 2020/21 if they both submit electronically?

O   Anna on 31 October 2021 and Franko on 31 January 2022

O   Both returns on 31 January 2022

O   Anna on 31 October 2022 and Franko on 13 March 2022

O   Anna on 31 January 2022 and Franko on 13 March 2022

Solution

2.2 Penalties for late filing

The penalty date for filing a late return is the day after the filing date.

Penalties for filing on or after penalty date are as follows:

0–3 months	£100
3–6 months	Further penalty: £10 per day (maximum 90 days)
6–12 months	Further penalty: greater of 5% of unpaid tax and £300
12 months +	Further penalty: greater of % of unpaid tax (conduct based) and £300

Essential reading

See the Essential reading for more details on penalties for late filing where the failure continues after the end of the 12-month period.

The Essential reading is available as an Appendix of the digital edition of the Workbook.

2.3 Penalties for errors

A common penalty regime applies to incorrect self-assessment tax returns, self-assessment corporation tax returns and misdeclarations on a value added tax (VAT) return.

Penalties are behaviour related and are based on the PLR as a result of the error. For example, if there is an understatement of tax, this understatement will be the PLR. Penalties can be reduced if taxpayer makes disclosure and are more generous if disclosure is unprompted.

The maximum and minimum amount of penalties are as follows:

Taxpayer behaviour	Maximum penalty	Minimum penalty – unprompted disclosure	Minimum penalty – prompted disclosure
Deliberate and concealed	100%	30%	50%
Deliberate but not concealed	70%	20%	35%
Careless	30%	0%	15%

Formula provided

The penalty percentages will be given to you in the Tax Rates and Allowances available in the exam.

Activity 2: Penalty for error

Alexander is a sole trader. He files his tax return for the tax year 2020/21 on 10 January 2022. The return shows his trading income to be £60,000. In fact, due to carelessness, his trading income should have been stated to be £68,000. Alexander has no other income.

Required

Compute the maximum penalty that could be charged by HMRC on Alexander for his error.

Solution

3 Self-assessment

A self-assessment is a calculation of the amount of taxable income and gains after deducting reliefs and allowances, and a calculation of income tax and CGT payable after taking into account tax deducted at source.

If the taxpayer is filing a paper return, they may make the tax calculation on their return or ask HMRC to do so on their behalf. In either case, this is treated as a 'self-assessment' by the taxpayer.

If the taxpayer wishes HMRC to make the calculation for Year 1, a paper return must be filed:

- On, or before, 31 October in Year 2; or
- If the notice to file the tax return is issued after 31 August in Year 2, within two months of the notice.

If the taxpayer is filing an electronic return, the calculation of tax liability is made automatically when the return is made online.

3.1 Amendments to self-assessments

3.1.1 Amendment by taxpayer

The taxpayer may amend their return (including the tax calculation) for Year 1 within 12 months after the filing date. For this purpose, the filing date means:

- 31 January of Year 2; or
- When the notice to file a return was issued after 31 October in Year 2, the last day of the three-month period starting with the issue.

3.1.2 Amendment by HMRC

A return may be amended by HMRC to correct any obvious error or omission in the return (such as errors of principle and arithmetical mistakes) or anything else that an officer has reason to believe is incorrect in the light of information available. The correction must usually be made within nine months after the day on which the return was actually filed. The taxpayer can object to the correction but must do so within 30 days of receiving notice of it.

4 Records

All taxpayers must retain all records required to enable them to make and deliver a correct tax return.

Records must usually be retained until the later of:

- Five years after the 31 January following the tax year where the taxpayer is in business (as a sole trader or partner or letting property). Note that this applies to all of the records, not only the business records;
- One year after the 31 January following the tax year otherwise.

The maximum penalty for each failure to keep and retain records is £3,000 per tax year.

5 Payment dates

PER alert

One of the competencies you require to fulfil Performance Objective 16 *Tax compliance and verification* of the PER is to determine the incidence (timing) of tax liabilities and their impact on cash flow/financing requirements. You can apply the knowledge you obtain from this section of the Workbook to help to demonstrate this competence.

5.1 Payments on account

Income tax and Class 4 NICs are payable by two equal payments on account by 31 January (during the tax year) and 31 July (following the end of the tax year). Each payment on account is equal to 50% of the previous tax year's income tax and Class 4 NIC payable by self assessment (the 'relevant amount'). This excludes any amounts deducted at source, eg PAYE.

Activity 3: Payments on account

Sue is a self-employed writer who paid tax for 2019/20 as follows:

	£
Total amount of income tax charged	9,200
This included tax deducted at source on company loan stock	1,200
She also paid Class 4 NIC	1,900

Required

Compute the payments on account for income tax and Class 4 NIC for 2020/21 and state by what dates they are due.

Solution

Essential reading

See the Essential reading for more details on the circumstances where payments on account are not required and on claims to reduce payments on account.

The Essential reading is available as an Appendix of the digital edition of the Workbook.

5.2 Balancing payment

Any balancing payment is payable by 31 January following the end of the tax year (which will also include all the Class 2 NICs).

5.3 CGT

CGT is payable by 31 January following the end of the tax year. However, for disposals of residential property a payment on account must be made within 30 days of completion of the disposal (as covered in Chapter 13).

5.4 Interest on late paid tax

PER alert

One of the competencies you require to fulfil Performance Objective 16 *Tax compliance and verification* of the PER is to explain tax filing and payment requirements and the consequences of non-compliance to clients. You can apply the knowledge you obtain from this section of the Workbook to help to demonstrate this competence

Interest is chargeable on late payment of payments on account and balancing payments from due date until day before actual payment date.

Exam focus point

This topic was tested in Question 32, Martin, in the September 2018 exam. The examining team commented that "answers for TX-UK need to be precise, so the explanation how HMRC will calculate interest should have said that this will be from the original due date to the date before the additional tax is paid. A general discussion of how HMRC charges interest was not sufficient."

5.5 Penalties for late paid tax

Where the balancing payment and/or CGT is paid late, the penalty date is 30 days after the due date.

The following penalties apply:

On or before penalty date	0%
Not more than five months after penalty date	5% of unpaid tax
Between five months and 11 months after penalty date	10% of unpaid tax
More than 11 months after penalty date	15% of unpaid tax

5.6 Interest on overpaid tax

Interest on overpaid tax (repayment supplement) is payable from the original date of payment until the day before the repayment of tax is made.

Repayment supplement paid to individuals is tax free.

Formula provided

For the purpose of Taxation (TX – UK), exams in June 2021, September 2021, December 2021 and March 2022, the **assumed rate of interest on underpaid tax is 2.75%,** and **on overpaid tax is 0.5%**. You will be given these rates of interest in the Tax Rates and Allowances available in the exam.

6 HMRC powers

PER alert

One of the competencies you require to fulfil Performance Objective 16 *Tax compliance and verification* of the PER is to correspond appropriately and in a professional manner with the relevant parties in relation to both routine and specific matters/enquiries. You can apply the knowledge you obtain from this section of the Workbook to help to demonstrate this competence.

6.1 Compliance checks

HMRC must give notice of a compliance check into a return by the first anniversary of the actual filing date if the return is filed on or before the filing date.

If the return is filed after the filing date, HMRC must give notice by the quarter day following the first anniversary of the actual filing date. The quarter days are 31 January, 30 April, 31 July and 31 October.

Essential reading

See the Essential reading for more details of HMRC powers in relation to determinations, discovery assessments and dishonest conduct of tax agents.

The Essential reading is available as an Appendix of the digital edition of the Workbook.

7 Appeals

Appeals must first be made to HMRC.

The taxpayer may be offered, or may ask for, an 'internal review', which will be made by an objective HMRC review officer not previously connected with the case.

If there is no internal review, or the taxpayer is unhappy with the result of an internal review, the case may be heard by the Tax Tribunal.

Essential reading

See Chapter 10 of the Essential reading for more details of appeals.

The Essential reading is available as an Appendix of the digital edition of the Workbook.

Activity 4: Self-assessment issues

Donatella is self-employed and submits her self-assessment tax return for the tax year 2020/21 on 28 March 2022. HMRC had issued a notice to file the return on 14 December 2021.

Donatella failed to include a sales invoice of £10,000 in the calculation of her trading income because she had misfiled an email with the invoice attached and she had not received the cash from the customer by her year end. As a result, her trading income assessment should have been £135,000.

Donatella also has a part-time employment where she earns £9,000 a year.

Required

1   Complete the following sentence about the latest date by which Donatella's self-assessment tax return can be amended.

HMRC can amend Donatella's self-assessment tax return by [   ] and

Donatella can amend her self-assessment tax return by [   ]

Pull down list

- 13 March 2023
- 14 September 2022
- 28 December 2022
- 28 March 2023

2   What is the latest date HMRC can give notice of its intention to commence a compliance check enquiry into Donatella's return?

O   31 January 2023

O   31 March 2023

○ 28 March 2023

○ 30 April 2023

3   What is the maximum penalty that can be charged in relation to the understated profits in the return (ignore interest and late payment penalties)?

○ £1,260

○ £1,200

○ £2,940

○ £4,200

4   Until which date must Donatella retain the records in relation to her 2020/21 income tax liability?

○ Employment records until 31 January 2023, all other records until 31 January 2027

○ Employment records until 13 March 2023, all other records until 13 March 2027

○ All records until 31 January 2023

○ All records until 31 January 2027

5   What penalty for late filing will be charged in connection with the 2020/21 return?

○ £nil

○ £100

○ £900

○ £1,000

Solution

Chapter summary

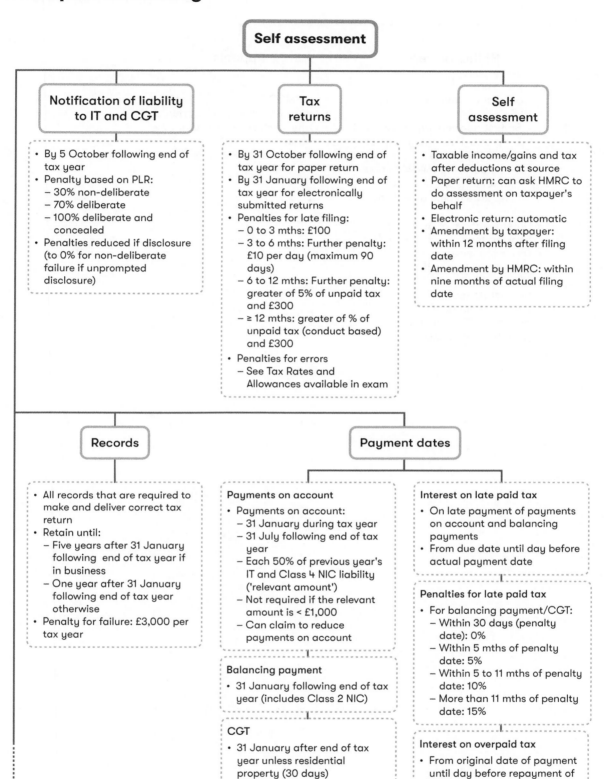

Self assessment

Notification of liability to IT and CGT

- By 5 October following end of tax year
- Penalty based on PLR:
  - 30% non-deliberate
  - 70% deliberate
  - 100% deliberate and concealed
- Penalties reduced if disclosure (to 0% for non-deliberate failure if unprompted disclosure)

Tax returns

- By 31 October following end of tax year for paper return
- By 31 January following end of tax year for electronically submitted returns
- Penalties for late filing:
  - 0 to 3 mths: £100
  - 3 to 6 mths: Further penalty: £10 per day (maximum 90 days)
  - 6 to 12 mths: Further penalty: greater of 5% of unpaid tax and £300
  - ≥ 12 mths: greater of % of unpaid tax (conduct based) and £300
- Penalties for errors
  - See Tax Rates and Allowances available in exam

Self assessment

- Taxable income/gains and tax after deductions at source
- Paper return: can ask HMRC to do assessment on taxpayer's behalf
- Electronic return: automatic
- Amendment by taxpayer: within 12 months after filing date
- Amendment by HMRC: within nine months of actual filing date

Records

- All records that are required to make and deliver correct tax return
- Retain until:
  - Five years after 31 January following end of tax year if in business
  - One year after 31 January following end of tax year otherwise
- Penalty for failure: £3,000 per tax year

Payment dates

Payments on account

- Payments on account:
  - 31 January during tax year
  - 31 July following end of tax year
  - Each 50% of previous year's IT and Class 4 NIC liability ('relevant amount')
  - Not required if the relevant amount is < £1,000
  - Can claim to reduce payments on account

Balancing payment

- 31 January following end of tax year (includes Class 2 NIC)

CGT

- 31 January after end of tax year unless residential property (30 days)

Interest on late paid tax

- On late payment of payments on account and balancing payments
- From due date until day before actual payment date

Penalties for late paid tax

- For balancing payment/CGT:
  - Within 30 days (penalty date): 0%
  - Within 5 mths of penalty date: 5%
  - Within 5 to 11 mths of penalty date: 10%
  - More than 11 mths of penalty date: 15%

Interest on overpaid tax

- From original date of payment until day before repayment of tax made

HMRC powers

- Compliance check notice by HMRC:
  - By first anniversary of actual filing date if return filed on or before filing date
  - By quarter day following first anniversary of the actual filing date if filed after filing date
- Determination: of amounts liable to tax
- Discovery assessment: to recover tax lost eg if careless/deliberate understatement
- Dishonest conduct of tax agents: HMRC may issue penalty up to £50,000

Appeals

- To HMRC
- Internal review may be offered
- Otherwise, cases heard by Tax Tribunal

Knowledge diagnostic

1. Taxpayer obligations

Individuals must notify their chargeability to income tax or CGT by 5 October following the end of the tax year. A common penalty regime applies to late notification of chargeability.

Tax returns must usually be filed by 31 October (paper) or 31 January (electronic) following the end of the tax year.

Two payments on account and a final balancing payment of income tax and Class 4 NICs are due. Class 2 NICs and CGT are payable at the same time as the balancing payment. Interest is payable on late paid tax.

2. Penalties

A penalty can be charged for late filing of a tax return based on how late the return is and how much tax is payable.

There is a common penalty regime for errors in tax returns, including income tax, NICs, corporation tax and VAT. Penalties range from 30% to 100% of the Potential Lost Revenue. Penalties may be reduced.

A penalty is chargeable where a balancing payment and/or CGT is paid after the due date and is based on the amount of the unpaid tax.

3. Compliance checks and disputes

A compliance check into a return can be started by HMRC within a limited period.

Disputes between taxpayers and HMRC can be dealt with by an HMRC internal review or by a Tribunal hearing.

Further study guidance

Question practice

Now try the following from the Further question practice bank (available in the digital edition of the Workbook):

Section A: Q73, Q74, Q75

Section B: Q76 Ash

Activity answers

Activity 1: Filing deadlines

The correct answer is: Anna on 31 January 2022 and Franko on 13 March 2022

The later of 31 January 2022 for the electronic returns and three months from the issue of a notice to file.

Activity 2: Penalty for error

Potential lost revenue (PLR) as a result of Alexander's error is: £68,000 − £60,000 = £8,000 × [40% (income tax) + 2% (Class 4 NICs] = £3,360.

Alexander's error is careless, so the maximum penalty for the error is: £3,360 × 30% = £1,008.

Activity 3: Payments on account

	£
Income tax paid by self assessment in 2019/20:	
Total income tax charged for 2019/20	9,200
Less tax deducted at source on loan stock for 2019/20	(1,200)
	8,000
Class 4 NIC	1,900
'Relevant amount'	9,900
Payments on account for 2020/21:	
31 January 2021 £9,900 × 50%	4,950
31 July 2021 £9,900 × 50%	4,950

Activity 4: Self-assessment issues

1   HMRC can amend Donatella's self-assessment tax return by   28 December 2022   and

    Donatella can amend her self-assessment tax return by   13 March 2023

    The return was due on the later of 31 January 2022 and 13 March 2022, ie 13 March 2022. It was actually filed on 28 March 2022 so it was filed late.

    The relevant deadlines are nine months from receipt for HMRC and 12 months from due filing date for the taxpayer.

2   The correct answer is: 30 April 2023

    12 months from the quarter date following actual submission because the return was late.

3   The correct answer is: £1,260

    £10,000 × (40% + 2%) × 30% = £1,260

    Income tax of 40%

    Class 4 NIC of 2%

    Non-deliberate (careless) error

4   The correct answer is: All records until 31 January 2027

    Donatella is in business so all relevant records must be kept for five years beyond the normal filing date.

5   The correct answer is: £100

The return is 15 days late (< three months).

Skills checkpoint 3

Tax administration and the payment of tax

Chapter overview

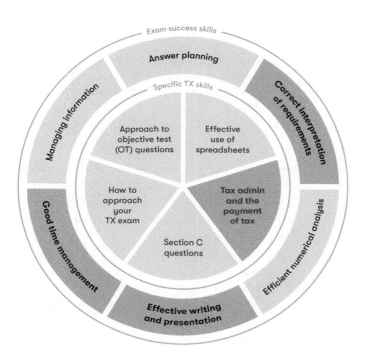

Introduction

As you can see from the TX syllabus diagram below, the tax system and its administration (Part A of the syllabus) feeds into all of the other areas of the TX syllabus.

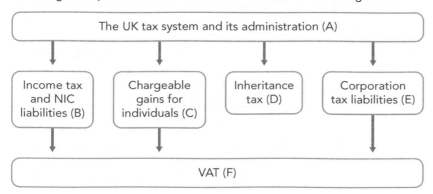

Although your TX exam will focus heavily on calculation questions, it is important not to neglect the administration part of the syllabus, because questions on this area can provide quick and easy exam marks. These types of question are often 'you know it or you don't' style questions and, therefore, if you know the correct answer, you can quickly select it, leaving more time for the calculation questions that require more care.

Tax administration and the payment of tax

The Sep 2019 examination team's report highlighted that the following question was not answered well:

In which of the following cases must an appeal be made directly to the Tribunal?

- A company appealing against a penalty for late filing of a corporation tax return
- A company appealing against a penalty for late filing of employer year-end returns
- An individual appealing against a penalty for late registration for value added tax (VAT)
- An individual appealing against a penalty for late payment of capital gains tax

The correct answer is 'An individual appealing against a penalty for late registration for value added tax (VAT)', because appeals relating to indirect taxes must be made directly to the Tribunal. Many candidates selected the first option, which is not correct because, for direct taxes, appeals must first be made to HM Revenue & Customs (HMRC).

The examination team's report said 'This is a challenging question on tax administration, an area which candidates often appear to struggle with. Candidates are reminded of the **importance of being prepared for questions on all aspects of the syllabus, including tax administration, which is an important aspect of TX-UK.**'

Section C questions may also ask you for dates.

The Dec 2019 examination team's report said:

'Where a question asks for dates, such as how long records used in preparing a self-assessment tax return should be retained, then these dates need to be precise – including the year relevant to the question.'

For example, a company must retain records for six years **after the end of the accounting period** (not just six years).

You will need to practise lots of TX questions in order to be able to pass the exam. However, the tax system and administration part of the syllabus can be approached using an old fashioned 'rote' learning method. You need to learn the information and then you can test yourself or ask a friend to test you. We have provided a list below that you can use for this purpose. It's a summary of the administration relating to all taxes in TX.

Test question	Answer
Appeals against HMRC decisions relating to direct taxes must first be made to whom?	HMRC. If relating to indirect taxes, appeals are made to Tribunal.
What does the First-tier Tribunal deal with?	Most cases
What does the Upper Tribunal deal with?	Complex cases
When is VAT registration compulsory?	See tax tables • At the end of any month taxable supplies over the previous 12 months have exceeded £85,000 (historical test); or • In the next 30 days, taxable supplies are expected to exceed £85,000 (future test).
When is VAT registration effective from?	The first day of the second month after the £85,000 was exceeded, or from an earlier date if they and the trader agree (historical test)

Test question	Answer
	Start of 30-day period if future 30-day test applies
What is the time limit in respect of claiming pre-registration input tax on goods?	VAT must have been incurred in the four years before registration date. (Services = six months before registration date.)
When is the tax point?	Earliest of: • When goods/service made available/completed (basic tax point) • Invoice issued date • Payment received If invoice issued within 14 days after basic tax point, invoice date can become the tax point.
What is a default and how long does it last?	Written notification for late VAT return or late payment. Until not been in default for 12 months
When are surcharges issued?	For every late payment during the default period
What about a late return during default?	No penalty if paid on time but extends the default period
What are the surcharge amounts during surcharge period?	1st - 2% VAT o/s - nil if <£400 2nd - 5% VAT /os - nil if <£400 3rd - 10% VAT o/s - but not less than £30 4th+ - 15% VAT o/s - but not less than £30
What errors can be corrected on the next VAT return?	• <£10,000 error • 1% x net VAT t/o for return period (max £50,000) Full disclosure is required to reduce possible penalty.
What is the common penalty regime?	Applies for failure to notify chargeability to, or liability to register for income tax, national insurance contributions (NICs), CGT, corporation tax and VAT Penalties are behaviour related, based on the 'potential lost revenue' (PLR): • Up to 30% of PLR if non-deliberate failure to notify • Up to 70% of PLR if deliberate failure to notify, increased to 100% if also concealment Penalties can be reduced if taxpayer makes disclosure.
Individuals	
Who needs to fill in a tax return?	Self employed, company directors, individuals with complicated affairs
When do individuals have to give notice of	5 October, following the end of the tax year

Test question	Answer
chargeability to HMRC?	
What are the filing dates for tax returns?	Paper returns – 31 October, following the end of the tax year Electronic returns – 31 January, following the end of the tax year OR Three months from HMRC issuing the notice to file a return (if later than 31 October)
How and when are income tax and Class 4 NIC paid?	Two payments on account: 1st POA – 31 January, during the current tax year 2nd POA – 31 July, after the tax year Balancing payment – 31 January AFTER the tax year, ie same as electronic filing date
When are CGT and Class 2 NIC paid?	31 January, after the end of the tax year But CGT on residential property - POA within 30 days of disposal
What are the penalties for late returns?	£100 automatic penalty If three - six months late, additional £10 per day (max 90 days) If 6 - 12 months late, greater of 5% of unpaid tax and £300 12 months+, greater of % of unpaid tax (conduct based) and £300
What is the interest amount for late payment of tax?	See tax tables Rate × Overdue tax × n/12
What is the penalty for late balancing payments?	One - six months late, 5% of unpaid tax 6 - 12 months late, 10% unpaid tax > 12 months late, 15% unpaid tax
What are the penalties for errors?	Penalty is based upon the potentially lost revenue. (See tax tables.)
When must HMRC amend obvious errors?	Within nine months of the actual filing date
When must the taxpayer make any amendments?	Within 12 months after the due filing date
When can HMRC make a compliance check?	Within 12 months of the return being actually submitted If filed late, can go to next quarter (31 January, 30 April, 31 July, 31 October) + 12 months Eg filed 14/2 - 30/4 + 12 months
How long must taxpayers retain records and what is the maximum penalty for not doing so?	Five years after the 31 January following the tax year where the taxpayer is in business (as a sole trader or partner or letting property) Note that this applies to all of the records, not

Test question	Answer
	only the business records; one year after the 31 January following the tax year otherwise. Maximum penalty £3,000 per tax year
When is IHT on lifetime transfers due?	If made between 6 April and 30 September, tax is due 30 April following the end of the tax year. Otherwise, six months from the end of the month of transfer.
When is IHT due on death tax on lifetime gifts?	Six months from the end of the month of the donor's death
When is IHT death tax on estate due?	Six months from the end of the month of death or on the delivery of account if earlier
Companies	
When must a company notify HMRC of its chargeability to corporation tax?	Within three months of the first accounting period
When is the filing date?	Later of: • 12 months after the end of the accounting period to which it relates • Three months from the date on which the notice requiring the return was made
When must the company make any amendments?	Same as individuals
Companies must keep records until when?	Later of: • Six years from the end of the accounting period • The date any compliance check enquiries are completed • The date after which a compliance check enquiry may not be commenced
When must HMRC give written notice of intention to conduct a compliance enquiry?	• First anniversary of due filing date (most group companies) or actual filing date (other companies); or • The quarter day following the first anniversary of the actual filing date, if the return is filed after the due filing date (quarter days are 31 January, 30 April, 31 July, 31 October)
When is corporation tax due for companies that are not large?	Nine months and a day after the end of the accounting period
When is corporation tax due for large companies?	Quarterly instalments in months 7, 10, 13 and 16 following the start of the accounting period. For short APs first payment in month 7 then every three months until final payment in fourth month after end of AP
What is the interest charged by HMRC on late	(See tax tables for rate.)

Test question	Answer
paid tax?	Rate × tax amount × n/12
What are the penalties for late filing?	• Up to three months late £100 • Up to six months late £200 • Up to 12 months late £200 + 10% of tax unpaid six months after the return was due • Over 12 months late £200 + 20% of tax unpaid six months after the return was due • If third consecutive late filing, £100 and £200 penalties are increased to £500 and £1,000
What is the penalty for failure to keep records?	Up to £3,000
What are the penalties for making errors?	Same as individuals

Exam success skills

The following question is worth 10 marks. It is on VAT which you have not yet covered so you may want to come back to this example at a later date.

For this question, we will also focus on the following exam success skills:

Correct interpretation of requirements. Read the requirement for each part first before you go through the detail in the scenario. Think about what you want to say before you start writing. Make sure that if there are two parts to a single requirement, you answer them both.

Effective writing and presentation. The markers want to see a clear layout with paragraphs that answer the requirement, and workings if relevant (eg for the calculation of the cumulative sales). They also want to see precise dates rather than simply explanations of dates.

Good time management. You need to look at the marks for the requirements to decide how much you need to write. Do not go over on 18 minutes for a 10-mark question.

Skills activity

Newcomer Ltd and Au Revoir Ltd

(a) Newcomer Ltd commenced trading on 1 November 2020. Its forecast sales are as follows:

		£
2020	November	18,500
	December	21,900
2021	January	23,400
	February	22,300
	March	22,700
	April	19,200

The company's sales are all standard-rated, and the above figures are exclusive of VAT.

Required

Explain when Newcomer Ltd will be required to compulsorily register for VAT.

(b) Au Revoir Ltd has been registered for VAT for many years and its sales are all standard rated. The company has recently seen a downturn in its business activities, and sales for the years ended 31 October 2020 and 2021 are forecast to be £77,000 and £75,500 respectively. Both of these figures are exclusive of VAT.

Required

Explain why Au Revoir Ltd will be permitted to voluntarily deregister for VAT, and from what date deregistration will be effective.

(4 marks)

Answer

Note. This question is a typical question on registration and deregistration. Note the importance of the dates.

(a) The registration threshold is £85,000 during any consecutive 12-month period. This is exceeded in February 2021:

		£
2020	November	18,500
	December	21,900
2021	January	23,400
	February	22,300
		86,100

Therefore, Newcomer Ltd must notify HM Revenue & Customs (HMRC) within 30 days of the end of the month the threshold was exceeded, ie by 30 March 2021.

Newcomer Ltd will be registered from the first day of the second month following the month in which the registration threshold was exceeded (ie from 1 April 2021), or an earlier date agreed between the company and HMRC.

(b) A person is eligible for voluntary deregistration if HMRC are satisfied that the amount of their taxable supplies (net of VAT) in the following one-year period will not exceed £83,000. However, voluntary deregistration will not be allowed if the reasons for the expected fall in value of taxable supplies is the cessation of taxable supplies or the suspension of taxable supplies for a period of 30 days or more in that following year. HMRC will cancel a person's registration from the date the request is made or an agreed later date.

Exam success skills diagnostic

Every time you complete a question, use the diagnostic below to assess how effectively you demonstrated the exam success skills in answering the question. The table has been completed below for the 'Newcomer Ltd and Au Revoir Ltd' activity to give you an idea of how to complete the diagnostic.

Exam success skills	Your reflections/observations
Correct interpretation of requirements	There are six marks available for requirement (a) so you need to make sure you write enough to justify this. Did you explain when Newcomer was required to register with an explanation of why (ie threshold exceeded)? Did you explain when Newcomer would be registered from? For part (b) there were two parts. Did you explain why deregistration was possible as well as the date?

Exam success skills	Your reflections/observations
Effective writing and presentation	Were you precise with the notification day, saying 1 March 2021 rather than just from the end of the month the threshold was exceeded?
Good time management	Did you manage your time to ensure you completed the question in the time available?
Most important action points to apply to your next question	

Summary

You must study the whole syllabus in order to pass the TX exam, but having the administration knowledge at your fingertips will give you extra time in the exam to answer the more difficult questions. In Section C questions, always be precise with your dates.

18 Inheritance tax: scope and transfers of value

Learning objectives

On completion of this chapter, you should be able to:

	Syllabus reference no.
Identify the persons chargeable.	D1(a)
Understand and apply the meaning of transfer of value, chargeable transfer and potentially exempt transfer.	D1(b)
Demonstrate the diminution in value principle.	D1(c)
Demonstrate the seven-year accumulation principle taking into account changes in the level of the nil rate band.	D1(d)
Understand the tax implications of lifetime transfers and compute the relevant liabilities.	D2(a)
Understand and compute the tax liability on a death estate.	D2(b)
Understand and apply the transfer of any unused nil rate band between spouses.	D2(c)
Understand and apply the residence nil rate band available when a residential property is inherited by direct descendants.	D2(d)
Understand and apply the following exemptions: (a) Small gifts exemption (b) Annual exemption (c) Normal expenditure out of income (d) Gifts in consideration of marriage (e) Gifts between spouses	D3(a)
Basic inheritance tax planning.	D3(b)
Identify who is responsible for the payment of inheritance tax and the due date for payment of inheritance tax.	D4(a)

Exam context

Inheritance tax (IHT) may be the subject of a 10-mark question in Sections B or C and you may also find specific aspects being tested in Section A such as tax on a single transfer of value. You will need to know when IHT is charged: transfers of value (basically gifts) and chargeable persons.

The concepts of potentially exempt transfers (PETs), chargeable lifetime transfers (CLTs) and the seven-year accumulation principle are all fundamental to an understanding of IHT. Once you have worked out the amount of a transfer of value, you need to be able to work out the IHT liability on it. This could be payable during the donor's lifetime and/or on death for a lifetime transfer and on death for a death estate. There are a number of exemptions which may be used to reduce IHT liability such as gifts between spouses/civil partners. Finally, you need to understand how IHT is paid and who pays it.

Chapter overview

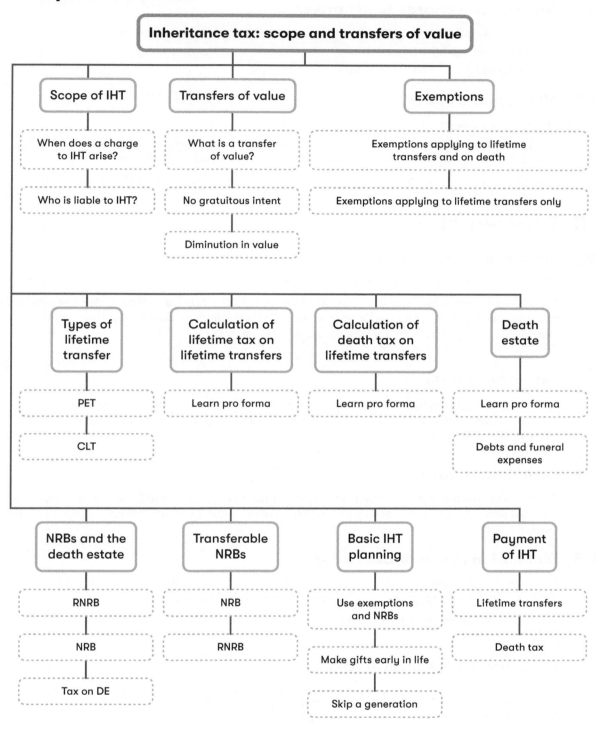

Inheritance tax: scope and transfers of value

Scope of IHT
- When does a charge to IHT arise?
- Who is liable to IHT?

Transfers of value
- What is a transfer of value?
- No gratuitous intent
- Diminution in value

Exemptions
- Exemptions applying to lifetime transfers and on death
- Exemptions applying to lifetime transfers only

Types of lifetime transfer
- PET
- CLT

Calculation of lifetime tax on lifetime transfers
- Learn pro forma

Calculation of death tax on lifetime transfers
- Learn pro forma

Death estate
- Learn pro forma
- Debts and funeral expenses

NRBs and the death estate
- RNRB
- NRB
- Tax on DE

Transferable NRBs
- NRB
- RNRB

Basic IHT planning
- Use exemptions and NRBs
- Make gifts early in life
- Skip a generation

Payment of IHT
- Lifetime transfers
- Death tax

1 Scope of inheritance tax (IHT)

1.1 When does a charge to IHT arise?

IHT is a tax on gifts, or transfers of value. There are two main chargeable occasions:

- Lifetime transfers
- Gifts made on death (death estate)

1.2 Who is liable to IHT?

Chargeable persons are individuals and trustees.

A trust is a legal structure where one person (the settlor) gives property to one or more people (the trustees) to be held for the benefit of one or more people (the beneficiaries).

Chargeable persons are taxed on all gifts of wealth (or transfers of value) that they make.

2 Transfers of value

2.1 What is a transfer of value?

IHT cannot arise unless there is a transfer of value.

A transfer of value is any gratuitous disposition (eg a gift) made by a person which results in them being worse off; that is, they suffer a diminution (ie reduction) in the value of their estate. An individual's estate is basically all the assets which they own.

> ### Exam focus point
>
> The examining team has stated that, as far as Taxation (TX – UK) is concerned, the terms 'transfer' and 'gift' can be taken to mean the same thing and that a transfer of value will always be a gift of assets.

2.2 Gratuitous intent

Transfers where there is no gratuitous intent are not chargeable to IHT. An example would be selling a painting for £1,000 at auction which later turns out to be worth £100,000 or other poor business deals.

2.3 Diminution in value/loss to donor

The value of the asset transferred for IHT is always measured as the reduction in value of the donor's wealth, 'loss to donor', **not** the amount gained by the donee.

In many cases, these two will be the same, as in the case of a gift of cash. However ,sometimes they will be different, for example where unquoted shares are gifted.

Illustration 1: Diminution in value (1)

Audrey holds 5,100 of the shares in an unquoted company which has an issued share capital of 10,000 shares. Currently Audrey's majority holding is valued at £15 per share.

Audrey wishes to give 200 shares to her son, Brian. However, the shares are worth only £2.50 each to Brian, since Brian will have only a small minority holding in the company. After the gift Audrey will hold 4,900 shares and these will be worth £10 each. The value per share to Audrey will fall from £15 to £10 per share since she will lose control of the company.

Required

What is the diminution in value of Audrey's estate?

Solution

The diminution in value of Audrey's estate is £27,500, as follows:

	£
Before the gift: 5,100 shares × £15	76,500
After the gift: 4,900 shares × £10	(49,000)
Diminution in value	27,500

Brian has only been given shares with a market value of 200 × £2.50 = £500. Remember, a gift is also a deemed disposal at market value for CGT purposes and it is this value that will be used in any CGT computation. IHT, however, uses the principle of diminution in value which can, as in this case, give a much greater value than the market value of the asset transferred.

Activity 1: Diminution in value (2)

Mr Jones owns 75% of Hill Jones Ltd, an unquoted investment company. He gives a 30% holding to his son.

Shareholdings on this date were valued at:

	£
75%	370,000
45%	200,000
30%	105,000

Required

What is the value for IHT and capital gains tax (CGT) purposes?

- ○ IHT: £105,000; CGT: £105,000
- ○ IHT: £105,000; CGT: £170,000
- ○ IHT: £170,000; CGT: £105,000
- ○ IHT: £170,000; CGT: £170,000

Solution

3 Exemptions

3.1 Exemptions applying to lifetime transfers and on death:

3.1.1 Gifts between spouses/civil partners

Any transfers of value between spouses/civil partners are exempt. The exemption covers lifetime gifts between them and property passing under a will or on intestacy.

3.2 Exemptions applying to lifetime transfers only:

3.2.1 Annual exemption (AE)

The first £3,000 of value transferred in any tax year is exempt.

Any unused annual exemption (or part thereof) may be carried forward for one year only, for use in the following tax year.

The current year annual exemption is used before the brought forward annual exemption.

The exemption is given in chronological order to the earliest gift(s) made in the tax year.

 Illustration 2: Annual exemptions

Frank has no unused annual exemption brought forward at 6 April 2019.

On 1 August 2019, he makes a transfer of £600 to his son Peter.

On 1 September 2019, he makes a transfer of £2,000 to his nephew Quentin.

On 1 July 2020, he makes a transfer of £3,300 to a trust for his grandchildren.

On 1 June 2021, he makes a transfer of £5,000 to his friend Rowan.

Required

Show the application of the annual exemptions.

Solution

	£
1.8.19 Gift to Peter	600
Less AE 2019/20	(600)
	0
1.9.19 Gift to Quentin	2,000
Less AE 2019/20	(2,000)
	0

The unused annual exemption carried forward is £3,000 − £600 − £2,000 = £400.

	£	£
1.7.20 Gift to trust		3,300
Less: AE 2020/21	3,000	
AE 2019/20 b/f	300	
		(3,300)
		0

The unused annual exemption carried forward is zero because the 2020/21 exemption must be used before the 2019/20 exemption brought forward. The balance of £100 of the 2019/20 exemption is lost, because it cannot be carried forward for more than one year.

2021/22	£
1.6.21 Gift to Rowan	5,000
Less AE 2021/22	(3,000)
	2,000

3.2.2 Gifts in consideration of marriage/civil partnership

The first £5,000 given by a parent on the occasion of a wedding is exempt. This applies per marriage.

The amount is lower for gifts by other parties:

- £2,500 by a lineal ancestor (eg grandparent) or one party of the marriage to the other
- £1,000 by any other person

3.2.3 Small gifts exemption

Gifts of up to £250 per donee per tax year are exempt.

The exemption cannot apply to gifts exceeding £250 per tax year in total to the same donee.

Also, the exemption cannot apply to gifts into trusts.

3.2.4 Normal expenditure out of income

Inheritance tax is a tax on transfers of capital, not income.

Therefore, cash gifts which are habitual are exempt if made out of income, as long as the gift does not result in a reduced standard of living of the donor.

As well as covering such things as regular presents this exemption can cover regular payments out of income such as a grandchild's school fees or the payment of life assurance premiums on a policy for someone else.

PER alert

One of the competencies you require to fulfil Performance Objective 17 *Tax planning and advice* of the PER is to mitigate and/or defer tax liabilities through the use of standard reliefs, exemptions and incentives. You can apply the knowledge you obtain from this section of the Workbook to help to demonstrate this competence.

Activity 2: Exemptions

Dale made a gift of £153,000 to her son on 17 October 2016 on the son's marriage. Dale gave £100,000 to her spouse on 1 January 2020. Dale gave £70,000 to her daughter on 11 May 2020. The only other gifts Dale made were birthday and Christmas presents of £100 each to her grandchildren.

Required

Compute the amount of the transfers of value after exemptions for each of these gifts.

Solution

---

4 Types of lifetime transfers

KEY TERM

Potentially exempt transfer (PET): A potentially exempt transfer (PET) is a lifetime transfer (other than an exempt transfer) made by an individual to another individual.

Chargeable lifetime transfer (CLT): Any other lifetime transfer by an individual (eg a gift to trustees) which is not an exempt transfer is a chargeable lifetime transfer (CLT).

4.1 Potentially exempt transfers (PET)

A potentially exempt transfer (PET) is a gift between individuals.

PETs are exempt from inheritance tax when the gift is made.

However, they may become chargeable to death tax if the donor dies within seven years of making the gift.

4.2 Chargeable lifetime transfers (CLT)

Any other lifetime transfers are chargeable lifetime transfers (CLTs) (eg gift to trust).

CLTs are chargeable during lifetime to lifetime tax.

Additional tax (death tax) may become payable if the donor dies within seven years of making CLT.

5 Calculation of lifetime tax on lifetime transfers

PER alert

One of the competencies you require to fulfil Performance Objective 15 *Tax computations and assessments* of the PER is to prepare or contribute to the computation or assessment of tax computations for individuals. You can apply the knowledge you obtain from this section of the Workbook to help to demonstrate this competence.

BPP
LEARNING
MEDIA

Follow this procedure:

Step 1 Prepare a **timeline** and **mark on CLTs** and **PETs**

Step 2 Value each **gift** remembering the **diminution in value** principle

Step 3 Deduct **exemptions** (see 'Exempt transfers' section above). Remember that annual exemptions are allocated against gifts in date order

Step 4 Ignore the PETs for now - because they become exempt if the donor survives for seven years.

For each CLT, look back seven years from the date of the transfer to see if any other CLTs have been made. If so, these transfers use up the nil rate band available for the current transfer. (This is called seven-year accumulation.) Work out the value of any nil rate band still available (**NRB at the time of the gift less any CLTs in the seven years before that gift**).

Step 5 Tax the **excess over the NRB** at 20/80 (ie 25% or ¼) **if the donor pays the IHT** (net transfer) or **20% if trustees pay the IHT** (gross transfer). If the question is silent, assume the donor pays the IHT

Step 6 Calculate the **gross value of the gift ('gross chargeable transfer')** for cumulation, ie to see how much of the NRB this gift will use up for future transfers.

= gift (after all reliefs and exemptions) **plus tax if donor pays**

= **just gift** (after all reliefs and exemptions) **if trust pays**

5.1 Lifetime tax: proforma

		£
Gift		X
Less AE		(X)
Less AE b/f		(X)
Net gift after exemptions		X
Less: NRB remaining:		
NRB at date of gift	X	
less CLTs in last 7 years before **gift**	(X)	
		(X)
		X
Tax @ 20% (donee paying) (or $^{20}/_{80,}$ donor paying)		X

The GCT which will use up the NRB for future gifts is calculated as follows:

	£
Net gift after exemptions	X
Tax IF paid by **donor** at $^{20}/_{80}$	X
Mark this GCT figure on your timeline.	GCT

Illustration 3: Lifetime tax (1)

Eric makes a gift of £336,000 to a trust on 10 July 2020. The trustees agree to pay the tax due.

Required

Calculate the lifetime tax payable by the trustees if Eric has made:

(a) A lifetime chargeable transfer of value of £100,000 in August 2012

(b) A lifetime chargeable transfer of value of £100,000 in August 2013

(c) A lifetime chargeable transfer of value of £350,000 in August 2013

Solution

(a) We need to start at step 3 (above)

Step 3: Value of CLT is £336,000 less £3,000 (AE 2020/21) and £3,000 (AE 2019/20) = £330,000.

Step 4: No lifetime transfers in seven years before 10 July 2020 (transfers after 10 July 2013). Nil rate band of £325,000 available.

Step 5:

	IHT
	£
£325,000 × 0%	0
£5,000 × 20%	1,000
£330,000	1,000

Step 6: GCT = '£330,000 (tax paid by trustees not donor)

(b) Step 3: Value of CLT is £330,000 as above

Step 4: Lifetime transfer of value of £100,000 in seven years before 10 July 2020 (transfers after 10 July 2013). Nil rate band of £325,000 – £100,000 = £225,000 available.

Step 5:

	IHT
	£
£225,000 × 0%	0
£105,000 × 20%	21,000
£330,000	21,000

Step 6: GCT = £330,000 (as above)

(c) Step 3: Value of CLT is £330,000 as above

Step 4: Lifetime transfer of value of £350,000 in seven years before 10 July 2020 (transfers after 10 July 2013). No nil rate band available as all covered by previous transfer.

Step 5:

	IHT
	£
£330,000 @ 20%	66,000

Step 6: GCT = £330,000 (as above)

Activity 3: Lifetime tax (2)

Mr Butcher put £337,000 into a trust on 13 August 2020 having already put £116,000 into a trust three years earlier (the GCT was £110,000).

Required

Calculate the IHT payable on the transfer to the trust in 13 August 2020 assuming:

(a) The trust agrees to pay the tax

(b) Mr Butcher pays the tax

Solution

Formula provided

The nil rate band for the current tax year and the lifetime rate will be given in the Tax Rates and Allowances available in the exam. Where nil rate bands are required for previous tax years, these will be given in the question.

The annual exemption is allocated to the first gift made in the tax year whether it is a PET or a CLT.

Remember, PETs do not use up any of the available NRB when performing lifetime tax calculations.

Activity 4: Lifetime tax (3)

Mr Beale put £343,000 into a trust on 13 August 2020 (trustees agreeing to pay the tax) having given £50,000 to his daughter on 15 March 2020. He gave £30,000 to his son on 19 August 2020.

Required

How much IHT is payable?

Solution

6 Calculation of death tax on lifetime transfers

IHT is charged on PETs and CLTs where the donor dies within seven years of making the gift.

Death tax is calculated at 40% and is payable by the **donee** of the gift.

6.1 Working out the tax on death

Follow this procedure:

Step 1 Use the **timeline** prepared for working out lifetime IHT. Mark **seven years** before the donor's death.

Step 2 Delete all PETs more than seven years before death. These are now exempt transfers.

Step 3 Start with the **earliest gift within seven years of death.**

Step 4 IHT is charged on the **value of the gift after reliefs and exemptions.**

Step 5 Deduct **available nil rate band (NRB)** which is the **NRB at the time of death less any previous chargeable transfers in the seven years before that gift.** Previous chargeable transfers are (1) CLTs and (2) PETs that have become chargeable.

Step 6 Tax **excess over available NRB at 40%.**

Step 7 **Deduct** any **taper relief.**

The **following table**, showing the percentage reduction depending on the period between date of gift (PET/CLT) and death, should be used to calculate the taper relief:

Years before death	Percentage reduction
Over 3 but less than 4	20%
Over 4 but less than 5	40%
Over 5 but less than 6	60%
Over 6 but less than 7	80%

Step 8 **Deduct** any **IHT paid in donor's lifetime** (CLTs only).

Formula provided

The taper relief table is given to you in the Tax Rates and Allowances available in the exam.

6.2 Proforma: death tax payable on lifetime gifts

DEATH TAX:

	£	£
Gross CLT/PET		X
Less NRB remaining:		
NRB on death	325,000	
Less GCTs in seven years **before gift**	(X)	
Available NRB		(X)
		X
Tax @ 40%		IHT
Less taper relief		
% × IHT		(X)
		X
Less lifetime tax (on CLT)		(X)
Death tax due		X

Illustration 4: Death tax on lifetime gift (1)

Mr Fowler made the following gifts during his lifetime:

3 March 2013	Gift to nephew	£40,000
14 October 2017	Gift to granddaughter on her marriage	£158,000
23 November 2018	Gift to son	£210,000

He died on 13 September 2020.

Required

Calculate the IHT payable and state by whom it is payable.

Solution

Lifetime tax:

None as all transfers are PETs

Death tax:

(i) PET March 2013:

   – more than 7 years before death ∴ exempt

(ii) PET October 2017:	£
Gift	158,000
– marriage exemption	(2,500)
– AE 2017/18	(3,000)
– AE 2016/17 b/f	(3,000)
PET	149,500

< NRB at date of death (£325,000) ∴ no tax due

GCT £149,500

(iii) PET November 2018:	£
Gift	210,000
– AE 2018/19	(3,000)
PET	207,000

	£	
Less NRB at date of death	325,000	
Less GCTs in seven years before **gift**	(149,500)	
		(175,500)
		31,500
Tax @ 40%		12,600

Payable by the son
(No taper relief as < three years before death)

Activity 5: Death tax on lifetime gift (2)

Mr Raymond made the following gifts during his lifetime:

13 May 2015	Gift to daughter	£130,000
23 August 2015	Gift into a trust	£334,000

He died on 7 June 2020.

Required

Calculate any IHT payable during life and on death. The nil rate band in 2015/16 was £325,000.

Solution

Exam focus point

Calculate lifetime tax on CLTs first. Then move on to death tax, working through all CLTs and PETs in chronological order. Remember: on death, PETs become chargeable so they must be taken into consideration when calculating the death tax on later CLTs.

7 Death estate

PER alert

One of the competencies you require to fulfil Performance Objective 15 *Tax computations and assessments* of the PER is to prepare or contribute to the computation or assessment of tax computations for individuals. You can apply the knowledge you obtain from this section of the Workbook to help to demonstrate this competence.

An individual's death estate consists of all the property they owned immediately before death (such as land and buildings, shares and other investments, cars and cash) **less debts and funeral expenses.**

The death estate also includes anything received as a result of death, for example the proceeds of a life assurance policy which pays out on the individual's death. The value of the policy immediately before the death is not relevant.

7.1 Death estate pro forma

X Deceased

Date of death .....

	£	£
Freehold property eg main residence	X	
Less interest-free/repayment mortgage and accrued interest	_	

	£	£
	(X)	
		X
Stocks and shares		X
Insurance policy proceeds		X
Leasehold property		X
Cars		X
Personal chattels		X
Debts due to deceased		X
Cash		X
		X
Less debts due from deceased (only if legally enforceable)		(X)
funeral expenses		(X)
Less exempt transfer to spouse		(X)
CHARGEABLE ESTATE		X

Essential reading

Further detail on which debts are deductible from the death estate and an Activity is contained within your Essential reading.

The Essential reading is available as an Appendix of the digital edition of the Workbook.

8 Nil rate bands and the death estate

8.1 Residence nil rate band (RNRB)

The residence nil rate band is an additional nil rate band used to compute IHT on the death estate (but not death tax on lifetime transfers, unlike the NRB).

The RNRB is relevant where:

- The deceased person died on or after 6 April 2017;
- The deceased person owned a home in which they lived (for Taxation (TX–UK) purposes called 'the main residence') which is **part of their death estate**; and
- The main residence passes (eg under a will) to one or more **direct descendants** of the deceased person (eg children, grandchildren).

The available RNRB is the lower of:

- The maximum RNRB which is:
  - £175,000; plus
  - Any transferred RNRB from a spouse or civil partner (see later in this Chapter); and
- The value of the main residence passing to direct descendent(s), after deducting any repayment mortgage or interest-only mortgage secured on the property.

If the value of the main residence passing to direct descendent(s) is less than the maximum RNRB, the unused RNRB may be transferred to the estate of a surviving spouse or civil partner (see later in this chapter).

Formula provided

The residence nil rate band amount for the current tax year will be given in the Tax Rates and Allowances available in the exam. The examining team has stated that **a question will not be set** where the residence nil rate band is available in respect of a death occurring prior to the tax year 2020/21.

> ### Exam focus point
>
> There are **other aspects** to the residence nil rate band. **None of the following are examinable** in Taxation (TX – UK):
>
> - **Tapering withdrawal** of the residence nil rate band where the net value of an estate exceeds £2 million
> - **Protection of the residence nil rate band** where an individual downsizes to a less valuable property or where a property is disposed of
> - **Nominating which property should qualify** where there is more than one main residence

8.2 NRB and the death estate

The available NRB for the death estate is:

- The maximum NRB which is:
  - £325,000; plus
  - Any transferred NRB from a spouse or civil partner (see later in this Chapter); less
- Lifetime transfers in the seven years before death (CLTs and PETs which have become chargeable).

8.3 Computing tax on the death estate

Follow this procedure:

Step 1   Compute the **value of the chargeable death estate**, ie after deducting exempt gifts to spouses/civil partners.

Step 2   Deduct the **available RNRB.**

Step 3   Deduct the **available NRB.**

Step 4   Charge the excess remaining at **40%. This IHT is payable by the personal representatives** (PRs) of the deceased.

Illustration 5: Tax on the death estate (1)

Laura dies on 1 August 2020, leaving a death estate valued at £530,000. In her will, Laura left cash of £80,000 to her husband and the remainder of her estate to her son which included her main residence valued at £200,000. Laura had made a gift of £171,000 to her sister on 11 September 2019.

Required

Compute the tax payable on Laura's death estate.

Solution

Death tax

Note. There is no death tax on the September 2019 PET which becomes chargeable as a result of Laura's death, as it is within the nil rate band at her death. However, it will use up part of the nil rate band.

		£
Chargeable estate (£530,000-£80,000)		450,000
Less: available RNRB		
(lower of £175,000 and £200,000)		(175,000)
available NRB		
NRB at date of death	325,000	
Less used in seven years before death		
(£171,000 less 2 x AE)	(165,000)	
		(160,000)
		115,000
Tax @ 40%		46,000

Activity 6: Tax on the death estate (2)

Rory died on 5 May 2020, leaving an estate comprising:

- 10,000 ABC plc shares, valued at £24,400
- Main residence worth £350,000
- Investment property valued at £84,000
- 1,000 XYZ Investment Ltd shares valued at £68,000

Rory had an outstanding loan of £5,750 to his bank at the time of his death.

Rory left a will directing that his wife should take the ABC plc shares, the main residence should go to his son and the rest of his estate should go to his daughter. He had made one gross chargeable transfer during his lifetime in 2014 of £232,000.

Required

Show the IHT payable on Rory's estate.

Solution

9 Spouses and civil partners – transferable nil rate bands

If one spouse or civil partner has already died, but did not use all of their NRB on death, the percentage of their NRB which was unused can be transferred across to the other spouse or civil partner and used in computing their death tax (for both lifetime transfers and death estate).

Unused RNRB can also be transferred to a spouse/civil partner if the second spouse dies on or after 6 April 2017 and can then be used in computing the tax on their death estate only. It does not matter whether or not the first spouse had a main residence in their death estate. If the first spouse died before 6 April 2017, they are deemed to have had a RNRB of £175,000, all of which is available for transfer.

Illustration 6: Transferable NRB

Robert and Claudia were married for many years until the death of Robert on 10 April 2020. In his will, Robert left his death estate valued at £100,000 to his sister. He had made no lifetime transfers.

Claudia died on 12 January 2021 leaving a death estate worth £850,000 to her brother, so the residence nil rate band is not relevant. Claudia had made a gross chargeable lifetime transfer of £50,000 in 2017.

Required

Calculate the inheritance tax payable on the death of Claudia, assuming that a claim is made to transfer Robert's unused nil rate band.

Solution

Claudia's CLT in 2017 is covered by the NRB

	£	
Chargeable estate		850,000
Less: available NRB		
NRB at date of death	325,000	
Robert's unused NRB (£325,000 - £100,000)	225,000	
Less used in 7 years before death	(50,000)	
		(500,000)
		350,000
Tax @ 40%		140,000

9.1 Changes in nil rate band between deaths of spouses/civil partners

If the nil rate band increases between the death of B and the death of A, the amount of B's unused nil rate band must be scaled up so that it represents the same proportion of the nil rate band at A's death as it did at B's death.

For example, if the nil rate band at Barbara's death was £300,000 and Barbara had an unused nil rate band of £90,000, the unused proportion in percentage terms is therefore £90,000/£300,000 × 100 = 30%. If Arthur dies when the nil rate band has increased to £325,000, Barbara's unused nil rate band is £325,000 × 30% = £97,500 and this amount is transferred to increase the nil rate band maximum available on Arthur's death.

The increase in the nil rate band maximum cannot exceed the nil rate band maximum at the date of Arthur's death, eg if the nil rate band is £325,000; the increase cannot exceed £325,000, giving a total of £650,000.

Claims to transfer the unused nil rate bands are usually made by the personal representatives of the second spouse or civil partner to die. The time limit for the claims is two years from the end of the month of their death (or the period of three months after the personal representatives start to act, if later) or such longer period as an officer of HMRC may allow in a particular case.

If the personal representatives do not make a claim, a claim can be made by any other person liable to tax chargeable on the second spouse or civil partner's death within such later period as an officer of HMRC may allow in a particular case.

10 Basic inheritance tax planning

> ### PER alert
>
> One of the competencies you require to fulfil Performance Objective 17 *Tax planning and advice* of the PER is to assess the tax implications of proposed activities or plans of an individual or entity with reference to relevant and up to date legislation. You can apply the knowledge you obtain from this section of the Workbook to help to demonstrate this competence.

10.1 Use exemptions

Donors should ensure that use is made of exemptions in relation to lifetime gifts, in particular the annual exemption, the marriage/civil partnership exemption, the normal expenditure out of income exemption and the spouse/civil partner exemption.

When considering how to pass on assets in the death estate, the spouse/civil partner exemption may be used to ensure that no inheritance tax is payable when the first spouse/civil partner dies. Remember that an election can be made to ensure that unused nil rate band of the first spouse/civil partner is available to be used against the estate of the surviving spouse/civil partner.

10.2 Make gifts early in life

The earlier that a gift is made in lifetime the more likely it is that the donor will survive for seven years after making it, thereby avoiding death tax on the transfer. If they survive at least three years, then taper relief will apply to reduce the death tax.

The values of lifetime transfers cannot increase and therefore it is good tax planning to give away assets which are likely to increase in value such as land and shares.

However, there are some situations where it may not be advantageous for the donor to make a lifetime transfer in terms of overall tax liability. One is where a gift of an asset would result in a large chargeable gain (either immediately chargeable or deferred under gift relief). In this case, it may be better for the donor to retain the asset until death as there is a tax-free uplift in value on death for capital gains tax purposes so that the donee will receive the asset at market value at the date of the donor's death. This is particularly relevant if the donor is unlikely to survive three years from the date of a lifetime gift and so death rates without the benefit of taper relief would apply to a lifetime transfer. Another is if the gift is residential property such that the residence nil rate band would apply in calculating tax on the death estate.

10.3 Make use of the nil rate bands

Gifts to trusts are chargeable transfers. If the gift is within the nil rate band, however, there will be no inheritance tax payable when the gift is made. Transfers are only cumulated for seven years and therefore, after that time has elapsed, a further gift within the nil rate band can be made to a trust, again without incurring any immediate payment of inheritance tax.

The residence nil rate band can only be used if the main residence is passed to direct descendants, not to other family members. Donors should consider making a will which uses the residence nil rate band by leaving the main residence to children or grandchildren and assets such as cash or shares to other family members such as brothers and sisters.

10.4 Skip a generation

Donors may consider giving assets to their children, either during lifetime or on death. Such assets may then be passed by those children to their own children, the grandchildren of the donor.

If the donor's children already have sufficient assets for their financial needs, it may be beneficial to skip a generation so that gifts are made to grandchildren, rather than children. This avoids a further charge to inheritance tax on the death of the children so that gifts will then only be taxed once before being inherited by the grandchildren, rather than twice.

11 Payment of IHT

PER alert

One of the competencies you require to fulfil Performance Objective 16 *Tax compliance and verification* of the PER is to determine the incidence (timing) of tax liabilities and their impact on cash flow/financing requirements. You can apply the knowledge you obtain from this section of the Workbook to help to demonstrate this competence.

11.1 Lifetime transfers

If the CLT is made between 6 April and 30 September, the tax is due by 30 April following the end of the tax year, otherwise the tax is due six months from the end of the month of transfer.

The donor is primarily liable for the tax due on chargeable lifetime transfers. However, the donee (ie the trustees) may agree to pay the tax out of the trust assets.

11.2 Death tax

The death tax on lifetime gifts is due six months from the end of the month of death, by the donee.

The death tax on the estate is due six months from the end of the month of death, or on delivery of the account if earlier, by the personal representatives of deceased.

Illustration 7: Payment dates

Lisa gave some shares to a trust on 10 July 2016. She gave a house to her daughter on 12 December 2016. Lisa died on 17 May 2020 leaving her death estate to her son.

Required

For each of these transfers of value, state who is liable to pay any inheritance tax due and the due date for payment.

Solution

10 July 2016

Chargeable lifetime transfer. Lifetime tax payable by Lisa (unless trustees agree to pay tax), due later of 30 April 2017 and 31 January 2017, ie 30 April 2017. Death tax payable by trustees, due 30 November 2020.

12 December 2016

Potentially exempt transfer – no lifetime tax. Death tax payable by daughter, due 30 November 2020.

17 May 2020

Death tax payable by personal representatives out of death estate, due on earlier of submission of account and 30 November 2020.

Chapter summary

Inheritance tax: scope and transfers of value

Scope of IHT

When does a charge to IHT arise?
- Lifetime transfers
- Death estate

Who is liable to IHT?
- Chargeable persons – individuals and trusts
- Taxed on all gifts of wealth

Transfers of value

What is a transfer of value?
- Any gift

No gratuitous intent
- Not chargeable to IHT

Diminution in value
- Value of asset transferred =
  - Loss to donor
  - Not amount gained by donee

Exemptions

Exemptions applying to lifetime transfers and on death
- Gifts between spouses/CPs

Exemptions applying to lifetime transfers only
- Annual exemption
  - £3,000 pa
  - Use current year first
  - Cf one year
  - Applies to gifts in chronological order
- Marriage/CP
  - £5,000 from parent
  - £2,500 from lineal ancestor or party of the marriage
  - £1,000 anyone else
- Small gifts
  - £250 per donee pa
  - > £250 all chargeable
- Normal expenditure out of income

Types of lifetime transfer

PET
- Gift between individuals
- Exempt when gift is made
- Becomes chargeable to death tax only if donor dies < seven years of gift

CLT
- Any other transfer (eg gift to trust)
- Chargeable to lifetime tax
- Chargeable to death tax if donor dies < seven years of gift

Calculation of lifetime tax on lifetime transfers

Learn pro forma
- Deduct NRB at date of gift (used up by GCTs in seven years before gift)
- Donor paying: 20/80 (assume)
- Donee paying: 20%

Calculation of death tax on lifetime transfers

Learn pro forma
- Deduct NRB at date of death (used up by GCTs in seven years before gift)
- 40%
- Taper relief
- Deduct any lifetime tax (no refund)

Death estate

Learn pro forma
- All assets owned at death
- Deduct exempt transfers to spouse/CP

Debts and funeral expenses
- Do not deduct promises or oral agreements

NRBs and the death estate

RNRB
- Lower of £175,000 (plus amount transferred from spouse) and value of residence
- Only available if passing main residence to direct descendant(s) in DE

NRB
- £325,000 (plus amount transferred from spouse)
- Used up by lifetime transfers in seven years before death (CLTs and PETs become chargeable)

Tax on DE
- Learn procedure

Transferable NRBs

NRB
- Transfer % of unused NRB on first spouse/CP's death

RNRB
- Transfer unused even if first spouse/CP died before 6.4.17

Basic IHT planning

Use exemptions and NRBs

Make gifts early in life

Skip a generation

Payment of IHT

Lifetime transfers
- Depends on timing of CLT
- Payable by donor or donee

Death tax
- On lifetime gifts: six months from end of month of death
- On DE: six months from end of month of death or on delivery of accounts if earlier
- Payable by PRs

Knowledge diagnostic

1. Scope of IHT

IHT is a tax on gifts or transfers of value during lifetime and on death.

2. Transfers of value

IHT is charged on the amount the donor loses, not what the donee gains (diminution in value principle).

3. Exemptions

Gifts to spouses/civil partners are exempt in lifetime and at death. Other exemptions (eg annual exemption) apply to lifetime gifts only.

4. Types of lifetime transfers

PETs are gifts by individuals to individuals. CLTs are transfers to a trust.

5. Calculation of lifetime tax on lifetime transfers

CLTs are chargeable to tax in lifetime. PETs are exempt. Deduct the nil rate band at the date of the gift (used up by GCTs in 7 years before the gift). Take care to determine who will pay the life tax - 20/80 or 20%.

6. Calculation of death tax on lifetime transfers

Death tax at 40% is paid on all gifts within seven years of death plus the death estate.

Taper relief is available to reduce the death tax on gifts made three to seven years before death.

7. Death estate

The death estate includes all assets that are owned at death. The RNRB and the NRB must be considered.

8. Spouses and civil partners - transferable nil rate bands

Any unused RNRB/NRB on first spouse's death can be transferred to surviving spouse.

9. Payment of IHT

Normally six months from end of month following gift or death.

Further study guidance

Question practice

Now try the following from the Further question practice bank (available in the digital edition of the Workbook):

Section A: Q77, 78, 79

Section B: Q80 Colin and Diane

Section C: Q81 Simona

Further reading

Part 1 of ACCA's article *Inheritance tax*, written by a member of the Taxation (TX – UK) examining team considers the scope of inheritance tax, transfers of value, rates of tax and exemptions. Part 2 covers the more difficult aspects of lifetime transfers, the calculation of the value of a person's estate, and the payment of inheritance tax.

Activity answers

Activity 1: Diminution in value (2)

The correct answer is: IHT: £170,000; CGT: £105,000

	£
Value before transfer	370,000
Less value after transfer	(200,000)
Transfer of value for IHT	170,000
CGT value (MV)	105,000

Activity 2: Exemptions

17 October 2016

	£
Gift to Dale's son	153,000
Less: Marriage Exemption	(5,000)
AE 2016/17	(3,000)
AE 2015/16 b/f	(3,000)
PET	142,000

1 January 2020

	£
Gift to Dale's spouse	100,000
Less spouse exemption	(100,000)
	0

11 May 2020

	£
Gift to Dale's daughter	70,000
Less: AE 2020/21	(3,000)
AE 2019/20 b/f	(3,000)
PET	64,000

The gifts to the grandchildren are covered by the small gifts exemption.

Activity 3: Lifetime tax (2)

(a)

	£
Gift (CLT)	337,000

		£
AE: 2020/21		(3,000)
2019/20 b/f		(3,000)
Net gift after exemptions		331,000
NRB at date of gift	325,000	
Less GCTs in previous seven years before gift	(110,000)	(215,000)
		116,000
Tax at 20%		23,200

Gross chargeable transfer is £331,000.

(b)

	£	£
Net gift after exemptions, as before		331,000
– NRB at date of gift	325,000	
Less GCTs in 7 years before gift	(110,000)	
		(215,000)
		116,000
Tax at 25% (20/80)		29,000

Gross chargeable transfer is £360,000 (£331,000 + £29,000).

Activity 4: Lifetime tax (3)

	£
Gift to daughter 15.3.20	
Gift	50,000
AE: 2019/20	(3,000)
2018/19 b/f	(3,000)
PET	44,000

No lifetime tax

	£
Gift to trust 13.8.20	
Gift	343,000
AE: 2020/21	(3,000)
2019/20 already used	–
Gross CLT	340,000
Less NRB at date of gift	(325,000)
	15,000
Tax @ 20%	3,000

Gift to son 19.8.20

	£
Gift	30,000
AE: 2020/21 and 2019/20 already used	–
PET	30,000

No lifetime tax.

Activity 5: Death tax on lifetime gift (2)

	£
Mr Raymond	
Lifetime tax:	
(i) PET 13.5.15:	
Gift	130,000
– AE 2015/16	(3,000)
– AE 2014/15	(3,000)
PET	124,000

No lifetime tax due on PETs

(ii) CLT 23.8.15		£
Gift		334,000
– AEs (all used)		Nil
CLT		334,000
	£	
Less NRB at date of gift	325,000	
Less GCTs in seven years before **gift**	(–)	(325,000)
		9,000
Tax @ 25% (20/80)		2,250

Gross chargeable transfer is £336,250 (334,000 + 2,250).

	£
Death tax:	
(i) PET 13.5.15	124,000

< NRB at date of death (£325,000) ∴ no death tax

GCT £124,000

£

	£	£
(ii) CLT 23.8.15		336,250
Less: NRB at date of death	325,000	
less GCTs in seven years before **gift**	(124,000)	(201,000)
		135,250
Tax @ 40%		54,100
Less taper relief (4–5 years) 40%		(21,640)
Less lifetime tax		(2,250)
Additional tax on death		30,210

Payable by trustees

Activity 6: Tax on the death estate (2)

Death estate

		£
ABC plc shares		24,400
Main residence		350,000
Investment property		84,000
XYZ Ltd shares		68,000
		526,400
Less: liabilities		(5,750)
spouse exemption (shares in ABC plc)		(24,400)
Chargeable estate		496,250
Less: available RNRB		
(lower of £175,000 and £350,000)		(175,000)
available NRB		
NRB at date of death	325,000	
Less used in seven years before death	(232,000)	
		(93,000)
		228,250
Tax @ 40%		91,300

Computing taxable total profits and the corporation tax liability

Learning objectives

On completion of this chapter, you should be able to:

	Syllabus reference no.
Define the terms 'period of account', 'accounting period', and 'financial year'.	E1(a)
Recognise when an accounting period starts and when an accounting period finishes.	E1(b)
Explain how the residence of a company is determined.	E1(c)
Recognise the expenditure that is allowable in calculating the tax-adjusted trading profit.	E2(a)
Recognise the relief which can be obtained for pre-trading expenditure.	E2(b)
Compute capital allowances (as for income tax).	E2(c)
Compute property business profits and understand how relief for a property business loss is given.	E2(d)
Recognise and apply the treatment of interest paid and received under the loan relationship rules.	E2(h)
Recognise and apply the treatment of qualifying charitable donations.	E2(i)
Compute taxable total profits.	E2(j)
Compute the corporation tax liability.	E4(a)

Exam context

One of the 15-mark questions in Section C will focus on corporation tax. Corporation tax may also be tested in 10-mark questions in Sections B or C. You should also expect to see one or more questions on corporation tax in Section A. When dealing with a corporation tax question in Section C, you must first be able to identify the accounting period(s) involved. Watch out for long periods of account. You must also be able to calculate taxable total profits; learn the standard layout so that you can easily slot in figures from your workings.

Chapter overview

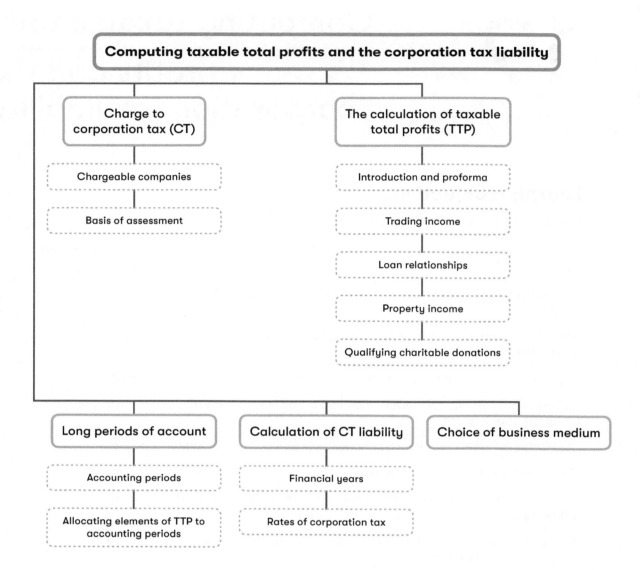

Computing taxable total profits and the corporation tax liability

Charge to corporation tax (CT)
- Chargeable companies
- Basis of assessment

The calculation of taxable total profits (TTP)
- Introduction and proforma
- Trading income
- Loan relationships
- Property income
- Qualifying charitable donations

Long periods of account
- Accounting periods
- Allocating elements of TTP to accounting periods

Calculation of CT liability
- Financial years
- Rates of corporation tax

Choice of business medium

1 Charge to corporation tax (CT)

Companies must pay corporation tax on their **taxable total profits** for each **accounting period**.

> **Company:** A **company** is any corporate body (limited or unlimited) or unincorporated association, eg sports club.

1.1 Chargeable companies

Companies resident in the UK are liable to pay CT on their worldwide profits. A company is UK resident if either:

- It was incorporated in the UK; or
- It was not incorporated in the UK but its central management and control (generally meetings of board of directors) are carried on in the UK

> **Exam focus point**
>
> This topic was tested in Question 33, Wretched Ltd, in the December 2016 exam. Candidates were required to state whether the company that was incorporated in the UK, but whose directors were all non-resident in the United Kingdom and whose board meetings were always held overseas, was resident or not resident in the UK for corporation tax purposes. The examining team commented that this requirement resulted in a very surprising amount of incorrect answers, with at least half the candidates deciding that the company was not resident because of its central management and control being exercised overseas.

1.2 Basis of assessment

CT assessments for a chargeable accounting period (AP) are normally based on a company's period of account.

> **Chargeable accounting period:** A **chargeable accounting period** is the period for which corporation tax is charged and cannot exceed 12 months. Special rules determine when a chargeable accounting period starts and ends.
>
> **Period of account:** A period of account is any period for which a company prepares accounts; usually this will be 12 months in length but it may be longer or shorter than this.

An accounting period starts on the earliest of:
- When a company starts to trade
- When the company otherwise becomes liable to corporation tax (eg it opens a bank account which pays interest)
- Immediately after the previous accounting period finishes

An accounting period finishes on the earliest of:
- 12 months after its start
- The end of the company's period of account
- The company starting or ceasing to trade
- The company entering/ceasing to be in administration
- The commencement of the company's winding up
- The company ceasing to be resident in the UK
- The company ceasing to be liable to corporation tax

Activity 1: Accounting periods

For each of the following companies, identify the accounting period(s).

(a) Jam Ltd, which has been trading for many years, prepares accounts for the 12 months to 30 September 2020.

(b) Klip plc is incorporated on 1 April 2020. On 1 June 2020, Klip plc starts to trade and prepares its first set of accounts to 31 August 2020.

(c) Learn Ltd, which has been trading for many years preparing accounts to 31 December each year, prepares accounts for the 11 months to 30 November 2020.

(d) Maker plc, which has been trading for many years preparing accounts to 31 July each year, prepares accounts for the 16 months to 30 November 2020.

Solution

Exam focus point

This topic was tested in Question 33(a), Ash Ltd, in the September 2018 exam. The examining team commented that 'This section was quite well answered. However, when considering accounting periods, it is very important not to confuse the corporate and unincorporated business rules. Applying the unincorporated business opening year rules to a limited company will obviously not achieve many marks.'

2 The calculation of taxable total profits (TTP)

PER alert

One of the competencies you require to fulfil Performance Objective 15 *Tax computations and assessments* of the PER is to extract and analyse data from financial records and filing information relevant to the preparation of tax computations and related supporting documents. You can apply the knowledge you obtain from this section of the Workbook to help to demonstrate this competence.

2.1 Introduction and proforma

A company's taxable total profits are arrived at by aggregating its various sources of income and its chargeable gains and then deducting losses and qualifying charitable donations. Here is a pro forma computation.

CT computation for the X months to...

	£	£
Trading income		
Adjusted profits	X	
Less capital allowances	(X)	
Trading profits (accruals)		X
Other income		
Interest income from non-trade loan relationship (accruals)		X
Property business income (accruals)		X
Miscellaneous income (accruals)		X
Net chargeable gains (receipts)		X
Total profits		X
Less qualifying charitable donations (QCDs) (payments)		(X)
Taxable total profits (TTP)		X

Note that the computation of chargeable gains and the use of losses by companies are dealt with later in this Workbook.

2.1.1 Points to note about the computation of TTP

- Dividends received from other companies (UK resident and non-UK resident), for the purposes of the Taxation (TX – UK) exam, are usually exempt and so **not included** in taxable total profits.
- Dividends paid are **not** deductible
- All figures are included **gross** in TTP.
- Companies pay CT (not capital gains tax) on chargeable gains (net of both current period and brought forward capital losses).
- All donations to charity are paid **gross** by companies (unlike individuals).
- **Patent royalties** received which do not relate to the trade are taxed as miscellaneous income. Patent royalties which relate to the trade are included in trading income normally on an accruals basis.
- Pre-trading expenditure incurred in the seven years prior to the commencement of trade is deductible under the same principles as seen for individuals in Chapter 7 of this Workbook.

2.2 Trading income

2.2.1 Adjustment of profits

The trading income of companies is derived from the profit before taxation figure in the statement of profit or loss, just as for individuals, adjusted as follows.

	£	£
Profit **before taxation**		X
Add expenditure not allowed for taxation purposes		X

	£	£
		X
Less: income not taxable as trading income		X
expenditure not charged in the accounts but allowable for the purposes of taxation		X
capital allowances		X
		(X)
Profit adjusted for tax purposes		X

The adjustment of profits computation for companies broadly follows that for computing business profits subject to income tax. There are, however, some minor differences. There is no disallowance for 'private use' for companies; instead the director or employee will be taxed on the benefit received.

Qualifying charitable donations which are not small donations to local charities are added back in the calculation of adjusted profit. They are treated instead as a deduction from total profits.

Investment income including rents or bank interest receivable is deducted from profit before taxation in arriving at trading income but brought in again further down in the computation (see below).

Exam focus point

An examination question requiring adjustment to profit will direct you to start the adjustment with the profit before taxation of £X and deal with all the items listed indicating with a zero (0) any items which do not require adjustment. Marks will not be given for relevant items unless this approach is used. Therefore, students who attempt to rewrite the statement of profit or loss will be penalised.

2.2.2 Capital allowances

The calculation of capital allowances follows income tax principles, but with the following differences:

- There is never any reduction of allowances to take account of any private use of an asset. The director or employee suffers a taxable benefit instead.
- A company's accounting period can never exceed 12 months. If the period of account is longer than 12 months it is divided into two; one for the first 12 months and one for the balance. The capital allowances computation must be carried out for each period separately.

Exam focus point

The calculation of trading income should be undertaken as a first step to the calculation of taxable total profits. However, it is important to realise that these are two distinct aspects when calculating a company's liability to corporation tax and you should not attempt to present them in one calculation.

2.3 Loan relationships

Loan relationship: If a company borrows or lends money, including issuing or investing in loan stock or buying gilts, it has a loan relationship.

2.3.1 Overview of loan relationship rules

Interest (and other debt costs such as arrangement fees) will arise as a consequence of any loan taken or extended.

Interest will be classified as trading or investment depending on the reason for the loan.

Interest is always dealt with on an **accruals basis** for companies.

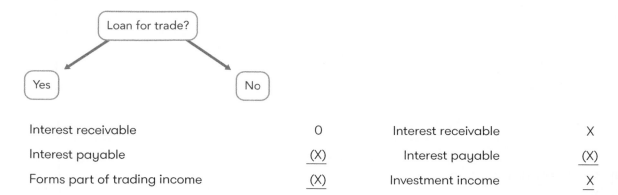

Interest receivable	0	Interest receivable	X
Interest payable	(X)	Interest payable	(X)
Forms part of trading income	(X)	Investment income	X

2.3.2 Trading loan relationships

Income and expenses on trading loans form part of trading income - therefore **no adjustment of profits is required.** Trading loan relationship **income** is unlikely unless the trade is one of money lending (eg a bank).

Loans taken out by a company for trade purposes include loans used to:

- Purchase plant and machinery
- Provide working capital
- Purchase property used for trading purposes such as an office, warehouse or factory

2.3.3 Non-trading loan relationships (NTLR)

If a loan relationship is not for trade purposes, an **adjustment of trading profits is required** for any debits or credits (eg interest payable or receivable) and these must be pooled. A net credit on the pool is chargeable as interest income.

You will not be expected to deal with net deficits (ie losses) on non-trading loan relationships in your exam.

Loans taken out by a company for non-trade purposes include loans used to:

- Purchase property which is then let out
- Acquire the share capital of another company

Creditor non-trading loan relationships include:

- Depositing cash on deposit at a bank
- Investing in loan stock or gilts

Interest payable to/receivable from HMRC on late or overpaid tax is always treated as a non-trade loan relationship.

Activity 2: Non-trade loan relationships

Armadillo Ltd is a UK-based manufacturing company with several subsidiaries.

Required

Which **TWO** of the following would be treated as non-trade loan relationship expenses for Armadillo Ltd?

☐ Mortgage interest payable on factory used to manufacture the company's products

☐ Interest payable on a loan to purchase shares in a trading subsidiary

☐ Interest received from HMRC on overpaid VAT

☐ Interest payable on a loan to purchase a small speculative shareholding in a property investment company

Solution

Essential reading

Further details on accounting for loan relationships, incidental costs of loan finance and capital costs of loan finance are contained in your essential reading.

The Essential reading is available as an Appendix of the digital edition of the Workbook.

2.4 Property business income

Unlike individuals, companies must use the accruals basis to calculate their property business income.

Deductibility of property expenses generally follows income tax principles set out earlier in this Workbook; however, there are some differences for companies.

- Property losses are relieved against total profits (see Chapter 21).
- Relief for interest payable on a loan to acquire or improve property is relieved under the loan relationship rules instead of being given as a tax reducer.

Essential reading

An example of the calculation of property business income for a company is included in your Essential reading.

The Essential reading is available as an Appendix of the digital edition of the Workbook.

2.5 Qualifying charitable donations

Qualifying charitable donations are deductible (on a **paid** basis) from total profits when computing taxable total profits.

Almost all donations of money to charity by a company can be qualifying charitable donations whether they are single donations or regular donations. There is no need for a claim to be made in order for a payment to be treated as a qualifying charitable donation (compare with gift aid donations where a declaration is required).

Donations to local charities which are incurred wholly and exclusively for the purposes of a trade are deducted in the calculation of the tax adjusted trading profits.

Activity 3: Calculation of taxable total profits

Abel Ltd, a UK resident trading company, produced the following results for the year ended 31 March 2021.

	£
Trading income	244,000
Property business income	15,000
Bank deposit interest received	4,000
Bank deposit interest accrued at 31 March 2020	1,000
Bank deposit interest accrued at 31 March 2021	2,000
Chargeable gains	42,000
Qualifying charitable donations paid	7,000
Dividends received	15,000

There were capital losses of £8,000 brought forward at 1 April 2020.

Required

(a) How much interest income (non-trade loan relationship income) should be included in the taxable total profits?

- O £4,000
- O £5,000
- O £6,000
- O £7,000

(b) What are the taxable total profits?

- O £298,000
- O £291,000
- O £299,000
- O £306,000

Solution

Essential reading

A comprehensive illustration of the calculation of TTP is included in your essential reading.

The Essential reading is available as an Appendix of the digital edition of the Workbook.

3 Long periods of account

KEY TERM

> **Long period of account (LPoA):** Any period of account exceeding 12 months

3.1 Accounting periods in a LPoA

No AP can **exceed 12 months** for CT purposes.

If a company has a period of account which is longer than 12 months it must be split into two APs.

- The **first** 12 months
- The **second** for the remaining months

3.2 Allocating elements of TTP to accounting periods

- **Trading income** before capital allowances and **property business income** are apportioned on a **time basis**.
- **Capital allowances** and balancing charges are **calculated for each accounting period**.
- **Other income is allocated to the period to which it relates** (eg interest accrued). Miscellaneous income, however, is apportioned on a time basis.
- **Chargeable gains and losses** are allocated to the **period in which they are realised**.
- **Qualifying charitable donations** are deducted in the accounting **period in which they are paid**.

Long period of account proforma

	First 12 months	Last n months
	£	£
Adjusted profit (time apportioned)	X	X
Less capital allowances (2 computations)	(X)	(X)
Taxable trading profits	X	X
Property business income (time apportioned)	X	X
Interest income (accruals basis)	X	X
Chargeable gains (receipts basis)	X	X
Less qualifying charitable donations (paid basis)	(X)	(X)
Taxable total profits	X	X

Illustration 1: Allocating TTP in a long period of account

Xenon Ltd makes up an 18-month set of accounts to 30 September 2021 with the following results:

	£
Trading income (no capital allowances claimed)	180,000
Interest income	
18 months @ £500 accruing per month	9,000
Chargeable gain (1 August 2021 disposal)	250,000
Less qualifying charitable donation (paid 31 March 2021)	(50,000)
	389,000

Required

What are the taxable total profits for each of the accounting periods based on the above accounts?

Solution

The 18-month period of account is divided into:

Year ending 31 March 2021

6 months to 30 September 2021

Results are allocated:

	Y/e 31.3.21 £	6m to 30.9.21 £
Trading income 12:6	120,000	60,000
Interest income		
12 × £500	6,000	
6 × £500		3,000
Chargeable gain (1.8.20)	–	250,000
Total profits	126,000	313,000
Less qualifying charitable donation (31.3.21)	(50,000)	
Taxable total profits	76,000	313,000

4 Calculation of CT liability

There is a single rate of corporation tax which is applied to a company's taxable total profits to compute the corporation tax liability.

4.1 Financial years

While TTP is calculated for accounting periods, CT is calculated with reference to financial years.

Financial year: A financial year runs from 1 April to the following 31 March and is identified by the calendar year in which it begins. For example, the year ended 31 March 2021 is the Financial year 2020 (FY 2020). This should not be confused with a tax year, which runs from 6 April to the following 5 April.

4.2 Rates of corporation tax

PER alert

One of the competencies you require to fulfil Performance Objective 15 *Tax computations and assessments* of the PER is to prepare or contribute to the computation or assessment of tax computations for single companies, groups or other entities. You can apply the knowledge you obtain from this section of the Workbook to help to demonstrate this competence.

The rates of corporation tax are fixed for financial years.

Since FY17, CT is charged at 19% of the taxable total profits.

If the rates for corporation tax are different in financial years and the AP falls into more than one financial year, taxable total profits are time apportioned between the financial years.

Exam focus point

The rates of corporation tax will be given in the Tax Rates and Allowances available in the exam.

Activity 4: Corporation tax for a LPoA

Delta plc has a 16-month period of account to 31 December 2020. The company has provided you with the following information for the 16-month period:

	£
Adjusted trading profit before capital allowances	3,600,000
Property business income	16,000
Chargeable gain	40,000
(sale of asset on 13 October 2020)	
Qualifying charitable donation	20,000
(paid annually on 31 July)	

The tax written down value of the main pool of plant and machinery qualifying for capital allowances at 1 September 2019 was £30,000. The only capital transaction during the 16-month period was the purchase of a new van for £8,000 on 15 November 2020.

Required

Calculate taxable total profits and the corporation tax liabilities for the accounting periods.

Solution

---

5 Choice of business medium

An individual can choose between trading as a sole trader or trading through a company. Trading through a company may reduce the overall tax and national insurance liability, in particular if profits are extracted in a tax-efficient manner.

 Essential reading

Analysis of the differences between these business mediums, including an illustrative example, is included in your essential reading.

The Essential reading is available as an Appendix of the digital edition of the Workbook.

Chapter summary

Computing taxable total profits and the corporation tax liability

Charge to corporation tax (CT)

Chargeable companies
- UK resident if:
  - UK incorporated or
  - UK central management and control
- UK resident assessable on worldwide income

Basis of assessment
- Compute TTP for each chargeable accounting period (AP)

The calculation of taxable total profits (TTP)

Introduction and proforma
- Aggregate income and gains, deduct losses and QCDs
- Dividend income not chargeable to CT
- Non-trade patent royalties = miscellaneous income
- Proforma:

	£	£
Trading income		
Adjusted profits	X	
Less capital allowances	(X)	
Trading profits (accruals)		X
Other income		
Interest income from non-trade loan relationship (accruals)		X
Property income (accruals)		X
Miscellaneous income (accruals)		X
Net chargeable gains (receipts)		X
Total profits		X
Less qualifying charitable donations (QCDs) (payments)		(X)
Taxable total profits (TTP)		X

Trading income
- Adjusted profits less capital allowances
- Adjustments similar to sole traders but no private use (PU) adjustments or PU assets

Loan relationships
- Loan for trade?
  - Yes: forms part of trading income (no adjustment required)
  - No: adjust in trading profit calculation and pool as interest income (NTLR)

Property income
- Calculated as for individuals except:
  - Always accruals basis
  - Interest on loans is NTLR expense, no tax reducer
  - Losses are relieved against total profits

Qualifying charitable donations
- Deductible on a paid basis from TTP
- Paid gross by companies

Long periods of account

Accounting periods
- Two APs:
  - First 12 months
  - Remaining months

Allocating elements of TTP to accounting periods
- Trading, property profits and misc income: time apportion
- Two CA comps
- Gains and QCDs: date received/paid
- Other income: accruals

Calculation of CT liability

Financial years
- FY20 = 1/4/20 – 31/3/21
- Used to determine tax rates

Rates of corporation tax
- FY17 – FY20: TTP × 19%

Choice of business medium

- Overall tax burden on trading profits can be lower with a company if profits extracted tax efficiently

Knowledge diagnostic

1. Charge to corporation tax

UK resident companies pay CT on worldwide profits. CT assessments are based on company's accounting period.

A company is UK resident if it is incorporated in the UK or if it is incorporated overseas and its central management and control are exercised in the UK.

2. The calculation of TTP

Taxable total profits comprise the company's income and chargeable gains (total profits) less some losses and qualifying charitable donations. It does not include dividends received from other companies.

Income includes trading income, property business income, income from non-trading loan relationships (interest) and miscellaneous income.

3. Long periods of account

Long periods of account are split into two accounting periods: the first 12 months and the remainder.

4. Calculation of CT liability

Tax rates are set for financial years.

Corporation tax is charged on taxable total profits for an accounting period, based on the tax rate(s) applicable to the relevant financial year(s).

5. Choice of business medium

An individual can choose between trading as a sole trader or trading through a company. Trading through a company may reduce the overall tax and national insurance liability, in particular if profits are extracted in a tax-efficient manner.

Further study guidance

Question practice

Now try the following from the Further question practice bank (available in the digital edition of the Workbook):

Section A: Q82, Q83, Q84

Section B: Q85 Red plc and Green plc

Section C: Q86 Elderflower Ltd

Activity answers

Activity 1: Accounting periods

(a) 1 October 2019 (immediately after previous accounting period finishes) to 30 September 2020 (12 months after start of accounting period and also the end of period of account).

(b) 1 June 2020 (company starts to trade) to 31 August 2020 (end of period of account). Incorporation does directly result in the start of an accounting period.

(c) 1 January 2020 (immediately after previous accounting period finishes) to 30 November 2020 (end of period of account).

(d) First accounting period: 1 August 2019 (immediately after previous accounting period finishes) to 31 July 2020 (12 months after start).

Second accounting period: 1 August 2020 (immediately after previous accounting period finishes) to 30 November 2020 (end of period of account).

Activity 2: Non-trade loan relationships

The correct answers are:

- Interest payable on a loan to purchase shares in a trading subsidiary

- Interest payable on a loan to purchase a small speculative shareholding in a property investment company

Mortgage interest on trading premises is an allowable trading expense. Interest payable on loans to purchase shares is always treated as a non-trade loan relationship, irrespective of the level of shareholding or type of company invested in. HMRC interest here was non-trade loan relationship income, rather than an expense.

Activity 3: Calculation of taxable total profits

(a) The correct answer is: £5,000

£4,000 (interest received) + £2,000 (closing accrual) − £1,000 (opening accrual)   = £5,000

The answer £4,000 is the interest received. The answer £6,000 does not take account of the opening accrual. The answer £7,000 adds the opening accrual instead of deducting it.

(b) The correct answer is: £291,000

Corporation tax computation for year ended 31 March 2021

	£
Trading income	244,000
Property business income	15,000
Interest income	5,000
Net chargeable gains (£42,000 − £8,000)	34,000
Total profits	298,000
Less qualifying charitable donation	(7,000)
Taxable total profits	291,000

Note. Dividends received are exempt from corporation tax.

The answer £298,000 is the total profits. The answer £299,000 does not deduct the capital loss brought forward. The answer £306,000 includes the dividends.

Activity 4: Corporation tax for a LPoA

	12 months to 31.8.20	4 months to 31.12.20
	£	£
Adjusted trading profit (12:4)	2,700,000	900,000
Less CA (W)	(5,400)	(9,476)
Taxable trading income	2,694,600	890,524
Property business income (12:4)	12,000	4,000
Gain	–	40,000
Less qualifying charitable donation	(20,000)	–
Taxable total profits	2,686,600	934,524
Corporation tax liability		
FY19/FY20 £2,686,600 × 19%	510,454	
FY20 £934,524 × 19%		177,560

Working

	AIA	Main pool	Allowances
	£	£	£
1.9.19–31.8.20			
Tax WDV b/fwd		30,000	
WDA (18%)		(5,400)	5,400
		24,600	
1.9.20–31.12.20			
Addition qualifying for AIA	8,000		
AIA @ 100% × £1,000,000 × $^4/_{12}$ (max)	(8,000)		8,000
WDA 18% × $^4/_{12}$		(1,476)	1,476
		23,124	9,476

20

Chargeable gains for companies

Learning objectives

On completion of this chapter, you should be able to:

	Syllabus reference no.
Compute and explain the treatment of chargeable gains.	E3(a)
Explain and compute the indexation allowance available using a given indexation factor.	E3(b)
Understand the treatment of disposals of shares by companies and the identification rules including the same day and nine-day matching rules.	E3(d)
Explain and apply the pooling provisions.	E3(e)
Explain and apply the treatment of bonus issues, rights issues, takeovers and reorganisations.	E3(f)
Explain and apply rollover relief.	E3(g)

Exam context

There will be a 15-mark question on corporation tax in Section C. This may include the gains of a company so it is important that you can deal with the aspects covered in this chapter.
Corporation tax on chargeable gains may also be tested in 10-mark questions in Sections B or C.
A Section A question may test a specific point such as computation of the indexation allowance.

Chapter overview

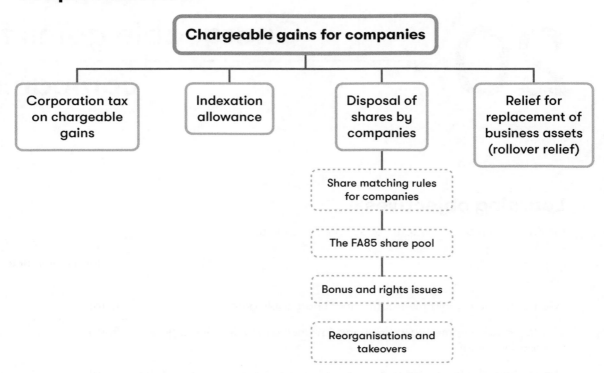

1 Corporation tax on chargeable gains

Companies do not pay capital gains tax. Their net chargeable gains for an accounting period are included in the taxable total profits (TTP) and are charged to corporation tax.

The calculation of the taxable gain/loss is similar to that of an individual except:

* There is a relief for inflation called indexation allowance (but this is frozen at December 2017);
* Different matching rules apply for the disposal of shares;
* Companies can only get one relief: replacement of business asset (rollover) relief; and
* No annual exempt amount is available.

Note that the treatment of capital losses for companies is covered in Chapter 21.

> ### Exam focus point
>
> Chargeable gains for companies were tested in the December 2017 exam. The examining team commented that candidates should be careful not to make basic mistakes such as deducting the annual exempt amount when calculating a corporate chargeable gain.

2 Indexation allowance

The purpose of having an indexation allowance is to remove the inflation element of a gain from taxation. However, the indexation allowance is frozen at December 2017 so that the inflation element of a gain beyond that date will be taxable.

Companies are entitled to an indexation allowance from the date of acquisition of the asset until the earlier of the date of disposal of the asset and December 2017.

The indexation factor is computed using the percentage rise in the RPI figures (expressed as a decimal and rounded to three decimal places).

> ### Exam focus point
>
> **The examining team will always give the indexation factor in the question.** You will not have to calculate the indexation factor using RPIs.

The indexation allowance is computed by multiplying the indexation factor by the relevant expenditure. Both the original cost and any enhancement expenditure will qualify for an indexation allowance (where incurred before January 2018).

The indexation allowance cannot increase or create a loss.

Expenditure incurred from January 2018 is not given an indexation allowance.

Illustration 1: Indexation allowance

An asset is acquired by Lenny Ltd on 15 February 2003 at a cost of £5,000. Enhancement expenditure of £2,000 is incurred on 10 April 2004 and further enhancement expenditure of £4,000 is incurred on 18 May 2018. The asset is sold for £30,500 on 20 August 2020. Incidental costs of sale are £500. The indexation factor between February 2003 and December 2017 is 0.551 and between April 2004 and December 2017 is 0.498.

Required

Calculate the chargeable gain arising.

Solution

The indexation allowance is computed as follows:

	£
0.551 × £5,000	2,755
0.498 × £2,000	996
	3,751

There is no indexation on the enhancement in May 2018 as it was incurred after December 2017. The computation of the chargeable gain is as follows:

	£
Proceeds	30,500
Less incidental costs of sale	(500)
Net proceeds	30,000
Less allowable costs (£5,000 + £2,000 + £4,000)	(11,000)
Unindexed gain	19,000
Less indexation allowance (see above)	(3,751)
Indexed gain	15,249

 ## Activity 1: Chargeable gain calculation

A company acquired an asset on 10 May 2005 at a cost of £12,000. Enhancement expenditure of £2,000 was incurred on 1 September 2010 and further enhancement expenditure of £3,000 was incurred on 1 August 2020. The asset is sold for £30,000 on 20 December 2020.

Indexation factors:

May 2005–December 2017 = 0.448

May 2005–December 2020 = 0.537

September 2010–December 2017 = 0.234

September 2010–December 2020 = 0.332

August 2020–December 2020 = 0.012

Required

1   What is the indexed gain in respect of this disposal?

    ○ £5,856

    ○ £5,892

    ○ £7,156

    ○ £10,156

2   What chargeable gain or allowable loss would have arisen on Karl Ltd if the proceeds had been £22,000 instead of £30,000?

Solution

Exam focus point

In an exam question, you may be given the indexation factor to the date of disposal (if later than December 2017) as well as the indexation factor to December 2017. This is to test that you know the rule that indexation is frozen to December 2017. Make sure you use the factor to December 2017!

3 Disposal of shares by companies

3.1 Share matching rules for companies

For companies, the matching of shares sold is in the following order:

- Shares acquired on the **same day**
- Shares acquired in the **previous nine days**, if more than one acquisition on a 'first in, first out' (FIFO) basis
- Shares from the FA 1985 pool (which includes purchases from 1 April 1982 (note not 1985) to 10 days prior to sale

The composition of the FA 1985 pool in relation to companies which are shareholders is explained below.

3.2 The FA 1985 share pool

We must keep track of:

- The **number** of shares
- The **cost** of the shares ignoring indexation
- The **indexed cost** of the shares

Disposals and acquisitions of shares which affect the indexed value of the FA 1985 pool are termed 'operative events'. Prior to reflecting, each such operative event within the FA 1985 share pool, a further indexation allowance (an 'indexed rise') must be computed from the date of the last such operative event up to the earlier of the date of the operative event concerned and December 2017. If the last operative event was in December 2017 or later, no further indexed rises will be calculated.

In the case of a disposal, following the calculation of the indexed rise to the earlier of the date of disposal and December 2017, the cost and the indexed cost attributable to the shares disposed of are deducted from the amounts within the FA 1985 pool.

The amounts deducted from the pool are then used in the computation of the chargeable gain, with **the indexation allowance being the difference between the cost and indexed cost figures.**

Proforma FA 1985 pool for a company

	No.	Cost	Indexed cost
		£	£
Addition	X	X	X
Index to purchase			X
Addition	X	X	X
	X	X	X
Index to earlier of disposal/December 2017			X
			X
Disposal	(X)	(X)	(X)
	X	X	X

Exam focus point

The examining team has stated that a detailed question will not be set on the pooling provisions. However, work through the examples below as you are expected to understand how the pool works.

Illustration 2: FA 1985 share pool

Smithers Ltd purchased 1,500 shares in Burns Ltd for £4,500 in May 1997, and another 3,000 shares in June 2017 for £8,000.

Smithers Ltd then sold 1,500 of its shares in Burns Ltd for £15,000 in May 2020.

Indexed rises:

May 1997–June 2017 = 0.736

June 2017–December 2017 = 0.021

Required

Compute the chargeable gain arising on the disposal.

Solution

The disposal is matched with the FA 1985 pool as there are no acquisitions on the same day or previous nine days.

FA 1985 share pool is constructed as follows:

	No.	Cost	Indexed cost
		£	£
May 1997	1,500	4,500	4,500
Index to June 2017			
0.736 × £4,500			3,312

	No.	Cost	Indexed cost
		£	£
			7,812
Addition June 2017	3,000	8,000	8,000
	4,500	12,500	15,812
Index to December 2017			
0.021 × £15,812			332
			16,144
Disposal May 2020	(1,500)	(4,167)	(5,381)
	3,000	8,333	10,763

The chargeable gain is therefore:

	£
Proceeds	15,000
Less cost of shares sold (from pool)	(4,167)
Less indexation allowance (£5,381 - £4,167)	(1,214)
Gain	9,619

Activity 2: Share matching rules and FA 1985 pool

ABC Ltd bought 1,000 shares in XYZ Ltd for £2,750 in August 1997 and another 1,000 for £3,250 in December 1997. On 2 July 2020, ABC Ltd purchased another 1,500 shares for £4,000.

ABC Ltd sold 3,000 shares on 10 July 2020 for £17,000.

Indexation factors:

August 1997–December 1997 = 0.023

December 1997–December 2017 = 0.738

Required

Calculate the gains and the value of the FA 1985 pool following the disposal.

Solution

3.3 Bonus and rights issues

Essential reading

The impact on the FA 1985 pool of bonus and rights issues is covered in your Essential reading

The Essential reading is available as an Appendix of the digital edition of the Workbook.

3.4 Reorganisations and takeovers

The rules on reorganisation and takeovers apply in a similar way for company shareholders as they do for individuals.

Essential reading

The application of the paper for paper rules for companies and a numerical example can be found in the essential reading.

The Essential reading is available as an Appendix of the digital edition of the Workbook.

4 Relief for replacement of business assets (rollover relief)

As for individuals, a gain may be deferred by a company where the proceeds on the disposal of a business asset are spent on a replacement business asset under rollover relief.

The conditions for rollover relief to apply to companies are the same as those for individuals seen in Chapter 15 of the Workbook, except that:

- Goodwill is not a qualifying asset for companies
- It is the **indexed** gain which is deferred (either by reducing the base cost of the replacement asset or, in the case of depreciating assets, by merely being charged at a later date)
- The deadline for making a claim for relief is the later of four years of the end of the accounting period in which the disposal of the old asset takes place and four years of the end of the accounting period in which the new asset is acquired.

Activity 3: Company rollover relief

Dream Ltd acquired a factory in April 2000 at a cost of £120,000. It used the factory in its trade throughout the period of its ownership.

In August 2020, Dream Ltd sold the factory for £250,000. The indexation factor between April 2000 and December 2017 is 0.635. In May 2020, it had acquired a replacement factory at a cost of £220,000.

Required

Calculate the gain chargeable on the sale of the first factory and the base cost of the second factory.

Note. Remember, any proceeds not reinvested must be charged immediately.

Solution

Chapter summary

Chargeable gains for companies

Corporation tax on chargeable gains

- Companies pay CT on gains not CGT
- Companies get indexation allowance but no AEA

Indexation allowance

- Rise in RPI (indexation factor) × cost. Indexation factors given in question
- Frozen at December 2017
- Indexation cannot create or increase a loss
- No indexation allowance on expenditure from January 2018

Disposal of shares by companies

Share matching rules for companies
- Same day
- Previous nine days
- FA85 pool

The FA85 share pool
- Record of number of shares, cost, and indexed cost
- Indexed to each operative event (ie acquisition or disposal)

Bonus and rights issues
- Shares added in to FA85 pool
- Rights issue is operative event, bonus issue is not

Reorganisations and takeovers
- Paper for paper treatment applies
- No gains until new shares disposed of

Relief for replacement of business assets (rollover relief)

- Operates for companies in the same way as for individuals
- Indexed gain may be deferred on reinvestment into new qualifying asset
- Goodwill not qualifying asset for companies

Knowledge diagnostic

1. Corporation tax on chargeable gains

Companies pay corporation tax on their gains. They do not get an annual exempt amount.

2. Indexation allowance

This is deducted from the gain calculation to remove the inflationary effect but is frozen at December 2017. It runs from date of expenditure to the earlier of the date of disposal and December 2017. Indexation cannot create or increase a capital loss.

3. Disposal of shares by companies

There are special rules for matching shares sold by a company with shares purchased. Disposals are matched with acquisitions on the same day, the previous nine days and the FA 1985 share pool. The FA 1985 pool is indexed to each operative event.

Rights issues are an operative event in the FA 1985 pool, but bonus issues are not.

4. Relief for replacement of business assets (rollover relief)

Rollover relief for replacement of business assets is available to companies to defer indexed gains arising on the disposal of business assets (not goodwill).

Further study guidance

Question practice

Now try the following from the Further question practice bank (available in the digital edition of the Workbook):

Section A: Q87, Q88, Q89

Section B: Q90 Long Ltd, Tall Ltd and Short Ltd

Section C: Q91 Xeon Ltd

Further reading

Part 1 of ACCA's article *Chargeable gains*, written by a member of the Taxation (TX – UK) examining team, looks at chargeable gains in either a personal or corporate context. Part 2 focuses on shares, reliefs, and the way in which gains made by limited companies are taxed.

Activity answers

Activity 1: Chargeable gain calculation

1 The correct answer is: £7,156

	£
Proceeds	30,000
Cost May 2005	(12,000)
Enhancement September 2010	(2,000)
Enhancement August 2020	(3,000)
Unindexed gain	13,000
Less: IA on cost May 2005 to December 2017 0.448 × £12,000	(5,376)
IA on enhancement September 2010 to December 2017 0.234 × £2,000	(468)
Indexed gain	7,156

There is no indexation on the enhancement in August 2020.

Be careful to choose the indexation factors to December 2017!

The answer £5,856 indexes all the expenditure to December 2020. The answer £5,892 indexes the pre-December 2017 expenditure to December 2020. The answer £10,156 ignores the August 2020 enhancement completely.

2 Answer: £nil

	£
Proceeds	22,000
Cost May 2005	(12,000)
Enhancement September 2010	(2,000)
Enhancement August 2019	(3,000)
Unindexed gain	5,000
Less: IA : £5,376 + £468, capped at	(5,000)
Indexed gain	0

Indexation allowance can reduce a gain to £nil but cannot create a loss.

Activity 2: Share matching rules and FA 1985 pool

	£
Match with acquisition in previous 9 days	
Proceeds (1,500/3,000 × £17,000)	8,500
Less cost	(4,000)
Gain	4,500

		£
Match with FA85 pool		
Proceeds (1,500/3,000 × £17,000)		8,500
Less indexed cost (W)		(7,903)
Gain		597

Total gains (£4,500 + £597) = £5,097

	No.	Cost	Indexed cost
		£	£
Working			
Aug 1997	1,000	2,750	2,750
Index to Dec 1997			
0.023 × £2,750			63
			2,813
Addition Dec 1997	1,000	3,250	3,250
	2,000	6,000	6,063
Index to December 2017			
0.738 × £6,063			4,474
			10,537
Disposal July 2020	(1,500)	(4,500)	7,903)
	500	1,500	2,634

Activity 3: Company rollover relief

Chargeable gain on sale of first factory

	£
Proceeds	250,000
Less cost	(120,000)
Unindexed gain	130,000
0.635 × £120,000	(76,200)
Indexed gain	53,800
Less rollover relief (balancing figure)	(23,800)
Chargeable gain: amount not reinvested (£250,000 – £220,000)	30,000

Base cost of second factory

	£
Cost of second factory	220,000
Less rolled over gain	(23,800)
Base cost	196,200

21

Loss relief for single companies

Learning objectives

On completion of this chapter, you should be able to:

	Syllabus reference no.
Compute property business profits and understand how relief for a property business loss is given.	E2(d)
Understand how trading losses can be carried forward.	E2(e)
Understand how trading losses can be claimed against income of the current or previous accounting periods.	E2(f)
Recognise the factors that will influence the choice of loss relief claim.	E2(g)
Explain and compute the treatment of capital losses.	E3(c)

Exam context

Losses could form part of a 15-mark question or a 10-mark question in Section C. They may also be included in Section A or B questions, for example dealing with carry forward loss relief. Dealing with losses involves a methodical approach: first establish what loss is available for relief, second identify the different reliefs available, and third evaluate the options. Do check the question for specific instructions; you may be told that loss relief should be taken as early as possible.

Chapter overview

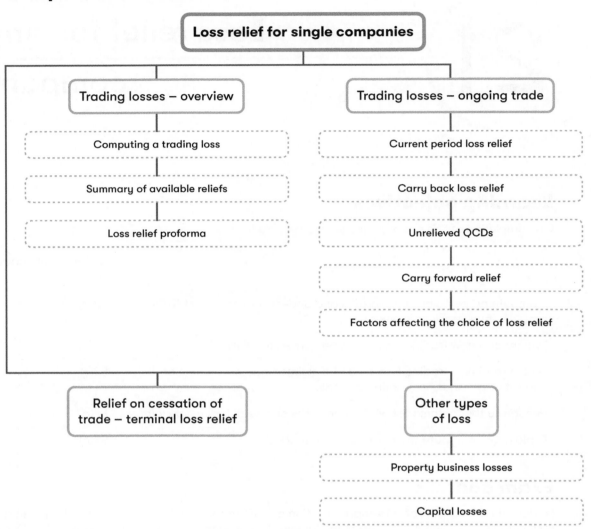

Loss relief for single companies

- Trading losses – overview
  - Computing a trading loss
  - Summary of available reliefs
  - Loss relief proforma

- Trading losses – ongoing trade
  - Current period loss relief
  - Carry back loss relief
  - Unrelieved QCDs
  - Carry forward relief
  - Factors affecting the choice of loss relief

- Relief on cessation of trade – terminal loss relief

- Other types of loss
  - Property business losses
  - Capital losses

1 Trading losses - overview

1.1 Computing a trading loss

A loss is computed in the same way as an adjusted trading profit:

		£
Profit/loss before taxation		X/(X)
Add:	expenditure not deductible for tax	X
Deduct:	items not taxed as trading income	
	– Income assessable under other categories	(X)
	– Non-taxable income	(X)
	capital allowances on plant and machinery	(X)
Trading loss		(X)

The trading income assessment for loss-making period is nil.

1.2 Summary of available reliefs

In summary, the following reliefs are available for trading losses incurred by a company:

- Claim to deduct the loss from current period total profits (current period relief)
- Claim to deduct the loss from earlier period total profits (carry back relief)
- Claim to deduct the loss usually from future period total profits (carry forward relief)

These reliefs may be used in combination. The options open to the company are:

- Current period relief only
- Current period relief, then carry back relief
- Current period relief, then carry forward relief
- Current period relief, then carry back relief, then carry forward relief
- Carry forward relief only.

These reliefs are explained in further detail later in this chapter.

1.3 Loss relief proforma

The following format is recommended for showing the loss relieved in each accounting period:

	2018	2019	2020	2021
Trading income	X	X	nil	X
Other income and gains	X	X	X	X
Total Profits	X	X	X	X
Current period			(X)	
Carry back		(X)		
Carry forward				(X)
Less QCDs	(X)	(X)	(X)	(X)
Taxable Total Profits (TTP)	X	X	X	X

2 Trading losses - ongoing trade

2.1 Current period loss relief

A claim may be made for a trading loss to be offset, as much as possible, against total profits, ie before qualifying charitable donations (QCDs) for the current accounting period.

This claim must be made within two years of the end of the accounting period in which the loss is **made**.

2.2 Carry back loss relief

Trading losses can be carried back and offset, as much as possible, against total profits (ie before QCDs) of the preceding 12 months.

However, a current period claim **must** be made first.

Any carry back is to more recent periods before earlier periods, ie on a last in first out (LIFO) basis. Losses can only be carried back for a maximum of 12 months prior to the start of the loss-making period, so if an accounting period falls partly outside this 12-month period, its total profits (before QCDs) must be pro-rated accordingly.

The claim must be made within two years of the end of the accounting period in which the loss is **made**.

2.3 Unrelieved QCDs

Losses offset in current period or carried back may result in QCDs becoming unrelieved because such donations are deducted from total profits after this loss relief to compute taxable total profits. The only way to get relief for these payments is via group relief (see chapter 22).

 Illustration 1: Carry back to a short accounting period

Tallis Ltd had the following results for the three accounting periods to 31 December 2020.

	y/e 30.9.19	3 months to 31.12.19	y/e 31.12.20
	£	£	£
Trading profit/(loss)	20,000	12,000	(39,000)
Building society interest receivable	1,000	400	1,800
Qualifying charitable donations	600	500	0

Required

Calculate the taxable total profits for all years and show any qualifying charitable donations which become unrelieved assuming that claims are made for current period and carry back trading loss relief. Identify any trading loss available for carry forward at 31 December 2020.

Solution

	y/e 30.9.19	3 months to 31.12.19	y/e31.12.20
	£	£	£
Trading profit	20,000	12,000	0
Interest income	1,000	400	1,800
Total profits	21,000	12,400	1,800
Less current period loss relief	-		(1,800)

	y/e 30.9.19	3 months to 31.12.19	y/e 31.12.20
	£	£	£
Less carry back loss relief	(15,750)	(12,400)	
Less qualifying charitable donations	(600)	0	0
Taxable total profits	4,650	0	0
Unrelieved qualifying charitable donations	0	500	0

Loss memorandum	£
Loss incurred in y/e 31.12.20	39,000
Less used y/e 31.12.20	(1,800)
Less used p/e 31.12.19	(12,400)
Less used y/e 30.9.19 £21,000 × 9/12 (max)	(15,750)
C/f	9,050

Notes.

1 The loss can be carried back to set against total profits of the previous 12 months. This means total profits in the y/e 30.9.19 must be time apportioned by multiplying by 9/12.

2 Losses remaining after the current period and carry back loss relief claims are available for carry forward loss relief.

2.4 Carry forward relief

If any loss remains unrelieved after current period and carry back claim(s) have been made, or no current period and carry back claims were made, then carry forward relief is available.

Any remaining losses will automatically be carried forward to the next accounting period.

A claim can be made to offset the brought forward loss, wholly or partly, against total profits (ie before QCDs).

With carry forward relief (unlike current period and carry back claims), the company can make partial claims to prevent QCDs becoming unrelieved.

If the loss is not fully relieved, the remaining loss is automatically carried forward to the next accounting period and the procedure is repeated until the loss is fully relieved.

A claim to utilise (and quantify) the loss relieved must be made within two years of the end of the accounting period in which the loss is **relieved**.

Exam focus point

There is a restriction on the amount of carried forward losses that can be relieved where the company has profits over £5 million but this restriction is not examinable in Taxation (TX – UK). Carried forward losses arising prior to 1 April 2017 are not examinable in Taxation (TX – UK) as different rules apply to such losses.

2.5 Factors affecting the choice of loss relief

PER alert

One of the competencies you require in order to fulfil Performance Objective 17 *Tax planning and advice* of the PER is to mitigate and/or defer tax liabilities through the use of standard reliefs, exemptions and incentives. You can apply the knowledge you obtain from this section of the Workbook to help to demonstrate this competence.

To decide on whether a loss should be relieved in the current period, carried back or carried forward will involve consideration of:

- Timing: current period and carry back claims give relief for the loss more quickly than carry forward, so generally preferable for cash flow reasons.
- Qualifying charitable donations: under current period and carry back relief, these may become unrelieved. Partial claims may be made for carry forward relief in order to keep qualifying charitable donations relieved.
- Tax rate: if the tax rate is changing then the cash tax saving should be considered, eg if the tax rate is expected to fall, relief may be preferable in earlier financial years.

Illustration 2: Choice of loss relief

Monster Ltd has the following results.

Year ended	31.3.18	31.3.19	31.3.20	31.3.21
	£	£	£	£
Trading profit/(loss)	2,000	(500,000)	100,000	120,000
Chargeable gains	35,000	250,000	30,000	45,000
Qualifying charitable donations	(30,000)	(20,000)	(20,000)	(20,000)

Required

Recommend appropriate loss relief claims, stating by when the claims should be made, and compute the corporation tax for all years based on your recommendations, showing any unrelieved qualifying charitable donations. Assume the rate of corporation tax is 19% for all financial years.

Solution

A current period loss relief claim for the year ended 31 March 2019 will be against total profits of £250,000 and obtain relief quickly. This outweighs the fact that the claim will waste the qualifying charitable donations of £20,000 so a current period claim should be made by 31 March 2021 (two years from the end of the loss-making period).

If a current period loss relief claim is made, a carry back relief claim can also be made for the year ended 31 March 2018. This will be against total profits of (£35,000 + £2,000) = £37,000. This claim will waste qualifying charitable donations of £30,000 and so would use £37,000 of loss to save tax at 19% on £7,000 (£35,000 + £2,000 − £30,000). A carry back claim should therefore not be made.

A carry forward relief claim will obtain relief in the year ended 31 March 2020 against total profits. The claim should be restricted to (£100,000 + £30,000 − £20,000) = £110,000 to keep £20,000 of total profit in charge to match the qualifying charitable donation. The remaining (£500,000 − £250,000 − £110,000) = £140,000 of the loss will be carried forward to the year ended 31 March 2021 to be set against total profits. These claims should be made by 31 March 2022 and 31 March 2023 respectively (two years from the end of the period in which the loss is relieved).

The corporation tax computations are as follows:

	31.3.18	31.3.19	31.3.20	31.3.21
	£	£	£	£
Trading income	2,000	0	100,000	120,000
Chargeable gains	35,000	250,000	30,000	45,000
Total profits	37,000	250,000	130,000	165,000
Less current period loss relief		(250,000)		
Less carry forward loss relief	-		(110,000)	(140,000)
Less qualifying charitable donations	(30,000)	0	(20,000)	(20,000)
Taxable total profits	7,000	0	0	5,000
CT at 19%	1,330	0	0	950
Unrelieved qualifying charitable donations	0	20,000	0	0

Activity 1: Trading loss relief

Malamah plc has the following results:

	31.12.18	31.12.19	31.12.20	31.12.21
	£	£	£	£
Trading income	20,000	30,000	(55,000)	5,000
Interest income	10,000	10,000	10,000	10,000
Qualifying charitable donations	(5,000)	(5,000)	(5,000)	(12,000)

Required

Calculate the TTP for the above periods assuming loss relief is claimed in the most beneficial manner. Show any unrelieved qualifying charitable donations and any loss unrelieved at 31 December 2021.

Solution

3 Relief on cessation of trade - Terminal loss relief

When a company ceases trading, carry forward relief will no longer be available.

Therefore, the carryback period is extended to 36 months for losses incurred in the 12 months prior to the cessation of trading. Losses can be carried back against total profits (ie before QCDs) of the preceding 36 months on last in, first out (LIFO) basis, ie most recent periods first.

As with the basic carryback relief, QCDs may be unrelieved.

Activity 2: Terminal loss relief

Khiva Ltd ceased trading on 31 March 2021. It had the following results for its last five accounting periods:

	Y/e 30.9.17	6 months to 31.3.18	Y/e 31.3.19	Y/e 31.3.20	Y/e 31.3.21
	£	£	£	£	£
Trading profit (loss)	3,000	9,000	16,000	12,000	(47,800)
Interest income	500	–	600	600	600
Chargeable gains	1,000	–	–	–	5,000
Qualifying charitable donations	300	–	300	300	–

Required

How much of the loss relating to the accounting period ended 31 March 2021 can be utilised against profits in the accounting period ended 30 September 2017?

O £nil

O £2,100

O £2,250

O £4,000

Solution

4 Other types of loss

4.1 Property business losses

These can be relieved:

- By offset against total profits, as much as possible, of the current accounting period. This treatment is **automatic** (no claim is required)
- Carried forward and claim made to offset, wholly or partly, against future total profits.

Any claims for carry forward loss relief must be made within two years of the end of the accounting period in which the loss is relieved.

No carry back relief is available for a property business loss.

4.2 Capital losses

These are relieved in the following order:

(a) Against current accounting period gains

(b) Against gains in future accounting periods

The loss must be relieved to the fullest extent possible and treatment is automatic (no claim is required).

Note that capital losses cannot be carried back, and can **never** be offset against income.

Chapter summary

Loss relief for single companies

Trading losses – overview

Computing a trading loss
- Loss adjusted in same way as trading profit

Summary of available reliefs
- Current period
- Carry back
- Carry forward

Loss relief proforma

	2018	2019	2020	2021
Trading income	X	X	nil	X
Other income and gains	X	X	X	X
Total Profits	X	X	X	X
Current period			(X)	
Carry back		(X)		
Carry forward				(X)
Less QCDs	(X)	(X)	(X)	(X)
Taxable Total Profits (TTP)	X	X	X	X
Unrelieved QCDs	X	X		

Trading losses – ongoing trade

Current period loss relief
- Against total profits in current AP
- All or nothing claim

Carry back loss relief
- Against profits in the previous 12 months
- Must have claimed current period relief first
- All or nothing claim

Unrelieved QCDs
- Current and prior period relief may result in wasted QCDs

Carry forward relief
- Against total profits of future APs
- Partial claims available to avoid wasting QCDs

Factors affecting the choice of loss relief
- Earlier relief (c/y then c/b) is beneficial for cash flow
- Consider impact of unrelieved QCDs

Relief on cessation of trade – terminal loss relief

- Carry back extended to 36 months
- Offset against total profits on LIFO basis

Other types of loss

Property business losses
- Automatic offset vs current period total profits
- Carry forward vs total profits (claim, partial claims allowed)

Capital losses
- Automatic offset vs current and future gains

BPP LEARNING MEDIA

Knowledge diagnostic

1. Trading losses – overview

Trading losses may be relieved by deduction from current period total profits, from total profits of earlier periods or from future period total profits

2. Trading losses – ongoing companies

Relief is given by offset against current period total profits and against total profits of the previous 12 months (LIFO). Must offset as much as possible. Current period claim must be made before carryback. QCDs may become unrelieved.

Trading losses carried forward can be offset, wholly or partly, against total profits. Can make partial claim to prevent QCDs becoming unrelieved.

3. Relief on cessation of trade – terminal loss relief

Trading losses in the last 12 months of trading can be carried back 36 months (LIFO) and offset against total profits.

4. Other types of loss

Capital losses can only be relieved against current and future chargeable gains.

Property losses are relieved automatically against total profits of the current period. Then carried forward to future periods for claim to relieve wholly or partly against total profits

Further study guidance

Question practice

Now try the following from the Further question practice bank (available in the digital edition of the Workbook):

Section A: Q92, Q93 and Q94

Section C: Q95 Ferraro Ltd

Activity answers

Activity 1: Trading loss relief

	31.12.18	31.12.19	31.12.20	31.12.21
	£	£	£	£
Trading income	20,000	30,000	–	5,000
Interest income	10,000	10,000	10,000	10,000
Total Profits	30,000	40,000	10,000	15,000
Current period	–	–	(10,000) (i)	–
	30,000	40,000	–	15,000
Carry back	–	(40,000) (ii)	–	–
	30,000	–	–	15,000
Carry forward	–	–	–	(3,000) (iii)
	–	–	–	12,000
Qualifying charitable donation	(5,000)	(5,000)	(5,000)	(12,000)
TTP	25,000	–	–	–
Unrelieved qualifying charitable donations		5,000	5,000	

	£
Loss memo	
Y/e 31.12.20	55,000
Current period	(i)(10,000)
Carry back (previous 12 months)	(ii) (40,000)
	5,000
Carry forward (partial claim to prevent QCD becoming unrelieved)	(iii) (3,000)
C/f at 31.12.21	2,000

Activity 2: Terminal loss relief

The correct answer is: £2,250

	Y/e 30.9.17	6 months 31.3.18	Y/e 31.3.19	Y/e 31.3.20	Y/e 31.3.21
	£	£	£	£	£
Trading income	3,000	9,000	16,000	12,000	–
Interest income	500	–	600	600	600
Gain	1,000	–	–	–	5,000
Total Profits	4,500	9,000	16,600	12,600	5,600
C/yr					(5,600) (i)

	Y/e 30.9.17	6 months 31.3.18	Y/e 31.3.19	Y/e 31.3.20	Y/e 31.3.21
	£	£	£	£	£
C/b	(2,250)*(v)	(9,000) (iv)	(16,600) (iii)	(12,600) (ii)	
	2,250	–	–	–	–
Qualifying charitable donation	(300)	–	–	–	–
TTP	1,950	–	–	–	–
Unrelieved qualifying charitable donation			300	300	

* £4,500 × 6/12 (36m carry back) = £2,250 maximum set-off

	£
Loss memorandum	
Y/e 31.3.21	47,800
Current	(5,600) (i)
C/b y/e 31.3.20	(12,600) (ii)
C/b y/e 31.3.19	(16,600) (iii)
C/b 6m to 31.3.18	(9,000) (iv)
C/b y/e 30.9.17	(2,250) (v)
	1,750

The answer £nil restricts the carry back as far as the six months to 31.3.18. The answer £2,100 incorrectly apportions the profit after QCDs for the year ended 30 September 2017 to determine the maximum set-off for that period. The answer £4,000 fails to time-apportion the profit for the year ended 30 September 2017 at all.

> **Tutorial note.** In answering an objective test question, there is no need to set out full computations; simply using a loss memo would suffice. The full computation is produced here for illustration purposes.

Groups

Learning objectives

On completion of this chapter, you should be able to:

	Syllabus reference no.
Define a 75% group, and recognise the reliefs that are available to members of such a group.	E5(a)
Define a 75% chargeable gains group, and recognise the reliefs that are available to members of such a group.	E5(b)

Exam context

Section A questions on groups could include the identification of members of a 75% group relief group or a 75% chargeable gains group. Groups may also feature in your examination as part of the 15-mark corporation tax question in Section C or in a 10-mark question in that Section or in Section B. Your first step in dealing with any group question must be to establish the relationship between the companies and identify what group or groups exist. You may find it helpful to draw a diagram. You must be aware that 75% group relief groups and 75% chargeable gains groups do not always coincide.

Chapter overview

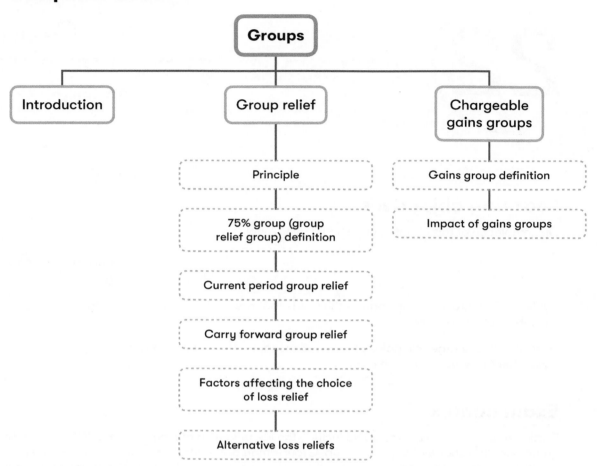

1 Introduction

A group exists for taxation purposes where one company is a subsidiary of another.

There are two types of relationship that you need to know:

- 75% groups for group loss relief
- 75% groups for chargeable gains

2 Group relief

2.1 Principle

The group relief provisions enable companies within a 75% group to transfer trading losses and certain other losses to other companies within the group, in order to set these against taxable total profits and reduce the group's overall corporation tax liability.

2.2 75% group (group relief group) definition

> **75% group (Group relief group):** Two companies are members of a 75% group where one is a 75% subsidiary of the other, or both are 75% subsidiaries of a third company.
>
> **75% subsidiary:** For one company to be a 75% subsidiary of another, the holding company must have:
>
> - At least 75% of the ordinary share capital of the subsidiary
> - A right to at least 75% of the distributable income of the subsidiary; and
> - A right to at least 75% of the net assets of the subsidiary were it to be wound up

Sub-subsidiaries may be included in a 75% group if the ultimate parent has at least a 75% effective interest.

A 75% group may include non-UK resident companies. However, losses may generally only be surrendered between **UK resident** companies.

> 🔍 **Exam focus point**
>
> Relief for trading losses incurred by an overseas subsidiary is not examinable in your exam.

Activity 1: 75% group

Consider the following group structure:

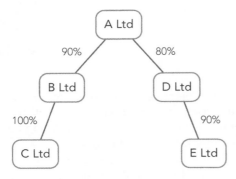

Required

Which companies are in the same 75% group as A Ltd?

O B Ltd, C Ltd and D Ltd only

O B Ltd and D Ltd only

O B Ltd and C Ltd only

O B Ltd, C Ltd, D Ltd and E Ltd

Solution

2.3 Current period group relief

2.3.1 Operation

A company which has made a current period loss (the surrendering company) may transfer all or part of this loss to another member of the 75% group (the claimant company).

2.3.2 Surrendering company

The surrendering company can transfer any amount of its current period available loss:

- Trade losses
- Excess qualifying charitable donations
- Excess property business losses

Any amount of loss can be surrendered so the company may specify an amount less than the maximum amount to be surrendered, and may also surrender trading losses by group relief that it could have used itself.

'Excess' qualifying charitable donations and property business losses refer to the losses in excess of the surrendering company's other profits (before any loss reliefs) in that period. These must, therefore, be first set off against the surrendering company's total profits before any remainder can be group relieved.

2.3.3 Claimant company

Sets loss against its taxable total profits (TTP) of **same period** as surrendering company's loss-making period.

The available profits for group relief are calculated assuming the claimant company uses any of its own current period losses first, even if such a claim is not made.

Essential reading

Your Essential reading contains details of the order in which losses are offset against a claimant company's total profits.

The Essential reading is available as an Appendix of the digital edition of the Workbook.

Activity 2: Available profits and losses

Verano Ltd owns 100% of the share capital of Invierno Ltd and several other group companies. Results for the year ended 31 March 2021 are as follows:

	£
Verano Ltd	
Trading loss	(100,000)
Trading loss brought forward at 1 April 2020	(17,000)
Non-trade loan relationship income	10,000
Property business loss	(15,000)
Invierno Ltd	
Trading loss	(100,000)
Trading loss brought forward at 1 April 2020	(12,000)
Chargeable gain	260,000

Required

1 What is the maximum loss that Verano Ltd can surrender to other group companies under current period group relief?

○ £100,000

○ £105,000

○ £115,000

○ £132,000

2 What is the maximum claim for current period group relief that Invierno Ltd can make?

○ £nil

○ £160,000

○ £148,000

○ £260,000

Solution

2.3.4 Corresponding accounting periods - time-apportioning of profits and losses

Under the following three situations, both available profits and losses must be time apportioned, so that only the results of the corresponding period may be offset under current period group relief.

- If the accounting period of a surrendering company and a claimant company are not the same dates.
- In the period of acquisition of a 75% subsidiary, current period group relief is only available after the date the subsidiary joins the group.
- In the period of sale of a 75% subsidiary, the selling group can only use current period group relief until there are 'arrangements in place' to sell the subsidiary.

Apportionment in periods of acquisition or disposal may be done using a different method if time-apportioning would give an unjust or unreasonable result.

Illustrations

(a) **Non-coterminous accounting periods**

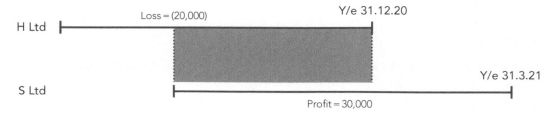

The maximum group relief in the overlapping period is the lower of:

$9/12 \times (£20,000) = £15,000$ and

$9/12 \times £30,000 = £22,500$

ie £15,000

Note that the remaining £5,000 loss could be surrendered to S Ltd in its year ended 31.3.20.

(b) **Company joining a group**

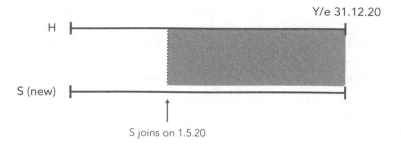

Y/e 31.12.20

S joins on 1.5.20

Group relief would only be available for the post-acquisition period, so both the loss and profit would be time apportioned by 8/12.

(c) **Company leaving a group**

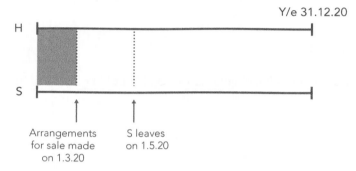

Y/e 31.12.20

Arrangements for sale made on 1.3.20

S leaves on 1.5.20

Group relief would only be available until arrangements for sale were in place, ie until 29 February 2020.

2.3.5 Group relief claims

- Any claim for current period group relief must be made within two years of the end of the claimant company's profit-making period.
- Made on claimant company's return supported by statement of consent from surrendering company.
- The claimant company can make a payment to the surrendering company in return for the loss which is ignored for corporation tax purposes as long as it does not exceed the amount of loss surrendered.

Activity 3: Group relief claims

Hot Ltd and its subsidiaries Set Ltd, Bag Ltd and Lip Ltd have the following results:

Hot Ltd	Year ended 31.3.21	–	trading income	£825,000
		–	other income	£180,000
Set Ltd	Year ended 31.3.21	–	trading income	£20,000
		–	property letting loss	£(40,000)
		–	non-trade loan relationship income	£30,000
Bag Ltd	Year ended 30.6.21	–	trading loss	£(105,000)
		–	other income	£5,000
Lip Ltd	Year ended 31.5.21	–	trading income	£75,000

Hot Ltd owns 90% of the share capital of Set Ltd. Set Ltd acquired 85% of the share capital of Lip Ltd on 1 September 2020 from an unrelated party. It was agreed with HM Revenue & Customs (HMRC) that sufficient arrangements were in place for Lip Ltd to leave its previous group on 31 July 2020.

Hot Ltd owned 75% of the share capital of Bag Ltd until it was sold to an unrelated party on

30 April 2021. It was agreed with HMRC that sufficient arrangements were in place for Bag Ltd to leave the Hot Ltd group on 28 February 2021.

Required

1   What is the maximum current period group relief claim possible by Hot Ltd in respect of Set Ltd's property letting loss in the year ended 31 March 2021?

- ○ £nil
- ○ £10,000
- ○ £9,000
- ○ £20,000

2   What is the maximum current period group relief claim possible by Lip Ltd in respect of Bag Ltd's trading loss?

- ○ £70,000
- ○ £50,000
- ○ £52,500
- ○ £37,500

3   Assuming a final and conclusive claim under current period group relief is made to offset Bag Ltd's trading loss against the taxable total profits of Hot Ltd, which of the following statements is correct?

- ○ Hot Ltd makes the claim supported by a statement of consent from Bag Ltd on or before 31 March 2023.
- ○ Hot Ltd makes the claim with or without a statement of consent from Bag Ltd on or before 30 June 2023.
- ○ Bag Ltd makes the claim with or without a statement of consent from Hot Ltd on or before 31 March 2023.
- ○ Hot Ltd makes the claim supported by a statement of consent from Bag Ltd on or before 28 February 2023.

Solution

2.4 Carry forward group relief

2.4.1 Principle

A company which has a loss carried forward (the surrendering company) may transfer all or part of this loss to another member of the 75% group (the claimant company).

2.4.2 Surrendering company

The surrendering company may surrender carried forward:

- trading losses and/or
- property business income losses

to other group companies under carry forward group relief.

Unlike current period group relief, a surrendering company can **only** surrender carried forward losses that it cannot deduct from its own total profits for the current period.

The company may specify an amount less than the maximum amount to be surrendered.

2.4.3 Claimant company

The claimant company must use its own (current period and brought forward) losses to the fullest extent possible in working out the available taxable total profits against which it may claim carry forward group relief.

Carry forward group relief is set against taxable total profits after all other reliefs for the current period but before relief for any amounts carried back from later periods.

2.4.4 Other points to note

Similar rules to current period group relief apply in relation to apportioning profits in non-coterminous accounting periods. The rules for claims are identical.

Exam focus point

There is a restriction on the amount of carried forward losses that can be relieved where the company has profits in excess of £5 million but this restriction **is not examinable** in Taxation (TX – UK). Also, a question **will not be set** involving carried forward losses arising prior to 1 April 2017 since carry forward group relief is not available for such losses

Activity 4: Carry forward group relief

Sage plc has owned 80% of Basil plc for many years. Both companies prepare accounts to 31 March each year. The companies always use loss relief and group relief as early as possible.

Results for the year ended 31 March 2021 are as follows:

	£
Sage plc	
Trading profit	75,000
Property business income	20,000
Trading loss brought forward at 1 April 2020	(120,000)

	£
Basil plc	
Trading profit	70,000
Property business loss	(50,000)

Required

1   Explain how Sage plc's trading loss brought forward can be relieved in the year ended 31 March 2021.

   Note. No calculations are required for this part.

2   Calculate the TTP (if any) for Sage plc and Basil plc for the year ended 31 March 2021, assuming the maximum carry forward group relief claim is made, and state any amount of trading loss for Sage plc to carry forward at 31 March 2021.

Solution

2.5 Alternative loss reliefs

Several alternative loss reliefs may be available, including group relief. In making a choice consider:

- **How quickly relief will be obtained:** obtaining loss relief by using current period group relief is quicker than carry forward loss relief and so generally preferable to carrying forward the loss for cash flow reasons.
- **The extent to which relief for qualifying charitable donations might be lost:** group relief is deducted after qualifying charitable donations in the claimant company, so relief for these donations is not lost. By contrast, if the surrendering company claims relief for the loss against its own current period total profits, relief for qualifying charitable donations in that company may be wasted.

3 Chargeable gains groups

3.1 Gains group definition

KEY TERM

> **Chargeable gains group:** A chargeable gains group consists of the top company plus companies in which the top company has a 50% effective interest, provided there is a 75% holding at each level.

A chargeable gains group exists where:

- A holding company owns at least 75% of a subsidiary's share capital; or
- Two subsidiaries are at least 75% owned by same parent company.

Sub-subsidiaries are included if the ultimate parent company's effective interest is at least 50%. The definition of a chargeable gains group is wider than that of a 75% group as only an effective 50% interest is needed compared to a 75% interest. However, a company can only be in one chargeable gains group although it may be a member of more than one 75% group.

Non-resident companies can be included in a chargeable gains group, but may generally not participate in any reliefs.

Essential reading

The Essential reading contains an illustration showing the difference between a 75% group relief group and a chargeable gains group.

The Essential reading is available as an Appendix of the digital edition of the Workbook.

3.2 Impact of gains groups

There are both practical and tax planning advantages to being in a chargeable gains group: asset transfers are tax-neutral; there is more chance of being able to use a group's capital losses, and more chance of rollover relief being available. These reliefs are explained in more detail below.

3.2.1 Intra-group transfers

Capital assets are transferred between group members at a no gain/no loss (NG/NL) value (being the eligible cost plus indexation to the earlier of the date of transfer and December 2017).

No election is needed, as this relief is compulsory.

Activity 5: Intra-group transfer

Hand Ltd owns 90% of Glove Ltd. On 6 June 2017, Hand Ltd transferred a building to Glove Ltd for £120,000. On this date, its market value was £275,000 and it had cost Hand Ltd £140,000 on 30 April 1996.

Required

1 What are the tax implications of this transfer?

2 Glove Ltd sells the building for £300,000 to a third party in September 2020.

   Required

   What is the chargeable gain arising?

Note. Indexation factors: April 1996–June 2017 = 0.784, June 2017–December 2017 = 0.021, June 2017–September 2020 = 0.073

Solution

3.2.2 Matching group gains and losses

- An election can be made to transfer all or part of a gain or a loss on disposal of an asset between group companies.
- Joint election within two years of end of accounting period by the company making the disposal.
- Only current period capital losses can be transferred, not brought forward losses (though a chargeable gain could be transferred to a company with brought forward capital losses).

Activity 6: Matching group gains and losses

Queen Ltd owns 90% of the ordinary share capital of Princess Ltd. Both companies prepare accounts to 31 March each year.

On 21 June 2020, Queen Ltd sold a building realising a chargeable gain of £96,000.

On 8 September 2020, Princess Ltd sold a building realising a capital loss of £28,000.

Princess Ltd also has unused capital losses from the previous accounting period of £32,000.

Required

Advise the group what action they should take in respect of these capital disposals for the year ended 31 March 2021 and the deadline for such action.

Solution

3.2.3 Group rollover relief

Companies in a chargeable gains group are treated as one unit for rollover relief, ie if:

- One company sells a qualifying asset at a gain
- Another company in the group reinvests in a new qualifying asset in the period 12 months before to three years after the disposal

The indexed gain can be deferred (by a joint claim between the two companies).

The new qualifying asset must be purchased from outside the group.

Chapter summary

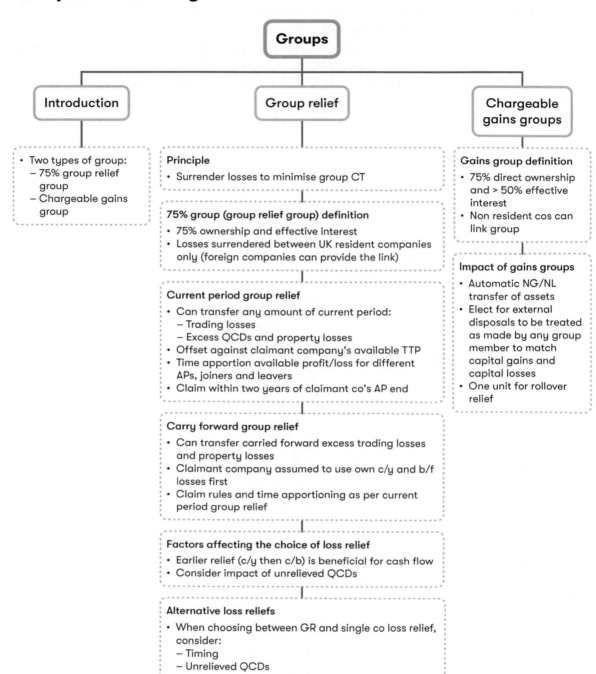

Groups

Introduction

- Two types of group:
  - 75% group relief group
  - Chargeable gains group

Group relief

Principle
- Surrender losses to minimise group CT

75% group (group relief group) definition
- 75% ownership and effective interest
- Losses surrendered between UK resident companies only (foreign companies can provide the link)

Current period group relief
- Can transfer any amount of current period:
  - Trading losses
  - Excess QCDs and property losses
- Offset against claimant company's available TTP
- Time apportion available profit/loss for different APs, joiners and leavers
- Claim within two years of claimant co's AP end

Carry forward group relief
- Can transfer carried forward excess trading losses and property losses
- Claimant company assumed to use own c/y and b/f losses first
- Claim rules and time apportioning as per current period group relief

Factors affecting the choice of loss relief
- Earlier relief (c/y then c/b) is beneficial for cash flow
- Consider impact of unrelieved QCDs

Alternative loss reliefs
- When choosing between GR and single co loss relief, consider:
  - Timing
  - Unrelieved QCDs

Chargeable gains groups

Gains group definition
- 75% direct ownership and > 50% effective interest
- Non resident cos can link group

Impact of gains groups
- Automatic NG/NL transfer of assets
- Elect for external disposals to be treated as made by any group member to match capital gains and capital losses
- One unit for rollover relief

Knowledge diagnostic

1. Introduction

There are two types of group relationships that exist:

- 75% group (group relief group) requires 75% direct and effective interest of parent in subsidiary.
- Chargeable gains group requires 75% direct interest at each level and a 50% effective interest in sub-subsidiaries.

2. Current period group relief

Within a 75% group, current period trading losses, excess property business losses and excess qualifying charitable donations can be surrendered between UK companies under current period group relief. Surrendering company can surrender any amount of its loss. The claimant company can only offset against current period TTP.

TTP and losses must be apportioned for non-corresponding accounting periods, and companies joining and leaving a group.

3. Carry forward group relief

Carried forward trading losses and property business losses can be surrendered between UK companies under carried forward group relief. Surrendering company assumed to use carried forward losses itself before considering surrender.

4. Chargeable gains groups

Chargeable gains groups allow assets to be transferred within the group at no gain/no loss or an election can be made to allocate a gain/loss to another group member. They are also treated as a single unit for rollover purposes.

Further study guidance

Question practice

Now try the following from the Further question practice bank (available in the digital edition of the Workbook):

Section A: Q96, Q97, Q98

Section C: Q99 Pixie Ltd

Further reading

ACCA's article *Groups*, written by a member of the Taxation (TX – UK) examining team, states that it is important that Taxation (TX – UK) candidates know the group relationship that must exist for reliefs to be available. Working through the examples in this article will prepare you for anything that could be set in the exam.

Activity answers

Activity 1: 75% group

The correct answer is: B Ltd, C Ltd and D Ltd only

A Ltd does not have a 75% effective interest in E Ltd (80% × 90% = 72%).

Note that D Ltd and E Ltd can form a separate 75% group; any losses incurred by E Ltd could be surrendered to D Ltd and *vice versa*.

Activity 2: Available profits and losses

1   The correct answer is: £105,000

    Verano Ltd can surrender its current year trade loss of £100,000 and its excess property business loss (£15,000 less £10,000) = £5,000, so £105,000 in total. Losses brought forward from previous periods cannot be surrendered or claimed via current period group relief.

    The answer £100,000 is just the current year trade loss. The answer £115,000 does not restrict the property business loss. The answer £132,000 does not restrict the property business loss and includes the trade loss brought forward.

2   The correct answer is: £160,000

    Invierno Ltd can claim up to its current year available TTP. If it makes a trading loss, assume that it makes a current year claim for relief. £260,000 less £100,000 = £160,000.

    The answer £nil assumes that the chargeable gain cannot be group relieved. The answer £148,000 deducts the loss brought forward. The answer £260,000 does not deduct the current year loss.

Activity 3: Group relief claims

1   The correct answer is: £nil

    Only excess property loss can be surrendered to group companies; the property loss is automatically offset against Set Ltd's taxable profits in the year of the loss.

    The answer £10,000 does not set off Set Ltd's loss against trading income. The answer £9,000 does not set off Set Ltd's loss against trading income and takes 90% of the loss – remember that once a 75% group relationship has been established the whole of a loss can be group relieved, not just the proportion relating to the shareholding. The answer £20,000 does not offset Set Ltd's loss against non-trading income.

2   The correct answer is: £37,500

    Bag Ltd could surrender 6/12 × £105,000 = £52,500 (1.9.20–28.2.21) but Lip Ltd can claim only 6/12 × £75,000 = £37,500 (1.9.20–28.2.21).

    The answer £70,000 is the amount which could be surrendered by Bag Ltd to the group as whole (1.7.20–28.2.21). The answer £50,000 assumes other income in Bag Ltd must be offset first. The answer £52,500 is the amount which could be surrendered by Bag Ltd.

    Remember, companies **joining** a group can only claim/surrender group relief from the date that they actually join the group. Companies **leaving** the group can only claim/surrender group relief until the date that arrangements to leave are in place, not the date they actually leave the group.

3   The correct answer is: Hot Ltd makes the claim supported by a statement of consent from Bag Ltd on or before 31 March 2023.

    It is the claimant company (Hot Ltd) which makes the claim, within two years of the end of its accounting period (year ended 31/3/21).

Activity 4: Carry forward group relief

1 Sage plc can claim to offset its trading loss brought forward against its current period total profits.

Any remaining loss which could not be used by Sage plc can be surrendered to Basil plc under carry forward group relief.

Basil plc must use its own losses as much as possible before claiming carry forward group relief.

2 **Sage plc and Basil plc – TTP for year ended 31 March 2021**

	Sage plc	Basil plc
	£	£
Trading income	75,000	70,000
Property business income	20,000	–
Total profits	95,000	70,000
Current period own loss relief	–	(50,000)
	95,000	20,000
Carry forward own loss relief	(95,000)	–
Carry forward group relief (£120,000 – £95,000) = £25,000 max	–	(20,000)
TTP	–	–

Sage plc will have £25,000 – £20,000 = 5,000 trading loss to carry forward at 31 March 2021.

Activity 5: Intra-group transfer

1 Building automatically transferred at NG/NL.

ie cost + indexation to date of transfer (earlier than December 2017)

ie £140,000 + (0.784 × £140,000) = £249,760

Glove Ltd has a base cost for the building of £249,760 for future disposal

2 Sale to third party in September 2020

	£
Proceeds	300,000
Cost (from (1))	(249,760)
Indexation allowance 0.021 × £249,760 (frozen to Dec 17)	(5,245)
Chargeable gain	44,995

Activity 6: Matching group gains and losses

Princess Ltd's unused capital loss of £28,000 and brought forward capital losses of £32,000 can be offset by transferring all or part of Queen Ltd's gain of £96,000.

If the whole of the gain is transferred, Princess Ltd will show the balance of the gain of £36,000 (£96,000 – £28,000 – £32,000) in its corporation tax computation. Alternatively, if Queen Ltd transfers only (£32,000 + £28,000) = £60,000 of the gain, the remaining £36,000 will be shown in Queen Ltd's corporation tax computation.

The two companies need to make a joint election by 31 March 2023.

23

Self assessment and payment of tax by companies

Learning objectives

On completion of this chapter, you should be able to:

	Syllabus reference no.
Explain and apply the features of the self-assessment system as it applies to companies, including the use of iXBRL.	A3(b)
Recognise the time limits that apply to the filing of returns and the making of claims.	A4(a)
Recognise the due dates for the payment of tax under the self-assessment system, and compute payments on account and balancing payments/repayments for individuals	A4(b)
Explain how large companies are required to account for corporation tax on a quarterly basis and compute the quarterly instalment payments.	A4(c)
List the information and records that taxpayers need to retain for tax purposes.	A4(d)
Explain the circumstances in which HM Revenue & Customs can make a compliance check into a self-assessment tax return.	A5(a)
Explain the procedures for dealing with appeals and First and Upper Tier Tribunals	A5(b)
Calculate late payment interest and state the penalties that can be charged.	A6(a)

Exam context

Section A questions on corporation tax administration could include the identification of filing dates and the calculation of interest on late paid tax or penalties. You may also be tested on these aspects in a Section B question. In Section C, you might be asked to explain an aspect of the tax administration system such as the appeals process.

Chapter overview

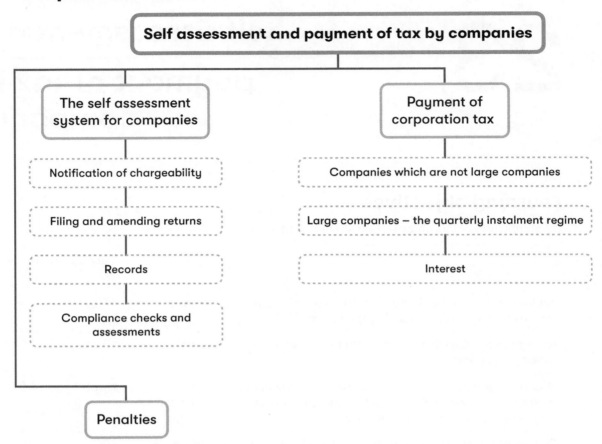

Self assessment and payment of tax by companies

The self assessment system for companies

Notification of chargeability

Filing and amending returns

Records

Compliance checks and assessments

Payment of corporation tax

Companies which are not large companies

Large companies – the quarterly instalment regime

Interest

Penalties

BPP
LEARNING
MEDIA

1 The self-assessment system for companies

The self assessment system relies upon the company completing and filing a tax return and paying the tax due. The system is enforced by a system of penalties for failure to comply within the set time limits, and by interest for late payment of tax.

PER alert

One of the competencies you require to fulfil Performance Objective 16 *Tax compliance and verification* of the PER is to explain tax filing and payment requirements and the consequences of non-compliance to clients. You can apply the knowledge you obtain from this section of the Workbook to help to demonstrate this competence.

1.1 Notification of chargeability

1.1.1 Notification of first accounting period

A company must notify HM Revenue & Customs (HMRC) when it becomes chargeable to corporation tax (eg when it starts to trade or if it acquires a source of income) within three months of the beginning of its first accounting period.

1.1.2 Notification of chargeability

HMRC will issue the company with a notice to file a corporation tax return. If no such notice is issued to the company then, if it is chargeable to corporation tax, the company must notify HMRC within 12 months of the end of the accounting period.

1.2 Filing and amending returns

PER alert

One of the competencies you require to fulfil Performance Objective 16 *Tax compliance and verification* of the PER is to verify and question client submissions and ensure timely submission of all relevant information to the tax authorities by the due date. You can apply the knowledge you obtain from this section of the Workbook to help to demonstrate this competence.

1.2.1 Filing date

An obligation to file a return arises only when the company receives a notice requiring a return. A return is required for each accounting period ending during or at the end of the period specified in the notice requiring a return. The filing date is normally the later of:

- 12 months after the end of the relevant period of account to which the return relates
- 3 months from the date on which the notice requiring the return was made

The relevant period of account is that in which the accounting period to which the return relates ends. Therefore, in a long period of account, the filing date for **both** returns is 12 months after the end of the period of account.

1.2.2 Required documents and format

Complete accounts and computations, including a self-assessment of tax payable, will be due on or before the filing date. All limited companies must file their return online and pay their corporation tax electronically. The filing of accounts must be done in inLine eXtensible Business Reporting Language (iXBRL).

Essential reading

Detail regarding iXBRL can be found in your Essential reading.

The Essential reading is available as an Appendix of the digital edition of the Workbook.

1.2.3 Amending a return

A company may amend a return within 12 months of the filing date.

HMRC may amend a return to correct any obvious errors or anything else that an officer has reason to believe is incorrect in the light of information available within nine months of the return being filed.

1.2.4 Claims

Wherever possible claims must be made on a tax return or on an amendment to it and must be quantified at the time the return is made.

Essential reading

Exceptions to this rule, and further detail regarding claim deadlines, can be found in your essential reading.

The Essential reading is available as an Appendix of the digital edition of the Workbook.

1.3 Records

Companies must keep records until the latest of:

- Six years from the end of the accounting period
- The date any compliance check enquiries are completed
- The date after which a compliance check enquiry may not be commenced

All business records and accounts, including contracts and receipts, must be kept or information showing that the company has prepared a complete and correct tax return.

If a return is demanded more than six years after the end of the accounting period, any records or information which the company still has must be kept until the later of the end of a compliance check enquiry and the expiry of the right to start one.

1.4 Compliance checks and assessments

1.4.1 Compliance checks

HM Revenue & Customs (HMRC) may decide to conduct a compliance check enquiry on a return, claim or election that has been submitted by a company, in the same way as for individuals.

The officer of HMRC must give written notice of his intention to conduct a compliance check enquiry. The notice must be given by:

- The first anniversary of the due filing date (most group companies) or the actual filing date (other companies), if the return was delivered on or before the due filing date; or
- The quarter day following the first anniversary of the actual filing date, if the return is filed after the due filing date. The quarter days are 31 January, 30 April, 31 July and 31 October.

1.4.2 Appeals and disputes

The procedure for HMRC internal reviews and appeals relating to individuals, discussed earlier in this Workbook, also applies to companies.

1.4.3 Assessment

The liabilities to pay tax on the due date and the filing date will arise automatically, without assessments being raised.

The tax return will include a self-assessment of the corporation tax payable for the period. If HMRC does not conduct a compliance check on the return within the required notice period, it will be treated as finalised.

2 Payment of corporation tax

PER alert

One of the competencies you require to fulfil Performance Objective 16 *Tax compliance and verification* of the PER is to determine the incidence (timing) of tax liabilities and their impact on cash flow/financing requirements. You can apply the knowledge you obtain from this section of the Workbook to help to demonstrate this competence.

2.1 Companies which are not large companies

Corporation tax is due for payment by **companies which are not large companies** (see below), **nine months and one day after the end of the chargeable accounting period**. For example, if a company, which is not a large company, has an accounting period ending on 31 December 2020, the corporation tax for the period is payable on 1 October 2021.

For a long period of account tax will be payable nine months and a day after **each** chargeable accounting period.

2.2 Large companies - the quarterly instalment regime

Large companies must pay their corporation tax in instalments.

2.2.1 Definition of a large company

Large company: A large company is a company whose augmented profits are above the profit threshold of £1.5 million for a 12-month accounting period (given in tax rates and allowances in exam).

Augmented profits: Augmented profits = TTP + dividends from unrelated (non-51% group) companies.

The profit threshold is divided by the number of related 51% group companies at the end of the immediately preceding accounting period.

The profit threshold is also time-apportioned for short chargeable accounting periods. For example, if a company has a three-month accounting period, the threshold is (£1.5m × 3/12) = £375,000.

Related 51% group company: A company (Company B) is a related 51% group company of another company (Company A), if Company A is a 51% subsidiary of Company B, or Company B is a 51% subsidiary of Company A, or both company A and company B are 51% subsidiaries of another company. Non-UK resident companies may be included as related 51% group companies. Companies which do not carry on a trade (dormant companies) are not related 51% group companies.

Illustration 1: Related 51% group companies

Yellow Ltd prepares accounts to 31 March each year. At 31 March 2020, Yellow Ltd had three wholly owned subsidiary companies – Verdant Ltd, Xeon Ltd and Zim Ltd – and owned 45% of the ordinary shares of Unicorn Ltd. Xeon Ltd did not carry on any trade or business during the year to 31 March 2020. Zim Ltd is not resident in the UK.

Yellow Ltd acquired 75% of the ordinary shares of Trident Ltd on 1 July 2020.

Required

What is the profit threshold for Yellow Ltd for determining corporation tax payment dates for the year ending 31 March 2021?

Solution

Verdant Ltd and Zim Ltd (residence not relevant) are related 51% group companies with Yellow Ltd so there are three related 51% group companies.

Xeon Ltd is not a related 51% group company because it is dormant.

Unicorn Ltd is not a related 51% group company because it is not a 51% subsidiary of Yellow Ltd.

Trident Ltd was not a related 51% group company at the end of the previous accounting period and so does not reduce the profit threshold of Yellow Ltd in respect of the year ending 31 March 2021.

The profit threshold for Yellow Ltd for the year ending 31 March 2021 is therefore (£1,500,000/3) = £500,000.

2.2.2 Exceptions

Transitional relief is available for companies in the first AP they are large. No quarterly payments are required if:

- Augmented profits ≤£10m for 12 month AP; and
- Not large in previous year.

The £10 million threshold is reduced proportionately by the number of related 51% group companies (including the company in question) at the end of the previous accounting period.

Any company whose corporation tax liability does not exceed £10,000 need not pay by instalments.

2.2.3 Quarterly instalment payments- 12-month accounting periods

Instalments are based on an estimate of the expected **current** accounting period (AP)'s liability.

For a 12-month AP, four quarterly instalments will be made in months 7, 10, 13 and 16 following the start of the AP. The instalments are due on the 14th of the month.

The correct instalment amounts for a 12-month period will be four equal amounts of 25% (3/12ths) of the corporation tax liability for the year.

Activity 1: Corporation tax due dates

A plc has taxable total profits (TTP) of £480,000 for the year ended 31 March 2021. In the year ended 31 March 2020, it had TTP of £600,000.

For many years, A plc has had investments in three other companies. The profits of those companies and the dividends paid to A plc in the year ended 31 March 2021 are as follows:

Company	% holding	TTP	Dividends paid to A plc
B Ltd	55%	£475,000	£10,000
C Ltd	75%	£600,000	£50,000
D Ltd	40%	£62,000	£25,000

All companies have a 31 March year end and none of them have any other related companies. There have been no other dividend receipts by any of the companies named above.

Required

1 What are the augmented profits of A plc in the year ended 31 March 2021 for the purposes of quarterly instalments of corporation tax?

○ £480,000

○ £505,000

○ £515,000

○ £565,000

2 Which of the above companies are large in the year ended 31 March 2021 for the purposes of quarterly instalments?

○ A plc and C Ltd only

○ A plc, B Ltd and C Ltd only

○ C Ltd only

○ None of these companies is large

3 When must the first corporation tax payment be made by A plc and B Ltd in respect of their liabilities for the year ended 31 March 2021?

○ A plc on 14 October 2020 and B Ltd on 1 January 2022

○ A plc on 14 October 2021 and B Ltd on 1 January 2021

○ A plc on 1 January 2022 and B Ltd on 1 January 2022

○ A plc on 14 October 2020 and B Ltd on 1 January 2021

Solution

Activity 2: Quarterly instalments for 12 month AP

F plc has a 31 March 2021 year end and has TTP of £2.1 million.

Required

Show the corporation tax instalments for the year ended 31 March 2021.

Solution

2.2.4 Short accounting period

If an accounting period is less than 12 months long, the first instalment is due on the 14th of the seventh months from the start of the accounting period (as for a 12-month period). Subsequent instalments are due at three monthly intervals but with the final payment **always** due by the 14th of the 4th month following the end of the AP regardless of the length of the period.

The amount of each instalment is computed by:

(a) Working out 3 × CT/n where CT is the amount of the estimated corporation tax liability payable in instalments for the period and n is the number of months in the period

(b) Allocating the smaller of that amount and the total estimated corporation tax liability to the first instalment

(c) Repeating the process for later instalments until the amount allocated is equal to the corporation tax liability

 ### Illustration 2: Instalments for short accounting period

B plc has a 10-month accounting period to 31 October 2020.

Required

When will the corporation tax be due if the total liability is expected to be £4 million?

Solution

Each instalment = 3 × (£4m/10) = £1.2m

	£m	
14.7.20	1.2	
14.10.20	1.2	
14.1.21	1.2	
	3.6	
14.2.21 (balance)	0.4	(4th month after AP end)
	4.0	

2.3 Interest

2.3.1 Interest charged by HMRC on late paid tax

Interest applies to tax paid after the due date (for non-large companies) and to underpaid instalments. This will run from the due date for tax. The rate of interest applied to underpaid tax is 2.75%. This rate will be given to you in your tax tables.

Activity 3: Late paid corporation tax

Forgetful Ltd paid its CT liability for the year ended 31 December 2020 on 31 December 2021 at the same time as filing its CT return for that accounting period. The CT liability was £200,000. Forgetful Ltd is not required to pay its corporation tax by quarterly instalments.

Required

How much interest will Forgetful Ltd be charged by HMRC in respect of the payment of CT for the year ended 31 December 2020?

- ○ £917
- ○ £5,500
- ○ £1,375
- ○ £nil

Solution

2.3.2 Interest from HMRC on overpaid tax

This will accrue at an annual rate of 0.50% (rate will be given to you in the exam) and will run from the later of:

- The due date for tax; and
- The date that the tax was originally paid.

Activity 4: Interest on overpaid corporation tax

Milton Ltd paid its CT liability for the year ended 31 December 2020 on 31 July 2021.

The final accounts showed an overpayment of £120,000 tax and HMRC paid this, along with the relevant interest to Milton Ltd on 31 October 2021.

Required

How much interest is payable by HMRC to Milton Ltd?

- ○ £nil
- ○ £50
- ○ £150
- ○ £100

Solution

2.3.3 Treatment for corporation tax

Interest paid/received on late payments or over payments of corporation tax is dealt with as investment income as interest paid/received on a non-trading loan relationship.

3 Penalties

Penalties may be levied for failure to notify the first accounting period, failure to notify chargeability for an accounting period, the late filing of returns, failure to keep records, and errors in returns.

> **PER alert**
>
> One of the competencies you require to fulfil Performance Objective 16 *Tax compliance and verification* of the PER is to explain tax filing and payment requirements and the consequences of non-compliance to clients. You can apply the knowledge you obtain from this section of the Workbook to help to demonstrate this competence.

3.1 Failure to notify chargeability

Failure to notify, and provide information about, the first accounting period can mean a penalty of £300 plus £60 per day the information is outstanding, and a penalty of up to £3,000 for fraudulently or negligently giving incorrect information.

The penalty for failing to notify HMRC of chargeability to CT for an accounting period is the same behaviour-based penalty as is applied to individuals (seen in Chapter 17 of this Workbook).

3.2 Late filing penalties

If the deadline for filing is not met, an automatic penalty will be imposed.

- Up to three months late: £100
- Up to six months late: £200
- Up to 12 months late £200 + 10% of tax unpaid six months after the return was due
- Over 12 months late £200 + 20% of tax unpaid six months after the return was due

If the returns for each of the two previous accounting periods were also late (ie this is the third consecutive late filing), the £100 and £200 penalties are increased to £500 and £1,000.

3.3 Failure to keep records

Failure to keep records can lead to a **penalty of up to £3,000** for each accounting period affected.

3.4 Errors in returns

The same common penalty regime for making errors in tax returns is applied to companies as is applied to individuals.

Chapter summary

Self assessment and payment of tax by companies

The self assessment system for companies

Notification of chargeability
- Notify first AP within three months
- Notify chargeability within 12m of AP if no notice to file issued

Filing and amending returns
- Deadline 12m from end of PoA, or 3m after notice to file if later
- Taxpayer can amend within 12m of due filing date, HMRC have 9m to correct errors

Records
- Must be kept for six years after AP end, or until enquiries complete

Compliance checks and assessments
- HMRC must notify intention to conduct compliance check:
  - Within 12m if delivered on time
  - Next following quarter date if late
- If no compliance check enquiry raised, self-assessment is considered final

Payment of corporation tax

Companies which are not large companies
- CT due 9m and 1d after end of each chargeable accounting period

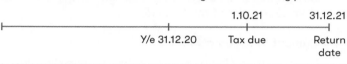

	1.10.21	31.12.21
Y/e 31.12.20	Tax due	Return date

Large companies – the quarterly instalment regime
- Large company is a company with Augmented Profits above the upper limit
  - Limit is £1.5 million multiplied by n/12 (n = no. months in AP) and divided by the number of related 51% group companies
  - Augmented profits = TTP + dividends received from unrelated companies
- Transitional relief. No quarterly instalments if:
  - Augmented Profits up to £10 million and
  - Not large in previous year
- 12m AP: QIPs due on 14th of months 7,10,13 and 16 from start of AP
- Short accounting period (AP)
  - Each instalment = 3 × CT/n (n = no. of months of AP)
  - Final instalment always due by 14th of 4th month following end of AP

14.07.20	14.10.20		14.01.21	14.04.21	31.12.21
Instal 1	Instal 2	Y/e 31.12.20	Instal 3	Instal 4	Return date

Interest
- Interest to HMRC on late paid tax runs from due date and is NTLR expense
- Interest from HMRC on overpaid tax runs from later of due date and date paid, and is NTLR income

Penalties
- Failure to notify chargeability – same as for individuals
- Late filing of tax return
  - Up to three months late £100
  - Up to six months late £200
  - Up to 12 months late £200 + 10% unpaid tax
  - Over to 12 months late £200 + 20% unpaid tax
- Failure to keep records – up to £3,000 per AP
- Errors in returns – same as for individuals

Knowledge diagnostic

1. Notification of chargeability

A company that does not receive a notice requiring a return to be filed must, if it is chargeable to tax, notify HMRC within 12 months of the end of the accounting period

2. Filing

A company must, in general, file a tax return within 12 months of the end of an accounting period.

3. Compliance checks

HMRC can carry out compliance check enquiries on returns. They must give notice normally within 12 months of the filing date.

4. Payment of corporation tax

Corporation tax is due nine months and one day after the end of an accounting period. However, large companies must pay their corporation tax by quarterly instalments.

Large companies are those whose augmented profits exceed the profit threshold.

Four quarterly instalments are made in months 7, 10, 13 and 16 following the start of a 12-month accounting period.

5. Penalties

Penalties may be levied for failure to notify the first accounting period, failure to notify chargeability for an accounting period, the late filing of returns, failure to keep records, and errors in returns.

Further study guidance

Question practice

Now try the following from the Further question practice bank (available in the digital edition of the Workbook):

Section A: Q100, Q101 and Q102

Section B: Q103 Skyblue Ltd and Turquoise plc

Section C: Q104 Cyan plc and Crimson plc

Activity answers

Activity 1: Corporation tax due dates

1   The correct answer is: £505,000

Augmented profits = TTP + dividends received from unrelated companies ie £480,000 + £25,000 = £505,000.

The answer £480,000 does not include any dividends. The answer £515,000 includes the dividend from B Ltd. The answer £565,000 includes all the dividends.

2   The correct answer is: A plc and C Ltd only

The profits limit is £1.5m ÷ 3 = £500,000. This is because there are three related 51% group companies (A plc, B Ltd and C Ltd). A plc and C Ltd have augmented profits of more than £500,000. Augmented profits are TTP plus dividends received from unrelated companies.

3   The correct answer is: A plc on 14 October 2020 and B Ltd on 1 January 2022

A plc is large for at least the second year running so must make its first payment on the 14th day of the 7th month of the accounting period to which the liability relates. B Ltd is not large so pays all of its liability nine months and a day after the accounting period ends.

Activity 2: Quarterly instalments for 12 month AP

F plc

CT: £2.1m × 19% = £399,000

Instalments:

	Y/e 31 March 2021
£399,000 ÷ 4 = £99,750	
Liability will be settled as follows:	£
14 October 2020	99,750
14 January 2021	99,750
14 April 2021	99,750
14 July 2021	99,750
	399,000

Activity 3: Late paid corporation tax

The correct answer is: £1,375

The tax was due on 1 October 2021. Working to the nearest whole month, this makes the payment three months late. The rate of interest for tax paid late is 2.75%, so the interest will be 2.75% × £200,000 × 3/12 = £1,375.

The answer £917 is two months' interest. The answer £5,500 is 12 months' interest. The answer £nil assumes that the payment was not overdue.

Activity 4: Interest on overpaid corporation tax

The correct answer is: £50

Normal due date (NDD) for year ended 31 December 2020 is 1 October 2021.

Original tax for year ended 31 December 2020 was paid on 31 July 2021.

Interest runs from the later of these two dates, ie 1 October 2021. So, a month's interest is payable at 0.50%, ie 0.50% × £120,000 × 1/12 = £50.

The answer £nil assumes that there was no overpayment. The answer £150 is three months' interest, ie from the payment date. The answer £100 is two months' interest (ie from the payment date to the due date).

Skills checkpoint 4

Section C questions

Chapter overview

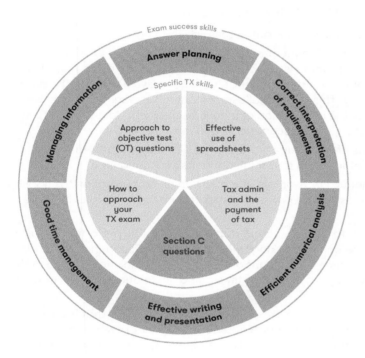

Introduction

Section C questions contain one 10-mark question and two 15-mark questions. The 10-mark question is slightly different from the 15-mark questions and the examining team have commented that many students struggle with the 10-mark question. One 15-mark question will focus on income tax and the other one will focus on corporation tax. This means that you know roughly what to expect and you can use proformas where relevant to help with the long calculations. Discursive elements will be relatively short. 10-mark questions often cover more than one tax and are designed to act as a bridge question between TX and the higher level exam, ATX. They require you to identify relevant information and its implications and this is why they may seem to be harder than the 15-mark questions.

Section C questions

The key steps for tackling Section C questions are outlined below and will be explained in more detail in the following section as the question 'Silvalean' is answered.

STEP 1 Read the requirements carefully first. You do not want to waste time calculating a tax liability if the question asks for taxable income. Knowing the requirements will help you focus on the information given in the scenario.

STEP 2 Learn and use the proformas where relevant. Once you have a proforma, you can start to work through the information in a methodical and time-efficient way.

STEP 3 Input easy numbers from the question directly into your proforma. This will make sure that you pick up as many easy marks as possible before dealing with more detailed calculations. Also, remember to include items even where no adjustment is required and input a zero in the computation.

STEP 4 Always use formulae to perform basic calculations. For small calculations, this can be done in a single cell, rather than including a separate working below the proforma (see Checkpoint 2 for more details on using the spreadsheet).

STEP 5 Show longer workings separately. Make sure they are easy for the marker to find, eg by labelling them and linking the figure to the main computation in the spreadsheet.

Exam success skills

The following question is an extract worth 12 marks from a 15-mark question.

For this question we will also focus on the following exam success skills:

- **Managing information.** It is easy for the amount of information contained in a Section C question to feel over-whelming. Active reading is a useful technique to use to avoid this. This involves focusing on the requirement first on the basis that, until you have done this, the detail in the question will have little meaning. This is especially important in 10-mark questions where you need to identify the relevance of the information you have been given. Note that you can highlight or strikethrough parts of the question scenario as you read through it.

- **Answer planning.** 10-mark questions often require more answer planning than 15-mark questions. You need to absorb the information and think about its implications.

- **Correct interpretation of requirements**. For example, the question on a corporation tax liability may tell you the operating profit or loss or the profit before tax figure to start with. There are no excuses for getting this wrong.

- **Efficient numerical analysis.** The key to success here is applying a sensible proforma for tax calculations, backed up by clear, referenced, workings wherever needed. Learning a standard proforma layout will save time and reduce the amount of planning and thinking required in the exam. Use the spreadsheet functionality. Do not waste time doing calculations manually when the spreadsheet can do them for you.

- **Effective writing and presentation.** You need to present your answer in a way that is easy for the marker to mark. For example, do not leave a huge gap between your answer and the workings. Use the cut and paste functions in the spreadsheet to improve the layout of your answer and workings.

- **Good time management.** Make sure you leave enough time to answer all parts of all of the Section C questions.

Skills activity

Silvalean Ltd is a manufacturing company that prepares accounts to 30 November each year and pays corporation tax in instalments. It has owned 45% of Goldchub Ltd and 90% of Bronzz Ltd for many years.

Silvalean Ltd prepared accounts for the year ended 30 November 2020. The following information is available:

- The operating profit for the year ended 30 November 2020 is £853,340. Depreciation of £30,380 has been deducted in arriving at this figure.

- On 1 June 2020, Silvalean Ltd acquired a newly-constructed freehold office building at a cost of £384,000. Legal fees on acquisition totalled £5,000 and these have been deducted in arriving at the operating profit figure. The office building was brought into use immediately on acquisition and was used for business purposes by Silvalean Ltd throughout the remainder of the year ended 30 November 2020.

- On 1 December 2019, the tax written down values of Silvalean Ltd's plant and machinery were as follows:

	£
Main pool	29,300
Special rate pool (consisting of car with CO_2 emissions of 176g/km)	16,100

		Cost/(Proceeds) £
1 March 2020	Purchased plant	25,600
5 June 2020	Sold the special rate pool car	(8,600)
20 July 2020	Sold a delivery van	(9,600)
31 October 2020	Purchased a car with CO_2 emissions 107g/km	10,300

The van sold on 20 July 2020 for £9,600 originally cost £20,500. The motor car purchased on 31 October 2020 is used by the sales manager: 25% of the mileage is for private journeys.

- On 1 July 2020, Silvalean Ltd made a loan to another company for non-trading purposes and £1,500 loan interest was accrued at 30 November 2020.
- On 12 September 2020, Silvalean Ltd sold a freehold office building to Bronzz Ltd for £293,600. The indexed cost of the office building was £242,800.
- During the year ended 30 November 2020, Silvalean Ltd received a dividend of £75,000 from Goldchub Ltd.
- On 5 September 2020, Silvalean Ltd made a qualifying charitable donation of £6,900.

Required

Calculate Silvalean Ltd's corporation tax liability for the year ended 30 November 2020.

Note. Your computation should commence with the operating profit of £853,340, and should also indicate by the use of zero (0) any items referred to in the question for which no adjustment is required.

(12 marks)

STEP 1 Read the requirements carefully first. You do not want to waste time calculating a tax liability if the question asks for taxable income. Knowing the requirements will help you focus on the information given in the scenario.

Note. This is a 12-mark question and at 1.8 minutes per mark, it should take approximately 22 minutes. The requirement is for a corporation tax liability calculation and it tells you to start with the operating profit of £853,340.

STEP 2 Learn and use the proformas where relevant. Once you have a proforma, you can start to work through the information in a methodical and time-efficient way.

Note. This means you can use a proforma for the computation and you can cut and paste as necessary if you need more rows. For example, you could set up your proforma look like this:

Note.

	A	B	C	D	E	F	G
1	Silvalean Ltd – Corporation tax computation for year ended 30 November 2020						
2						£	
3	Operating profit					853,340	
4							
5							
6							
7							
8							
9							
10							
11	Capital allowances						
12	Adjusted profit						
13	Property business income						
14	Interest income from non-trading loan relationships						
15	Miscellaneous income						
16	Chargeable gains						
17	Total profits						
18	Less losses deductible from total profits						
19	Less qualifying charitable donations						
20	Taxable total profits						
21							
22	CT @ 19%						

STEP 3 Input easy numbers from the question directly into your proforma.

Note. There are some easy numbers from the question that you can input straight into your proforma such as the operating profit, depreciation, interest from non-trading loan relationships and the deduction for qualifying charitable donations. This will make sure that you pick up as many easy marks as possible before dealing with more detailed calculations.

STEP 4 Always use formulae to perform basic calculations.

Note. For the corporation tax liability, the marker will be able to see your working very clearly by clicking on the cell G15 (in the answer below) and viewing the spreadsheet formulae (ie TTP*19%). This means that there is no value in spending time on explanations of simple calculations such as this.

STEP 5 Show longer workings separately. Make sure they are easy for the marker to find. The examining team have complained that some students leave a very big gap between the answer and the workings. Make it easy for the markers!

Note. Clear workings are needed here for the structures and buildings allowances and the plant and machinery capital allowances. Take the additions and disposal information from the question and make use of the spreadsheet formulae to calculate the WDAs. Link the cells for the total allowances from your working back into the TTP proforma. This makes it easier for your marker to clearly follow through your logic.

◢	A	B	C	D	E	F	G	H	I
1	Silvalean Ltd – Corporation tax computation for year ended 30 November 2020								
2							£		
3	Operating profit						853,340		
4	Depreciation						30,380		
5	Legal fees on acquisition						5,000		
6	SBA						(5,760)		
7	Capital allowances						(31,450)		
8	Adjusted profit						851,510		
9	Interest income from non-trading loan relationships						1,500		
10	Dividends						0		
11	Chargeable gains						0		
12	Total profits						853,010		
13	Less qualifying charitable donations						(6,900)		
14	Taxable total profits						846,110		
15									
16	Corporation tax liability						**160,761**		
17									
18									
19	**SBA**								
20	Cost		384,000						
21	WDA		(5,760)						
22	TWDV c/f		378,240						
23									
24									
25	**Capital allowances**					AIA	Main pool	Special rate pool	Allowances
26						£	£	£	£
27	TWDV b/f						29,300	16,100	
28	Additions qualifying for AIA								
29	1.3.20 Plant					25,600			
30	AIA					(25,600)			(25,600)
31	Additions not qualifying for AIA								
32	31.10.20 Car						10,300		
33	Disposals								
34	5.6.20 Car							(8,600)	
35								7,500	
36	20.7.20 Van						(9,600)		
37							30,000		
38	WDA @18%						(5,400)		(5,400)
39	WDA @6%							(450)	(450)
40	TWDV c/f						24,600	7,050	
41	Allowances								(31,450)

Exam success skills diagnostic

Every time you complete a question, use the diagnostic below to assess how effectively you demonstrated the exam success skills in answering the question. The table has been completed below for the 'Silvalean' activity to give you an idea of how to complete the diagnostic.

Exam success skills	Your reflections/observations
Managing information	Did you remember that dividends received from other companies are never included in arriving at the TTP?
	Did you note that the office building was newly constructed and therefore SBAs were available (and remember that they needed to be time-apportioned due to the building being purchased mid-year)?
	Did you remember that the private use of the car by the employee is not relevant for capital allowance purposes? No adjustment is ever made to a **company's** capital allowances to reflect the private use of an asset.
Answer planning	Did you use a proforma to make sure that you did not forget anything? Did you ensure that you dealt with each item in the scenario?

Exam success skills	Your reflections/observations
Correct interpretation of requirements	You needed to calculate the corporation tax liability. Did you do this, or did you stop at the TTP?
Efficient numerical analysis	Did you use the functions in the spreadsheet to help with numerical accuracy?
Effective writing and presentation	Did you present a neat set of figures in a proforma with appropriate workings that would have been easy for a marker to follow?
Good time management	Did you manage your time to ensure you completed the calculations in the time available, leaving yourself enough time to attempt any additional elements such as discussion in part (b)?
Most important action points to apply to your next question	

Summary

Section C of the TX exam is worth 40 marks, most of which will need to be answered using a spreadsheet.

The best way to score well in Section C questions is to practise them frequently. You need to have both good technical knowledge and good exam technique. It is important to be aware that in the exam you will be dealing with detailed calculations under timed exam conditions and time management is absolutely crucial. For good exam technique you therefore need to ensure that you:

- Read the requirements carefully.
- Use a clear, standard proforma where relevant.
- Use spreadsheet formulae to perform basic calculations.
- Score well on the easier parts of the question.
- Show clear workings for more complex areas.

24

An introduction to VAT

Learning objectives

On completion of this chapter, you should be able to:

	Syllabus reference no.
Recognise the circumstances in which a person must register or deregister for VAT (compulsory) and when a person may register or deregister for VAT (voluntary).	F1(a)
Recognise the circumstances in which pre-registration input VAT can be recovered.	F1(b)
Explain the conditions that must be met for two or more companies to be treated as a group for VAT purposes, and the consequences of being so treated.	F1(c)
Calculate the amount of VAT payable/recoverable.	F2(a)
Understand how VAT is accounted for and administered.	F2(b)
Recognise the tax point when goods or services are supplied.	F2(c)
Explain and apply the principles regarding the valuation of supplies.	F2(e)
Recognise the principal zero rated and exempt supplies.	F2(f)
Recognise the circumstances in which input VAT is non-deductible.	F2(g)
Recognise the relief that is available for impairment losses on trade debts.	F2(h)
Understand the treatment of the sale of a business as a going concern.	F2(i)

Exam context

Section A questions on basic value added tax (VAT) topics could include identification of the date for registration and dealing with impairment losses. Section B questions could also include computing the amount of VAT payable or recoverable. In Section C, registration requirements may be examined in more detail. Make sure that you know the difference between the historical test and the future test, and the dates by which HMRC must be notified and registration takes effect. Do not overlook pre-registration input VAT. You may also be required to calculate the VAT due for a return period. Watch out for non-deductible input tax and check the dates if there are impairment losses.

Chapter overview

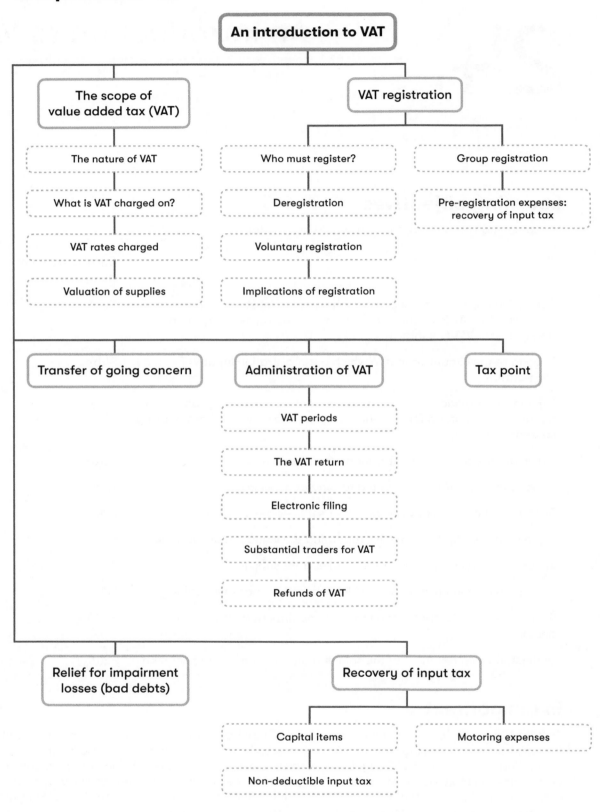

An introduction to VAT

The scope of value added tax (VAT)
- The nature of VAT
- What is VAT charged on?
- VAT rates charged
- Valuation of supplies

VAT registration
- Who must register?
- Deregistration
- Voluntary registration
- Implications of registration

Group registration
- Pre-registration expenses: recovery of input tax

Transfer of going concern

Administration of VAT
- VAT periods
- The VAT return
- Electronic filing
- Substantial traders for VAT
- Refunds of VAT

Tax point

Relief for impairment losses (bad debts)

Recovery of input tax
- Capital items
- Non-deductible input tax
- Motoring expenses

1 The scope of value added tax (VAT)

1.1 The nature of VAT

Value added tax (VAT) is a tax on turnover, not on profits. The basic principle is that the VAT should be borne by the final consumer. Registered traders may deduct the tax which they suffer on supplies to them (input tax) from the tax which they charge to their customers (output tax) at the time this is paid to HM Revenue and Customs (HMRC). So, at each stage of the manufacturing or service process, the net VAT paid is on the value added at that stage.

Illustration 1: The VAT charge

During 2020, a forester sells wood to a furniture maker for £100 plus VAT. The furniture maker uses this wood to make a table and sells the table to a shop for £150 plus VAT of 20%. The shop then sells the table to the final consumer for £300 plus VAT.

Required

Show how VAT will be accounted for on these transactions.

Solution

VAT will be accounted for to HMRC as follows:

	Cost	Input tax 20%	Net sale price	Output tax 20%	Payable to HMRC
	£	£	£	£	£
Forester	0	0	100	20	20
Furniture maker	100	20	150	30	10
Shop	150	30	300	60	30
					60

Because the traders involved account to HMRC for VAT charged less VAT suffered, their profits for income tax or corporation tax purposes are based on sales and purchases net of VAT.

1.2 What is VAT charged on?

VAT is charged on taxable supplies of goods and services made in the UK by a taxable person in the course or furtherance of any business carried on by them. It is also chargeable on the import of goods into the UK (whether they are imported for business purposes or not, and whether the importer is a taxable person or not) and, on certain services received from abroad, if a taxable person receives them for business purposes.

> **Taxable supply:** A **taxable supply** is a supply of goods or services made in the UK, other than an exempt supply. This means that standard-rated supplies and zero-rated supplies are taxable supplies.

> **PER alert**
>
> In order to fulfil Performance Objective 15 Tax computations and assessments of the PER, you must demonstrate that you can prepare or contribute to computations or assessments of indirect tax liabilities. You can apply the knowledge you obtain from this chapter to help to demonstrate this competence.

1.3 VAT rates charged

A **taxable supply** is either **standard-rated** or **zero-rated**. The standard rate is 20%.

Certain supplies, which fall within the classification of standard rate supplies, are charged at a reduced rate of 5%. An example is the supply of domestic fuel.

Zero-rated supplies are taxable at 0%. A taxable supplier whose outputs are zero rated but whose inputs are standard rated will obtain repayments of the VAT paid on purchases.

An **exempt supply is not chargeable to VAT.** A person making exempt supplies is unable to recover VAT on inputs. Therefore, the exempt supplier has to shoulder the burden of VAT. Of course, they may increase their prices to pass on the charge, but they cannot issue a VAT invoice which would enable a taxable customer to obtain a credit for VAT, since no VAT is chargeable on their supplies.

Supply	Examples
Standard-rated	• Most goods/services
Zero-rated	• Non-luxury food • Books • Children's clothes and footwear
Exempt	• Burial/cremation services • Health services • Non-profit-making education • First and second class postage stamps

Essential reading

See Chapter 24 Section 1 of the Essential reading for an example showing the effect on businesses of having standard-rated, zero-rated and exempt outputs and details on what is meant by 'supplies'.

The Essential reading is available as an Appendix of the digital edition of the Workbook.

1.4 Valuation of supplies

> **Value of supply:** The value of a supply is the VAT-exclusive price on which VAT is charged.
>
> **Consideration of supply:** The consideration for a supply is the amount paid in money or money's worth.

Using the standard rate of 20%:

Value + VAT = consideration

£100 + £20 = £120 VAT-inclusive price

Formula to learn

The VAT proportion of the consideration is known as the 'VAT fraction'. It is:

$$\frac{\text{Rate of tax}}{100 + \text{rate of tax}} = \frac{20}{100 + 20} = \frac{1}{6}$$

For example, the VAT element of the VAT-inclusive price of £120 is £120 × 1/6 = £20.

Provided the consideration for a bargain made at arm's length is paid in money, the value for VAT purposes is the VAT exclusive price charged by the trader. If it is paid in something other than money, as in a barter of some goods or services for others, it must be valued and VAT will be due on the value.

If the price of goods is effectively reduced with money off coupons, the value of the supply is the amount actually received by the taxpayer.

VAT is calculated on the invoice price less all trade discounts. If a prompt payment discount is offered, VAT must be calculated on the actual amount received. The trader must either provide details of the discount on the invoice or must invoice for the full amount and then issue a credit note if the discount is taken up.

2 VAT registration

2.1 Who must register?

(a) Registration is compulsory if:

    (i)   At the end of any month, taxable supplies over the previous 12 months have exceeded £85,000 (historical test); or

    (ii) In the next 30 days, taxable supplies are expected to exceed £85,000 (future test).

(b) This requirement may be waived if the trader can satisfy HM Revenue & Customs (HMRC) that taxable supplies in the following 12-month period will be less than £83,000.

(c) Taxable supplies is the VAT-exclusive value of all zero rated and standard rated supplies.

(d) The trader has 30 days to notify HMRC.

(e) Registration is effective from:

    (i)   The first day of the second month after the £85,000 was exceeded, or from an earlier date if they and the trader agree (historical test); and

    (ii) Start of 30-day period if future 30-day test applies.

(f) When determining the value of a person's taxable supplies for the purposes of registration, supplies of goods and services that are capital assets of the business are to be disregarded, except for non zero rated taxable supplies of interests in land.

Note that if a trader does not register when they should, output VAT will still be due from the date that they should have registered for VAT.

> **Exam focus point**
>
> The registration limit and deregistration limit are given in the tax tables.
>
> Be sure you know the difference between the historic and future tests.

Illustration 2: VAT registration and dates

At the end of every month, a trader must calculate their cumulative turnover of taxable supplies for the previous 12 months to date.

Fred started to trade cutlery on 1 January 2020. Sales (excluding VAT) were £8,000 a month for the first nine months and £8,500 a month thereafter.

Required

From what date should Fred be registered for VAT?

Solution

Sales to 31 October 2020	£80,500
Sales to 30 November 2020	£89,000 (exceeds £85,000)

Fred must notify his liability by 30 December 2020 (**not 31 December**) and will be registered and charge VAT from 1 January 2021.

Activity 1: Notifying HMRC

Jack commenced trading on 1 January 2020. His quarterly turnover (spread evenly over the quarter) is as follows:

Quarter ended	Turnover £
31 March 2020	7,500
30 June 2020	13,500
30 September 2020	18,000
31 December 2020	24,000
31 March 2021	33,000
30 June 2021	39,000

Required

By what date is Jack required to notify HMRC that he is liable to register for VAT?

Solution

Activity 2: Notification and registration dates

Jill commenced trading on 1 January 2020 with monthly sales as follows:

Goods	Turnover per month £
Goods ABC (standard rated)	8,000
Goods DEF (zero rated)	7,000
Service GHJ (exempt)	10,000

On 14 April 2020, Jill signed a contract to provide £30,000 of Goods ABC and £47,000 of Goods DEF on 2 May 2020 in addition to the monthly supplies detailed above.

Required

By what date is Jill required to notify HMRC that she is liable to register for VAT, and from which date must she be registered?

○ Notify by 30 June 2020 and register from 1 July 2020

○ Notify by 30 May 2020 and register from 1 June 2020

○ Notify by 14 April 2020 and register from 14 April 2020

○ Notify by 13 May 2020 and register from 14 April 2020

Solution

2.2 Deregistration

If the business ceases to make taxable supplies, it must deregister. If in the next year, VAT-exclusive taxable supplies will be below £83,000, the business may deregister.

There is a deemed supply of business assets such as plant, equipment or trading inventory when a business ceases to be VAT registered. However, if the transfer is of a going concern, it is outside the scope of VAT.

2.3 Voluntary registration

A person making taxable supplies which do not exceed the registration threshold may nonetheless register for VAT voluntarily.

Advantages:

- Able to reclaim input VAT
- Imposes discipline on the business to keep accurate records
- Lends credibility to a business

Disadvantages

- Adds to administrative costs
- Reduces the competitive edge and deters business if the customers are not VAT registered

For example, consider a trader who has one input during the year which cost £1,000 plus £200 VAT; they work on the input which becomes their sole output for the year and they decide to make a profit of £1,000.

- If they are not registered, they will charge £2,200 and will not be able to reclaim the £200 VAT on the original purchase.
- If they are registered, they will charge £2,000 plus VAT of £400. Their customer will have input tax of £400 which they will be able to recover if they, too, are registered.

2.4 Implications of registration

(a) Traders making standard or zero rated supplies must charge VAT on all taxable supplies using tax invoices.

(b) These traders can recover related input tax suffered.

(c) However, input tax is not recoverable on:

    (i) Cars (unless involved in motor trade)

    (ii) UK customer entertaining

    (iii) Non-business purchases

(d) Exempt traders (eg an insurance company):

    (i) Cannot register (as they make no taxable supplies)

    (ii) Cannot recover input VAT suffered

Activity 3: Reclaiming VAT

Chester Ltd, which is registered for VAT, incurred the following expenditure (including VAT) during the quarter ended 31 December 2020.

	£
New car for salesman (private use)	14,500
Three new motor vans	28,200
Second-hand container lorry	29,370
Entertaining – UK customers	4,935
– employees	5,250

Required

How much VAT can be reclaimed in respect of the above and on what amount will Chester be entitled to claim capital allowances?

Solution

2.5 Group registration

Companies may apply for group VAT registration. The effects and advantages of group registration are as follows:

- Allows group companies to nominate one company in the group to prepare one VAT return for the companies in the group (the 'representative member').
- Intra-group transactions are disregarded for VAT purposes.
- It is administratively much easier.
- All members of group registration are jointly and severally liable for VAT liability.

2.5.1 Who can form a group?

The holding entity must **control subsidiaries** (ie by voting power) and the entities within the group registration must have **a fixed establishment in the UK**. The **holding** entity can be a **company, sole trader or partnership** but the **rest of the group members must be corporate**. The holding entity must control the UK company(/ies) that they wish to form a group with.

Entities must elect to form a VAT group, it is not automatic, and not all eligible entities need to be included.

2.6 Pre-registration expenses: recovery of input tax

VAT incurred on goods and services before registration can be treated as input tax and recovered from HMRC subject to certain conditions.

If the claim is for input tax suffered on **goods** purchased prior to registration, the following conditions must be satisfied.

(a) The goods were acquired for the purpose of the business which either was carried on or was to be carried on by them at the time of supply.

(b) The goods have **not been supplied onwards or consumed before the date of registration** (although they may have been used to make other goods which are still held).

(c) The VAT must have been incurred in the **four years prior to the effective date of registration**.

If the claim is for input tax suffered on the supply of **services** prior to registration, the following conditions must be satisfied.

(a) The services were supplied for the purposes of a business which either was carried on or was to be carried on by them at the time of supply.

(b) The services were supplied within the **six months prior to the date of registration**.

Input tax attributable to **supplies made before registration** is not deductible even if the input tax concerned is treated as having been incurred after registration.

Activity 4: Input VAT

Bilbo Ltd commenced trading on 1 August 2020 and applied to register for VAT with effect from 1 October 2020.

Prior to registration, it had incurred VAT on the following VAT exclusive amounts:

	£
Accountancy fees – invoice dated 10 March 2020	5,000
Van purchased new on 23 June 2020	8,000
Inventory of spare parts as on 30 September 2020	12,000

Required

What input VAT can Bilbo Ltd claim in respect of each of these items assuming the van and inventory are still held on 1 October 2020?

Accountancy fees £ [   ]

Van £ [   ]

Inventory £ _____

Solution

---

3 Transfer of going concern

When the assets of a VAT registered business are sold, each asset will be subject to VAT at the appropriate rate.

When, however, the **whole business is sold as a going concern** then the supply of assets is outside the scope of VAT and **no VAT is chargeable**.

There are conditions for the transfer of a going concern to apply:

- The purchaser of the business must also be VAT registered.
- The same kind of business will be carried on.
- There is no significant break in trading.

4 Administration of VAT

The administration of VAT is dealt with by HM Revenue and Customs (HMRC).

Local offices are responsible for the local administration of VAT and for providing advice to registered persons whose principal place of business is in their area. They are controlled by regional collectors.

From time to time, a registered person will be visited by HMRC staff from a local office to ensure that the law is understood and is being applied properly. If a trader disagrees with any decision as to the application of VAT given by HMRC, they can ask their local office to reconsider the decision.

If HMRC believe that a trader has failed to make returns, or if they believe those returns to be incorrect or incomplete, they may issue **assessments of the VAT** due to the best of their judgement. The time limit for making assessments is normally four years after the end of a VAT period, but this is extended to 20 years in the case of fraud, dishonest conduct, certain registration irregularities and the unauthorised issue of VAT invoices.

A trader may appeal to the Tax Tribunal in the same way as an appeal may be made for income tax and corporation tax (see earlier in this Workbook). VAT returns and payments shown thereon must have been made before an appeal can be heard.

4.1 VAT periods

The VAT period (also known as the tax period) is the period covered by a VAT return. It is usually three calendar months. The return shows the total input and output tax for the tax period.

HMRC allocate VAT periods according to the class of trade carried on (ending in June, September, December and March; July, October, January and April; or August, November, February and May), to spread the flow of VAT returns evenly over the year. When applying for registration, a trader can ask for VAT periods which fit in with their own accounting year. It is also possible to have VAT periods to cover accounting systems not based on calendar months.

A registered person whose input tax will regularly exceed their output tax can elect for a one-month VAT period, but will have to balance the inconvenience of making 12 returns a year against the advantage of obtaining more rapid repayments of VAT.

Certain small businesses may submit an annual VAT return (see later in this chapter).

4.2 The VAT return

The regular VAT return to HMRC is made on form VAT 100.

Input and output tax figures must be supported by the original or copy tax invoices, and records must be maintained for six years.

4.3 Electronic filing

Nearly all VAT registered businesses must file their VAT returns online and make payments electronically.

The time limit for submission and payment is one month plus seven days after the end of the VAT period. For example, a business which has a VAT quarter ending 31 March 2021 must file its VAT return and pay the VAT due by 7 May 2021.

4.3.1 Making tax digital (MTD)

For VAT periods starting on or after 1 April 2019, most businesses which are VAT-registered and have a taxable turnover above the registration threshold must follow the Making Tax Digital (MTD) rules. Other VAT-registered businesses (eg those who are voluntarily registered) can choose to follow the MTD rules.

Many VAT records must be kept digitally under MTD. These include business name and address, registration number, and details of the supplies the business makes and receives (eg time of supply, value of supply and VAT rate charged or input tax reclaimed). The records can be kept by using a software package, which is also used to submit the return directly to HMRC, or other software such as spreadsheets to keep the records which are then submitted using bridging software to connect to HMRC.

Businesses which do not follow MTD rules continue to submit their returns electronically through the HMRC website.

The time for submission of returns and payment of VAT are not changed by the introduction of MTD.

4.4 Substantial traders for VAT

Once a trader's **total VAT liability for the 12 months or less to the end of a VAT period exceeds £2.3 million, the trader must start making payments on account of each quarter's VAT liability during each quarter.**

Two payments on account of each quarter's VAT liability must usually be made. The first is due one month before the end of the quarter and the second is due at the end of the month which is the final month of the quarter. The amount of each payment on account made during the quarter is 1/24 of the trader's annual VAT liability in the period in which the threshold is exceeded. For the purposes of calculating the payments on account (but not for the purposes of the £2.3 million threshold for entry into the scheme), a trader's VAT due on imports from outside the EU is ignored.

If the VAT liability for the quarter exceeds the total of the payments on account, a balancing payment is due one month after the end of the quarter to bring the total payments for that quarter to the amount of the VAT liability. If the VAT liability for the quarter is less than the total of the payments on account, HMRC will make a repayment to the trader.

Payments must be made and the quarterly VAT return submitted by the last day of the relevant month ie there is no additional seven days. Payments must be made electronically.

The default surcharge (see later in this chapter) applies to late payments.

Illustration 3: Substantial traders

Large Ltd is liable to make payments on account of VAT calculated at £250,000 each for the quarter ended 31 December 2020.

Required

What payments/repayment are due if Large Ltd's VAT liability for the quarter is calculated as:

(a) £680,000?

(b) £480,000

Solution

(a)

Date	Payment
30 November 2020	Payment on account of £250,000
31 December 2020	Payment on account of £250,000
31 January 2021	Balancing payment of £680,000 – £250,000 – £250,000 = £180,000 with submission of VAT return for quarter

(b)

Date	Payment/repayment
30 November 2020	Payment on account of £250,000
31 December 2020	Payment on account of £250,000
31 January 2021	Repayment by HMRC of £480,000 – £250,000 – £250,000 = £20,000 on submission of VAT return for quarter

Once a trader is in the scheme, the payments on account are reviewed annually at a set time. However, the trader **can apply to reduce payments on account at any time if the total VAT liability for the latest four returns is less than 80% of the total on which the payments on account are currently based**, ie the VAT liability decreases by 20% or more. Conversely, **HMRC may increase the payments on account in between annual reviews if the trader's total 12-month VAT liability increases by 20% or more**, ie the VAT for the last four periods is at least 120% of the amount on which the payments on account are currently based. A trader can apply to **leave the scheme if their 12-month VAT liability is below £1,800,000**. A trader whose VAT liability at the annual review was below £2.3 million will be automatically removed from the scheme six months later.

A trader may elect to pay their actual VAT liability monthly instead of making payments on account. For example, the actual liability for January would be due at the end of February. The trader can continue to submit quarterly returns as long as HMRC is satisfied the trader is paying sufficient monthly amounts.

4.5 Refunds of VAT

 There is a four-year time limit on the right to reclaim overpaid VAT. This time limit does not apply to input tax which a business could not have reclaimed earlier because the supplier only recently invoiced the VAT, even though it related to a purchase made some time ago. Nor does it apply to overpaid VAT penalties.

 If a taxpayer has overpaid VAT and has overclaimed input tax by reason of the same mistake, HMRC can set off any tax, penalty, interest or surcharge due to them against any repayment due to the taxpayer and repay only the net amount. In such cases, the normal four-year time limit for recovering VAT, penalties, interest, etc by assessment does not apply.

HMRC can refuse to make any repayment which would unjustly enrich the claimant. They can also refuse a repayment of VAT where all or part of the tax has, for practical purposes, been borne by a person other than the taxpayer (eg by a customer of the taxpayer) except to the extent that the taxpayer can show loss or damage to any of their businesses as a result of mistaken assumptions about VAT.

5 Tax point

Each tax invoice is assigned to a return period according to its tax point.

The basic tax point is when goods are made available, or when services are completed.

If the invoice is issued or payment is received before the basic tax point, the earlier date becomes the tax point.

If the earlier date rule does not apply and the invoice is issued within 14 days after the basic tax point, the invoice date can become the tax point.

Illustration 4: Tax point

Julia sells a sculpture to the value of £1,000 net of VAT. She receives a payment on account of £250 plus VAT on 25 April 2020. The sculpture is delivered on 28 May 2020. Julia's VAT return period is to 30 April 2020. She issues an invoice on 4 June 2020.

Required

Outline the tax point(s) and amount(s) due.

Solution

A separate tax point arises in respect of the £250 deposit and the £750 balance payable.

Julia should account for VAT as follows.

Deposit

25 April 2020: tax at 20% × £250 = £50

This is accounted for in her VAT return to 30 April 2020. The charge arises on 25 April 2020 because payment is received before the basic tax point (which is 28 May 2020 – date of delivery).

Balance

4 June 2020: tax at 20% × £750 = £150

This is accounted for on the VAT return to 31 July 2020. The charge arises on 4 June because the invoice was issued within 14 days of the basic tax point of 28 May 2020 (delivery date).

Activity 5: Tax points

1   On 31 May, Bang Ltd ordered a new printing machine and on 16 June paid a deposit of £6,000. The machine was despatched to Bang Ltd on 30 June. On 18 July, an invoice was issued to Bang Ltd for the balance due of £54,000. This was paid on 23 July.

2   What is the tax point for the £6,000 deposit?

3   What is the tax point for the balance of £54,000?

Solution

6 Relief for impairment losses (bad debts)

A trader may claim a **refund of VAT on amounts unpaid by debtors** if:

(a) They have accounted for VAT

(b) The debt is **over six months old; and**

(c) The debt has been **written off** in the creditor's accounts.

If the debtor later pays all (or part) of the amount owed, the corresponding amount of VAT repaid must be paid back to HMRC.

Impairment loss relief claims must be made within **four years of the time the impairment loss became eligible for relief** (in other words, within four years and six months from when the payment was due).

 ## Illustration 5: Impairment loss relief

Elixir Ltd has VAT accounting periods ending on 31 March, 30 June, 30 September and 31 December. The company sold standard rated goods to Ben on 1 July 2020. The VAT inclusive amount on the invoice was £2,000 and payment was due by 15 July 2020. Ben paid Elixir Ltd £500 as part payment on 1 October 2020 but then became untraceable and Elixir Ltd has written off the remaining debt.

Required

State how much impairment loss relief can be claimed by Elixir Ltd and the earliest VAT return on which the claim can be made.

Solution

The amount of the loss is £2,000 − £500 = £1,500.

The VAT on the loss is £1,500 × 1/6 = £250, so this amount can be claimed as impairment loss relief.

Payment was due on 15 July 2020 and so the six-month period ended on 15 January 2021. The earliest VAT return on which an impairment loss relief claim is that for the quarter ending 31 March 2021.

7 Recovery of input tax

Not all input VAT is deductible. For input tax to be deductible the payer must be a taxable person in the course of their business.

7.1 Capital items

There is no distinction between capital and revenue expenditure for VAT. A manufacturer paying VAT on the purchase of plant to make taxable supplies will be able to obtain a credit for all the VAT immediately.

7.2 Non-deductible input tax

The following input tax is **not deductible**:

(a) **VAT on purchased motor cars** not used wholly for business purposes. VAT on cars is never reclaimable unless the car is acquired new for resale or is acquired for use in or leasing to a taxi business, a self-drive car hire business or a driving school (see below for treatment of motor expenses).

(b) **50% of the VAT on leased motor cars which are 'qualifying cars'.** The 50% restriction covers any private use of the car. A qualifying car is one on which input tax has not already been irrecoverable.

(c) **VAT on business entertaining** where the cost of the entertaining is not a tax deductible trading expense unless it is entertainment of overseas customers in which case the input tax is deductible.

(d) VAT on expenses incurred on domestic accommodation for directors or proprietors of a business

(e) **VAT on non-business items passed through the business accounts.** If goods are bought partly for business use, the purchaser may:

   (i)   Deduct all the input tax, and account for output tax in respect of the private use; or

   (ii)   Deduct only the business proportion of the input tax.

(f) VAT which does not relate to the making of supplies by the buyer in the course of a business

7.3 Motoring expenses

7.3.1 Accessories and maintenance costs

Input VAT can be reclaimed if accessories for business use are fitted after the original purchase of a car and a separate invoice is raised.

If a car is used for any business purposes (even if it is also used for private purposes) any VAT charged on repair and maintenance costs can be treated as input tax.

7.3.2 Fuel

If a business pays for fuel which is only used for business purposes, it can claim all the input tax paid on that fuel. However, many businesses will pay for fuel which is used for private motoring by employees.

If a business does provide fuel for private and business use to an employee, but the employee reimburses the business the full cost of the private fuel, there is an actual taxable supply by the business valued at the amount received from that employee. The business can claim its input tax on all fuel, but then must account for output tax on the amount paid by the employee. HMRC will accept that the full cost of all private fuel has been reimbursed where a log is kept recording private miles and the employee pays a fuel-only mileage rate that covers the average fuel cost (on its website, HMRC publishes a set of such rates for different sizes of engine).

If a business provides fuel to its employees for private use without charge or at a charge below the full cost, there is a deemed taxable supply. The business then has the following options for how to account for VAT on fuel:

(a) **Not to claim any input tax in respect of fuel** purchased by the business. **No output tax is charged**. In effect, the fuel is not brought into the VAT system at all.

(b) **Claim input VAT only on the fuel purchased for business journeys**. This requires the business to keep detailed mileage records of business and private use. **No output tax is charged in respect of private use.** In effect, the private fuel is not brought into the VAT system.

(c) **Claim input tax on all fuel purchased and charge output tax based either on the full cost of the private fuel supplied** (again, this requires detailed mileage records to be kept) **or the VAT fuel scale charge** which reflects the deemed output in respect of private use. The fuel scale charge is based on the CO_2 emissions of the car.

Illustration 6: Fuel scale charge

Iain is an employee of ABC Ltd. He has the use of a car with CO_2 emissions of 176g/km for one month and a car with CO_2 emissions of 208 g/km for two months during the quarter ended 31 August 2020.

ABC Ltd pays all the petrol costs in respect of both cars without requiring Iain to make any reimbursement in respect of private fuel. Total petrol costs for the quarter amount to £390 (including VAT). ABC Ltd wishes to use the fuel scale charge as detailed records of private mileage have not been kept.

VAT scale rates (VAT inclusive) for three-month periods:

CO_2 emissions	£
175	362
205	450

Required

What is the VAT effect of the above on ABC Ltd?

Solution

Value added tax for the quarter:

	£
Car 1	
£362 × 1/3 =	121
Car 2	
£450 × 2/3 =	300
	421
Output tax:	
1/6 × £421	£70
Input tax	
1/6 × £390	£65

Activity 6: Fuel

John is an employee of BBT Ltd. He has the use of a car which is used for both business and private mileage for the current VAT quarter.

BBT Ltd pays all the petrol costs in respect of the car totalling £1,200 of which 20% is for private mileage.

The relevant quarterly scale charge is £508.

Both figures are inclusive of VAT.

Required

1 What is the VAT effect of the above on BBT Ltd if it uses the quarterly scale charge?

   ○ Output VAT of £85, input VAT of £40

   ○ Output VAT of £85, input VAT of £200

   ○ Output VAT of £17, input VAT of £200

   ○ Output VAT of £17, input VAT of £40

2 What is the VAT effect of the above on BBT Ltd if it charges John for the private fuel?

   ○ Output VAT of £40, input VAT of £48

   ○ Output VAT of £48, input VAT of £48

   ○ Output VAT of £48, input VAT of £200

   ○ Output VAT of £40, input VAT of £200

Solution

Chapter summary

An introduction to VAT

The scope of value added tax (VAT)

The nature of VAT
- Tax on turnover, borne by final consumer
- Registered traders deduct input tax from output tax and pay net VAT to HMRC

What is VAT charged on?
- Taxable supplies of goods/services made in the UK by a taxable person
- Import of goods into the UK

VAT rates charged
- Standard 20%
- Zero 0%
- Exempt

Valuation of supplies
- Value of supply = VAT exclusive price
- Consideration for a supply = amount paid ie value + VAT
- VAT fraction = 1/6

VAT registration

Who must register?
- If taxable turnover exceeds £85,000 in past 12 months (historic) or will be in next 30 days (future)

Deregistration
- If cease to make taxable supplies
- Voluntary if taxable supplies next year will be below £83,000

Voluntary registration
- Able to reclaim input VAT
- But adds to admin costs

Implications of registration
- Must charge VAT on taxable supplies
- Can recover related input VAT
- Exempt traders cannot register nor recover input VAT

Group registration
- Group nominates 'representative member' who prepares one VAT return for entire group
- Intragroup sales are ignored
- All members of group are jointly and severally liable

Pre-registration expenses: recovery of input tax
- Goods/services acquired/supplied for the purpose of the business
- Goods not supplied onwards or consumed before registration date
- VAT on goods must have been incurred in 4 years before registration date
- Services supplied within 6 months before registration date

Transfer of going concern

- If assets sold each has VAT at the appropriate rate
- If a transfer of a going concern (TOGC) then no VAT chargeable
- Conditions to be met:
  – Purchaser VAT registered
  – Same kind of business carried on
  – No significant break in trade

Administration of VAT

VAT periods
- Quarterly – normal

The VAT return
- Form VAT 100
- Maintain records for six years

Electronic filing
- Most must file returns and make payments online
- Due a month and seven days after end of VAT period

Substantial traders for VAT
- Payments on account if VAT liability exceeds £2.3 million

Refunds of VAT
- 4 year limit on right to reclaim overpaid VAT

Tax point

- Earliest of:
  – Despatch date
  – Invoice date
  – Cash received

Relief for impairment losses (bad debts)

- Refund of VAT on bad debts if:
  – Trader has accounted for VAT
  – Debt is over six months old
  – Debt has been written off in the creditor's accounts

Recovery of input tax

Capital items
- No distinction between capital and revenue expenditure for VAT

Non-deductible input tax
- Cars
- 50% of VAT on leased cars that are qualifying cars
- Business entertaining
- Expenses incurred on domestic accommodation for directors/proprietors
- Non-business items
- VAT not related to making of supplies by buyer in course of business

Motoring expenses
- Input VAT on accessories and maintenance after original purchase can be reclaimed
- Input VAT can be reclaimed on fuel used only for business purposes
- Several options if business provides fuel for private use

Knowledge diagnostic

1. Charge to value added tax (VAT)

VAT is charged on taxable supplies made by taxable persons in the course of their trade.

Some supplies are taxable (standard rate, reduced rate, zero rate). Others are exempt. Make sure you understand the difference and can work out VAT from the VAT-exclusive and VAT-inclusive price.

2. Registration

A trader becomes liable to register for VAT if its taxable supplies over a 12-month period exceeds £85,000 or in the next 30 days its taxable supplies will exceed £85,000. A trader may also register voluntarily.

Group registration allows only one VAT return to be prepared for the group as a whole.

3. Transfer of going concern

VAT is not charged on the transfer of a going concern.

4. Administration of VAT

VAT periods can be a month, a quarter or a year. Payment made electronically usually by seven days from the end of the month following the VAT period. Substantial traders must make payments on account.

5. Tax point

Basic tax point is when goods are made available or when services are completed. Actual tax point can be earlier or later.

6. Impairment losses (bad debts)

A trader can claim refund of output tax on impairment losses which remain unpaid six months from the time that payment is due and have been written off

7. Recovery of input tax

General principle is that input tax is only recoverable in relation to business use. No input tax is recoverable on cars with private use and business entertaining (other than overseas customers). Input tax can be recovered on fuel but output tax may be charged on private fuel using the fuel scale charge.

Further study guidance

Question practice

Now try the following from the Further question practice bank (available in the digital edition of the Workbook):

Section A:

Q105, Q106, Q107

Section B: Q108 Justin

Section C: Q109 Ongoing Ltd

Further reading

There are two technical articles available on ACCA's website on VAT, called *Value added tax – Parts 1 and 2*. The first article considers VAT registration and deregistration, and output and input VAT. These topics are covered in this chapter.

There is also an article called *Motor cars* that explains the implications of acquiring, running or having the use of a motor car for income tax, corporation tax, value added tax (VAT) and national insurance contribution (NIC).

You are strongly advised to read these articles in full as part of your preparation for the TX exam.

Activity answers

Activity 1: Notifying HMRC

Annual turnover does not exceed £85,000 until 31 March 2021 (on a month by month basis) therefore Jack does not become liable to register until then. He must then notify HMRC within 30 days ie by 30 April 2021. He will then be registered from 1 May 2021 or an earlier date by mutual agreement.

Month	Supplies £	Cumulative 12 months' sales £
January 2020	2,500	
February 2020	2,500	
March 2020	2,500	
April 2020	4,500	
May 2020	4,500	
June 2020	4,500	
July 2020	6,000	
August 2020	6,000	
September 2020	6,000	
October 2020	8,000	
November 2020	8,000	
December 2020	8,000	63,000

Month	Supplies £	Cumulative 12 months' sales £
January 2021	11,000	71,500
February 2021	11,000	80,000
March 2021	11,000	88,500
April 2021	13,000	97,000
May 2021	13,000	105,500
June 2021	13,000	114,000

Activity 2: Notification and registration dates

The correct answer is: Notify by 13 May 2020 and register from 14 April 2020

The historical test would be breached on 31 May 2020. Taxable supplies in the first five months amount to 5 × (£8,000 + £7,000) = £75,000, plus the special orders placed in May take the total to above £85,000.

The future test is breached on 14 April 2020 because, on that date, Jill knows her taxable supplies in the next 30 days will exceed the registration threshold: £8,000 + £7,000 + £30,000 + £47,000 =

£92,000. Notification is required 30 days from the test (count 14 April as day 1) and registration takes effect from 14 April 2020.

Activity 3: Reclaiming VAT

Input tax reclaimed

	£
Vans (£28,200 × 1/6)	4,700
Lorry (£29,370 × 1/6)	4,895
Entertaining employees (£5,250 × 1/6)	875
	10,470

Capital allowance values

		£
Car		14,500
Vans	(£28,200 − £4,700) =	23,500
Lorry	(£29,370 − £4,895) =	24,475

Activity 4: Input VAT

Accountancy fees £ 0

Van £ 1,600

Inventory £ 2,400

	£
Accountancy fees – not recoverable as > 6 months prior to registration	0
Van – in use post-registration £8,000 × 20%	1,600
Inventory – still held at date of registration £12,000 × 20%	2,400
	4,000

Activity 5: Tax points

2   16 June

The basic tax point is the date the goods are made available on 30 June. However, the actual tax point for the deposit is the earlier payment.

3   30 June

The basic tax point is the date the goods are made available on 30 June. The later issue of the invoice does not displace this date because the invoice was issued more than 14 days after the basic tax point.

Activity 6: Fuel

1   The correct answer is: Output VAT of £85, input VAT of £200

If John is not charged for the private fuel, BBT Ltd can reclaim input VAT of £200 (£1,200 × 20/120) and will have to account for output VAT of £85 (£508 × 20/120) based on the scale charge. The answers output VAT of £17 or input VAT of £40 reduces the VAT based on the private mileage percentage which is not 'elevant when using the quarterly scale charge.

2   The correct answer is: Output VAT of £40, input VAT of £200

If John is charged £240 (£1,200 × 20%) for the private fuel then BBT Ltd will reclaim input VAT of £200 and will have to account for output VAT of £40 (£240 × 2/6) based on the charge to John. The answer £48 assumes £240 is the VAT exclusive price, ie VAT is 20% x £240.

Further aspects of VAT

Learning objectives

On completion of this chapter, you should be able to:

	Syllabus reference no.
List the information that must be given on a VAT invoice.	F2(d)
Understand when the default surcharge, a penalty for an incorrect VAT return, and default interest will be applied.	F2(j)
Understand the treatment of imports, exports and trade within the European Union.	F2(k)
Understand the operation of, and when it will be advantageous to use, the VAT special schemes:	
• Cash accounting scheme	F3(a)(i)
• Annual accounting scheme	F3(a)(ii)
• Flat rate scheme	F3(a)(iii)

Exam context

The topics in this chapter could be examined in any of Sections A, B or C. Penalties are an important topic as they are used to enforce the VAT system, but the special schemes are designed to make life simpler for small businesses. You may be asked to advise on the VAT treatment of imports and exports outside the European Union (EU) and on trade within the EU. The flat rate scheme may also lead to a small extra profit for the business, depending on the flat rate percentage and the level of inputs.

Chapter overview

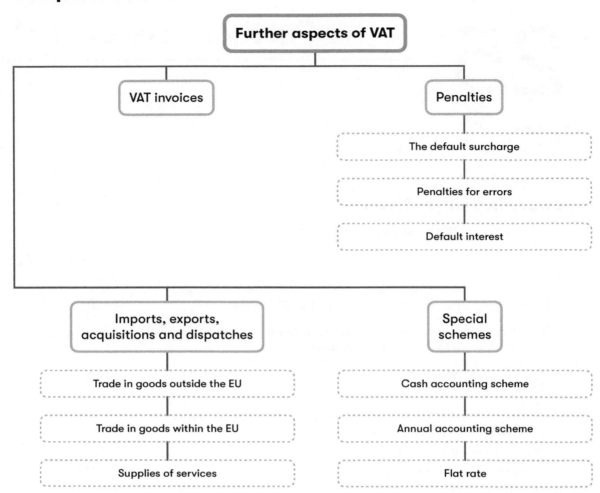

1 VAT invoices

A taxable person making a taxable supply to another VAT registered trader must supply a VAT invoice within 30 days of the time of supply, and must keep a copy. There is no requirement to supply a VAT invoice if the supply is exempt or if the supply is to a non-VAT registered customer.

The invoice must show:

(a) The supplier's name, address and registration number

(b) The date of issue, the tax point and an invoice number

(c) The name and address of the customer

(d) A description of the goods or services supplied, giving for each description the quantity, the unit price, the rate of VAT and the VAT exclusive amount

(e) The rate of any cash discount

(f) The total invoice price excluding VAT (with separate totals for zero-rated and exempt supplies)

(g) Each VAT rate applicable and the total amount of VAT

If an invoice is issued, and a change in price then alters the VAT due, a credit note or debit note to adjust the VAT must be issued.

Credit notes must give the reason for the credit (such as 'returned goods'), and the number and date of the original VAT invoice. If a credit note makes no VAT adjustment, it should state this.

A less detailed VAT invoice may be issued by a taxable person where the invoice is for a total including VAT of up to £250. Such an invoice must show:

(a) The supplier's name, address and registration number

(b) The date of the supply

(c) A description of the goods or services supplied

(d) The rate of VAT chargeable

(e) The total amount chargeable including VAT

Zero-rated and exempt supplies must not be included in less detailed invoices.

VAT invoices are not required for payments of up to £25 including VAT which are for telephone calls, or car park fees, or made through cash operated machines. In such cases, input tax can be claimed without a VAT invoice.

Every VAT registered trader must **keep records** for **six years**.

Essential reading

See Chapter 25 Section 1 for information on keeping VAT records.

The Essential reading is available as an Appendix of the digital edition of the Workbook.

2 Penalties

2.1 The default surcharge

A default occurs when a trader either submits their VAT return late, or submits the return on time but pays the VAT late. A default surcharge is applied if there is a default on payment during a default surcharge period.

- Written notification of a default (surcharge liability notice) will be given to a trader after the first default (ie first late payment/return).

- Once issued, it remains in force until the trader has not been in default for 12 months.

- While notice is in force the trader will be liable to a surcharge each time they default. This will only be for late payment of tax; no penalty exists for submission of late return provided the tax was paid on time. The late return, however, will extend the notice period.

The surcharge depends on the number of defaults involving late payment of VAT which have occurred in respect of periods ending in the surcharge period, as follows:

Default involving late payment of VAT in the surcharge period	Surcharge as a percentage of the VAT outstanding at the due date	
First	2%	No surcharge if < £400
Second	5%	No surcharge if < £400
Third	10%	But not less than £30
Fourth or more	15%	But not less than £30

Illustration 1: Default charge

Peter has an annual turnover of around £300,000. His VAT return for the quarter to 31 December 2018 is late. He then submits returns for the quarters to 30 September 2019 and 31 March 2020 late as well as making late payment of the tax due of £12,000 and £500 respectively.

Peter's VAT return to 31 March 2021 is also late and the VAT due of £1,100 is also paid late. All other VAT returns and VAT payments are made on time.

Required

Outline Peter's exposure to default surcharge.

Solution

A surcharge liability notice will be issued after the late filing on the 31 December 2018 return, outlining a surcharge period extending to 31 December 2019.

The late 30 September 2019 return is in the surcharge period, so the period is extended to 30 September 2020. The late VAT payment triggers a 2% penalty. 2% × £12,000 = £240. Since £240 is less than the £400 *de minimis* limit it is not collected by HMRC.

The late 31 March 2020 return is in the surcharge period, so the period is now extended to 31 March 2021. The late payment triggers a 5% penalty. 5% × £500 = £25. Since £25 is less than the £400 *de minimis* limit it is not collected by HMRC.

The late 31 March 2021 return is in the surcharge period, so the period is extended to 31 March 2022. The late payment triggers a 10% penalty. 10% × £1,100 = £110. This is collected by HMRC since the £400 *de minimis* does not apply to penalties calculated at the 10% (and 15%) rate.

Peter will have to submit all four quarterly VAT returns to 31 March 2022 on time and pay the VAT on time to avoid the default surcharge regime.

The application of the default surcharge regime to small businesses is modified. **A small business is one with a turnover below £150,000**. When a small business is late submitting a VAT return or paying VAT, it will receive a letter from HMRC offering help. No penalty will be charged. If a further default occurs within 12 months, a surcharge liability notice will be issued.

2.2 Penalties for errors

The common penalty regime for making errors in tax returns discussed in Chapter 17 also applies to VAT returns.

Errors on a VAT return not exceeding the greater of:

- £10,000
- 1% × net VAT turnover for return period (maximum £50,000)

may be **corrected on next return**.

Other errors should be notified to HMRC in writing, eg by letter or email.

In both cases, a penalty for the error may be imposed. Correction of an error on a later return is not, of itself, an unprompted disclosure of the error and fuller disclosure is required for the penalty to be reduced.

Default interest (see next) on the unpaid VAT as a result of the error is only charged where the limit is exceeded for the error to be corrected on the next VAT return.

2.3 Default interest

Interest (not deductible in computing taxable profits) is charged on VAT which is the subject of an assessment (where returns were not made or were incorrect), or which could have been the subject of an assessment but was paid before the assessment was raised. This interest is sometimes called 'default interest'. It runs from the date the VAT should have been paid to the actual date of payment but cannot run for more than three years before the assessment or voluntary payment.

3 Imports, exports, acquisitions and dispatches

The terms **import and export** refer to purchases and sales of goods with countries **outside the European Union (EU)**.

The terms **acquisition and dispatch** refer to purchases and sales of goods with countries **in the EU**.

> ### Exam focus point
>
> The UK left the EU in January 2020 but, for exams in the period 1 June 2021 to 31 March 2022, it will be assumed that the EU acquisition rules continue to apply.

3.1 Trade in goods outside the EU

Export/import outside the EU	VAT treatment
UK VAT registered trader exports (sale of goods) outside the EU	Zero-rated sales
UK trader imports (purchases) from outside the EU	• Treated same way as goods purchased within the UK • Account for VAT at point of entry • Reclaim on next VAT return

3.2 Trade in goods within the EU

	VAT treatment
Sales (dispatches) by a UK registered trader within the EU	Zero rated if to a VAT registered customer, otherwise standard rated

Purchases (acquisitions) in the UK by a VAT registered trader from the EU	• UK trader accounts for output VAT at point of acquisition. Earlier of:
	   - 15th day of month following month of acquisition; and
	   - Date of issue of an invoice
	• Treated as input VAT (provided tax invoice issued by supplier)

VAT treatment
• VAT neutral*

*The acquisition transaction is entered on the UK trader's VAT return as an output and an input, so the effect is usually neutral. Thus, the UK trader is effectively in the same overall position as they would have been if they had acquired the goods from another UK VAT registered trader.

Although the end result is the same as with an import from outside the EU, the difference with an EU acquisition is that there is no need to actually pay the VAT prior to its recovery as input VAT.

3.3 Supplies of services

(a) The general rule is that supplies of services to any business customer are charged where the customer is established/situated.

(b) If a UK VAT registered trader is supplied with services from another country (EU, or non-EU), the place of supply is deemed to be the UK. The UK trader accounts for output VAT on the supply but the equivalent amount is the input VAT for the supply. So, the transaction is usually neutral.

(c) Supplies of services from a UK VAT registered trader to another business outside the UK are usually outside the scope of UK VAT as the place of supply is not in the UK.

4 Special schemes

> **PER alert**
>
> One of the competencies you require to fulfil Performance Objective 15 *Tax computations and assessments* of the PER is to explain the basis of tax calculations, and interpret the effect of current legislation and case law. You can apply the knowledge you obtain from this section of the Workbook to help to demonstrate this competence.

Special schemes can make VAT accounting easier and ease cash flow for certain types of trader.

4.1 Cash accounting scheme

(a) A trader whose annual taxable turnover (exclusive of VAT) does not exceed £1.35 million can apply for it.

(b) A trader can join only if all returns and VAT payments are up to date.

(c) VAT can be accounted for on the basis of cash paid and received, thus giving automatic impairment loss (bad debt) relief.

(d) A trader must cease using the cash accounting scheme as soon as turnover exceeds £1.6 million; however, the trader can continue to bring outstanding VAT into account on a cash basis for a further six months after leaving the scheme.

4.2 Annual accounting scheme

(a) Only available to traders who are up to date with VAT payments and regularly pay VAT to HMRC (not to those who normally receive payments).

(b) Available for traders whose taxable turnover (exclusive of VAT) for the 12 months starting on their application to join the scheme is **not expected to exceed £1.35 million**.

(c) All traders with turnover of up to £1.6 million can stay in the scheme.

(d) Only file one return per year but make payments on account (POA) throughout the year via direct debit.

(e) POA = 90% previous year's net VAT liability in nine monthly payments starting at the end of the fourth month of the year.

(f) Balance and return due within **two months after year end**.

Advantages of annual accounting:

- Only **one VAT return each year** so fewer occasions to trigger a default surcharge
- Ability to **manage cash flow** more accurately
- **Avoids need for quarterly calculations for input tax recovery**

Disadvantages of annual accounting:

- Need to **monitor future taxable supplies** to ensure turnover limit not exceeded
- **Timing of payments have less correlation to turnover** (and hence cash received) by business
- **Payments based on previous year's turnover may not reflect current year turnover** which may be a problem if the scale of activities has reduced.

4.3 Flat rate scheme

(a) The optional flat rate scheme simplifies the way in which small traders calculate their VAT liability.

(b) The scheme can be used if VAT-exclusive taxable turnover for the next 12 months is not expected to exceed £150,000.

(c) To calculate the VAT liability, simply apply a flat rate percentage to total (VAT-inclusive) turnover.

(d) The flat rate percentage will usually depend upon the trade sector into which the trader falls. If the trader makes no, or limited, purchases of goods, a rate of 16.5% applies so there is very little advantage to using the scheme.

(e) A 1% reduction off the flat rate % can be made by businesses in their first year of VAT registration.

(f) No input VAT is recovered.

(g) The scheme means there is no need to calculate and record output and input VAT; however, VAT at 20% is still treated as being charged where a supply is made to a registered trader, and therefore a VAT invoice must still be issued.

(h) A trader must leave the scheme if total annual VAT-inclusive turnover > £230,000.

Exam focus point

The flat rate percentage will be given to you in your exam.

Illustration 2: Flat rate scheme

Brian is an accountant who has been registered for VAT for many years and undertakes work for individuals and for business clients. In a VAT year, the business client work amounts to £70,000 and Brian issues VAT invoices totalling £84,000 (£70,000 plus VAT at 20%). Turnover from work for individuals totals £18,000, inclusive of VAT. Brian provides some exempt financial services which amount to £2,000 in a VAT year. The flat rate percentage for an accountancy business is 14.5%. Brian also incurs annual standard rated expenses of £4,800 inclusive of VAT relating to the taxable supplies.

Required

Advise Brian whether he should register for the flat rate scheme.

Solution

Under the flat rate scheme VAT due to HMRC will be £84,000 + £18,000 + £2,000 = £104,000 (VAT inclusive amount) × 14.5% = £15,080.

Under the normal VAT rules, the net VAT due to HMRC would be:

	£
£70,000 × 20%	14,000

	£
£18,000 × 1/6	3,000
Output VAT	17,000
Less input VAT £4,800 × 1/6	(800)
VAT due to HMRC	16,200

Brian should therefore register for the flat rate scheme as he will save VAT of £16,200 – £15,080) = £1,120. The reduced VAT administration cost of using the flat rate scheme should also be taken into account.

Activity 1: Flat rate or not flat rate

Cool Kids Ltd has annual turnover of £84,900. 85% of the sales are standard rated and 15% are zero rated. Standard rated expenses are £14,100.

All figures are exclusive of VAT.

The relevant flat rate percentage for Cool Kids Ltd trade is 11%.

Required

1   What is the VAT liability if Cool Kids Ltd does not use the flat rate scheme?

  ○ £9,677

  ○ £14,160

  ○ £11,613

  ○ £14,433

2   What is the VAT liability if Cool Kids Ltd does use the flat rate scheme?

  ○ £9,339

  ○ £11,207

  ○ £10,927

  ○ £8,107

Solution

Chapter summary

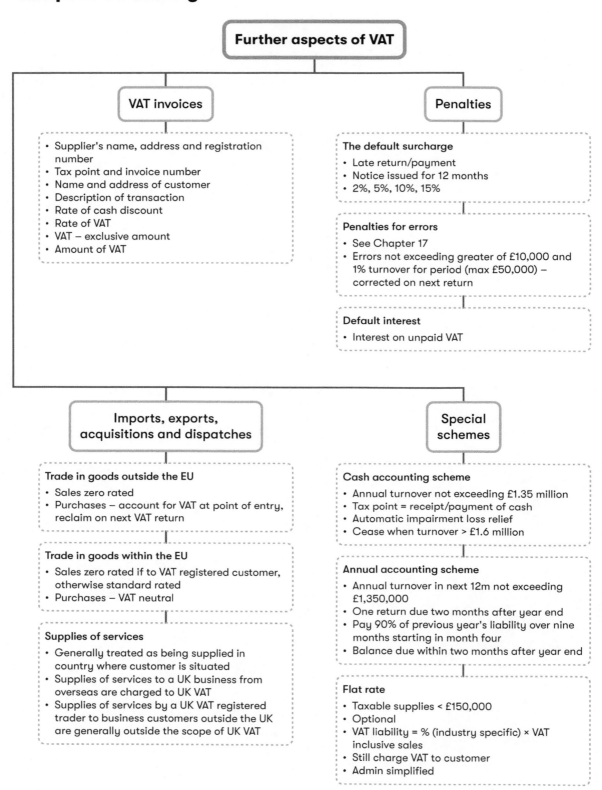

Further aspects of VAT

VAT invoices

- Supplier's name, address and registration number
- Tax point and invoice number
- Name and address of customer
- Description of transaction
- Rate of cash discount
- Rate of VAT
- VAT – exclusive amount
- Amount of VAT

Penalties

The default surcharge
- Late return/payment
- Notice issued for 12 months
- 2%, 5%, 10%, 15%

Penalties for errors
- See Chapter 17
- Errors not exceeding greater of £10,000 and 1% turnover for period (max £50,000) – corrected on next return

Default interest
- Interest on unpaid VAT

Imports, exports, acquisitions and dispatches

Trade in goods outside the EU
- Sales zero rated
- Purchases – account for VAT at point of entry, reclaim on next VAT return

Trade in goods within the EU
- Sales zero rated if to VAT registered customer, otherwise standard rated
- Purchases – VAT neutral

Supplies of services
- Generally treated as being supplied in country where customer is situated
- Supplies of services to a UK business from overseas are charged to UK VAT
- Supplies of services by a UK VAT registered trader to business customers outside the UK are generally outside the scope of UK VAT

Special schemes

Cash accounting scheme
- Annual turnover not exceeding £1.35 million
- Tax point = receipt/payment of cash
- Automatic impairment loss relief
- Cease when turnover > £1.6 million

Annual accounting scheme
- Annual turnover in next 12m not exceeding £1,350,000
- One return due two months after year end
- Pay 90% of previous year's liability over nine months starting in month four
- Balance due within two months after year end

Flat rate
- Taxable supplies < £150,000
- Optional
- VAT liability = % (industry specific) × VAT inclusive sales
- Still charge VAT to customer
- Admin simplified

Knowledge diagnostic

1. VAT invoice

There are various items of information that must be shown on a VAT invoice which is used to charge VAT.

2. Penalties

Various penalties exist for breaching the VAT legislation. Make sure you know when each one applies.

3. Imports, exports, acquisitions and despatches

Imports from outside the EU are subject to VAT and exports outside the EU are zero rated.

Taxable acquisitions from EU states are treated as a sale and a purchase by the UK trader.

Despatches to EU states are zero rated.

4. Special schemes

Special schemes exist to aid traders.

Cash accounting gives automatic relief for impairment losses.

Annual accounting simplifies the submission of VAT returns.

Flat rate scheme makes the calculation of the VAT liability easier.

Further study guidance

Question practice

Now try the following from the Further question practice bank (available in the digital edition of the Workbook):

Section A:

Q110, Q111, Q112

Section C: Q113 Kiln Ltd and Log Ltd

Further reading

There are two technical articles available on ACCA's website, called *Value added tax – Parts 1 and 2*. The second article covers VAT returns, VAT invoices, penalties, overseas aspects of VAT and special VAT schemes.

You are strongly advised to read these articles in full as part of your preparation for the TX exam.

Activity answers

Activity 1: Flat rate or not flat rate

1   The correct answer is: £11,613

		£
Output VAT		
£84,900 × 85% × 20%		14,433
Input VAT		
£14,100 × 20%		(2,820)
VAT payable		11,613

The answer £9,677 treats the amounts as VAT-inclusive. The answer £14,160 calculates output tax on total sales. The answer £14,433 does not deduct input tax.

2   The correct answer is: £10,927

Using the flat rate scheme

((£84,900 × 85% × 1.20) + (£84,900 × 15%)) × 11% = £10,927

The answer £9,339 is the VAT-exclusive amount times the flat rate. The answer £11,207 calculates the VAT-inclusive amount on all sales, ie (£84,900 × 1.20) × 11%. The answer £8,107 deducts the input VAT which is only recoverable under the normal VAT rules.

Skills checkpoint 5

How to approach your TX exam

Chapter overview

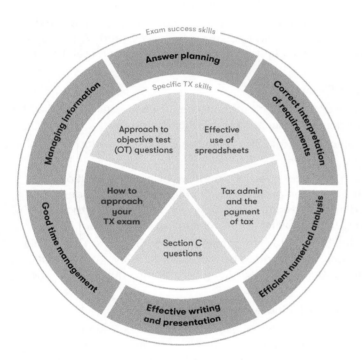

Introduction

You can answer your TX exam in whatever order you prefer. It is important that you adopt a strategy that works best for you. We would suggest that you decide on your preferred approach and practise it by doing a timed mock exam before your real exam.

Remember your TX exam will be structured as follows:

Section A: 15 individual OT questions worth two marks each. Questions in Section A can come from any syllabus area. There will be a mix of numerical and discursive style questions and you may find that some questions are easier than others.

Section B: Three OT case questions worth 10 marks each. Each case question will consist of five individual OT questions worth two marks each. There will normally be a mix of numerical and discursive questions. You do not have to answer these questions in order as the answer from one will not be required for subsequent questions. Again, questions in Section B can come from any syllabus area but each case will examine a single tax in the context of the given scenario.

Section C: Section C will contain one 10-mark and two 15-mark questions which will be scenario based and may contain both discursive and computational elements. The two 15-mark questions will focus on income tax and corporation tax and the 10-mark question can cover any part of the syllabus. The majority of the 40 marks in Section C will need to be done on a spreadsheet (see Checkpoint 2).

This Skills Checkpoint will provide you with one suggested approach for tackling your TX exam.

Good luck!

How to approach your TX exam

We would suggest the following approach for tackling your TX exam. It is important that you adopt an approach that works best for you and practise it by completing a mock exam to time prior to your real exam.

Complete Section A first - allocated time 54 minutes

- Tackle any easier OT questions first. Often discursive style questions such as those on the administration of tax (see Checkpoint 3) can be answered quickly, saving more time for calculations. Do not leave any questions unanswered. Even if you are unsure, make a reasoned guess. Skills Checkpoint 1 covers how to approach OT questions in more detail.

- If you do not feel that you need the full 54 minutes to complete Section A, you can carry this time forward to your Section C questions which tend to be more time pressured. With practice, it may be possible for you to complete Section A up to ten minutes quicker than the allocated time of 54 minutes.

Complete Section B next - allocated time 54 minutes

- You will have 18 mins of exam time to allocate to each of the three OT case questions in Section B. Use the same approach to OT questions as discussed for Section A.

- Each individual case tends to focus on a single tax. Start with the OT case question you feel most confident with.

- Each case will typically contain three numerical questions and two discursive questions (like 'Delroy and Marlon' and 'Opal' in the specimen exam) or two numerical questions and three discursive questions (like 'Glacier Ltd' in the specimen exam). Again, it is better to tackle the discussion type questions first as they tend to be less time consuming.

- If you do not feel that you need the full 54 minutes to complete Section B you can carry this time forward to your Section C questions which tend to be more time sensitive. With practice, it may be possible for you to complete Section B approximately five minutes quicker than the allocated time of 54 minutes.

Finally, complete Section C – allocated time 72 minutes

- Section C will contain one 10-mark and two 15-mark questions which will be scenario based and will contain both discursive and computational elements. Allocate at least 18 minutes to the 10-mark question and 27 minutes to each 15-mark question (remembering to split your time between each of the sub requirements) and but you may have up to 15 minutes of extra time if you have completed Sections A and B of the exam in less than the allotted time.

- Start with the question you feel most confident with. The first sub-requirement will normally involve some detailed calculations, and these tend to be very time sensitive. If possible, answer the discursive sub-requirements first. This will ensure that you do not spend too much time on the calculations and then lose out on the easier discursive marks. Make it clear to your marker which sub-requirement you are answering.

- Skills Checkpoints 2 and 4 look specifically at the techniques you should use answering the scenario-based questions in Section C. It is very likely that you will need to use spreadsheets so make sure you are confident using the techniques covered in Skills Checkpoint 2.

- You must practise questions in full to time, as this is the only way to acquire the necessary skills to tackle tax questions in the exam. Continuous effort in practising these skills (particularly spreadsheet skills) will lead to an increased chance of success in your exam.

Set some time aside to practise this approach through the completion of a mock exam to time.

Appendix 1: Tax Tables

Supplementary information

(a) Calculations and workings need only be made to the nearest £.

(b) All apportionments should be made to the nearest month.

(c) All workings should be shown in Section C.

Tax rates and allowances

The following tax rates and allowances are to be used in answering the questions.

Income tax

		Normal rates	Dividend rates
Basic rate	£1 – £37,500	20%	7.5%
Higher rate	£37,501 – £150,000	40%	32.5%
Additional rate	£150,001 and over	45%	38.1%

Savings income nil rate band	– Basic rate taxpayers	£1,000
	– Higher rate taxpayers	£500
Dividend nil rate band		£2,000

A starting rate of 0% applies to savings income where it falls within the first £5,000 of taxable income.

Personal allowance

	£
Personal allowance	12,500
Transferable amount	1,250
Income limit	100,000

Where adjusted net income is £125,000 or more, the personal allowance is reduced to zero.

Residence status

Days in UK	Previously resident	Not previously resident
Less than 16	Automatically not resident	Automatically not resident
16 to 45	Resident if 4 UK ties (or more)	Automatically not resident
46 to 90	Resident if 3 UK ties (or more)	Resident if 4 UK ties
91 to 120	Resident if 2 UK ties (or more)	Resident if 3 UK ties (or more)
121 to 182	Resident if 1 UK tie (or more)	Resident if 2 UK ties (or more)
183 or more	Automatically resident	Automatically resident

Child benefit income tax charge

Where income is between £50,000 and £60,000, the charge is 1% of the amount of child benefit received for every £100 of income over £50,000.

Car benefit percentage

The relevant base level of CO_2 emissions is 55 grams per kilometre.

BPP LEARNING MEDIA

The percentage rates applying to petrol-powered motor cars (and diesel-powered motor cars meeting the RDE2 standard) with CO_2 emissions up to this level are:

51 grams to 54 grams per kilometre	13%
55 grams per kilometre	14%

A 0% percentage applies to electric-powered motor cars with zero CO_2 emissions.

For hybrid-electric motor cars with CO_2 emissions between 1 and 50 grams per kilometre, the electric range of a motor car is relevant:

Electric range

130 miles or more	0%
70 to 129 miles	3%
40 to 69 miles	6%
30 to 39 miles	10%
Less than 30 miles	12%

Car fuel benefit

The base figure for calculating the car fuel benefit is £24,500.

Company van benefits

The company van benefit scale charge is £3,490, and the van fuel benefit is £666.

Individual savings accounts (ISAs)

The overall investment limit is £20,000.

Property income

Basic rate restriction applies to 100% of finance costs relating to residential properties.

Pension scheme limits

Annual allowance	£40,000
Minimum allowance	£4,000
Income limit	£240,000

The maximum contribution that can qualify for tax relief without any earnings is £3,600.

Approved mileage allowances: cars

Up to 10,000 miles	45p
Over 10,000 miles	25p

Capital allowances: rates of allowance

Plant and machinery

Main pool	18%
Special rate pool	6%

Motor cars

New cars with CO_2 emissions up to 50 grams per kilometre	100%

CO_2 emissions between 51 and 110 grams per kilometre	18%
CO_2 emissions over 110 grams per kilometre	6%

Annual investment allowance

Rate of allowance	100%
Expenditure limit	£1,000,000

Commercial structures and buildings

Straight-line allowance	3%

Cash basis accounting

Revenue limit	£150,000

Cap on income tax reliefs

Unless otherwise restricted, reliefs are capped at the higher of £50,000 or 25% of income.

Corporation tax

Rate of tax: Financial year 2020	19%
Financial year 2019	19%
Financial year 2018	19%
Profit threshold	£1,500,000

Value added tax (VAT)

Standard rate	20%
Registration limit	£85,000
Deregistration limit	£83,000

Inheritance tax: nil rate bands and tax rates

	£
Nil rate band	325,000
Residence nil rate band	175,000
Rate of tax on excess over nil rate band – Lifetime rate	20%
– Death rate	40%

Inheritance tax: taper relief

Years before death	Percentage reduction
More than 3 but less than 4 years	20%
More than but less than 5 years	40%
More than 5 but less than 6 years	60%

Years before death	Percentage reduction
More than 6 but less than 7 years	80%

Capital gains tax

		Normal rates	Residential property
Rates of tax:	Lower rate	10%	18%
	Higher rate	20%	28%
Annual exempt amount			£12,300

Capital gains tax: business asset disposal relief (formerly entrepreneurs' relief) and investors' relief

Lifetime limit - business asset disposal relief	£1,000,000
- investors' relief	£10,000,000
Rate of tax	10%

National insurance contributions

Class 1 Employee	£1 to £9,500 per year	Nil
	£9,501 to £50,000 per year	12%
	£50,001 and above per year	2%
Class 1 Employer	£1 – £8,788 per year	Nil
	£8,789 and above per year	13.8%
	Employment allowance	£4,000
Class 1A		13.8%
Class 2	£3.05 per week	
	Small profits threshold	£6,475
Class 4	£1 to £9,500 per year	Nil
	£9,501 to £50,000 per year	9%
	£50,001 and above per year	2%

Rates of interest (assumed)

Official rate of interest	2.25%
Rate of interest on underpaid tax	2.75%
Rate of interest on overpaid tax	0.50%

Standard penalties for errors

Taxpayer behaviour	Maximum penalty	Minimum penalty – unprompted disclosure	Minimum penalty – prompted disclosure
Deliberate and concealed	100%	30%	50%
Deliberate but not concealed	70%	20%	35%
Careless	30%	0%	15%

Index

BPP
LEARNING
MEDIA

Bibliography

Cases	
Bamford v ATA Advertising Ltd 1972	**[1972]** 48 TC 359
Blackwell v Mills 1945	**[1945]** 2 All ER 655
Brown v Bullock 1961	**[1961]** 3 All ER 129
Brown v Burnley Football and Athletic Co Ltd 1980	**[1980]** 53 TC 357
Caillebotte v Quinn 1975	**[1975]** 50 TC 22
Cape Brandy Syndicate v CIR 1921	**[1921]** 1 KB 64
Carmichael and Anor v National Power plc 1999	**[1999]** UKHL 47
CIR v Fraser 1942	**[1942]** 24 TC498
CIR v Scottish and Newcastle Breweries Ltd 1982	**[1982]** 55 TC 252
Cole Brothers Ltd v Phillips 1982	**[1982]** 55 TC 188
Donald Fisher (Ealing) Ltd v Spencer 1989	**[1989]** STC 256
Edwards v Clinch 1981	**[1981]** STC 617
Elwood v Utitz 1965	**[1965]** 42 TC 482
Fitzpatrick v IRC 1994	**[1994]** STC 237
Hall v Lorimer 1994	**[1994]** IRLR 171
Hampton v Fortes Autogrill Ltd 1979	**[1979]** 53 TC 691
Harvey v Caulcott 1952	**[1952]** 33TC159
Jarrold v John Good and Sons Ltd 1963	**[1963]** 40 TC 681
Law Shipping v CIR 1923	**[1923]** 12 TC 621
Lucas v Cattell 1972	**[1972]** 48 TC 353
Lupton v Potts 1969	**[1969]** 45 TC 643
Mallalieu v Drummond 1983	**[1983]** 57 TC 330
Martin v Lowry 1927	**[1927]** 1 KB 550
McKnight (HMIT) v Sheppard (1999)	**[1999]** STC 669
McLaren v Mumford 1996	**[1996]** 69 TC 173
Munby v Furlong 1977	**[1977]** 50 TC 491
Odeon Associated Theatres Ltd v Jones 1971	**[1971]** 48 TC 257
Pickford v Quirke 1927	**[1927]** 13 TC 251
Rutledge v CIR 1929	**[1929]** 14 TC 490
Samuel Jones & Co (Devondale) Ltd v CIR 1951	**[1951]** 32 TC 513
Sanderson v Durbridge 1955	**[1955]** 36 TC 239

Cases	
Smith v Abbott 1994	**[1994]** STC 237
Strong & Co of Romsey Ltd v Woodifield 1906	**[1906]** AC 448
Vodafone Cellular Ltd and others v Shaw 1995	**[1995]** 69 TC 376
Wimpy International Ltd v Warland 1988	**[1988]** 61 TC 51
Wisdom v Chamberlain 1969	**[1969]** 45 TC 92
Yarmouth v France 1887	**[1887]** 19 QB D

Tell us what you think

Got comments or feedback on this book? Let us know.
Use your QR code reader:

Or, visit:
https://bppgroup.fra1.qualtrics.com/jfe/form/SV_9TrxTtw8jSvO7Pv